Families and Health Care

Psychosocial Practice

MODERN APPLICATIONS OF SOCIAL WORK

An Aldine de Gruyter Series of Texts and Monographs

SERIES EDITOR

James K. Whittaker

Ralph E. Anderson and Irl Carter, **Human Behavior in the Social Environment: A Social Systems Approach** (fourth edition)

Richard P. Barth and Marianne Berry, **Adoption and Disruption: Rates, Risks, and Responses**

Richard P. Barth, Mark Courtney, Jill Duerr Berrick, and Vicky Albert, **From Child Abuse to Permanency Planning: Child Welfare Services Pathways and Placements**

Kathleen Ell and Helen Northen, **Families and Health Care: Psychosocial Practice**

Marian Fatout, **Models for Change in Social Group Work**

Mark W. Fraser, Peter J. Pecora, and David A. Haapala, **Families in Crisis: The Impact of Intensive Family Preservation Services**

James Garbarino, **Children and Families in the Social Environment** (second edition)

James Garbarino, Patrick E. Brookhouser, Karen J. Authier, and Associates, **Special Children—Special Risks: The Maltreatment of Children with Disabilities**

James Garbarino, Cynthia J. Schellenbach, Janet Sebes, and Associates, **Troubled Youth, Troubled Families: Understanding Families At-Risk for Adolescent Maltreatment**

Roberta R. Greene, **Social Work with the Aged and Their Families**

Roberta R. Greene, **Human Behavior Theory: A Diversity Framework**

Roberta R. Greene and Paul H. Ephross, **Human Behavior Theory and Social Work Practice**

André Ivanoff, Betty J. Blythe, and Tony Tripodi, **Involuntary Clients in Social Work Practice: A Research-Based Approach**

Paul K. H. Kim (ed.), **Serving the Elderly: Skills for Practice**

Jill Kinney, David A. Haapala, and Charlotte Booth, **Keeping Families Together: The Homebuilders Model**

Robert M. Moroney, **Shared Responsibility: Families and Social Policy**

Robert M. Moroney, **Social Policy and Social Work: Critical Essays on the Welfare State**

Peter J. Pecora, Mark W. Fraser, Kristine Nelson, Jacqueline McCroskey, and William Meezan, **Evaluating Family-Based Services**

Peter J. Pecora, James K. Whittaker, Anthony N. Maluccio, Richard P. Barth, and Robert D. Plotnick, **The Child Welfare Challenge: Policy, Practice, and Research**

Norman A. Polansky, **Integrated Ego Psychology** (second edition)

John R. Shuerman, Tina L. Rzepnicki, and Julia H. Littell, **Putting Families First: An Experiment in Family Preservation**

Betsy S. Vourlekis and Roberta R. Greene (eds). **Social Work Case Management**

Heather B. Weiss and Francine H. Jacobs (eds.), **Evaluating Family Programs**

James K. Whittaker, Jill Kinney, Elizabeth M. Tracy, and Charlotte Booth (eds.), **Reaching High-Risk Families: Intensive Family Preservation in Human Services**

James K. Whittaker and Elizabeth M. Tracy, **Social Treatment, 2nd Edition: An Introduction to Interpersonal Helping in Social Work Practice**

Families and Health Care

Psychosocial Practice

Kathleen Ell and Helen Northen

Aldine de Gruyter
New York

About the Authors

Kathleen Ell is Associate Professor, Director of the Hamovitch Social Work Research Center, and past Chair of the Health Concentration at the School of Social Work of the University of Southern California. She has published numerous articles and chapters in these areas. She teaches graduate courses in human behavior and is Consulting Editor for *Health and Social Work.*

Helen Northen, Ph.D. from Bryn Mawr College, School of Social Work and Social Research is Professor Emeritus and Consultant to the University of Southern California, School of Social Work. She is a noted social work practice theorist, as evidenced in several major social work practice books including: *Social Work with Groups, Clinical Social Work, and Theories of Social Work with Groups.* She has been elected to the National Academies of Practice as a Distinguished Practitioner of Social Work.

ALDINE DE GRUYTER
A Division of Walter de Gruyter, Inc.
200 Saw Mill River Road
Hawthorne, New York 10532

Library of Congress Cataloging-in-Publication Data
Ell, Kathleen Obier, 1940–
Families and health care: psychosocial practice / Kathleen Ell and Helen Northen.
p. cm.—(Modern applications of social work)
Includes bibliographical references.
ISBN 0-202-36059-8.—ISBN 0-202-36060-1 (pbk.)
1. Family—Medical care—Psychological aspects. 2. Sick—Family relationship. 3. Family—Psychological aspects. 4. Medical social work. I. Northen, Helen. II. Title. III. Series.
[DNLM: 1. Family. 2. Social Work. WA 309 E44f]
RA418.5.F3E35 1990
362.1'04—dc20
DNLM/DLC
for Library of Congress 89-18560
CIP

Manufactured in the United States of America

10 9 8 7 6 5 4 3 2

Contents

Foreword

From its earliest beginnings, social work practice in health care has recognized the importance of environmental factors as contributing to both the onset and successful treatment of physical illness. A significant part of that environment is the family crucible in which health related attitudes and behaviors are learned and which is, most frequently, the context for healing and renewal. In a work that is at once theoretically satisfying and practical in application, Ell and Northen explore the knowledge base that underpins health related social work interventions. This rich introduction to basic content on coping, stress and adaptation sets the stage for specific chapters on a variety of family centered interventions including assessment and the evaluation of practice. Beginning students of social work in health care as well as seasoned practitioners will find much of value here. The authors communicate their concepts easily and with a judicious use of practice examples. Attention to the research literature is clear and the bibliography is excellent.

Families and Health Care is yet another example of social work's recognition and support of family caregiving roles and of the importance of family centered practice. The authors write from a rich and distinguished background in social work practice and research. In part as a result of their work, the social work practice task, in general, will become more responsive to family caregiving responsibilities. This book offers an antidote to the "medicalization" of health care. It is wholistic in its approach. It respects family values and culture. It is a sensibly written book for a practical profession. Its practice prescriptions call to mind what the great British social policy analyst, Richard Titmuss (1974, p. 150)* had in mind when he spoke, in another context, about what "a compassionate society can achieve when a philosophy of social justice and public accountability is translated into a hundred and one detailed acts of imagination and tolerance." The kind of family focused social work practice in health care offered by Ell and Northen in this very substantial volume brings us closer to that vision.

James K. Whittaker
The University of Washington

*Titmuss, R. M. (1974). *Social Policy,* London: George Allen & Unwin Ltd.

Preface

Knowledge about families and about families and the health status of individual family members has advanced significantly in recent years. At the same time, trends in the financing and delivery of health care services place increasingly greater caregiving responsibilities on families in the face of illness or disability, but fail to ensure adequate provision of supportive services to assist families. The existing literature, however, is extremely limited in the attention given to the roles of social workers and other health care practitioners in helping families with their health-related tasks and functions. In an effort to be comprehensive, we review the knowledge base that underpins family-health-related interventions as it is represented in theoretical developments, research, social and organizational policies, and practice. In so doing, we present an argument intended to encourage practitioners to enhance their work with families and rise above the many barriers and disincentives to family intervention in health promotion and health care.

In this book, the family is conceptualized as a primary social system interacting with the broader social environmental system. From this perspective, multiple relationships and interactions between families and health and illness are highlighted. Empirical research and clinical observation provide convincing evidence that families influence significantly the health status of individual family members and that the illness of one member often has adverse effects on other members and on family relationships and family functioning. For example, there is compelling evidence of the normative influence of the family on members health beliefs and practices. The family as a source of potential support and of stress is also implicated in the onset and course of illness. On the other hand, when illness or disability strikes a family member, its effects reverberate throughout the family system. Spouses, children, or siblings may experience serious distress and in extreme cases may themselves become ill as a result of this distress. Usual family functioning processes may be adversely affected as well. Close examination also reveals the family's dependence on environmental resources to effectively carry out its health-related roles. On the basis of the overwhelming empirical evidence presented throughout the book, the call for family interventions to assist families in the health promotion and illness response roles is compelling.

The family is commonly regarded as the basic unit of society. Today, there is evidence from all over the world that despite massive social change, the family is also one of the most resilient of social institutions (Kendall, 1988; Reiss & Lee, 1988; Zimmerman, 1980). Family structure is diverse and subject to change over time. Widespread awareness of major changes in families and in family life in recent years has been heightened by discussions in multiple forums ranging from the popular media to national policy debates among social and political leaders and academic scholars.

Demographic data confirm that, indeed, the family is undergoing numerous changes in household structure, role performance, and overall lifestyle (Berlin, 1988; Chilman, 1988a; Macklin, 1988; Masnick & Bane, 1980; Watkins, Menken & Bongaarts, 1987). An emphasis on current forms of family life does not suggest that families did not vary in the past or that families were ever static social structures. To the contrary, family life in the United States has always varied among different sociocultural groups (Fulmer, 1988; Hines, 1988; McGoldrick, 1988; Wagner, 1988a; Woehrer, 1978). Furthermore, family life varies as it moves through developmental transitions over time. A thoughtful consideration of contemporary families and individual health and illness demands, therefore, that we be ever mindful of the rich diversity of this primary social institution, including family variations in structure, lifestyle, and sociocultural practices. Throughout subsequent discussions of theory, research, and policy, we will draw attention to implications of family diversity for the family's health-related functions and tasks. The practice implications of family diversity will also be highlighted (Dillon, 1985).

It is anticipated that this text will be invaluable to social workers in health care and other health care practitioners as well. Moreover, the book is organized so that chapters might be assigned to students in health concentrations as the specific topics relate to courses in practice, behavior, policy and research. The book will also be relevant to practitioners in the fields of mental health, family and child welfare, gerontology, education, and industrial practice.

We would like to thank numerous colleagues on the faculty of the University of Southern California, School of Social Work for their review and comments on selected portions of the book: Maurice Hamovitch, Alan Levy, John Brekke, Richard Sullivan, and Karen Subramanian. A note of thanks also to colleagues who contributed case examples: June Simmons, Senior Care Network and Huntington Memorial Hospital, Pasadena, California and students from the School of Social Work. Another thank you to Linda Mediansky for help in preparing the manuscript. KE would also like to thank her family for their support and patience during the writing of this book.

Kathleen Ell
Helen Northen

1
Relevant Theoretical Frameworks

The theoretical base that underpins a discussion of family-focused health promotion and family-focused medical care is a product of synthesizing scientific and epistemological movements within and across disciplines. Indeed, a chronicle of relatively recent theoretical developments in the fields of public health and medicine dramatically illustrates this knowledge synthesis in an evolutionary response to new information. Kuhn (1970) proposed that when faced with unanswered questions or a need for new explanations of observed phenomena, long-held assumptions or paradigms undergo a shift or, in the most extreme case, are replaced with a new paradigm. Consistent with this proposition, the emergence of the general systems paradigm (a paradigm that was originally formulated in the face of similar empirical observations within many different scientific fields) and parallel developments in the field of ecology spurred a dramatic shift in thinking about the human organism and its relationship to its environment. These developments, in turn, provided the impetus for shifting and refining underlying assumptions about interactions between people and their environments as they affect health and illness. At the same time, the influence of the systems and ecological paradigms can be traced in social work theory and family theory.

In this chapter, we examine this theoretical progression as it converges to support our basic contention, namely, that health promotion and health care should include a primary focus on the family. In an overview of paradigm shifts and theoretical convergence, we trace the influence of the general systems paradigm and the ecological perspective as overarching conceptual frameworks within public health, medicine, health psychology, social work, and family therapy. Social stress, social integration, and transactional stress models are presented in some detail as they are related to the family-health/illness connection. The ecosystemic and biopsychosocial models are described as synthesizing meta-theoretical frameworks. Finally, we review emerging perspectives on the family, including the family systems model and family stress and coping models. Overall, the progression of knowledge within each of the cited disciplines and health professions parallels the trend toward synthesis that characterizes the scientific community as a whole (Schwartz, 1982). It is this integration and progression of knowledge that provides the rationale for including a family perspective in health care practice.

The General Systems Paradigm

The general systems paradigm was first formulated in the 1950s, and its influence has been widespread (Bertalanffy, 1974; Boulding, 1956; Buckley, 1968). Analyzing recent paradigm shifts in such diverse fields as physics, chemistry, ecology, mathematics, biology, psychology, and others, Schwartz and Ogilvy (1979) have identified radical shifts in a view of the world that can be traced to the influence of the systems paradigm, including: (1) a shift from a simple and probabilistic world toward a view of its complexity and diversity; (2) a shift from a view of a hierarchically ordered world to a world ordered by heterarchy that emphasizes interactive influence, mutual constraints, and simultaneous interests; (3) a shift from the image of a mechanistic and machine-like universe toward one that is holographic, recognizing that everything is interconnected with each part containing information about the whole; (4) a shift from an assumption of direct causality to assumptions of mutual causality; and (5) a shift from the notion that complex systems are merely the sum of more simple units toward the metaphor of morphogenesis which describes the creation of new forms.

The process of explicating the general systems paradigm within specific disciplines was begun in the 1950s and continues today. For example, numerous applications to social work practice have been elaborated and the paradigm's underlying assumptions have been recognized as consistent with the profession's long-held focus on the person and environment (Coulton, 1981; Germain, 1977; 1987; Hearn, 1969; Hollis, 1981; Meyer, 1983a; Northen, 1969, 1988). Although frequently referred to as general systems theory, the paradigm is more accurately viewed as an overarching framework, an abstract meta-theory or a model about relationships among objects (Buckley, 1968). The paradigm is best characterized as a way of thinking and a means of organizing our perceptions of relatedness and dynamic processes. Therefore, it has been termed "the skeleton of science" (Boulding, 1956). The paradigm is not specific to a single discipline but, rather, proposes a common language to be used among many disciplines. For this reason, it is a particularly useful paradigm for integrating knowledge across disciplines. In fact, the emergence of new interdisciplinary fields such as psychoneuroimmunology and social psychophysiology has been attributed to the systems perspective (Schwartz, 1982).

Several basic assumptions are intrinsic to the general systems paradigm (Buckley, 1968). Living and nonliving forms can be regarded as a system, having discrete properties that can be observed and studied. Systems are organized wholes, not just the sum of their separate parts, and consist of elements that are related in varying mutual or unidirectional, nonlinear, and intermittent causal networks. Of prime importance, living systems are assumed to be capable of primary as well as reactive change and evolution. Finally, living systems maintain their differentiation through continuous inputs from and outputs to their environment. In the subsequent discussion of family systems theory, we will illustrate the application of these assumptions at a lower level of abstraction.

The emergence of the general systems paradigm can be characterized as a scientific revolution in Kuhnian terms (1970) because it challenged existing paradigms that were held within various disciplines. Pertinent to our discussion, the paradigm provides a framework from which to reframe questions about mind–body relationships and person and environment transactions as an object of legitimate scientific inquiry in the matter of health and disease (Viney, Clarke, & Benjamin, 1986).

The Ecological Perspective

Ecology is the study of relations between organisms and their environments (Catalano, 1979). Specifically, ecologists study adjustment or adaptation to environmental change. Originally, the perspective was applied to analyze phenomena among animal and plant life. Early ecologists tried to explain changes in the size, mix, spatial distribution, and behavior of subhuman populations in a given geographic area. An ecosystem referred to habitats and the relationships among organisms living there (Catalano, 1979).

Major assumptions of the ecological perspective include: (1) that individual behavior is best explained within the total environmental context in which individuals are embedded; (2) that human environments are extremely complex and include physical dimensions as well as elaborate social, economic, and political structures; and (3) that individuals must maintain an adaptive mutuality with their environments as persons and environments are reciprocally influenced (Catalano, 1979; Germain, 1977; Germain & Gitterman, 1980; Holahan, Wilcox, Spearly, & Campbell, 1979). Application of the ecological perspective by social and behavioral scientists challenges theorists to describe and conceptualize the complex social environment. In this vein, Bronfenbrenner (1979) has proposed envisioning the environment as a nested arrangement of circumjacent contexts, including the microsystem or person, the mesosystem or interpersonal relations within family, school, and work contexts, the exosystem or social structures and institutions, and the macrosystem or overarching cultural patterns, values, and ideologies. Each of these environmental contexts is recognized to have potential effects on health and illness (Winett, 1985).

As early as the 1920s, sociologists began applying the ecological perspective to the human community in attempts to understand the nature, location, and growth of cities (Catalano, 1979). In recent years, this conceptual framework has been borrowed by social and behavioral scientists to better understand human adaptation in relation to changing environments (Barker, 1978; Micklin & Choldin, 1984; Moos & Insel, 1974). An underlying assumption of the early sociologists persists among social ecologists of today, namely, that major sources of physical illness and abnormal behavior or psychopathology are adaptation-related disorders that occur in interaction with community, social, and economic change (Catalano, 1979) and with characteristics of the environment (Moos & Insel, 1974).

A Social–Ecological Perspective in Public Health

Paradigm shifts are most evident in recent population-based studies of health and illness. Epidemiology, the study of the origin and spread of disease in human populations, has always been a central line of inquiry in the field of public health. Early in its history, the discipline focused on infectious disease and operated primarily from the germ paradigm (Catalano, 1979). In the face of new information, however, the field expanded its focus to include more emphasis on chronic disease and on illnesses associated with individual lifestyles (Moos, 1979). In recent years, a distinct subfield, social or psychosocial epidemiology, has emerged (Polinkas, 1985). Two major research thrusts have characterized much of this line of epidemiological research: the relationship between stress and physical and mental illness; and the direct or indirect effects of social integration, social network membership, and social support on health and on the stress–illness relationship. Knowledge gained from this social epidemiological research has spurred the development of theoretical models that can be applied in conceptualizing relationships between families and health.

Social Stress and Illness

The common sense and intuitive observation made by practitioners that illness often, although not always, followed stressful periods in the lives of individuals, was probably the earliest recognition of the potential health effects of life stress. It was not until the 1940s, however, that accumulating evidence began to suggest that the central nervous system was a plausible mechanism to explain the observed associations. Historical antecedents of the proposition that stressful life events have an etiological role in illness are found in the work of Cannon, who illustrated that stressful life events can be harmful, and by Adolf Meyer, who proposed that such events were etiological factors in illness (Dohrenwend & Dohrenwend, 1981).

In the progression of knowledge concerning social stress, the work of Selye marks a critical landmark. His research provided a physiological basis for future conceptualizations regarding social stress and the biological organism (Selye, 1956). Consistent with a biological paradigm, Selye envisioned stress as a bodily state, rather than as an external component of the environment. He posited that all stressors, regardless of type, produced the same pattern of physiological response, a pattern that he termed the general adaptation syndrome (GAS). In early laboratory studies, he identified the natural state of the organism to be one of equilibrium with its environment. Change in one part of the organism was seen to result in disequilibrium among all parts. The struggle to reestablish homeostasis was proposed to involve several processes including an alarm phase, in which the organism is mobilized for fight or flight, and a resistance phase, during which the organism copes with the change. If the organism fails to overcome the threat over time, a state of exhaustion is said to occur, eventually resulting in diseases of adaptation. The contribution of Selye's seminal research is reflected in the voluminous literature that has followed his work. Criticisms of his contribution have not detracted from its importance. Rather, knowledge about the physiological processes underlying stress responses has undergone major advances in recent years (McCarthy, Horwatt, & Konarska, 1988; Stein & Schlieifer, 1985; Williams, 1985).

Life Event Research

The influence of Selye's stress model is clearly reflected in the epidemiological research on stressful life events. In this body of research, stress is conceptualized as the readjustment or change in usual behavior required by the individual in response to specific life events. These studies test the hypothesis that the intensity or magnitude of threat, disruption, or readjustment evoked by life events is associated with emotional arousal and neuroendocrine changes, which, if prolonged, may result in impaired functioning or illness (Gunderson & Rahe, 1974). Individuals are inventoried regarding their stressful life experiences within a specified time period (Dohrenwend & Dohrenwend, 1981). In general, numerous studies have identified associations (albeit in most cases small) between stress scores and illness onset. Criticisms of this seminal work have centered on: (1) methodological weaknesses; (2) its failure to distinguish positive versus negative stressors and the extent to which the individual had control over the event; (3) inadequate consideration of daily strains and chronic stress; and (4) perhaps most important from a clinical standpoint, the failure to take into account mediating processes. Recognizing that stress is a fact of life, theoretical refinements and improved research methods are currently being applied to further explicate the relationship between social stress and health (Fleming, Baum, & Singer, 1984; Kaplan, 1983; Kasl & Cooper, 1987; Vingerhoets & Marcelissen, 1988; Weinberger, Hiner, & Tierney, 1985; Zales, 1985). As will be observed in Chapter 2, most stress inventories include a significant proportion of family-related events, thereby highlighting the family as a source of stress with potential effects on health.

Social–Structural Stress

Social epidemiologists have also examined the influence of social–structural phenomena on health. Guided by an ecological perspective, these studies hypothesize that macroenvironmental events generate individual stress and thereby influence individual health. For example, total mortality, infant mortality, child abuse, and psychiatric admissions have been traced to unemployment policies and economic fluctuations (Brenner, 1984). Other studies have demonstrated the negative effects of unemployment on adult physical and mental health (Kessler, House, & Turner, 1987). Studies have demonstrated increases in the incidence of stressful life events (Catalano & Dooley, 1977) and suicide rates (Brenner, 1985) associated with economic decline. Community-wide stressors, such as widespread unemployment and the Three Mile Island nuclear accident, also have negatively affected health (Dew, Bromet, & Schulberg, 1987). Haan, Kaplan, and Camacho (1987) conclude that the consistent finding of poorer health status among the poor is attributable to the health hazards that are ubiquitous in the environment of the poor. As the primary social unit, the family is crucial in buffering the health-related impact of social change and social environments on individual family members. We will return to this issue in Chapter 3 as we discuss the social context and specific social policies that influence the family-health/illness connection.

Stressful Physical Environments

In still other research guided by a social–ecological perspective, physical aspects of the environment have been demonstrated to have health effects (see Moos, 1979, for a review). For example, physical and mental illness and mortality rates are higher in urban than rural areas and highest in crowded cities (Maddocks, 1980; Moos, 1979). Of particular import is evidence that the physical environment, as manifested in household crowding, is related to problems in family functioning in areas of parental discipline and the marital relationship (Moos, 1979).

Other research has drawn attention to the influence of treatment environments on individual health behavior (Greenley & Davidson, 1988; Moos, 1985; Whitehead, Fusillo, & Kaplan, 1988). These studies have enhanced our understanding about the differential effects of the physical setting, as well as organizational structures on patient outcomes and on family behavior. For example, physical and structural aspects of rehabilitation hospitals have been shown to deter or promote independent behaviors of patients with spinal cord injuries (Willems & Halstead, 1978). In other work, the social structure of emergency and intensive care units has been shown to negatively affect family members of patients with a heart attack (Speedling, 1982).

Social Integration, Social Networks, Social Support, and Health

One of the earliest social epidemiological studies was Durkheim's (1951) study of suicide in which he found that suicide rates were related to community divorce rates and religious participation. He concluded that these findings were attributable to the negative effects of social isolation and its resultant normlessness or anomie. For this seminal work, Durkheim is considered a forerunner of contemporary research on social integration and social network participation. In later studies, Leighton (1974) proposed that communities could be plotted on a continuum of community integration–disintegration. He suggested that individual mental health is, to some extent, a product of community integration and mutual obligation. In contrast, poorly integrated communities are perceived to be stressful, especially insofar as they fail to provide access to needed resources. In more recent studies, Warren (1981) has identified differences in the "social health" of communities by assessing patterns of helping networks.

Evidence of the physical health effects of primary social network membership began accumulating from epidemiological studies conducted during the 1960s. Bruhn and colleagues (Bruhn, Chandler, Miller, Wolf, & Lynn, 1966; Bruhn, Phillips, & Wolf, 1982) found that rates of coronary heart disease differed between neighboring communities in Pennsylvania. Closer examination indicated that the community life of the population with lower rates of illness was characterized by close-knit family and neighborhood relationships. Other studies have implicated sociocultural mobility (resulting in severed social ties) in the etiology of illness (Syme, 1984).

It was in the mid-1970s that the emergence of social support theory appeared, linking concepts of social integration, social networks, and social support to physical health. In two seminal articles, Cassel (1976) and Cobb

(1976) reviewed more than 30 human and animal studies that found social relationships to be protective of health. They concluded that future research and theory-building take into account the potential direct and buffering roles of the social support that is exchanged within social relationships as it might influence health directly by enhancing individual well-being and indirectly by mediating the stress–illness relationship. House, Landis, and Umberson (1988) conclude that although the studies that these investigators reviewed were methodologically flawed, large-scale prospective studies conducted within the past 10 years have established a theoretical basis and strong empirical evidence for a causal impact of social relationships on health.

Theory concerning social relationships and social support and health is still in a formative stage. Although the research in this area has been characterized by little definitional consensus and the absence of standardized measures, findings are remarkably consistent in identifying influences on health. Future theoretical refinement and research is needed to enhance not only our understanding of the mechanisms through which social relationships affect health but also the factors that promote or inhibit the development and maintenance of social relationships (House et al., 1988). We will review results of research on social support with special attention to the supportive role of the family in the following chapter.

Transactional Stress Models: Interactional Processes and Mediating Factors

The hypothesized relationship between stress and illness has been the subject of extensive work by theorists, researchers, and practitioners. Increasingly, emphasis has shifted beyond a narrow focus on the reactive state of the organism to include a focus on multicausal and interactive processes. For example, in a significant shift in assumptions from Selye's general adaptation model, Lazarus (1966, 1981, Lazarus & Folkman, 1984) has proposed a more psychologically focused stress model that includes potential mediating factors in stress response. This theoretical model emphasizes the role of cognitive appraisal in individuals' perceptions of stress and in their subsequent response to stress. From this perspective, stress is believed to occur through transactions between persons and their environments. In this model, stress is neither an environmental stimulus, a characteristic of the person, nor a biological response, but rather it is experienced in the face of the individual's perception of a balance between demand and the availability of resources to respond to the demand. No events are universally stressful, unless perceived as stressful by the individual.

Pearlin and colleagues (1981) also define stress as resulting from interactions among multiple factors, including life events, chronic life strains, self-concepts, coping, and social supports. Lazarus places greater emphasis on the cognitive phenomenological view of stress in that he proposes that stress follows primary and secondary cognitive appraisal processes (in the former, the individual assesses the implications of the stressor; in the latter, resources are evaluated). Pearlin emphasizes the importance of chronic role strains and a process, over time, that produces stress. Both theorists assume that people are rarely passive in the face of life events and strains, but that they seek to change what they can, and, when they cannot bring about change in the stressor, they actively attempt to influence the personal meaning of the stressor or their emotional response to the stressor. These cognitive, emotional, and behavioral strategies constitute coping.

Antonovsky (1979) has proposed an integrative stress and health model. He suggests that there is widespread consensus about many stressors, and, more importantly, because stressors are ubiquitous, most individuals are continually exposed to life stressors. He suggests, therefore, that the important question concerns why most individuals do not regularly breakdown or become ill. Thus, he departs from the emphasis on cognition that is a hallmark of Lazarus and other cognitive theorists and proposes instead a more existential focus. Based on studies of holocaust survivors and others who have demonstrated successful coping in the face of adversity, he concludes that what distinguishes these individuals is their "sense of coherence." He defines sense of coherence as "a global orientation that expresses the extent to which one has a pervasive, enduring, though dynamic feeling of confidence that one's internal and external environments are predictable, and that there is a high probability that things will work out as well as can reasonably be expected" (Antonovsky, 1979, p. 123). The sense of coherence is proposed to be a product of sufficient "generalized resistance resources" which he defines as all personal, social, and environmental forces that an individual brings to bear in coping with stress.

To date, transactional models have not been applied in epidemiological studies, primarily because operationalizing these models is methodologically difficult and costly to incorporate in large-scale surveys. Several recent studies, however, suggest that chronic daily stressors and role strains might have even greater negative effects than more major life events, because they are so common and repeatedly activate an organismic response (Brantley, 1988; Kanner, Coyne, Schaefer, & Lazarus, 1981). Future research and theory building concerning human response to stress will undoubtedly be enhanced to the extent that interactional processes and mediating factors are examined. The social support literature already attests to the potential merits of including resources when studying individual response to the vicissitudes of life. Transactional models of person and environment interactions are also of clinical import insofar as they suggest avenues for intervention in the etiological stress–illness relationship. In subsequent chapters, we will present a broad range of interventions that are targeted to the family's role in the stress process that so often accompanies serious illness.

Ecological Systems: Paradigm Synthesis in Social Work

In yet another illustration of knowledge synthesis, social work theorists have found that integrating systems theory with the ecological perspective provides a useful overarching conceptual framework for the profession's traditional focus on person and environment (Allen-Meares & Lane, 1987; Carlton, 1984; Germain, 1977; 1978; 1987; Meyer, 1976; Northen, 1969; 1988; Siporin, 1975; 1980; Whittaker, Schinke, & Gilchrist, 1986). An ecosystemic perspective enlarges the unit of attention to include the individual, social institutions, culture, and the interactions and transactions among systems and within specific systems (Germain & Gitterman, 1980; Holahan et al., 1979). Furthermore, the perspective provides a framework from which to examine reciprocal processes between persons and environments, such as interpersonal transactions, social support exchange, coping behaviors, role-taking, social learning, resource acquisition, social stress, and the effects of social policies.

The ecosystemic perspective appears to be an especially useful conceptual framework for better understanding the family-health/illness connection and most important for delineating avenues for professional intervention. For example, from an ecosystemic viewpoint, it is possible not only to conceptualize community health problems and to analyze relationships between a community wellness center or health care facility and its broader community and between families and their environments, but also to examine the influence of culture on health-related family behavior. From this perspective, appropriate targets for health-related intervention with families include deficits in the environment, dysfunctional transactions between families and their environments, and the adaptive strategies of families.

In a model of person–environment fit, Coulton (1981) has explicated the traditional social work focus on person–environment interaction as it effects people's health. She proposes that life events, crises, and changes; resources, demands, and opportunities characteristic of the environment; needs, capabilities, and aspirations of the person; and physical health, mental health, and feeling of well-being influence person–environment fit. Presumably, lack of fit is perceived as stressful. She indicates an interaction effect between fit and health. However, we suggest that the model would more accurately reflect reality by incorporating mutual interactions among all factors. As we will demonstrate in the following chapter, families are often sources of stress for individual members as well as support. Therefore, the family plays a critical role in the degree of person–environment fit, and therein lies one mechanism through which the family influences the health of its members.

The Biopsychosocial Model: A Transactional Systems Perspective

The biomedical or disease model has long dominated scientific research and practice in the field of medicine. In the face of new observations about health and illness, however, the validity and adequacy of the model have been seriously questioned (Dubos, 1959). Antonovsky (1979) asked, given a common pathogenic environment, why many people stay well. In reframing this basic question to focus on health rather than illness, he made a compelling argument that what he terms *salutogenesis* (in contrast to pathogenesis) should be a legitimate focus of scientific inquiry in medicine, public health, and social science. We have already described other data documenting the impact of economic and social change (Catalano, 1979) and social and physical environments (see Moos, 1979 for a review) on health. These observations appear to fall well outside of the purview of a narrow biomedical model of illness. Furthermore, and perhaps most convincing, critics of the disease model have pointed to the fact that medical technology is woefully inadequate in addressing the chronic diseases that are preeminent in contemporary society. For example, the Center for Disease Control of the United States Health Service indicates that up to 50 percent of mortality from the 10 leading causes of death in the United States can be traced to lifestyle (Bruhn, 1988). These and other critics (Fuchs, 1975; Pratt, 1982; Thomas, 1977) underscore the need for a model that includes a focus on the role of individual health behaviors and lifestyles and on social and institutional environments and policies as they jointly and interactively affect individual and community health.

If it is conceded that the biomedical or disease model is inadequate because it neglects consideration of critical causal factors in health and illness, then a new paradigm is needed. In recent history, psychosomatic, holistic, and biobehavioral or behavioral medicine are sometimes referred to as alternatives to the disease model (Di Matteo & Friedman, 1982). Each of these movements has merit and represents attempts to conceptually link mind and body. None, however, represents a dynamic theoretical framework for the *interdisciplinary* study of multiple, complex, and reciprocal interactions that are presumed to be associated with health and illness.

Recently, the biopsychosocial model is emerging as an alternative to traditional paradigms (Engel, 1977, 1980; Leigh & Reiser, 1980; Schwartz, 1982). The coining of the term, *biopsychosocial,* has obvious appeal insofar, as it is on the surface, inclusive rather than exclusive. In our view, however, its ultimate value will be assessed in terms of its usefulness in guiding future theoretical development, scientific inquiry, and practice. Indeed, this is the ultimate test of all scientific paradigms.

As originally set forth by Engel (1977; 1980), the model is based on the general systems paradigm and proposes that disease and illness can only be truly understood by evaluating all potential contributing factors, and that these include the social and psychological context. In a further attempt to specify and extend the model, Schwartz (1982) has observed that the emerging paradigm shift is a logical result of the recognition that health and illness, and problems associated with both, are inherently multidimensional in nature. Drawing on earlier philosophical writings and more recent research, he proposes a relational and organismic (systemic) view of health, disease, and illness as it exists in humans. He contrasts this way of thinking about health and disease from mechanistic approaches that are more characteristic of the biomedical model. He goes on to describe a contextual thinking style as assuming multicausality rather than single-causality and proposes that organistic thinking focuses attention on the interaction among multiple causes. He concludes that traditional ways of thinking consistent with the disease model, while undoubtedly useful in advancing medical technology, are insufficient in accounting for the multiple variables that interact and affect health and illness.

The biopsychosocial model is best understood as an overarching conceptual framework or metaphor derived from the general systems paradigm and applied to the study of human health and disease. From this perspective, behavior and disease are viewed as subject to genetic, biological, psychological, sociocultural, and ecological factors (Gentry, 1984). By its nature, the model is interdisciplinary. From this umbrella framework, it is possible to conceptualize a broad range of relationships and processes that ultimately can be tested as to their contribution to health and illness. For example, under this framework, the continued exploration of physiological reactivity, disease, and the Type A coping style (coronary-prone coping behavior) (Matthews & Rakaczky, 1986), as well as examination of the hypothesis that Type A behavior is a product of Western cultures (Margolis, McLeroy, Runyan & Kaplan, 1983), are legitimate lines of inquiry. Similarly, the relationship between human behavior and cancer etiology and treatment falls within this model (Levy, 1985). Even more important, this framework raises both social–psychological and social–structural avenues of intervention to an equal plane with physiological interventions (Cassileth & Hamilton, 1979; Derogatis, 1986a; Greene, 1983; Leigh & Reiser, 1980; McHugh & Vallis, 1985). In subsequent chapters, we will review extensive data that underscores the family's equally vital role in health promotion, health maintenance, and in the management of illness. These family-health interfaces can be best examined from a biopsychosocial perspective. In Chapter 3, the powerful and pervasive effects of social–structural environments on family-health activity will be examined. This discussion is also appropriate under a biopsychosocial model.

Family Systems Theory

In what by now can be seen as a pattern in knowledge synthesis, knowledge progression influenced by new information and converging perspectives can also be traced throughout the relatively recent development of family systems theory. In contrast to the development of many other social and behavioral science theories, the growth and refinement of family systems theory has been based in practice, occurring predominantly within the field of family therapy. Its earliest origins have been traced to the work of Freud who proposed, what was then a new paradigm, namely, that emotional illness developed in relationship to significant others (Kerr, 1981). Over time, many mental health practitioners concluded that a patient's therapy was related, in many ways, to the response of his or her family. At the same time, some of these clinicians, who were to become pioneers in family therapy, recognized the need to conceptualize and describe relationships within the family (Kerr, 1981). Psychiatrists and social workers found that personality and individual functioning theories were inadequate in explaining family processes. Therefore, in the 1950s and 1960s, these early family theorists borrowed extensively from the emerging general systems paradigm (Doherty & Baird, 1983).

The influence of systems thinking in the evolution of family theory is clearly evident. Indeed, the most important element in paradigm progression in family theory was the focus of attention on interactional processes. During the 1970s and up to today, numerous theoretical models of family functioning have emerged, varying primarily in the specific aspect of family functioning that is emphasized. In recent years, however, increasing attention is focused on the family system's interaction with its broader physical and social environment, thereby reflecting an expansion of the family perspective as it is influenced by the ecological perspective. Therefore, although there is no single integrated family theory at this time, consensus is emerging among family therapists and theorists that an overarching ecosystemic perspective has the greatest utility for understanding families (Forman & Hagan, 1983).

At this point, it is useful to examine several general assumptions that appear in more than one, but not all, systemic theoretical orientations to the family. A family systems perspective focuses attention on the family as a discrete entity rather than as a collection of individuals. Hartman and Laird (1983) have underscored several propositions about living systems that have been applied to our thinking about families. Living systems are assumed to: (1) be open systems, with boundaries that are to some extent permeable and open to new information from their environments, which in turn determines the systems potential for growth and change (a closed system is assumed to move toward entropy or lack of organization and differentiation); (2) strive toward internal balance or inner integrity; and (3) require, in order to survive, a sustained adaptive balance with their environment. Consistent with the general systems paradigm, the family is viewed as an open, transactive, and adaptive system, capable of either self-directed or externally directed growth and change.

As already noted, family theorists have focused their attention on the specific interactional processes in which families engage and on the structure of families. A family is, to a great extent, a product of its own historical development (Hartman & Laird, 1983). This intergenerational perspective is a central theme throughout the family therapy literature.

Systems are assumed to have boundaries, a line separating the system from its environment. Boundary is an important concept in understanding both individual member boundary as it relates to separateness and connectedness within the family system, as well as the family's interaction with its environment (Doherty & Baird, 1981). "In the case of a family, the boundary consists of an invisible set of loyalties, rules and emotional connections" (Hartman & Laird, 1983, p. 81). Families' internal boundaries range on a continuum from close-knit or enmeshed to loosely tied or disengaged. At the same time, it is recognized that families must open their boundaries to routinely interact with other systems. Indeed, the ability to obtain resources from environmental systems is a critical factor in the survival of the family. Zimmerman (1988) has noted that family boundaries are becoming more permeable in that government is increasingly less reluctant to interact directly on family life.

Systems theory suggests that boundary maintenance means that system boundaries are well-defined (Buckley, 1968). Boss (1988), however, has drawn attention to family "boundary ambiguity." She suggests that the ambiguity centers on who is in or out of the family system. The issue of boundary ambiguity emerges frequently in health practice in questions about whether the patient is included or excluded in family system work, and in questions about which members are to be included when working with complex family structures, such as step-families.

Minuchin and his co-workers are perhaps best known for delineating the internal family structure (1975; 1978). From this theoretical perspective, families are assumed to be complex systems with intricate organizational structures. Families are proposed to carry out their functions through subsystems such as the parental, marital, and sibling subsystem. Lines of authority and power, role behavior, and rules are additional aspects of family structure (Doherty & Baird, 1981).

Family Stress and Coping Theory: Integrative Models

A consideration of family stress and coping theory is included in our discussion for several reasons. First, and most important, from a clinical perspective, this body of knowledge highlights the family's ability to grow and to change and, thus, is the rationale for presuming that families can be helped through professional intervention. Having witnessed the strength and resilience of the family system in response to life stressors and to illness, we believe it is necessary to learn about family strengths so as to be better guided in our attempts to assist families who are having difficulties. Second, as will be described later, family stress is experienced by most, if not all, families at all stages of family development. Third, the family's response to life stressors is presumed to affect the family's overall health promotion and health maintenance work, with important effects on the health of individual family members. Fourth, illness is presumed to be a family stressor event, and the family's response to this stressor is recognized as affecting the course of illness, the well-being of individual family members, and the family system. Finally, and perhaps most important, the evolutionary development of knowledge in this area provides a basis for the belief that we can intervene successfully in the area of family stress management. Furthermore, although family stress theories are not practice theories (in that specific intervention, techniques derived from specific theoretical frameworks are not prescribed), the conceptualization of family stress and response provides the practitioner with direction as to areas to which interventions might be targeted.

It is noteworthy that one of the earliest formulations of family stress theory (Hill, 1949; 1958; 1981) has withstood the test of time and continues to underpin contemporary family stress literature (Boss, 1988; Burr, 1973; McCubbin, 1979; McCubbin et al., 1980; McCubbin & Patterson, 1982). The underlying base for the majority of family stress formulations is the general systems paradigm, perhaps accounting for the general consistency across theoretical approaches. Briefly stated, Hill's model proposes that:

> A (the event)—interacting with B (the family's crisis-meeting resources)—interacting with C (the definition the family makes of the event)—produces X (the

crisis). The second and third determinants—the family resources and definition of the event—lie within the family itself and must be seen in terms of the family's structures and values. The hardships of the event, which go to make up the first determinant, lie outside the family and are an attribute of the event itself (Hill, 1958).

At the time, Hill also proposed that family adjustment involved several stages resulting in a new level of family organization. It is noteworthy that Hill first presented his theoretical model to practicing social workers (Boss, 1988).

Whereas the basic components of family stress theory were set forth in this early work, the task of rendering clarity and empirical support to these early conceptualizations continues today (Boss, 1988; Burr, 1973; McCubbin et al., 1980; McCubbin & Patterson, 1983; McCubbin, 1988). The first part of Hill's formulation has spurred attempts to define its specific components, including the stressor event, family resources, family definitions of the stressor, and the family crisis. The second part of the model has been recently explicated in the study of family coping, family adjustment, and family adaptation (Boss, 1988).

In contrast to conceptualizations about stress within individuals, approaches to family stress theory have been grounded in sociology, rather than medicine, biology, or psychology. However, similar conceptual and methodological difficulties confront both individual and family stress theorists. For example, how should family stress be defined? Is the stress inherent in the stressor or in the family's response to the stressor? Indeed, can these be distinguished (McCubbin et al., 1980)? Are there events about which there is consensus as to their stressful nature? If so, then what factors account for differential family responses to these events? What components of the family system are of practical concern in terms of the family's response to stress: its overall organization, its relationship with other social systems in its environment (i.e., its social community), its adaptive capacity? Each of these questions has obvious practical implications for the family's health-related functioning.

Stressor Events

Family stress theorists and researchers commonly distinguish stressor events from a state of family stress. Family stressors are frequently classified as normative and nonnormative events. Among the former are family transitions, such as the transition to parenthood, child launching, the empty nest period, retirement, widowhood, and relocation and commonly occurring stressors of contemporary society, such as divorce, drug use, dual careers, working mothers, single-parenting, step-parenting, and economic fluctuations (McCubbin & Figley, 1983). Others have called attention to chronic environmental stress associated with the minority status of families (Peters & Massey, 1983). Nonnormative or catastrophic events include substance abuse, abandonment, chronic illness, bereavement, unemployment, rape, natural disasters, war, and captivity (Figley & McCubbin, 1983). There is also recognition of the importance of the accumulation of clustering of events wherein the family's coping capacity may fail under the burden of exposure to an overload of stressors (Geismar et al., 1979; McCubbin & McCubbin, 1988). This line of reasoning is closely analogous to Selye's notion of exhaustion that has been operationalized in the individual life event research referred to earlier.

Boss (1988) has proposed a detailed classification of events according to characteristics that have apparent implications for the family's perception of the event and its ability to cope. Using a dialectic approach, she distinguishes internal, normative, ambiguous, volitional, chronic, and cumulative from external, nonnormative, nonambiguous, nonvolitional , acute, and isolated events. Internal events are precipitated within the family, such as a member getting drunk or committing suicide or running for election, whereas external events begin outside the family. Illness-related stressors have also been shown to vary along the dimensions of ambiguity, time, and responsibility for the event (Tomlinson, 1986).

Family Stress

Among family stress theorists, consensus is emerging that stress occurs as a result of the family's definition or perception of the event. Furthermore, the family's perception of the event is presumed to be influenced by family resources and community norms and perceptions concerning the stressor (McCubbin & Patterson, 1983; Reiss & Oliveri, 1983). In this context, family stress is a situation-dependent perceived demand-capability imbalance (McCubbin & Patterson, 1987) or a change in the family's equilibrium (Boss, 1988). Family stress is distinguished from family distress which is defined by its perceived unpleasant or disorganized family state (McCubbin & Patterson, 1983) or family crisis wherein the family system is blocked, immobilized, and incapacitated (Boss, 1988). Boss (1988) suggests that families are either in crisis or are not, whereas families experience stress along a continuum reflecting degrees of stress. A family crisis is also defined as being distinct from family stress insofar as it is characterized by the family's failure to restore stability and reduce ongoing pressure for change in the family (McCubbin & Patterson, 1983). This transactional perspective of family stress is akin to the individual stress theories described earlier.

Family Resources

In recent years, family members' personal resources, the family system's internal resources, social support, and coping have been studied as they are assumed to constitute Hill's B factor (the family's crisis-meeting resources (McCubbin et al., 1980; Pilisuk & Parks, 1983). Family resources are proposed to include its individual member and collective strengths available at the time the stressor event occurs (Boss, 1988). Personal resources of individual family members include demographic and sociocultural characteristics, member's physical health, and psychological resources such as self-esteem, sense of control or mastery, and personality characteristics (Ell, 1985, 1986; Pearlin & Schooler, 1978; Pearlin, Schooler, Lieberman, & Menaghan, 1981).

Family resources that have been most frequently elaborated on theoretically, as well as examined empirically, are family cohesion, adaptability, and communication. Family cohesion and adaptability and related concepts are salient in the theoretical formulations of a broad range of family theorists, researchers, and therapists (Beavers & Voeller, 1983; Olson & McCubbin, 1982; Olson, Sprenkle, & Russel, 1979; Minuchin, 1974). Although theorists vary in their conceptions of family cohesion and adaptability, these constructs are derived from the systems paradigm, with the former referring to family integration or degree of bonding or connections among family members, and the latter to the ability of the family to change in the face of external demand. Family communication is seen as a process affecting both family cohesion and adaptability. In the Circumplex Model of Family Functioning developed and tested by Olson and his associates, it is hypothesized that families that are balanced on the dimensions of change and cohesion will function more adequately than families assessed to be at extremes. Communication is presumed to be a facilitating dimension in that it facilitates movement of families on cohesion and adaptability (Olson, 1986). In an attempt to identify family resources that are most applicable to its health-related functions, Pratt (1976) has described the "energized family" as being characterized by flexible internal organization and role relationships, shared power, individual member autonomy, and a supportive environment for individual member growth.

In recent history, social support has been the most extensively studied resource in stress management (Cohen, 1988a, Cohen & Syme, 1985). Social support research pertaining to family stress response has been far more limited. Nonetheless, the utility of this resource for families is also well-documented in recent literature, especially as it prevails in family coping with illness. (This evidence will be reviewed in detail in the following chapter.) Interest in social support as it pertains to family stress response has ranged to include a focus on: supportive exchanges within the family system, such as within the husband-wife helping relationship (Burke & Weir, 1982, Coyne & DeLongis, 1986; Waltz, 1986a,b); supportive exchange between the family system and its extended primary social network (Pilisuk & Parks, 1983); and extending supportive resources through encouraging family participation in a broad range of mutual and self-help support groups (Wassermann & Danforth, 1988). The latter intervention has been most visible in attempts to assist families with the transition to parenthood (Gray, 1982; Wandersman, 1982), during illness (as reviewed in Chapter 5), and bereavement (Jeter, 1983; Videka-Sherman & Lieberman, 1986).

Family Coping

Family coping theory is (as is individual coping theory) in an early stage of development. Building on Hill's earlier conceptualizations of family adjustment and regenerative power as processes following the crisis, family theorists are only now beginning to examine family coping processes (Boss, 1988; McCubbin & McCubbin, 1987; Patterson, 1988b). In contrast to individual coping, family coping always involves interpersonal processes (Klein & Hill, 1979; Menaghan, 1983). McCubbin and his colleagues (1980) have described the multifaceted task confronting the stressed family system, suggesting that the family must simultaneously: (1) maintain satisfactory internal organization and communication; (2) promote member independence and self-esteem; (3) maintain family bonds and coherence; (4) maintain and develop social supports; and (5) attempt to control the impact of the stressor and the amount of change in the family unit. The individual member and collective cognitive, affective, and behavioral responses of the family to achieve these goals constitute family coping (Patterson, 1988b) or stress management (Boss, 1988). In an example of a family stress model, the Family Adjustment and Adaptation Response (FAAR) Model, defines coping behavior as attempts to reduce or manage a demand (McCubbin & Patterson, 1983). From this perspective, family coping behaviors can involve: (1) direct action to reduce the number and/or intensity of demands; (2) direct action to acquire additional resources; (3) maintaining existing resources; (4) managing tension; and (5) attempts to cognitively restructure the meaning of a situation (Patterson, 1988b).

In highlighting the importance of coping repertoires and strategies, family theorists have asked a question similar to that raised by Antonovsky (1979) about what factors distinguish persons who stay well in a pathogenic environment. What factors distinguish those families who never reach a state of crisis and who remain durable and resilient even in the face of extreme adversity (McCubbin & McCubbin, 1988)? In this regard, rigidity and disorganization in accommodating change or stress are regarded to be dysfunctional coping responses, whereas flexibility and stability are purported to be effective strategies.

Family stress theory also directs our attention to the family's definition of the stressor (Hill, 1958) or the family's perception of the stressor event (Boss, 1988). In this context, attention is drawn to the perceived meaning of the stressor event or situation, and the question is raised as to whether there is a shared family perception (an issue that is important in relation to from whom to obtain assessment data). In the FAAR Model, situational meanings include the family's subjective definition of the demands, their capabilities, and these factors relative to each other (Patterson, 1988b). At another level, global family meanings are proposed as influencing the family stress process (Patterson, 1988b). These are referred to as the family schema or the family paradigm. The former is proposed to include five discrete dimensions: (1) a shared family purpose; (2) perception of itself in relation to its broader community; (3) family outlook; (4) a family's view of its current experience in relation to other experiences; and (5) its perception of shared control over life circumstances (Patterson, 1988b).

In a similar vein, Reiss (1981, 1982) has identified the family paradigm to be a critical factor in collective family problem-solving. He proposes that each family is guided in its transactions with its social world by its own family paradigm, namely its collective or shared constructions, expectations, and fantasies about its social world (Reiss, 1981). The family paradigm model is a synthesizing model in that it focuses on transactions between the family and its social environment, emphasizing the family's adaptability and creativity in the face of external social forces. In related work, Reiss and Oliveri (1983) observe that a family's perceived meaning of a stressful event, such as illness, will be strongly influenced by community perceptions of the event. In an important related theoretical development, Antonovsky and Sourani (1988) have begun to measure the collective perceived coherence of family life. In preliminary research, these investigators found that a strong family sense of coherence defined as family life being comprehensible, manageable, and meaningful was associated with spouses satisfaction with family life following a disabling illness.

Family Stress Outcomes

Attention to outcomes in family stress theory recognizes the nonstatic, ever-changing, evolutionary, and growth characteristics of family systems. Hill wrote about this process as the family's regenerative power. In a similar vein, Boss (1988) underscores the fact that even families in crisis do not remain in an immobilized and incapacitated state. Others observe that illness has the effect of changing the family system in numerous ways (Cassileth, & Hamilton 1979).

McCubbin and Patterson (1983) and Patterson (1988) have extended Hill's original formulation beyond the family crisis stage to incorporate processes in the family's adaptation over time. The Double ABCX Model, therefore, extends the original ABCX Model to include both acute adjustment and long-term adaptation (McCubbin & Patterson, 1983). In so doing, these family theorists have underscored the regenerative power of the family as it undergoes reorganization following a crisis.

Family coping theory and adaptation theories are vital theoretical links to practice with families. These conceptualizations highlight the belief that families can be helped in their management of stress, and, most important, they delineate avenues for clinical assessment and intervention. Recently there is recognition that the stress experience will vary among families of different sociocultural groups (Peters & Massey, 1983).

The Future: Continued Theory Integration and Refinement

It should now be clear that an important step in advancing theory as it underpins family-focused health and medical care is the synthesis or integration of family theory within the biopsychosocial model. Integrating family theory within a biopsychosocial model of health and illness requires a further paradigm shift from traditional medical science (Beavers, 1983; Bloch, 1983, 1984; Ramsey, 1989) and, to a lesser extent, from the heavy emphasis on individual behavior within health psychology (Kerns & Turk, 1985). Unquestionably, knowledge about individual behavior and health and illness will continue to be applied in the theoretical refinement of family theory as it applies to health. However, a biopsychosocial model of the family-health/illness connection will necessarily focus on the family system, including the multiple and reciprocal interactions among family members as they affect individual member health and well-being.

Fortunately, attempts to conceptualize linkages between the family and member health and illness have begun (Newbrough, Simpkins, & Maurer, 1985; Patterson, 1988a; Ramsey, 1989 Rolland, 1988a,b). These theoretical linkages will continue to draw on family functioning theory, conceptualizations about a family life cycle or developmental stages, and family stress and coping theory. Wikler's (1986) elaboration of family stress theory as applied to families with a developmentally disabled child provides a valuable example of the merits of examining families and illness connections from a theoretical perspective.

Families undergo change in form and lifestyle in conjunction with the life-span of individual family members. Some theorists and practitioners have gone so far as to delineate a family life cycle (Carter & McGoldrick, 1988). The family life cycle is described as moving through developmental stages marked by legal beginnings and terminations and social exits and entrances. Examples of the former are marriage, retirement, and death of a spouse. The latter commonly focus on the birth of children, their exit from the home into the school arena, and their subsequent launching into independent adult life. The model has been useful in outlining the family tasks associated with these transition points and during the stages between the critical events. Health care practitioners have found the model to be useful in highlighting the potential impact of illness or disability on families' ability to master these developmental tasks (Brown, 1988; La Voie, 1985; Rolland, 1988a,b) as well as differences in a family's adaptation to illness that are attributable to its stage in the family life cycle (Levy, 1988). Recent criticism of the family life cycle model is derived from its original emphasis on the so-called traditional nuclear family with children. A consideration of the model in attempts to understand the family-health/illness connection will need to incorporate the diversity in family structures that characterizes society today.

In the continued development and refinement of a family perspective on health, it will also be necessary to go beyond a consideration of the family system to include the family's relationship to its social, economic, cultural, and physical environment. Inclusion of this ecological perspective will help ensure that environmentally induced hazards and environmental resources are not neglected in designing interventions to enhance family-health roles (Franklin, 1988). We will elaborate on this perspective in Chapter 3.

The further development and refinement of social support theory, as it is applied to health, will undoubtedly contribute to the elaboration and specification of the biopsychosocial model. Furthermore, integrating family theory with support theory will become an increasingly important knowledge base for enhancing our understanding of the family-health/illness connection (Ell, 1989; Perlman & Rook, 1987; Pilisuk & Parks, 1983). Whereas, social support theory applied to health is relatively new in the health sciences, the social support construct is not new to social work. The profession also has a rich heritage of work with families, as evidenced in Chapter 6. Social workers, therefore, are poised strategically and, in our view, obligated to assume leadership both in further refining social support theory and in explicating relationships between support, families, and health, (Ell, 1989). This is especially the case as it pertains to evaluating the effectiveness of interventions and service-delivery technologies that are aimed at influencing relationships between social integration, social networks, and social support and health and illness as they are enacted within and influenced by family systems.

A specific area for further study, and one about which social work is particularly knowledgeable, is the relationship between community, especially the human service community, and family health-related functions and tasks. Social workers traditionally have advanced the belief that community and primary network support are major contributors to individual and family well-being (Geismar, 1980; Geismar et al., 1979; Selby, 1959; 1979). Moreover, ensuring access to basic human services and resources within one's community has been a cornerstone of the profession's advocacy efforts. There is considerable evidence from clinical experience and from early research that the ability of the family system to make linkages to the broader community system is a critical resource in the family's ability to function, especially in the face of stress (Geismar, 1980; Geismar et al., 1979; Pilisuk & Parks, 1983). Sources of support outside the family include friends and neighbors, religious and organizational affiliations, and a community network of resources. Of particular interest is evidence that the family's ability to promote the health of its members is positively affected by its regular interaction with community organizations and resources (Pratt, 1982). Social workers have been in the forefront in documenting the importance of social integration and access to human services in fostering early child development (Zigler & Weiss, 1985), mitigating the stresses of family life (Dooley, Prochaska, & Klibanoff, 1983; Geismer, 1980; Geismar et al., 1979), in preventing child abuse (Garbarino et al., 1987), and in maintaining people with physical and psychological impairments in their communities (Ell, 1985; Gray, 1982; Collins & Pancoast, 1976; Wassermann & Danforth, 1987; Whittaker et al., 1983; Whittaker, Schinke, & Gilchrist, 1986). The merits of expanding the profession's contribution in refining practice theories and in developing new service technologies to influence the social integration, network participation, and social support exchange of families toward the goal of maximizing health are unquestionable.

As the foregoing clearly demonstrates, the theoretical groundwork for advancing knowledge regarding the role of the family in health has been laid. Social workers are on the front lines in providing a broad range of family health-related services. Continued theoretical development will advance more quickly and be applied more readily in practice to the extent that practitioners actively participate in future knowledge-building efforts.

2
Research on Health, Illness, and Families

In the preceding chapter, we have presented a theoretical rationale for the argument that the family should be a primary unit for health care intervention. The proposition that families influence individual health and illness and, conversely, that families are affected by individual members' health status is also consistent with clinical observation. In this chapter, we selectively review extant research as it provides empirical evidence of the interactive relationships between families and health and illness. In recent years, a growing body of research documents: (1) relationships between families and individual member's health and development of illness; (2) family effects on illness outcomes; and (3) the impact of illness on family systems and family functioning. These relationships are discussed separately to enhance clarity, although we recognize that they are interactive and not mutually exclusive. Indeed, as the family affects an illness, the illness may be changing the family simultaneously (Campbell, 1986). Organizing a discussion of the research in this way also serves to highlight areas for psychosocial intervention.

Individual Health Status

Relationships between families and individual members' health status can be viewed from a biological, developmental, and ecosystemic perspective. Family genetic influences on predisposition to illness as well as on hereditary illness are well-documented. More recently, researchers have begun to examine family social processes as they may influence members' overall health. These studies have generally addressed family influences on individual development, interactional processes within families, as well as transactional processes between families and the broader social environment (Venters, 1989).

Genetic Influences

Families transmit disease and predisposition to disease genetically. Examination of the mechanisms of this family relationship to illness falls primarily within the domain of the biological sciences and will not be reviewed here. Social and behavioral scientists, however, have become engaged in several related areas of scientific inquiry. One such area concerns the extent to which physiological reactivity to stress may be genetically influenced (Matthews & Rakaczky, 1986). To date, the question remains largely an unproven hypothesis (Matthews & Rakaczky, 1986). Whether similarity in risk factors (e.g., cardiovascular disease, blood pressure) among family members is genetically determined or results from aspects of family environment is another area of interdisciplinary research (Baranowski & Nader, 1985). Additional questions of interest to the social scientist concern marriage and childbearing decision-making processes in the face of known genetic risks; (Black, 1980; Katz, 1980; Schoenfeld, Berkman, Myers, & Clark, 1984). Recent research suggests that genetic counseling reduces negative psychological responses, but it has little effect on childbearing practices (Neal-Cooper & Scott, 1988). There is also evidence that parental discussion of prenatal testing distresses their preschool children (Black & Furlong, 1984). The family context and influence on individual health practices, when confronted with inherited predisposition to disease, is also of research interest. The latter is of concern, for example, in light of evidence that smoking increases risk of coronary illness when there is a family history of cardiovascular disease (Khaw & Barrett-Connor, 1986).

Social Processes

Evidence to support the proposition that families influence member's health by way of social processes is converging from several different lines of research. In general, family social processes are believed to exert their influence on health by shaping member's health practices and health service use, influencing psychological health, and providing access to environmental resources. The first is concerned with the family as a primary socializing agent. The family is assumed to play a vital role in directly and indirectly shaping, from childhood, member's beliefs and attitudes about health-related practices and lifestyle and conveying family norms about what constitutes illness and what are appropriate illness behaviors (Geertsen, Klauber, Rindflesh, Kane, & Gray, 1978; Lau & Klepper, 1988; Shapiro, 1983). Cultural differences in family customs and practices have long been recognized, attesting to the rich diversity of family life (Hines, 1988; McGoldrick, 1988; Wagner, 1988a,b; Woehrer, 1978). Family socialization effects on health practices are profoundly influenced by families' cultural and socioeconomic milieus (Harwood, 1981). Family functioning styles have also been shown to influence health practices (Pratt, 1976). Families can be expected, therefore, to exhibit similar health habits, lifestyles, symptom recognition and response, as well as medical care utilization patterns.

The relationships between psychological health and physical health and between environmental factors and physical health have long been recognized. It is interesting, however, that only recently have investigators focused their research on these potential areas of interaction between families and health and illness. Increased interest among researchers in studying the family-health/ illness connection has been spurred by recognition of the importance of lifestyle and other personal and environmental forces that combine to influence health. In this scientific climate, the merits of undertaking family research are increasingly recognized.

Health Practices

Health-related behaviors including diet, exercise, smoking, and alcohol use are, in large part, presumed to be learned and maintained within the family. Recent evidence of similar health practices among family members is consistent with a family socialization hypothesis (see Sallis & Neder, 1988; and Venters, 1986, for reviews).

In light of the irrefutable evidence that smoking has ill effects on health, the degree to which the family influences this health-related behavior is an important empirical and practical question. In this regard, women's smoking has been found to predict birth weight of their children, physical development, and accidents among preschoolers (Graham, 1987). Other data indicate that family processes are critical influences on smoking behavior (Doherty & Whitehead, 1986). Children of parents who smoke are consistently found to be more likely to become smokers themselves, especially if it is the mother who smokes. There is also evidence that smoking habits are reinforced within families. For example, smoking among significant others, especially partners, hinders long-term abstinence after initial smoking cessation (Coppotelli & Orleans, 1985; Mermelstein, Cohen, Lichtenstein, Baer, & Kamarck, 1986).

In a similar vein, other evidence indicates that children are rarely obese if their parents are not also obese, and that family environments are frequently related to individual diet and nutrition practices (see Baranowski & Nader, 1985, for a review; Garn, Bailey, & Higgins, 1980). There is evidence, for example, of familial genetic and interactive contributions to the etiology and course of anorexia and bulimia (Strober & Humphrey, 1987). These data have spurred numerous calls for a family approach in medical care (Geyman, 1977; Schaffer, 1983; Schmidt, 1978), focusing attention on the value of detailed family assessment by all health care practitioners (Doherty

& Campbell, 1988). At the same time, there is little evidence of relationships between family factors and children's concepts of health and illness, perhaps due in part to conceptual and methodological inadequacies in the research to date (see Gochman, 1985, for a review). Least well-researched is the question of family influence on health-promoting behavior (Gochman, 1985).

Other evidence underscores the potential positive effects of families on health practices. Of interest, age-adjusted mortality rates have been shown to be higher for the unmarried (Berkman & Syme, 1979; Blazer, 1982; House, Robbins & Robbins & Metzner, 1983) and nonparents (Kobrin & Hendershot, 1977) than for the married and parents. Spurred by these data, a recent study examined mechanisms that might explain these findings. Analyzing data from a national sample of nearly 2000 respondents, the investigator found that marriage and the presence of children in the home had a deterrent effect on negative health behaviors (Umberson, 1987). The investigator suggested that family roles may promote social control of health behaviors which, in turn, affect subsequent member mortality.

Health Care Utilization

Recently, families have been shown to exhibit similar patterns of symptom reporting, doctor visits (Gorton, Doerfler, Hulka, & Tyroler, 1979; Newacheck & Halfon, 1986), and medicine use (Osterweis, Bush, & Zuckerman, 1979). Maternal medical care use and employment and family stressors and social network structure have been related to children's use of pediatric care (Alexander & Markowitz, 1986; Cafferta & Kasper, 1985; Horowitz, Morgenstern & Berkman, 1985; Newacheck & Halfon, 1986). An area of family influence on health service use that has received recent attention concerns symptoms appraisal and response and the decision to seek professional medical care. Recent evidence suggests that individuals engage in several stages or processes of symptom recognition and evaluation before initiating contact with the formal medical care system (Berkanovic, Telesky, & Reeder, 1979; Matthews, Siegel, Kuller, Thompson, & Varat, 1983; Safer, Tharps, Jackson, & Leventhal, 1979). Not well-examined is the actual decision-making process leading to obtaining professional medical care (Alonzo, 1986; McKinlay, 1972).

It is known, however, that 70–90 percent of all sickness episodes are handled outside the formal health care system, and individuals engage in self-treatment often with the aid of the family (Demers, Altamore, Mustin et al, 1980; Hulka, Kupper, & Cassel, 1972; Pratt, 1976; Turk & Kerns, 1985). Furthermore, consultation with family members is commonly engaged in during physical symptom appraisal and in decision making prior to seeking health care services (Berkanovic & Telesky, 1982; Doherty & Campbell, 1988; Mckinlay, 1973). Under some circumstances, consultation with family members leads to delay in obtaining care for cancer (Leventhal, Leventhal & Nguyen, 1985), and emergency care for an acute coronary event (Alonzo, 1986). On the other hand, elderly persons without family in their geographic area were more likely to use emergency room services for non-urgent care than persons with family access (Coe, Wolinsky, Miller, & Prendergast, 1985). Family members may redefine symptoms, encourage denial or the use of home remedies, or strongly encourage or initiate the decision to seek professional care. These appraisal and decision-making processes are also subject to cultural influences. Further study of family influences on prediagnostic and care-seeking phases is needed as many important questions remain unanswered (Leventhal et al. 1985). Cultural influences on help-seeking behavior and use of health care services is especially relevant among the poor and minority groups. Data indicate that these groups delay seeking professional care, and despite overall poorer health their use of medical care has been less than or at most equal to the nonpoor (Starr, 1986). In addition to the structural barriers to health care documented in Chapter 3, there is need to learn more about cultural influences on service use. Indeed, throughout this book, we will observe the special needs of socioeconomically disadvantaged persons with respect to health.

Psychological Health

The influence of the family on psychological health has been well-documented in both the theoretical and empirical literature. Emerging evidence suggests that there may be specific psychological pathways through which families influence member's physical health. For example, there is some preliminary evidence that the affective climate of the family and family loss events may be etiologically implicated in the development of cancer, although the mechanisms for such a relationship are largely unknown (Grassi & Molinari, 1987). Similarly, family coping styles have been implicated in the development and reinforcement of Type A coping behavior in individual family members (Matthews & Rakaczky, 1986). This finding is of concern in light of the strong evidence that Type A behavior is an independent risk factor in coronary heart disease. Familial etiology of chronic pain behavior, implicating various dimensions of family functioning, is also being examined (Violon, 1985). Adolescent somatization is less likely to occur among more cohesive and more adaptable families (Walker, McLaughlin, & Greene, 1988).

Spanning the past two decades, a burgeoning body of social epidemiological research documents consistent negative relationships between stress and illness onset (Craig & Brown, 1984; Dohrenwend & Dohrenwend, 1981; Gunderson & Rahe, 1974; Kasl, 1984) and positive relationships between social network membership and illness onset and overall mortality (Berkman & Syme, 1979; Blazer, 1982; House, Robbins, & Metzner, 1983; House, Landis, & Umberson, 1988; Orth-Gomer & Johnson, 1987; Smith, Mercy, & Conn, 1988). Each of these lines of research is closely tied to families. Families are primary sources of stress for individual family members, and families are commonly looked to first for social support (Pearlin & Turner, 1987). Research instruments used to assess life stressors generally include a preponderance of family-related events (Holmes & Rahe, 1967). Similarly, in epidemiological studies, access to immediate family and extended kin are included in assessing social networks and social integration. Studies of social support and health commonly assess emotional, informational, and tangible support from primary network members (Cohen & Syme, 1985; Ell, 1985).

Furthermore, families are critical in developing individual member relational and social skills. Analyzing research indicating that individuals who cannot or will not establish social relations in the broader community in culturally appropriate ways are more likely to be infertile, suffer more illness, and have higher mortality rates than more socially appropriate persons. Schwartzman (1985) concludes that family socialization processes are closely linked to physical health by influencing members' social skills. In turn, social relational skills are a critical factor in determining one's access to social support (Cohen, Sherrod, & Clark, 1986).

Despite numerous conceptual and methodological problems inherent in stress research (Campbell, 1986; Cohen, 1982), this body of work contributes substantially to understanding the relationship between family and health. In studies of stressful life events, people commonly rank family events as requiring the greatest adjustment (Campbell, 1986; Pearlin & Turner, 1987). For example, death of a spouse is ranked as the most stressful event on the widely used Schedule of Recent Life Events (Holmes & Rahe, 1967). The health consequences of bereavement have been studied extensively as indicated in recent reviews (Bowling, 1987; Jacobs & Ostfeld, 1977; Klerman & Clayton, 1984; Susser, 1981). The strongest evidence indicates that male mortality rates increase after the death of their spouses. Divorce is frequently ranked the second most disturbing life event. There is some evidence of negative health effects following divorce; however, the issue merits further study (Campbell, 1986; Verbrugge, 1977). On the other hand, there is evidence that positive family events reduce depressive symptoms among older adults (Krause, 1988).

Families undoubtedly influence early stress experience, attitudes toward stress, and the coping styles of individual members (Baltrusch & Waltz, 1986). The influence of family stress on members' health is visible early on (Crnic, Greenberg, Ragozin, Robinson, & Baskman, 1983). For example, maternal stress has been related to pregnancy complications, neurological impairments in infants, and neonatal deaths (Herrenkohl, 1988). Furthermore, children, especially preschoolers, are more susceptible to a range of physical illnesses and more likely to seek medical care and exhibit behavior problems in the face of stressful family events, including developmental crises (Beautrais, Fergusson, & Shannon, 1982; Hall & Farel, 1988; Meyer & Haggarty, 1962; Shapiro, 1983).

There is also evidence of stress contagion among family members. Data from the well-known Framingham study of coronary heart disease suggests that a woman's occupational stress is associated with increased risk of her husband developing heart disease (Eakes, Haynes, & Feinleib, 1983; Haynes, Eakes, & Feinleib, 1983). Family problems have also been associated with the development of angina pectoris (Medalie et al., 1973), and family dysfunction has been associated with teen-age pregnancy, which carries its own risks to child health (Romig & Thompson, 1988).

On the other side of the continuum, studies of social integration, social networks, and social support and health attest to the health protective effects of social relationships, especially family ties (see Broadhead, Kaplan, James et al., 1983; Cohen & Syme, 1985; Ell, 1984, for extensive reviews). These findings come as no surprise to practitioners as the role of the family as the primary support system has long been recognized (Caplan, 1976; Selby, 1956; Selby, 1979). There is evidence that social support is health protective insofar as it enhances general well-being and mediates life stress. Following a comprehensive examination of vulnerability and immunity, Antonovsky (1979) suggests that social support is a general resistance factor that reduces "breakdown" (i.e., impaired physical, psychological, and social functioning) and enhances coping throughout the life cycle.

Evidence suggests that the relationship between family stress and childhood illness may be moderated by social support (Haggerty, 1980) and that social support may moderate the immune response to stress among elderly adults (Thomas, Goodwin, & Goodwin, 1985) and mitigate the use of medical care in the face of life stress (Pilisuk, Boylan, & Acredolo, 1987). In the prospective study of 10,000 men referred to previously, support from wives mediated the likelihood of developing angina among highly anxious men (Medalie & Goldbourt et al., 1973). Finally, several studies of pregnancy highlight the health benefits of family support (Nuckolls, Cassell & Kaplan, 1972; Norbeck & Tilden, 1983; Smilkstein et al., 1984). Moreover, during childbirth, spousal support has been associated with less pain and less medication use among wives (Copstick et al., 1986). In striking contrast, the negative health effects of seriously impaired support-giving within families is demonstrated among some infants exhibiting nonorganic failure to thrive (Goldson, Millon, & Bentovim, 1985).

Environmental Resources and Hazards

Influences on health may also derive from familial access to environmental resources and from exposure to environmental hazards. A primary determinant of family–environmental interaction is socioeconomic and sociocultural status. This is especially true for children. Indeed, the poor have higher rates of most illnesses and higher mortality rates (Berkman & Syme, 1979; Haan, Kaplan, & Comacho, 1987). Despite increased access to medical care resulting from public health care financing mechanisms (progress that is currently undergoing potentially severe erosion in the face of changing financing mechanisms as documented in the following chapter) and advances in medical technology in the early detection and treatment of serious illness, the poor continue to have lower utilization rates of preventive health care services, are less likely to have access to a regular source of care (Guendelman & Schwalbe, 1986; Hayward, Shapiro, Freeman, & Corey, 1988; McDonald & Coburn, 1988; Wolinsky, 1982), are more likely to postpone seeking care until advanced stages of illness (Perkins & Boyle, 1986), have longer hospital stays (Epstein, Stern, Tognetti, Begg et al., 1988), and have been slower to experience the overall population decline in coronary heart disease mortality (Sempos, Cooper, Kovar, & McMillen, 1988; Wing et al., 1988). There is also evidence that the poor have fewer nonfamilial extended social network relationships (Antonucci, 1985; Auslander & Litwin, 1988) and thereby may be disadvantaged in coping with general life stressors and with illness.

Similarly, evidence of poorer health status among some minority groups undoubtedly results from economic disadvantages (Sandefur & Tienda, 1988) as well as culturally based health practices and barriers to preventive health care (Bailey, 1987; Chesney, Chavira, Hall, & Gary, 1982; Cox, 1986). Especially alarming, the Task Force on Black and Minority Health recently found that 60,000 excess deaths occur each year in minority populations (CDC, 1986). Excess deaths were defined as the difference between the number of deaths observed in the minority populations and the number that would have been expected if the minority population had the same age- and sex-specific death rates as the nonminority population.

Furthermore, data documents ethnocultural variation in patient knowledge about the signs and symptoms of and treatment for cancer (ACS, 1981;

1985b) and initial response to symptoms (Axtell & Meyers, 1974; Chirokos, Reiches, & Moeschberger, 1984; Stavraky, Kincade, Stewart, & Donner, 1987). For example, black and Hispanic persons, especially those with lower income, report less knowledge about cancer and are less frequently diagnosed at localized stages of the disease (ACS, 1986; Michielutte & Diseker, 1982). Other preliminary data suggest that blacks are less likely to receive specialized early cardiac diagnostic procedures and treatment (Peniston et al., 1987), and in the face of a suspected heart attack, they are more likely to delay seeking emergency services longer than whites (Cooper, Simmons, Castaner, Prasad, Franklin, & Ferlinz, 1986). Some evidence suggests that Mexican Americans are less knowledgeable about the prevention of coronary heart disease (Hazuda et al., 1983). In addition, black and Hispanic patients comprise a disproportionate number of all patients with AIDS (Ell, Larson, Finch, Sattler, & Nishimoto, 1989). Of special concern to social workers is evidence that poor and minority patients are less likely to participate in cancer support groups (Taylor, Falke, Shoptaw, & Lichtman, 1986) and are more likely to benefit from psychosocial services that have been tailored to their specific needs (Ell, Mantell, & Hamovitch, 1989; Subramanian & Ell, in press).

The negative effects of poverty on the health of children is also well-documented (Dutton, 1985). Especially disturbing is the persistent inverse association between economic status and the probability that a new-born infant will not survive the first year of life (Stockwell, Swanson, & Wicks, 1988). Related data indicate that the highest rates of adolescent pregnancy are found among low-income black adolescents (Franklin, 1988). Increased prevalence of chronic illness (Egbuono & Starfield, 1982), problematic illness course (Nevin, Johnston, & Merrett, 1981), and increased mortality rates among children have been associated with poverty (Nersesian, Petit, Shaper, Lemieux, & Naor 1985; Wise, Kotelchuck, Wilson, & Mills, 1985).

Furthermore, single motherhood in combination with poverty is increasingly recognized as potentially increasing the health risks of many children. For example, a high prevalence of depression has been found among mothers seeking pediatric care who were living alone and either low-income or black (Orr & James, 1984), and single mother's depression scores have been shown to predict her child's health (Angel & Worobey, 1988). In a recent study, when background stress factors (i.e., high life stress, loss of a parent through death or divorce, living in a single-parent family, and family discord) were combined, poorer and minority children were three times more likely to exhibit psychosocial dysfunction than more advantaged children (Murphy & Jellinek, 1988). In a similar vein, family structure, namely having two parents and older siblings, reduced the negative effects of life stress among poor young school children (Sandler, 1980). In contrast, there is evidence that absent black fathers provide a substantial amount of support to mothers caring for ill children (Slaughter & Dilworth-Anderson, 1988).

Many members of minority ethnic groups are at dual risk, because they are not only subject to experiencing cultural barriers in receiving services (Guendelman, 1985; Harwood, 1981; Schaefer, 1983), but also are disproportionately represented among the poor. Indeed, disentangling the probable interactions between ethnicity and socioeconomic status remains a direction for future comparative research. For example, although black children have been shown to be at increased risk of hospitalization for asthma, evidence indicates that much of this increase is related to poverty (Wissow, Gittelsohn, Szklo, Starfield, & Mussman, 1988). Thus it is not yet clear whether observed ethnic and racial differences are merely masking the effects of social class resulting from the persistent socioeconomic differences between some minority groups and whites in the United States (Bain, Greenberg, & Whitaker, 1986; Dayal, Power, & Chiu, 1982; Dayal, Polissar, Yang, & Dahlberg, 1987; Page & Kuntz, 1980; Satariano, Belle, & Swanson, 1986).

In Chapter 3, the influence of the social environment on family health-related functions and tasks will be examined in greater detail, with particular attention to the role of social, health, and organizational policies.

Families and Illness Outcomes

Until very recently, studies of psychosocial response to illness have concentrated on patients' internal emotional processes (Quinn & Herndon, 1986). That patients are embedded in a primary ecosystem, namely their family, was for the most part ignored in studies of adult illness. Currently, the overall management of and response to illness is increasingly recognized as a family affair. Family influences on patients' recovery and survival, on adaptation and quality of life, and on compliance and rehabilitation processes have been documented. To a great extent, families have been shown to have salutary effects on patients' illness outcomes by way of the emotional, informational, and tangible support they provide to patients and through family coping processes, such as open family communication and flexible role allocation. Conversely, negative family influences on patient outcomes result from the absence of these supports or when family intended "support" is misinformed, misdirected, and ineffective (Ell & Dunkel-Schetter, in press). Moreover, when family functioning has been traditionally characterized by conflict and poor communication or when families are themselves overwhelmed or debilitated by the illness (the latter to be discussed in greater detail in the next section), the effects of the family on patient outcomes are also likely to be negative.

Recovery and Survival

Evidence of the salutary effects of family social support on recovery from serious and life-threatening illness is persuasive. Three large-scale studies have examined mortality. In a 10-year prospective study of 1400 patients with myocardial infarction (MI), those who were married at the time of MI were significantly less likely to die during hospitalization and over the following 10 years (Chandra, Szkol, Goldberg, & Tonanscia, 1983). Ruberman and colleagues (1984) found that high stress in combination with social isolation was associated with higher death rates and poorer recovery among post-MI patients. Some of the stress indicators involved family events. In each of these studies, the positive effect of the social support variable was maintained when potentially confounding physical risk factors were controlled.

The effects of marital status on the diagnosis, treatment, and survival of patients with cancer were recently examined in population-based data on 27,779 cancer cases. Unmarried persons with cancer had decreased overall survival, were more likely to be diagnosed at more advanced stages of the illness, and were more likely to be untreated (Goodwin, Hunt, Key, & Samet, 1987). Even after adjusting for stage and treatment, unmarried persons still had poorer survival. The investigators suggest that the benefits of marriage on survival are mediated by social, psychological, and economic forces.

There is convincing evidence that family support enhances recovery and rehabilitation outcomes (Ell, 1984; Wallston, Allagna, DeVellis, & DeVellis, 1983). For example, better long-term recovery in terms of return to work (Finlayson & McEwen, 1977) and overall role-functioning (Ell & Haywood, 1984) has been associated with family support. Cancer prognosis and recovery have been favorably affected by support (Funch & Marshall, 1983; Stolar, 1982).

Family functioning has also been associated with the course of illness. In a longitudinal study, the health status of diabetic children deteriorated with greater family disruption (Koski & Kumento, 1975). Family stress and parents' poor marital relationship have also been associated with poor diabetic control (Gath, Smith, & Baum, 1980; Simonds, 1977). A pile-up of stressful family events has been associated with declining pulmonary functioning among children with cystic fibrosis (Patterson & McCubbin, 1983). Finally, Minuchin and colleagues have specified a model of family functioning and diabetic control; however, its generalizability remains to be tested (Coyne & Anderson, 1988; Minuchin, Rosman, & Baker, 1978; Rosman & Baker, 1988).

Adaptation and Quality of Life

The negative psychological sequelae, most frequently represented by dysphoric emotions, accompanying serious illness and impairment has been well-documented in the clinical literature. Numerous empirical studies of the prevalence and extent of psychological distress among patients with serious illness have confirmed the common occurrence of psychological distress. They have also uncovered additional facts about the nature of the distress and its extent.

First, it seems that much of the dysphoria frequently observed by practitioners during acute illness states is time-limited. Not surprisingly, the vast majority of patients with MI experience significant distress during hospitalization, most commonly anxiety, denial, and depression (Davidson, 1979; 1983). For example, the percentage of patients reporting depression ranges from 21 to 73 percent (Block, Boyer, & Imes, 1984). However, the majority of patients with MIs experience fairly rapid psychological recovery and demonstrate little or no long-term psychosocial or affective impairment (Lloyd & Cawley, 1983; Mayou, 1981). Similar results have been found among patients with cancer. Psychiatric morbidity has been found to be common, albeit, of a relatively minor nature (mainly depressive disorder) (Dean, 1987; Derogatis, Morrow, Fetting et al., 1983). Prolonged distress of a more serious nature has been found to occur among less that one-third of patients with MIs, cardiac surgery (Lloyd & Cawley, 1982; Mayou, 1981), or cancer (Ell, Nishimoto, Mantell, & Hamovitch, 1988a; Maguire, Lee, Bevington et al., 1978; Morris, Greer, & White, 1977).

Finally, a broader focus on adaptation to life-threatening and chronic illness has led to what are generally termed quality of life studies (Aaronson & Beckmann, 1987). These studies examine physical, social, and psychological well-being following illness. Indeed, several recent studies have demonstrated the value of examining both positive and negative feeling states when studying adaptation to illness (Ell, Mantell, & Hamovitch, 1988a; Waltz, 1986a,b). When viewed together, research findings underscore the merits of more closely examining adaptive processes in response to illness.

To date, research on family influences on adaptation to illness has been relatively sparse. Far more research has focused on the negative impact of illness on families, as discussed in the next section. Recognition of family adaptive and, in some cases, maladaptive influences on illness outcomes has emerged, somewhat secondarily, from the rapidly expanding research on social support, as well as from studies of family functioning. The majority of support and illness studies have focused on support from intimate social relationships, most frequently the marital partner.

Effects of Family Support

The adjustment of dialysis (Peyrot, McMurray, & Hedges, 1988; Rounds & Israel, 1985; Siegel, Calsyn, & Cuddihee, 1987), MI (Ell & Haywood, 1984; Ell, 1985–86; Waltz, 1986a,b; Waltz, Badura, Pfaff, & Schott, 1988), and cancer (Bloom & Spiegel, 1984; Dempsey et al., 1975; Dunkel-Schetter, 1984; Ell, Nishimoto, Morvay, Mantell, & Hamovitch, 1989; Funch & Marshall, 1983; Quinn, Fontana, & Reznikoff, 1986; Smith, Redman, Burns, & Sagert, 1985; Taylor & Daykof, 1988), patients has been shown to be positively influenced by support. In most of these studies, emotional support from intimate relationships was perceived to be most beneficial. For example, in one study of adolescents with cancer, mothers and fathers were reported to be primary sources of support (Tebbi, Stern, Boyle, Mettlin, & Mendell, 1985).

If intervention is to be guided by the knowledge gained from this research (Ell & Dunkel-Schetter, in press), there is a need to understand the processes by which social support influences health outcomes (Cohen & Syme, 1985; Dunkel-Schetter & Wortman, 1982). Social support from significant others is assumed to enhance adjustment to illness by assuring patients that they continue to be cared for and loved, esteemed and valued, and that they have access to tangible coping resources insofar as they are members of a network of mutual obligation in which others can be counted on if needed (Cobb, 1976). Specifically, support is presumed to maintain or enhance self-esteem, sense of personal control and mastery, and enhance coping in the face of illness-related threats. For most patients, the family is the primary source of support following the onset of illness or trauma.

Single constructs rarely capture the complexities of the human enterprise; so it is that conceptual ambiguities and methodological inadequacies pervade the social support research. For example, although support is generally assumed to have salutary effects, emerging evidence confirms the sometimes negative effects of support (Coyne, Wortman, & Lehman, 1988; Lehman, Ellard, & Wortman, 1986). These findings are leading social support investigators to recognize that support results from an interactive process between recipients and providers that is subject to misunderstandings. It is equally important to remember that support provision is only one process among many that occurs within the context of long-standing and complex social relationships, such as the marital relationship (Coyne & DeLongis,

1986; Waltz, 1986a) and family relationships in general. Family social support following illness undoubtedly is influenced by the nature of the relationship in which the support is provided.

The majority of seriously ill patients indicate that they are well-supported by their families, however, a substantial minority report stress or strain from family relationships (Lichtman et al., 1987; Smith et al., 1985). In those studies, the stress or strain had a negative influence on patient adaptation. For example, family conflict during acute stages of coronary events increased patient distress (Carter, 1984; Ell & Dunkel-Schetter, in press). Other studies indicate that patients with cancer are stressed by inadequate communication with family members and by the withdrawal of significant others (Peters-Golden, 1982). Anxious and overprotective families have been shown to give advice to patients with heart attacks in direct conflict with directions patients received from medical staff (Speedling, 1982). Some families have unnecessarily discouraged return to work following MI (Garrity, 1973; Hyman, 1972). Well-intentioned family support has also been shown to exacerbate feelings of despair and dependency (Revenson, Wollman, & Felton, 1983) and to cut off communication of distressful feelings (Dunkel-Schetter & Wortman, 1982) among patients with cancer. Preliminary evidence suggests that unhelpful supporters may cancel out the helpful support of others in recovery from MI (Ell and Haywood, 1984) and that negative social interactions impact negatively on adjustment following stroke (Stephens, Kinney, Norris, & Ritchie, 1987). Negative effects of support-giving have also been demonstrated in that elderly spouses caring for their partners become susceptible to illness themselves (Minkler, Satariano, & Langhouser, 1984). Some patients with cancer experience a desire for greater family closeness, especially with spouses, than actually occurs (Friedman et al., 1988). High social network density (network members being more likely to know and interact with one another) was found to be associated with higher distress among parents of children with spina bifida (Kazak & Marvin, 1984).

Effects of Family Functioning

Research focusing on patterned family functioning processes, as discussed in the preceding chapter, highlights the family's contextual influence on adaptation to illness. In these studies, varying family processes including family cohesion, adaptability, conflict, and moral and religious orientation have been examined using a variety of measures including unstructured interviews, the Family Environment Scale (Moos & Moos, 1983), or instruments based on the Circumplex Model of family functioning (Olson et al., 1979). In general, better patient adaptation is shown to be associated with greater cohesion, adaptability, and less conflict (Johnson, 1985). Adaptive coping by individual family members also has been associated with better patient adjustment (Johnson, 1985; Lichtman, Taylor, & Wood, 1987). In two interesting studies, spousal–patient incongruence with respect to coping styles and strategies were correlated with better long-term cardiac rehabilitation (Bar-On & Dreman, 1987) and with outcome following dialysis home training (Marshall, Rice, O'Mera, & Shelp, 1975). On the other hand, spousal agreement with patients' self-evaluation of functional status has been associated positively with patients' rehabilitation (New, Ruscio, Priest et al., 1968). It is important to note, however, that these studies leave the question of causality unanswered. Cohesive families may enhance patient adaptation; however, it is equally plausible that patient adaptation may influence family processes. Longitudinal studies are needed to further clarify this issue.

It is noteworthy that the majority of studies examining the relationship between family functioning and adjustment to illness has focused on childhood illness and handicap. In general, poor family functioning increases the likelihood that the ill child's adjustment will be problematic, while good family functioning enhances adjustment (see Johnson, 1985, and Shapiro, 1983, for reviews). For example, in a study of 209 children with documented chronic illness, children who were ill and lived in dysfunctional families had a higher incidence of psychological distress than healthy controls (Pless, Roghman, & Haggerty, 1972). Family coping style has also been associated with the adjustment of adolescents with cystic fibrosis (Boyle, di Sant'Agnese, Sack et al., 1976) and cancer (Blotcky, Raczynski, Gurwitch, & Smith, 1985). Closed family communication has been shown to negatively impact children with cancer (Spinetta & Maloney, 1978). High maternal stress has been associated with lower self-concept among children with myelomeningocele (Kazak & Clark, 1986). There is also evidence that children mimic parental attitudes toward the illness (Johnson, 1985). The most disturbing body of research identifies the occurrence of family maltreatment of handicapped children (see Ammerman, Van Hassell, & Herson, 1988; and Garborino, Brookhouser, Authier, et al., 1987, for reviews). On the other hand, creativity in family problem-solving and supportive fathers characterized well-adjusted versus maladjusted children with cystic fibrosis (Kucia, Drotar, Doershuk, et al., 1979). In a study of 20 children with diabetes, aged 7–13, better adjustment of the children was associated with parental self-esteem and optimal family functioning (Grey, Genel, & Tamborlane, 1980).

Studies of family functioning and adult illness have been more rare. Increased communication of affection and an increased desire for physical closeness (but not sexual intercourse) has been reported by patients with cancer and their spouses (Leiber, Plumb, Gerstenzang, & Holland, 1976). Better adjustment among patients with cancer has been associated with family expressiveness and less conflict (Spiegel, Bloom, & Gottheil, 1983), family cohesiveness (Bloom, 1982), and marital relationship (Dean, 1987).

Studies of adult pain behavior suggest that spouses may engage in reinforcing pain behavior that perpetuates the pain cycle (Kremer, Sieber, & Atkinson, 1985; Roy, 1985). Families perceived to be low in conflict and organization and oriented to achievement predicted better adult diabetic control (Edelstein & Linn, 1985). Finally, there is evidence that problematic family relationships preceding the onset of illness are associated with poorer patient adaptation (Carter, 1984; Coyne, Wortman, & Lehman, 1988; Wellisch, Jamison, & Pasnau, 1978).

Adherence to Treatment Regimens

Patient's adherence to prescribed medical regimens and lifestyle changes as well as participation in rehabilitation programs have been associated with family support and family functioning, although research in this area is sparse (Caplan, Van Harrison, Wellons, & French, 1980; Masters, Cerreto, & Mendlowitz, 1983; O'Reilly, 1986; Schultz, 1980) and, in some cases, methodologically flawed (Levy, 1983). In general, family support and family cohesiveness and adaptability have been shown to increase patient's compliance (Becker & Green, 1975; Doherty & Baird, 1983; Wallston et al., 1983) and to increase participation in rehabilitation programs (Ell, 1984). The role of the family in long-term adherence or lifestyle change is less clear, although, in one study of 290 participants in the national cardiac Multiple Risk Factor Intervention Trial (MRFIT), specific support from family members was associated with long-term maintenance of risk-reducing behaviors (O'Reilly, 1986).

Family support has been shown to increase compliance among arthritis patients (Carpenter & Davis, 1976), and overall family functioning has been shown to predict adherence to long-term dialysis treatment (Sherwood, 1983; Steidl, Finklestein, Wexler, et al., 1980). Spousal support has also been correlated with patients' compliance with a cholesterol-lowering drug (Doherty, Schrott, Metcalf, & Iasiello-Vailas, 1983). There is evidence that the prospect of returning to a family unit increased patients' willingness to engage in rehabilitation therapy programs (D'Afflitti & Weitz, 1974) and that family support enhanced participation in a work-site antihypertensive program (Alderman & Shoenbaum, 1975) and an exercise program for men with significant cardiac risk factors (Heinzelman & Bagley, 1970). In contrast, patients' perceived family support was not a strong predictor of long-term dietary restriction among dialysis patients (Brown & Fitzpatrick, 1988).

Perhaps because long-term medication use is critical, indeed life-saving, in the management of childhood diabetes, numerous studies have examined factors associated with compliance with treatment protocols and diabetic control. In general, adherence to treatment regimens is enhanced by well-functioning families and by parental support (Hanson & Henggeler, 1987). On the other hand, lack of compliance, in part resulting from lack of parental support, has been associated with poor compliance with treatment regimens by children and adolescents with cancer (Dolgin, Katz, Doctors, & Siegel, 1986; Lansky, Smith, Cairns, & Cairns, 1978).

The role of environmental resources was underscored in a study of treatment compliance following renal transplantation. Children living in fatherless households and of lower socioeconomic status were less likely to comply (Korsch, Fine, & Negrete, 1978). Similarly, children with cystic fibrosis were more likely to adhere to complex medical regimens if they were living with both parents (Oppenheimer & Rucker, 1980) and if mothers were not employed (Patterson, 1985).

Impact of Illness on Families

A growing body of research attests to the fact that illness is a family experience. The mutuality of illness experience becomes clear in light of the growing evidence of illness effects on family marital, parental, and sibling subsystems and on family relationships with extended social networks, including the medical care system and the broader community. Family functioning is also affected, including family communication, affective climate, coping, rule-making, and role allocation. A sudden illness or accident may propel a family into crisis, dramatically affecting the maintenance of the family system. Chronic illness or long-term rehabilitation may alter family systems (Stuifbergen, 1987), especially if the demands of the illness are in conflict with the developmental tasks of a particular stage in the family life cycle (Rolland, 1987a). In some cases, family adjustments may linger beyond the requirements of the illness, becoming entrenched so as to appear almost irreversible (Penn, 1983; Sheinberg, 1983). Finally, in examining the impact of illness on families, two areas of related research, bereavement and caregiving studies, merit inclusion. Taken together, empirical evidence of interactions between illness and families documents the need for ensuring that families have access to psychosocial interventions as they cope with illness and its sequelae.

Impact on Family Subsystems

Marital Subsystem. The impact of illness or trauma on the marital system is experienced directly by the spouse and/or through its effects on the marital relationship. Spouses of seriously ill or physically impaired patients have been shown to experience both physical and psychological distress. For example, wives of cardiac patients have been found to be more frequently distressed than patients during acute hospitalization (Mayou, Foster, & Williamson, 1978; Speedling, 1982). In one study, lack of control of hospital events, lack of opportunities to express distress, lack of information, and inadequate or poor social support from well-meaning friends were reported to be major spousal stressors following coronary artery bypass surgery (Gilliss, 1984). High anxiety, depression, and illness coincident with coronary events have also been found among spouses (Bedsworth & Molen, 1982; Dhooper, 1983; Stern & Pascale, 1979). Homecoming and the first weeks of convalescence also are periods of significant distress for spouses of patients with myocardial infarction and bypass surgery (Bramwell, 1986; Carter, 1984; Dhooper, 1983; Finlayson & McEwen, 1977; Gilliss, 1984; Speedling, 1982). In many of these studies, marital conflict about patients' recommended general activity level is a major source of the distress. Much of this conflict, in turn, is attributable to spouses having been given little or no information about recommended patients' activity levels, including sexual activity (Papadopoulos, Larrimore, Cardin, & Shelley, 1980).

Spouses of patients with cancer also experience significant distress (Northouse, 1985; Northouse & Swain, 1987; Nuehring & Barr, 1980). For example, husbands of patients with breast cancer have reported difficulties with sleeping, eating, and concentration on work (Wellisch, Jamison, & Pasnau, 1978). Moreover, spouses reported physical symptomatology since the onset of the patient's illness has been associated with their psychological adaptation (Ell et al., 1988a,b). Spousal distress, including fear of cancer recurrence and of the patient's death and social isolation have been shown to be greater than that of patients (Goldberg, Wool, Glicksman, & Tull, 1984; Gotay, 1984; Lichtman et al., 1987; Oberst & James, 1985). There is also evidence that patient and spouse pairs experience similar psychological adaptation to cancer (Cassileth et al., 1985; Plumb & Holland, 1977), and that patients demonstrate greater psychological vulnerability (Ell et al., 1988a,b). It is also noteworthy that change in spouses' usual daily routines, including juggling work and home responsibilities, has been found to be distressful for both spouses and patients (Ell et al., 1988a,b; Northouse & Swain, 1987).

Several investigators have reported increased psychological distress and the occurrence of physical or pain symptoms in spouses of chronic pain patients (Kerns & Turk, 1985). The stress and depression among spouses of patients with serious head injuries (Brown & McCormick, 1988; Lezak, 1978), burns (Reddish & Blumenfield, 1984; 1986), spinal cord injuries (Kester, Rothblum, Lobato, & Milhous, 1988; Romano, 1975), and stroke (Coughlan & Humphrey, 1982; Tompkins, Schulz, & Rau, 1988) are also well-documented. Early clinical observation indicates that family members of patients with AIDS are severely distressed (Macklin, 1988).

On a strikingly positive note, evidence indicates that most marital relationships remain the same or improve following a cancer diagnosis (Lichtman et al., 1987). Evidence from cardiac studies also attest to the resiliency of this relationship in the face of numerous illness-related stressors (Carter, 1984; Croog & Fitzgerald, 1978; Finlayson & McEwen, 1977; Meddin & Brelje, 1983; Radley & Green, 1986). If negative effects do occur, they are most likely to result from poor communication between spouses. For example, less satisfactory reallocation of roles, more role conflict and role strain, less family cohesion, and greater family conflict has been found to result from poor communication between cancer patients and their spouses (Lichtman et al., 1987; Vess, Moreland, & Schwebel, 1985a,b). Problematic sexual interactions occur among may seriously ill patients and their partners (Anderson & Hacker, 1983; Anderson & Jochimsen, 1985; Flor, Turk, & Scholzs, 1987; Frank et al., 1978; Morris et al., 1977; Taylor, Lichtman, Wood, et al., 1986; Papadoupolis et al., 1980; Wellisch, Jamison, & Pasnau, 1978), presumably, in part, also related to communication difficulties. There is also evidence that sexual dissatisfaction impacts negatively on patients' adjustment (Taylor et al. 1986). Open communication has been associated with greater affection between wives and husbands during later stages of progressive cancer (Hinton, 1981). On the other hand, absence of open communication might not be problematic for couples for whom this a comfortable life-long pattern (Chekryn, 1984).

Evidence of the effects of childhood illness and handicap on the marital relationship is contradictory; in some studies negative effects are reported, whereas others find little effects or even positive effects on the marriage (Evans, Burlew, & Oler, 1988; Johnson, 1985; Lansky, et al., 1978; Martin, 1975; Sabbeth & Leventhal, 1984; Satterwhite, 1978). Levels of marital satisfaction among parents of myelomeningocele children have been found to be similar to comparison groups (Kazak & Marvin, 1984), and having a handicapped child or a child with cancer has been shown to bring about increased marital closeness and family cohesion (Barbarin, Hughes, & Chesler, 1985; Kazak & Clark, 1986).

Parental Subsystem. Serious childhood illness and handicap has been shown to have a major impact on parents and on parental coping and parenting (see Fife, 1980, Foster & Berger, 1985, Johnson, 1985, Masters, Cerreto, & Mendlowitz, 1983, and Shapiro, 1983, for reviews). The impact on parents is pervasive (Chesler & Barbarin, 1984). Parents of affected children experience physical illness, depressive disorder, and high anxiety (Burr, 1985; McAndrew, 1976; Shapiro, 1983). There is some evidence that reported levels of dysphoric mood among parents are greater than that which exists in the general population (Fielding, Moore, Dewey et al., 1985), that distress may persist long after the acute diagnosis or trauma (Cella, Perry, Kulchycky, & Goodwin, 1988; Kratochivil & Devereux, 1988; Wikler, Wasow, & Hatfield, 1981), and that single parents might be especially vulnerable (Evans, Burlew, & Oler, 1988).

Parents frequently also experience serious financial strain (Jacobs, McDermott, 1989; & Satterwhite, 1978; Stein & Riessman, 1980) and little hope of accomplishing previously determined life goals (Shapiro, 1983). Withdrawal from social activities, increased social isolation (Burr, 1985; Shapiro, 1983), problematic relationships with extended social networks (Stein & Riessman, 1980) and with health professionals (Barbarin & Chesler, 1984), and an increase in general life stressors (Shapiro, 1983) are experienced by many parents. In the case of AIDS, parental isolation is observed to be extreme (Frierson, Lippman, & Johnson, 1987; Urwin, 1988).

There is evidence that mothers experience greater or at least different stressors from that of fathers in caring for a handicapped child (Breslau, Staruch, & Mortimer, 1982; Johnson, 1985; Kazak & Marvin, 1984; Schilling, Schinke, & Kirkham, 1985), and that mothers and fathers may have different styles of coping (Shapiro & Shumaker, 1987). Married women caring for a handicapped child are also less likely to be employed (especially if they are a minority and poor) (Breslau, Salkever, & Staruch, 1982). Much less is known about fathers' experiences with childhood illness (Johnson, 1985; Schilling et al., 1984), however, there is evidence that fathers' coping behavior is equally important to the overall well-being of the child and the family (McCubbin, Nevin, Cauble, et al., 1982; McCubbin, McCubbin, Patterson, Cauble, et al., 1983). Moreover, wives rate spousal support in terms of the degree to which their husbands participate in the care of ill children (Barbarin et al., 1985). Conversely, husbands associate spousal support with their wives time spent at home vs. in the hospital (Barbarin et al., 1985).

Other data attest to the impact of childhood illness on parental coping and parenting from a family functioning perspective. Burr (1985) has recently reviewed the potential impact of having a chronically ill child on a family's ability to accomplish eight categories of family developmental tasks: physical maintenance; allocation of resources; division of labor; socialization of family members; maintenance of order and establishment of communication; reproduction, release, and recruitment of members; placement of members in the larger society; and maintenance of motivation and morale. She found substantial evidence that families with a chronically ill child face serious threats to their ability to successfully carry out each of these tasks. Indeed, the fact that the majority of families meet these challenges successfully is testimony to their strength and courage (Johnson,

1985; Kupst & Schulman, 1980). In this vein, researchers have recently begun to examine effective family coping (Trute & Haruch, 1988).

Study findings also indicate, however, that a substantial minority of parents are especially disadvantaged because they lack adequate coping repertoires. One study directs attention to specific areas of family functioning. A qualitative study of parents of 32 pediatric cancer patients in remission identified five themes of family reaction: increased experience of negative affect; rules prohibiting emotional expression; health and behavior problems appearing or becoming exacerbated following the diagnosis; role changes; and increased closeness among family members (Koch, 1985a). Negative reactions and increased closeness were found to vary with family rules regarding emotional expression and role changes (Koch, 1985b). Preliminary evidence suggests that some families reorganize the family system to include the ill child in the parental subsystem (Velasco de Parra, de Cortazer, & Covarrubias-Espinoza, 1983) or form parent–child alliances against the other parent (Penn, 1983; Walker, 1983) with potential adaptive or maladaptive results. Finally, there are data indicating that problems in parental communication are common, and that child-rearing practices may be negatively affected (Shapiro, 1983). On the other hand, open family communication has been shown to be associated with positive coping strategies in their children (Spinetta & Maloney, 1978), and family closeness following preterm birth has been related to fewer parenting problems (Siefert, Thompson, Bensel, & Hunt, 1983).

Children. It is noteworthy that research on the impact of parental illness on children has been almost nonexistent (Peters & Esses, 1985). The documented impact of illness on spouses and parents would suggest that children will be affected by the serious illness of a parent. Peters and Esses (1985) found that children of parents with multiple sclerosis perceived their families as more conflicted and less cohesive than comparison controls. The investigators suggest that research in this area has been limited by methodological and conceptual problems, but that future research will be enhanced by focusing on the family as a system.

Several studies have examined children's responses to a parent's cancer. Wellisch (1979) found an increase in acting out behavior among adolescents whose parents had cancer, and Power (1977) found significant distress among adolescents with a parent with Huntington's disease. In a study of mother–daughter relationships among patients with breast cancer, the majority of relationships remained strong or grew stronger following the diagnosis (Lichtman, Taylor, Wood et al., 1987). Deteriorating relationships occurred in 12 percent of the relationships, and these were associated with patients' poor prognosis, more severe surgery, and poorer psychological adjustment. Children of dialysis patients were found to be more likely to be depressed and have school problems (Tsaltas, 1976) and to exhibit latent aggressive feelings toward the sick parent (Friedlander & Viederman, 1982). In contrast, one study found no differences on various measures between children of fathers paralyzed as a result of spinal cord injury and children whose parents were not disabled (Buck & Hohmann, 1981).

Siblings. Empirical studies of the effects of illness on siblings have been relatively rare (see Drotar & Crawford, 1985, McKeever, 1983; and Sourkes, 1980, for reviews). Sibling distress has been most frequently reported from clinical observation, however, as is generally the case, clinical populations probably differ from nonclinical samples. Indeed, some of the contradictions in the literature result from different sampling strategies (Thomas, 1987) and different methodologies (Lobato, Faust, & Spirito, 1988). To date, the majority of studies has focused on identifying adverse reactions among siblings.

In one study, mothers' reports indicated that 81 percent of the families had siblings who developed maladaptive behavior changes following the diagnosis of childhood leukemia (Powazek, Payne, & Goff, 1980). Similarly, siblings of children with spina bifida have been found to be more poorly adjusted than siblings of control children (Tew & Laurence, 1973), and siblings of cardiology, hematology, and plastic surgery patients were found to be more withdrawn and irritable (Lavigne & Ryan, 1979). Although severity of the illness was not found to be significantly related to the siblings' adjustment, siblings of children with visible handicaps had greater emotional and behavioral problems than siblings of children with nonvisable handicaps. In a study of siblings of children with cancer, the siblings showed even more distress than the patients in the areas of perceived isolation and fear of expressing negative feelings (Cairns, Clark, Smith, & Lansky, 1979).

On the other hand, in a study of 239 families of pediatric patients with cystic fibrosis, cerebral palsy, myelodysplasia, and multiple handicaps, mothers completed a measure of psychological functioning, the Psychiatric Screening Inventory, for a randomly selected sibling of the patient who was 6–18 years old (Breslau, Weitzman, & Messenger, 1981). Siblings of disabled children did not manifest higher rates of severe psychologic impairment or greater overall symptomatology when compared to data on 1034 randomly selected children from a cross-section of Manhattan households. However, siblings of disabled children scored significantly higher than controls on interpersonal aggression with peers and in school. In that study, type and severity of disability were not associated with the psychological functioning of the siblings. In a comparison of teacher reports of school behavior of siblings of children suffering from renal failure with a healthy control group, no significant differences were found (Fielding, Moore, Dewey et al., 1985). In a controlled study of children with nephrotic syndrome, problems among siblings were less common than expected, however, parental ratings indicated that their physical and emotional health was significantly worse than that of the healthy controls (Vance, Fazan, Satterwhite, & Pless, 1980). In that study, siblings of the children with kidney disease had lower academic performance, self-acceptance, and social confidence than did the controls.

Few studies of sibling response to childhood illness have examined aspects of family functioning as it mediates the experience of siblings (Lobato et al., 1988). There is evidence that problems of siblings frequently stem from the likelihood that parents and medical personnel fail to communicate openly with them (Koch-Hattem, 1986). A very recent study draws attention to the characteristics of effective coping among siblings, an area that also has been studied inadequately (Tritt & Esses, 1988).

Bereavement and Families

Earlier in the chapter, we discussed the physical health consequences of bereavement when a spouse dies. There is also substantial evidence of short- and long-term psychological stress associated with family grief (Lehman, Wortman, & Williams, 1987; Osterweis, Soloman, & Green, 1984). Only a few studies have examined the effects of parental death on middle-aged adults (Horowitz Krupnick, Kaltreider, Wilner, et al., 1981; Sanders, 1978), however, negative emotional sequelae is common. Goldberg (1973) has cogently reviewed the family tasks and reactions associated with bereavement, highlighting the need for role realignment.

Evidence suggests that the death of a child reverberates throughout the family system and may have the most long-standing effects (Hamovitch, 1964; Payne, Goff, & Paulson, 1980; Rando, 1985; Videka-Sherman & Lieberman, 1985). For example, in an early investigation of the impact of death from childhood leukemia on 20 families, the investigators found both anticipatory as well as subsequent grief reactions were widespread affecting parents and siblings (Binger, Ablin, Feurstein, et al., 1969). In more recent studies, an unexpectedly high incidence of incomplete mourning by parents following the death of a child with cystic fibrosis was found (Kerner, Harvey, & Lewison, 1979). Similar ongoing distress was found among parents of children with cancer up to 3 years after the death of their child (Moore, Gilliss, & Martinson, 1987; Rando, 1985). There is also evidence that self-help groups, such as Compassionate Friends, and psychotherapy fail to help bereaved parents as much as would be hoped (Videka-Sherman & Lieberman, 1985). Access to an ongoing support person and open communication with child prior to death have characterized better parental adjustment (Spinetta, Swarner, & Sheposh, 1981).

Reactions to the death of an adult child are far less well-researched; however, the experience has been shown to exact a severe toll on parents (Shanfield, Benjamin, & Swain, 1984). This issue is recently highlighted by the AIDS epidemic. Although systematic research has yet to be conducted on families of patients with AIDS, clinical experience and some preliminary data attest to the myriad of problems facing family members as they cope with the emotional and social sequelae of the illness and the death of their child (Cleveland, Walters, Skeen, & Robinson, 1988; Maloney, 1988).

Impact on Family Caregivers

Families are primary providers of care in the face of illness and disability. Given continued growth in the numbers of persons surviving trauma and life-threatening illness as well as the skyrocketing cost of professional care, families, undoubtedly, will be called on to increase their caregiving activity. It is likely, therefore, that a substantial proportion of the population will participate in various caregiving roles. These trends have spurred investigators to examine the impact of the caregiving experience on the caregiver and, to a lesser extent, on the recipient of care.

The bulk of the research has been conducted on spousal care and on adult children providing care to their parents. Very recently, parents caring for ill or handicapped children have been the subject of study (Krauskopf & Akabas, 1988). With increasing emphasis on home care, more and more children with disabilities and chronic illness will be cared for at home (Feinberg, 1985). Evidence suggests that mothers assume much of this caregiving responsibility, however, neither mother's nor father's caregiving experience has been well-researched (Johnson, 1985). One study found mothers caring for a severely disabled young adult were more likely to be ill themselves, to experience significant psychological distress, and to be less likely to be employed (Hirst, 1985). The long-term effects of "high tech" homecare on the family system remains to be evaluated (Feinberg, 1985).

In an extensive review of caregiving, Horowitz (1985) notes that families provide 80 percent of all home health care for frail elderly, and that 80 percent of all older persons depend primarily on their family to meet home health care needs. Spouses provide the most extensive and comprehensive care, but they also report the highest level of stress when compared to other caregivers (Horowitz, 1985; Johnson, 1985). Despite numerous methodological and theoretical problems in the research to date (Bass, Tausig, & Noelker, 1988, 1989; Raveis, Siegel, & Sudit, 1988, 1989), stressors associated with caregiving have been well-documented.

Several investigators have identified the vulnerability of caregiving spouses. In a survey of 678 elderly residents of Alameda County, California, respondents who reported their spouses as being ill in the last 6 months were more likely to report their own health as poorer than those respondents whose spouses were not ill (Satariano, Minkler, & Langhauser, 1984). In a comparison of caregiving groups (spouses, children, other relatives, friends, and neighbors), spouses were found to experience the greatest degree of physical and financial strain (Cantor, 1983). In that study, although the majority of caregivers were women, men were equally represented among spouse caregivers. The investigator suggested that the stress experienced by these spouses may be in part attributable to their carrying out personal and household tasks that might represent a role reversal that is in itself stressful. Jones and Vetter (1984) found that spousal caregivers experienced significant reductions in their social participation. Similarly, Bryan and Evans (1980) found that spouses were most likely to assist home dialysis patients and curtail their outside social activities.

Parent caretaking by adult children has become so commonplace that Brody (1985) has termed it a normative family stress. Indeed, there is overwhelming preference across generations for children (especially daughters) to provide affective support to their aging parents (Brody, Johnson, & Fulcomer, 1984), and there is evidence that filial affection is a primary motivator among female caregivers (Finley, Roberts, & Banahan, 1988). Unfortunately, there is substantial evidence that women, and working women in particular, experience numerous stresses in maintaining multiple roles (Brody, Kleban, Johnsen et al., 1987; Fitting, Robins, Lucas, & Eastham, 1986; Perlman & Giele, 1983). For example, women caregivers of patients with cancer have encountered hostility, fear, and withdrawal from co-workers (Feldman, 1987), and working spouses of home dialysis patients encounter greater role strain than nonworking women (Peterson, 1985). There is also evidence that caretakers desire assistance in carrying out the caregiving tasks (Reece, Walz, & Hageboeck, 1983). For example, support from other family members and friends is viewed by caregivers of patients following a stroke as primary enabling resources in the caregiver's ability to cope with numerous stressors (Silliman, Earp, & Wanger, 1988).

The psychosocial costs of caregiving are substantial (Belle, 1982; Finch & Groves, 1983; Sommers & Shields, 1987). Noteworthy, the finding that women predominate among all caregivers has been linked to other research demonstrating greater reported stress among women as compared to men (Kessler & McLeod, & Wethington 1985). Whereas data document the negative impact across a wide spectrum of caregiving, there is considerable variation in the degree of stress reported by caregivers (Horowitz, 1985), and reported distress is frequently less than would be expected (Burr, Guyer, Todres, & Abrahams, 1983; Cain, Kelly, & Shannon, 1980; Stone, Cafferata, & Sangl, 1987). Evidence of the variable impact of caregiving suggests that potential moderating factors be examined. These generally include personal and environmental resources of the caregiver and use of formal care services. For example, there is data suggesting that racial and socioeconomic status will influence significant others' experience (Mindel, Wright, & Sarrett, 1986). Other data suggest that caregiving burden and cost are greater among poor caretakers (Belle, 1983) and among those living with the patient (George & Gwyther, 1986). Existing data indicate that the caregiver–patient relationship is associated with distress (Cox, Parson, & Kimboko, 1988; George & Gwyther, 1986; Zarit, Todd, & Zarit, 1986), that interpersonal conflict between caregiver and recipient increases caregiver strain and negative affect (Sheehan & Nuttall, 1988), and that social support can reduce the risk of caregivers' psychological distress (Baillie, Norbeck, & Barnes, 1988).

Research underscores the complementary roles of informal network caregiving and formal systems care, suggesting that optimal outcomes result when each support system performs those caretaking tasks for which it is best suited (Hoch & Hemmens, 1987; Litwak, 1985). There is some evidence, for example, that informal caregivers are better able to more closely match service with specific patient need (Greene, 1983). Unfortunately, there is also evidence that the formal system may fail to provide those services that would most effectively reduce caregiver strain (Hooyman, Gonyea, & Montgomery, 1985), and that counseling services targeted to reduce the subjective burden of family members are frequently unavailable (Cox et al., 1988). Moreover, use of the formal care system has been shown to occur only after the care needs exceed caregivers' resources (George & Gwyther, 1986; Stone et al., 1987), with increasing perceptions of stress by the caregiver (Zarit, Todd, & Zarit, 1986) and lack of support (Casserta, Lund, Wright, & Redburn, 1987). Unfortunately, sociocultural differences in family caregiving experiences have been neglected in the research to date (Cox et al., 1988; Morycz, Malloy, Bozich, & Martz, 1987).

Family Coping Resources

In the Face of Illness

Least well-researched in studies of the impact of families on illness or of the impact of illness on families are psychosocial factors that may influence adaptation. The lack of extensive research on coping resources that may mediate familial response is unfortunate because this knowledge is needed to aid practitioners in the development of appropriate intervention strategies (Ell, 1985–1986). Familial access to and activation of social network supports as well a familial coping strategies are, however, well-documented as critical factors in the family's response to serious illness, handicap, or trauma (Barbarin, 1988; Kazak & Marvin, 1984; Peterson, 1984; Northouse & Northouse, 1988). Furthermore, there is evidence that support influences parental response to high risk infants and reduces the negative consequences for families rearing a handicapped child (see Dunst, Cooper, & Bolick, 1987, for a review). For example, help with daily chores, a male supporter, and emergency child care were found to positively influence neonatal morbidity among urban indigent mothers (Pascoe, Chessare, & Baugh, 1985), and support has been associated with better parental adjustment (Philipp, 1984).

The finding that social network support is important in families' response to the stressors accompanying illness (Fife, Norton, & Groom, 1987; Finlayson & McEwen, 1977; Kazak, 1986; Morrow, Carpenter, & Hoagland, 1984; Schilling, Gilchrist, & Schinke, 1984; Unger & Powell, 1980) is consistent with family stress theory. Unfortunately, far less is known about potential impediments to support exchange in the management of illness and about optimal ways to maximize family's support experience. For example, under some circumstances, a family's ability to obtain needed social supports may be impaired. Thus, a family's preoccupation with an ill child may reduce social participation and thereby also reduce ready access to obtaining support from others. Furthermore, illness-related physical and emotional demands might impede a family's ability to provide support to other network members, and in this way, impair the family's receipt of needed supports because reciprocity is known to enhance supportive relationships and, under some circumstances, to be a condition of receiving support from others. Data attest to the salutary effects of reciprocal exchange of support among families coping with childhood illness, while paradoxically, also suggesting that these families may have reduced access to relationships characterized by reciprocity (Friedrich & Friedrich, 1981; Kazak & Wilcox, 1984). Finally, there is evidence that under some circumstances the poor lack access to informal network support (Camasso & Camasso, 1986).

Other studies raise questions about the effects of illness on supportive exchange within the marital dyad (Burke & Weir, 1982). In view of evidence that wives are husbands' primary source of support (Peplau & Gordon, 1985), to whom do men turn when their wives are ill? Three recent studies suggest that men may be disadvantaged under these circumstances. In one study, husbands of patients with breast cancer reported hesitation in seeking emotional support from their wives (Lichtman et al., 1987). In other studies, spouses reported significantly less perceived adequacy of support than patients, a disturbing finding in light of the fact that support was related to spouses psychological adaptation (Ell et al., 1988a,b; Northouse, 1988). In one of the studies, spouses and patients reported less access to more distant social relationships than nonspouse significant others (Ell et al., 1988a,b). It would appear, therefore, that spouses may also experience the social isolation that has been found to distress patients (Dunkel-Schetter & Wortman, 1982).

Studies also attest to inherent difficulties in support experience. For example, support from family members and friends reduces the negative effects of caregiving (Horowitz, 1985; Scott, Roberts, & Hutton, 1986), but caregivers frequently delay requesting assistance until they experience declining physical health (Synder & Keefe, 1985). Paternal support during childhood illness is needed, however, fathers may need encouragement in this role (Wasilewski, Clark, Evans, Feldman et al., 1988). Furthermore, in a disturbing paradox (with important clinical implications), access to a larger social network has been shown to be more important to health status for those less able to utilize network resources effectively (Hibbard, 1985). Consistent with an earlier observation, obtaining social supports from others requires social skills (Cohen et al., 1986), however some families may be less skillful in reaching out to and maintaining network ties than others. Equally disturbing is evidence that family members frequently report that they receive inadequate or misguided support from family and friends (Oberst & James, 1985; Papadopoulos et al., 1980; Northouse & Swain, 1987) and that support from others declines over time (Hobfoll & Lerman, 1989). For example, advice-giving and encouraging recovery are reported to be unhelpful by bereaved spouses and parents (Lehman, Ellard, & Wortman, 1986; Videka-Sherman, 1987). In light of these research findings, practitioners are advised to assess social network support, initiate appropriate intervention strategies to enhance families' access to social network support, and intervene to reduce the occurrence of miscarried helping by primary network members (Coyne et al., 1988).

Of special concern to practitioners is evidence that families report receiving inadequate support from health care professionals (Northouse & Swain, 1987; Oberst & James, 1985; Papadopoulos et al., 1980). Whereas family members repeatedly express their need for information from health professionals (Baldwin & Glendinning, 1983; Chesler & Barbarin, 1984; Coffman, 1983; Horner, Rawlins, & Giles, 1987; Tarran, 1981; Welch, 1981), they also report great difficulty in obtaining the information (Chenoweth & Spencer, 1986; Ell & Dunkel-Shetter, in press; Krant & Johnson, 1977, 1978; Northouse & Northouse, 1988; Sebring & Moglia, 1987; Welch, 1981; Wright & Dyck, 1984). Moreover, all too often, health professionals fail to respond to family members' need for repeated or ongoing information (Chesler & Barbarin, 1984).

In addition, family members report a desire for emotional support and counseling from health professionals (Morrow, Carpenter, & Hoagland, 1982) and appear to benefit when allowed to actively participate in the choice of treatment (Morris & Royle, 1988). It is not surprising that family members report inadequate access to psychosocial care in light of other evidence indicating that service to families is least likely to be included in routine psychosocial service in acute hospitals (Sikes & Rhodenhauser, 1987), that service to siblings is also not routinely provided (Lavigne, 1980), and that follow-up service to bereaved is a major gap in oncological follow-up (Kupst, 1980; Kupst & Schulman, 1980). Finally, extended family members are underserved, despite evidence of their beneficial support, such as in the case of grandparents assisting mothers following preterm birth (Pederson, Bento, Chance et al., 1987).

Again, consistent with family stress theory, research also underscores the potential mediating role of family coping strategies in response to illness. Families who actively seek informational and emotional support, who maintain open lines of communication and family cohesion, flexibly reallocate roles, and creatively problem-solve are more likely to make optimal adjustments. There is also some evidence that denial may be a useful coping strategy to enable families to pace the numerous assaults of serious illness (Fife et al., 1987; Slaby & Glicksman, 1985). At the same time, the negative effects of family denial are also evident when families maintain unhealthful behaviors, such as in the the case of alcoholism (Boss, 1988), or give advice that deters prompt receipt of vital medical care (Leventhal et al., 1985).

In studies of parents of children with cystic fibrosis, coping strategies, such as endowing the illness with meaning and sharing the burdens of the illness, predicted long-term family adaptation (Venters, 1981) and compliance with home treatment (Patterson, 1985). Other data underscore the families need for effective coping strategies in order to sustain emotional bonding and maintenance of boundaries (Quinn & Herndon, 1986), separateness and connectedness (Maurin & Schenkel, 1976), and to manage internal and external relationships and adapt to illness-generated change, while preserving continuity (Barbarin, 1988). Coping by having another child, or increasing one's investment in a surviving child, or adopting a new role have been found to be beneficial to bereaved parents (Videka-Sherman, 1987). Families may require, therefore, counseling and social skill training to enhance ability to obtain needed social supports and to enhance coping repertoires (Whittaker, Schinke, & Gilchrist, 1986). Fortunately, there is evidence that coping skill training can be accomplished through structured parent groups (Schilling, Gilchrist, & Schinke, 1984).

In Chapter 1, family perception of the event was purported to be a critical factor in their stress response. This factor has been less frequently studied, however. As is true for individuals, illness often precipitates a need for families to revise their view of life, their shared view of social reality (Reiss, 1981). Adaptative familial response to illness requires that families engage in a range of actions to adapt to this changing reality (Krausz, 1988; Mishel & Murdaugh, 1987).

Family-illness transactions are also presumably influenced by interactions among structural characteristics of the family including its life cycle and sociocultural context, the nature of the illness, and by characteristics of the family's adaptation prior to the illness (Reiss & Oliveri, 1983). Few studies, however, have examined potential relationships among these factors. This line of inquiry must be included in a future research agenda.

Individual family members' personal resources are also worthy of mention. In this regard, locus of control and sense of control, self-efficacy, or mastery have recently been the subject of increasing research on individual coping (Folkman, 1984; Taylor, 1983). The utility of this personal resource in family coping merits study. There is evidence that personal resources, such as personal sense of control and an internal locus of control, influence spousal adaptation in the face of serious illness (Ell et al., 1988a,b; Schoeneman & Reznikoff, 1983). In contrast, perceived lack of control over life circumstances has been associated with dysphoric mood among spouses of chronic pain patients (Flor et al., 1987). In an interesting study of caregivers, many preferred coping without outside assistance (Barusch, 1988). The investigator suggested that educational programs include techniques that emphasize ways in which caregivers can enhance their coping skills and thereby enhance their self-esteem and sense of personal control. In the same vein, data attest to a desire on the part of family members to be treated as competent and effective individuals (Chesler & Barbarin, 1984). Finally, families need access to a network of community-based services. This issue will be discussed in detail in the following chapter.

Toward Health Promotion

Research on family resources as applied to its health promotion and illness prevention roles is only now emerging as a potentially fertile area of exploration (Venters, 1986). Of theoretical import, the extensive empirical data are consistent with the interactive biopsychosocial model of health and illness presented in Chapter 1. Taken together, the research reviewed provides compelling empirical support for a family-oriented approach to health promotion. Opportunities to enhance families' health-maintenance work will be discussed in greater detail in subsequent chapters.

3
The Social Environment and Family-Focused Health Care

In Chapter 1, we presented an epistemological argument for using a macroscopic (de Rosnay, 1975) conceptual lens to view the family's relationship to the health of its individual members. In making this argument, we drew primarily on two meta-theoretical conceptualizations: the general systems paradigm and the ecological paradigm. Subsequently, we presented a large body of research findings that are of primary concern to practitioners. We concluded that this growing knowledge-base documents the interdependence of family members as it pertains to health promotion and health maintenance and emphasizes the reciprocal relationship between families and the physical impairment of one of its members. We also alluded to the influence of the environment on the family's health-related functions. In this chapter, however, we underscore that these environmental forces are powerful, pervasive, and have potentially negative as well as positive effects not only on families but on their ability to carry out health-related tasks.

In the preceding chapters, we have emphasized a view of the family as a primary social system. In this chapter, we emphasize that the family is, at the same time, a part of the broader systems that make up its social environment. In this context, we repeat that the social environment of the family includes other mesosystems such as school and work contexts, the exosystem or social structures and institutions, and the macrosystem or overarching cultural patterns, values, and ideologies (Bronfenbrenner, 1979). An in-depth discussion of each of the social environmental influences on family health functions, however, is beyond the scope of one book, much less one chapter. In selectively highlighting social–structural trends and developments that impact on families' health-related roles, we establish the proposition that failure to give equal attention to environmental forces impinging on families results in an excessive emphasis on family responsibility and, indeed, ignores the social reality. This issue is most dramatically illustrated in the case of the poor.

A consideration of the social–structural environment affecting family health roles inevitably focuses our attention on social policies and institutional arrangements, bringing to the fore a series of complex questions and historical traditions. Social policies and institutions inherently involve value-laden choices and complex political processes. In the United States, governmental institutions and policies have been guided by overarching value traditions that hold individualism, freedom, independence, and, therefore, minimum governmental intervention as the highest good (Wilensky & Lebeaux, 1965). Public policy is marked by these value traditions insofar as policy entails the operationalization of social goals. It is not surprising, then, that under a flag of societal goals that emphasizes individualism, freedom, independence, and minimal government, the United States has failed to articulate and operationalize either a coherent family policy or health policy. Indeed, the family's inviolate right to freedom and privacy, as a widely held social value, has long served to delay a social policy response to serious problems such as incest, child abuse, and sexual education in the schools. In a similar vein, freedom to choose one's health care provider has been a powerful argument against calls for a national health service.

Given a social reality that lacks a coherent policy and institutional infrastructure for either families or health care, we are left with the need to examine the effects of a fragmented series of policies, organizations, and programs as they converge, and all too often conflict, in their effects on the family-health/illness connection. We will first examine social policy and the family with specific reference to health issues. Subsequently, we will explore areas in which health policy and programs impinge on or interact with the health maintenance and caretaking roles of the family. In each of these discussions, the plight of the socioeconomically disadvantaged family will be underscored as will issues precipitated when a policy or program ignores, or is in conflict with, the changing family structures that characterize society today. We will look closely at the organizational structure of hospitals and health care institutions to determine their effects on families and on the ability of health care practitioners to provide family-focused health care. Family support programs and mutual aid groups will be discussed insofar as they reflect a collective community response to family needs. Finally, bioethical decision making, a task confronting many families today, will be presented to illustrate a special case of environmental demand placed on families in the absence of clear social norms or community supports. In this way, we demonstrate that the health-related functions, tasks, and problems of the family are not solely a family responsibility, but rather, that the success or failure that families experience in carrying out these is inextricably related to factors in their social environment.

Social Policy, Families, and Health

We have already suggested that the United States lacks a coherent family policy, however, a family perspective on social policy is increasingly recognized in policy formulation and in assessing the impact of policies on families (Zimmerman, 1988). In this respect, policies are viewed from a family perspective as distinct from an individual perspective. From this stance, policies can be distinguished as to whether family goals and objectives are implicit or explicit (Zimmerman, 1988). Indeed, all social policies can be examined in light of the needs of families as well as in terms of their effects on families.

Social Policy and Family Well-being

In earlier chapters, we reviewed both theoretical and empirical evidence supporting the conclusion that a family's general well-being is a critical factor in its ability to carry out its health-related roles. An ecosystemic view of family well-being focuses attention on the family's interaction with the community in which it is embedded. In turn, this interaction, or family–environment fit, is influenced by a series of social and institutional policies. Indeed, the majority of social policies impact families. For example, economic, employment, housing, retirement, tax, and income maintenance policies all have implicit implications for family well-being; that is, although family goals and objectives are not necessarily inherent in the policy, specific components in these policies and their resulting programs affect families and family well-being (Zimmerman, 1988). Family policy analysts have long observed, however, that while the vast array of social policies and programs benefit individual family members, they were not designed to ensure the viability of the family as a social system (Myrdal, 1968; Schorr, 1972; Zimmerman, 1976; 1978).

A striking example of a negative program effect on families is manifested in the Aid to Families with Dependent Children (AFDC) program. Although intended to provide financial support to needy families, the eligibility requirements of the program have effectively penalized two-parent families and have encouraged separate parental living arrangements (Moroney, 1987). This negative effect has long been recognized (Garfinkel & McLanahan, 1986), however, beginning attempts to remedy this negative impact on families were recently addressed in the Welfare Reform Act of 1988. Indirect effects on health are also potentially related to such a policy. For example, in Chapter 2, we reviewed data suggesting that family structure and living arrangements can influence coping with serious childhood illness insofar as two-parent families are likely to experience more stress and in some cases poorer health outcomes. A policy that effectively discourages parents from living together also potentially reduces the ability of the same parents to meet the needs of an ill child.

At the other end of the spectrum, lack of, or failed, social policy can also indirectly influence family well-being. For example, teen birthrates have been associated with low state welfare expenditures and high unemployment rates (Zimmerman, 1988). Furthermore, while male joblessness has been documented to be a critical factor in the continued erosion and poverty of the black family, the issue has all but been ignored in recent policy deliberations (Nichols-Casebolt, 1988; Sampson, 1987; Wilson & Neckerman, 1986). Unfortunately, when a primary family member is unemployed, the family is also less likely to have health insurance. In addition, unemployment has been associated with increased health problems and family stress. Thus, failure to address joblessness potentially results in a three-way negative influence on family health-related functions: (1) through family poverty; (2) by reducing access to health care; and (3) by negatively impacting member's health.

Beyond indirect effects on family well-being, general social policies also can have specific effects on public health and, in this way, influence family well-being. Environmental, food, and drug regulation (or absence of regulation), nuclear energy, hazardous waste, and highway safety policies all have potential effects on individual and community health. Increased rates of illness in communities adjacent to hazardous dumps are a clear example of this effect. Defense policy and defense spending influence public spending on both family and health programs and thus influence family well-being. Family proponents suggest, therefore, that all policies be evaluated in terms of their effects on families (Zimmerman, 1988).

Numerous policies and programs are structured toward explicit family-related goals and objectives. These include: child protection services, foster care, adoption services, family-planning programs, maternal and child health programs, and an emerging body of family law pertaining to such issues as child support and custody, marriage and divorce, and cohabitation (Zimmerman, 1988). Insofar as these policies influence family well-being they also influence health-related activities.

Social policies typically emerge out of an uneven mix of multiple, conflicting, and complex rational and emotional processes (Kane & Kane, 1987; Zimmerman, 1988). In recent years, the family has become a rallying focus for conflicting political, social, and philosophical debate, as evidenced in the daily media. On the one hand, nostalgic reminiscences, tempered by selective recall, spur calls for social policies that support the once common nuclear family and its "traditional values" (including its effectiveness as an institution of social control) (Stoesz, 1987b). On the other hand, changing family structures are viewed as enhancing individual family members' growth, and policies are proposed to strengthen this aspect of family life and mediate its accompanying stressors (Kagan & Shelley, 1987; Moroney, 1987; Zimmerman, 1988).

Striking paradoxes are also evident. For example, on the one hand, family planning services linked to high schools are currently attacked on the grounds that parental responsibility is inviolate. In stark contrast to a "right of families" approach, considerable governmental intervention was marshalled several years ago in prosecuting parents for failing to do all in their power to prolong the life of a severely deformed infant (Kane, 1985). In related contradictions, Kulys and Meyer (1985) note that the life of a newborn child who will never be independent or self-supporting is maintained at great expense, while at the same time, there is a reluctance to give sufficient resources to an AFDC mother to provide her children with a nutritious diet, thereby increasing the likelihood that these children will become unhealthy.

Such ideological themes (and paradoxes) continue to influence current discussions of social policy related to families, demonstrating, once again, the powerful value context surrounding the formulation of public policy. Under these circumstances, an important task of the professional and academic community is to marshall the relevant empirical data to inform future policy debates (Stoesz, 1987a). In this vein, it is important that we not lose sight of the fact that a measure of the strength of family life is not its adherence to a single structure, but rather its resilience and ability to adapt its structure in the face of ever-changing environments. In our view, family well-being, and therefore the family's success in its health-related functions and tasks, will most likely be enhanced to the extent that social policies reduce the serious socioeconomic disadvantages of a substantial proportion of families and aim to strengthen all families, regardless of their particular form or structure.

Health Policy and Families

As indicated previously, discussions of health care policy in the United States frequently refer to the lack of such, or at best suggest that the policy pursued most vigorously has been a seemingly concerted effort to avoid the formulation of a national health care policy. As a result,

> At the present time, the American health care system is a far-flung, eclectic, and internally unrelated collection of separate institutions, programs, and personnel—a genuine nonsystem, to use a much overused term. There is no central organizing or controlling force, either nationally or locally, that can ensure that any portion of the health care system will respond to the highest social priorities if those priorities are ever set (Williams and Torrens, 1984).

Indeed, there is as yet no agreement that health care is a right of all individuals. Kane (1985) has portrayed the uneven history of landmark policies and programs during this century, a history that has been characterized by incremental, remedial, and inconsistent policymaking. All of these issues have been presented in depth elsewhere (Califano, 1985; Fuchs, 1986b). This patchwork and fragmented approach is clearly illustrated when health care programs are assessed in terms of their responsiveness to the needs of families.

An Historical Overview

A brief historical overview of landmark health care legislation provides a contextual framework to enhance our understanding of the role of the social environment in determining families' access to health-related resources. In 1935, Title V of the Social Security Act created the Maternal and Child Health Service and the Crippled Children's Service. Prior to this period of landmark legislation, public health and the health needs of families were not distinguished from attempts to address general social issues (Kane, 1985). During those early years, the health needs of individuals and families were served under Charity Organization Societies, settlement houses, and in conjunction with voluntary hospitals. Social work pioneers were in the forefront of social reform movements that included a heavy emphasis on public health (Kane, 1985). For example, in 1912, the Children's Bureau was established and the first task undertaken was its study of infant mortality (Lesser, 1985). The Shepard–Towner Act of 1921 established the first public health grants-in-aid program under the auspices of the Children's Bureau, with the goal of establishing a network of state-administered programs and improving existing services to promote the health of mothers and infants (Lesser, 1985; Mantell, 1984). This legislation was responsive to the higher U.S. maternal and infant mortality rate at the time when compared to almost all other Western countries (Lesser, 1985). It is noteworthy that today, the United States continues to rank poorly in infant mortality among industrialized nations.

Since 1935, a progression of federal health laws and programs were enacted to address a broad range of health concerns, including a national school lunch program, regulations for labeling food and drugs, a federal program to support the construction of hospitals, and the establishment of the National Institutes of Health to sponsor research (Bracht, 1978; Kane, 1985). In 1960, the Kerr–Mills amendment to the Social Security Act provided state grants for medical assistance for the elderly, and in 1965, Titles XVIII and XIX created Medicare and Medicaid to assist in meeting the medical care needs of the elderly and the poor. In 1967, under the Office of Economic Opportunity, neighborhood health centers were established, and in the same year, the Children and Youth Projects were enacted with the goal of providing comprehensive preventive and medical care services to children and youth. Kane (1985 p. 264) characterizes this period:

> Overall, this period can be summarized as one of attention to special populations—migrants, coal miners, alcohol and drug abusers, preschoolers, trauma victims, abused children, the elderly, the mentally ill, rape victims, and so on. Many national programs were installed to deal with specific disease entities or problems, and the model of a decentralized program, administered by states but oiled by federal dollars, was firmly established. By the early 1970s, however, the health care buying spree was over. . . . By 1980, dialogues about health policy were flavored with disillusionment and even despair. The cost of care was frightening and likely to rise. . . .

Indeed, during the 1980s, we have seen a general shift in social values that has resulted in deemphasizing society's collective responsibility for those at risk in our society, with a renewed emphasis on individualism, decentralization, and minimum governmental intervention. As a result, many of the existing human service programs have suffered serious cutbacks in funding or are undergoing major structural changes. As we will demonstrate later in this chapter, the poor and minority families are especially disadvantaged by gaps in this health care nonsystem and by failure to commit adequate resources to meet the needs of less fortunate members of society.

With the exception of the Medicare Catastrophic Coverage Act of 1988, legislation in the 1980s was aimed at cost-saving, rather than at extending benefits. In fact, this legislation was withdrawn in 1989 in light of widespread criticism because the program extended benefits, but with the recipients of medicare bearing the full cost of these increased benefits. Although the Health Maintenance Organization Act was originally enacted in 1973, it was not until the 1980s, that the potential cost-saving benefits of this approach to financing health care captured widespread interest and was incorporated into some state Medicaid programs. During this period, governmental regulation programs became more visible in legislation mandating peer and utilization review processes to oversee health care providers and, in so doing, to reduce unnecessary medical care and hospital stays. At the same time, regulations mandating specific ancillary services such as social services, were weakened, as were requirements concerning the qualifications of social service providers. Each of these thrusts was aimed at cost reduction.

In 1983, with little debate, Congress dramatically changed the method of financing hospitalization under Medicare. Cost-based reimbursement to hospitals was discontinued and, in its place, a prospective payment to hospitals by diagnosis-related groups (DRGs), a fee-per-case system as apposed to fee-for-service, was instituted (Caputi & Heiss, 1984). This legislation is a radical step in reforming Medicare and is aimed at giving hospitals an incentive to reduce costs (Austin, 1986; Garner, 1986; Starr, 1986). This major structural change in health care financing has dramatically altered the delivery of medical care and the way in which social work departments deliver services (Caputi & Heiss, 1984; Coulton, 1984; Holden, 1989).

Family-Focused Health Programs

Government sponsored programs targeted to the health needs of families can be roughly divided into those with: a primary goal of prevention or health promotion; and those intended to assist families in coping with illness or trauma. In general, these programs are categorical; that is, they are established to serve specific groups or specific conditions. Over the years, successive amendments to Title V of the 1935 Social Security Act have expanded community health services for mothers and children. For example, the Maternal and Infant Care (MIC) program was enacted as part of Title V of the Social Security Act in 1963. It is distinguished from Medicaid, in that it extends reimbursement for medical care to include comprehensive prenatal and well-child care services (including social services) for low-income families in high-risk urban and rural areas (Combs-Orme, 1987). An array of other programs addresses specific health-related needs of families, including the food stamp program, the Supplemental Food Program for Women, Infants, and Children (WIC), early periodic screening, detection, and treatment programs, and the Improved Pregnancy Outcome (IPO) programs (Poole & Carlton, 1986). During the past 20 years, the positive effects of these specialized programs as well as of Medicaid have been documented (see Combs-Orme, 1987, Poole & Carlton, 1986, and Starr, 1986, for reviews). It is especially disturbing, therefore, that political support for these programs has wavered during the 1980s. For example, between 1981 and 1983, maternal and child health funding was cut 30 percent overall, and 47 states had reduced such services (Combs-Orme, 1987). Although it is premature to assume a causal relationship, infant mortality increased in some states during 1984, despite a modest nationwide decrease (Wegam, 1984).

Far fewer resources are designated for prevention, screening, and early detection among adults. In fact, a common criticism of Medicare concerns its emphasis on acute care and inadequate reimbursement for preventive and long-term care. Nutritional programs for older Americans are provided within Senior Centers; however, these programs have been cut in recent years. Furthermore, Medicare has not been immune to further cost-saving measures in the current political climate, with the result that recipients incur increasing out-of-pocket expenses.

Whereas the Maternal and Child Health Program, today housed within the Public Health Service, has been the central program for meeting families health promotion and prevention needs, the Crippled Children's Program (also originally established by Title V of the Social Security Act of 1935), is the preeminent national program administered by states to assist families in mitigating the social, emotional, and economic costs of caring for a chronically ill or handicapped child. Early in its history, children with orthopedic conditions were most commonly served; however, over the years, the program has extended its services to include all chronic and disabling conditions. Eligibility for the program's services are more liberal than those generally adopted for public assistance or Medicaid, taking into account not only family income and size, but also diagnosis, estimated cost of care, including aftercare, and ongoing additional costs of caring for a handicapped child (Lesser, 1985). Enacted in 1976, the Supplemental Security Income Program for Disabled Children provides some measure of income security for families with a handicapped child up to age 16; however, income eligibility requirements frequently demand that families deplete their own resources first (Rudolf, Andrews, Ratcliff, & Downes, 1985). Indeed, on reaching adulthood, recipients of Crippled Children's assistance are at risk because the only programs to which they are entitled to seek aid are public assistance and Medicaid. During the 1960s, legislation was enacted to establish Regional Centers to provide comprehensive services for families with a developmentally disabled child. Current proponents for improving services to all handicapped children point to the success of this program and call for similar regional models to address the needs of children and families with handicapping physical conditions (Hobbs & Perrin, 1985; The Children's Roundtable of Los Angeles, 1989).

The need for a coherent policy addressing the long-term care needs of adults is now well-recognized. Long-term disability and the need for long-term aftercare, all too often, pose serious risks to family systems. For example, up until now families of impaired adults were required to "spend down" to poverty status before becoming eligible for Medicaid payment for long-term care. In the most extreme example, the integrity of the family system was destroyed, when spouses were driven to obtain an unwanted divorce in order to protect life savings needed to maintain their own independence. Fortunately, one of the least controversial provisions of the Medicare Catastrophic Coverage Act protects spousal income, assets, and homes when the patient enters a nursing home. This provision became effective in late 1989. Some states have elected to include this provision in their Medicaid program.

We next examine this patchwork network of health programs in terms of access and the degree to which care is comprehensive and coordinated. Indeed, the complex array of health and related social services becomes, for families and human service practitioners alike, an all to often bewildering maze of fragmented, specialized programs and services with many differing eligibility or entitlement requirements. In a striking example, programs for children with spina bifida and their families can be found under the Crippled Children's Services, SSI, Medicaid, Education for All Handicapped Children, and community mental health clinics (Rudolf et al., 1985).

Structural Issues Affecting Families Access to Services

Medical Care

In the United States, the vast majority of health-related services is purchased in the marketplace. Indeed, a free-enterprise marketplace mentality has dominated health policy in America (the most notable exception being health care for veterans). From their inception, the two flagship governmental health care programs, Medicare and Medicaid, approached the marketplace structure as sacrosanct. Therefore, while, in 1965, Medicare shifted health care for the aged into the framework of universal social insurance, its provisions entailed the payment of prevailing medical fees (in addition, doctors could charge more than paid by Medicare), and hospitals were payed on the basis of their stated costs (Starr, 1986). Medicaid, while established within a means-tested public assistance model for the "helpless" and "deserving" poor, allowed states discretion in setting physician fee schedules but also reimbursed hospitals on the basis of their costs. The architects of this legislation admittedly designed these programs to obtain the support of organized medicine and the powerful national association of hospitals (Starr, 1986). Not surprisingly, the effect of these major government programs on the health care market was to infuse the market with new financing that, in turn, resulted in dramatically escalating overall health care costs. Furthermore, the inherent structural incentives resulted in what many believe to be an excessive focus on acute medical care and hospital care over preventive, health maintenance, and long-term care.

Today, although the evidence is mixed, there is reason to conclude that these programs have contributed to the overall improvement in the health of the American people (Starr, 1986). Certainly, the programs have reduced the numbers of uninsured and extended access to medical care. There is also evidence that additional funding for medical research and advances in medical technology has payed off in reducing infant mortality (Starr, 1986).

Questions remain, however, about whether the disproportionate emphasis on acute medical care results in the greatest benefits or whether a more even emphasis on personal lifestyles and health promotion (Califano, 1985), prevention, community-based and out-patient care, and in-home services might result in even greater health benefits and reduced costs as well. For example, community health centers are an effective means to improve health and to reduce rates of hospitalization (Starr, 1986), and preventive maternal and child care programs have resulted in decreased infant mortality (Combe-Ormes, 1987; Poole & Carlton, 1986). In recent years, however, and erosion in the political commitment to child health and prevention programs has occurred, with substantial negative effects on the poor and minority families (Jones & Rice, 1987).

Despite evidence of the overall effectiveness of many governmental programs in improving the health of Americans (Starr, 1986), almost all programs have experienced substantial funding cuts in recent years. The cost-saving measures in Medicare have been subtle, reflecting the more favored status of this program due to its large middle-class consistency and its link to an employee tax-base (Starr, 1986). However, as already noted, recipients of Medicare are experiencing increased out-of-pocket costs (a trend likely to continue), and these costs effectively reduce access to health care among poor elders (Petchers & Milligan, 1988).

Cutbacks in the Medicaid program have been less subtle, presumably due, in large part, to its widespread perception as a public welfare program. A major source of cost-saving in this program has been through the reduction of those eligible for care under the program, with a significant proportion of the reduction occurring among AFDC recipients and thereby falling on children (Starr, 1986). Continued escalating costs of the program are attributable to increasing hospital and nursing home costs, with the net results that public money has been shifted from primary and preventive health care (such as that provided in community health centers) to pay for acute care (Starr, 1986). We will elaborate further on the impact of this shifting policy on the poor later in this discussion. However, here we underscore that program changes are effectively reducing access to less costly and at least equally beneficial health care services for the poor.

It is noteworthy that in the current cost-conscious social climate, the marketplace free-enterprise structure continues to thrive. Initially spurred by the influx of money for health care from Medicare and Medicaid, in recent years health care has become a thriving industry with all of the trappings of the corporate community (Califano, 1985; Starr, 1982; Stoesz, 1986; Wohl, 1984). Thus public payment for private profit has radically shifted the delivery of health care services from voluntary nonprofit and tax-supported public centers to the private for-profit sector.

The rapid growth of for-profit health care corporations has been nothing short of remarkable in recent years (Gray, 1986; Marmor, Schlesinger, & Smithey, 1986; Navarro, 1975; Wohl, 1984). In a recent analysis, only 2 of 45 corporations lost money during 1984, while 6 demonstrated revenue growth between 50 and 100 percent, and an additional 13 reported an annual growth rate of over 100 percent (Stoesz, 1986). Large-scale mergers in the nursing home industry are leading to projections that in the near future, all nursing home beds will be controlled by as few as 30 corporations (Stoesz, 1986). Health Maintenance Organizations and home health care firms are also growing corporations (Stoesz, 1986).

This revolution in health care delivery is spurred by cost concerns and is reflected in several structural changes in the overall delivery system, including the emergence of preferred provider organizations, self-contained employer health care programs, and unique partnerships between health care providers such as hospitals and insurance companies (Kiesler & Morton, 1988). Although there is little debate about the direction and strength of these shifts in health care policy and delivery, the ultimate effects on the health of individuals and families in the United States is uncertain. The pitfalls and dangers of the commercialization of health care are purported to include: (1) escalating costs in the face of marketing unnecessary services; (2) failing to provide services that are most needed, but less profitable; and (3) declining quality of care as a result of the declining influence of professional ethics (Relman, 1980). Other arguments hold that the shifts bode well insofar as consumer desires are more likely to be considered (Havighurst, 1986), and that the quality of care provided by managed care programs will be more easily evaluated by consumer groups (Hale & Hunter, 1988).

Large-scale research is yet to be conducted on the effects of these structural shifts on the health of Americans. However, preliminary studies comparing for-profit and nonprofit providers suggest that results fall far short of proponents expectations of increased efficiencies that are presumed to occur from market competition (Stoesz, 1986). In fact, some evidence of patient neglect and operational inefficiencies has been found on the part of health care corporations (Stoesz, 1986). The strongest evidence indicates that this structural shift further exacerbates unwarranted disparities between care for the poor and the nonpoor (Starr, 1982; Stoesz, 1986). At the same time, there is widespread consensus that for-profit managed care programs will predominate the health care market in the foreseeable future (Hale & Hunter, 1988).

Supportive Community Services to Assist Families

Of direct relevance to the overarching theme of this book, Pratt (1982) has convincingly delineated the implications of a changing health and illness paradigm on families. She proposes:

> As we come to accept a redefinition of health, every aspect of life is opened up as a potential influence on health that must be evaluated and managed—job, community, home, military service, recreation, and aspects of personal conduct such as sex, diet, exercise, smoking, alcohol, stress, exposure to chemicals, and risks of accident. . . . While medicalizing of health meant taking a problem out of its social–psychological–environmental context and isolating it for treatment, the new life-style construction of health means that any health problem must be examined in terms of the full complexity of the person's and family's life situation and in terms of past, present, and future life situation. . . . The responsibility for health care shifts largely to families because they are more knowledgeable than the professionals about their own pattern of life; only they can reform their living habits . . . and only they can be expected to sustain the long-term commitment to the person's destiny that is the basis for managing health as a lifelong enterprise. This changed time perspective on health is one of the major implications of the emerging theory of health (Pratt, 1982, p. 77).

Herein, Pratt has set forth the vital role of families in health promotion and health maintenance. Families' success in promoting and maintaining the health of its members is undoubtedly a product of its ability to obtain the social resources vital to maintaining family well-being and the extent to which a family's social environment is supportive rather than hazardous.

At the other end of the spectrum, the ability of children and adults to remain at home, while managing chronic and disabling physical conditions over long periods, requires extensive family participation. Indeed, as already observed in Chapter 2, there is overwhelming evidence that families are continuing to provide a very large proportion of caregiving and that they desire to do so (Creedon, 1988; Doty, 1986; Moroney, 1983;). Community-based social and health-related services are essential to assist patients and their families in promoting health and in maintaining a maximum level of independent living and quality of life in the face of illness (Ell, 1985; Poole, 1987; Reichert, 1982). Increasingly, however, families are expected to coordinate fragmented services, including out-patient medical care, community mental health services, nursing homes, hospices, church-related services, home care, private practitioners (Pollin & Cashion, 1984), and voluntary health agencies (Black, Dornan, & Allegrante, 1986), and to perform caregiving tasks previously carried out by health care professionals (Dunn, & Watson, 1988; Kulys & Meyer, 1985; Heagerty, Sheridan, 1985). Families will be aided in carrying out these roles if adequate community supportive services are available and if they are informed about effective ways to coordinate and use these resources (Freedman, Pierce, & Reiss, 1987).

To what extent do Medicare, Medicaid, and other governmental programs support the family's health promotion and maintenance functions and family caregiving? In general, the answer is, less than adequately. The gaps in health care financing and programs are vividly demonstrated in a recent national study of child health in the United States (National Association of Children's Hospitals and Related Institutions (NACHRI), 1989). Preventive health care affecting children is shown to be seriously uneven across both socioeconomic and geographic boundaries.

In the face of illness or disability, program policies actually result in impeding family caregiving efforts or in placing excessive burdens on family caregivers. For example, as previously discussed, eligibility requirements for Medicaid stipulate that families "spend-down" or exhaust any savings before receiving benefits. Other policies effectively operate as disincentives to family caretaking, even going so far as to penalize those families who bring a family member home rather than institutionalizing the member (Motwani & Herring, 1988). As already noted, long-term care costs effectively impoverish a substantial number of elderly families (Branch, Friedman, Cohen et al., 1988), and the overall economic impact of a child's physical handicap is substantial for most families (Salkever, 1985). Limited financing for home-based psychosocial services also acts to deter social workers and other health care practitioners from providing after-care services (Rosengarten, 1986). Indeed, lack of financing for in-home care, case management, and community-based services to support families electing to provide care to children dependent on medical technology results in undesirable dependence on hospital and institutional care (Burr, Guyer, Todres et al., 1983; The Children's Roundtable of Los Angeles, 1989; Task Force Report, 1988).

Failure to enact policies aimed at alleviating the stressors associated with family caregiving is also in direct conflict with existing data on caregivers needs and preferences (Doty, 1986; Moroney, 1983). Several waiver and pilot programs that address care recipients' and caregivers' needs are currently undergoing evaluation. For example, adult day care programs have been emphasized as an alternative to nursing home placement in the Medicaid Home and Community Care waiver program enacted in the Omnibus Budget Reconciliation Act of 1981 (Dilworth-Anderson, 1987; Harder, Gornick, & Burt, 1986).

The introduction of DRGs as a cost-saving measure has introduced a structural change into the system with major implications for the way in which care is delivered, the type of care to be delivered, and pursuant to our discussion, the care-giving activities of families. Although early evidence suggests that DRGs are relatively effective at controlling acute care hospital costs, they do not prevent cost-shifting to alternative levels of care, such as rehabilitation, nursing home care, and home health care (Poole, 1987). The extent to which economic, social, and emotional costs are shifted to family members needs to be examined. It is already known that patients are going home "quicker but sicker," however, questions, about the long-term impact on families and family caregivers remain largely unanswered. Moreover, the prospects for increased federal funding for long-term care are uncertain, however, the private sector will undoubtedly expand its efforts in this area.

Therefore, the question arises as to the extent to which nongovernmental programs address the needs of families. As will be discussed later, the impact of extending vital services through the marketplace is fraught with known and unknown hazards. To what extent family needs and assessments of the impact on families will influence the development of service packages remains to be evaluated. Families already face a continuing care system that is specialized, fragmented, complex, uncoordinated, and incomplete (Ell, 1985; The Children's Roundtable of Los Angeles, 1989; Poole, 1987; Reichert, 1982; Wood & Estes, 1988). It is difficult to envision that such a nonsystem will be improved by greater dependence on the for-profit private sector.

The structural changes that are occurring as a result of reduced federal spending, increased beneficiary cost-sharing, and the shift to for-profit care are not limited to the delivery of medical services but increasingly include those social services that are critical in long-term in-home management of illness. Reichert (1982; 1983) has decried the increasing intrusion of the market system and its ideology into the arena of health-related community and social services. He characterizes the health care nonsystem as complicated further by increasing market penetration, increasing regulation, increasing fragmentation of services, and astronomical costs. He identifies the incursion of the marketplace from three directions: the increasingly common practice by public agencies of contracting for services from both voluntary agencies and private enterprises (Kramer & Grossman, 1987), the expansion of private corporation social services, and the increasing modeling of profit sector management approaches by nonprofit agencies (Lewin, Eckels, & Miller, 1988).

Voicing similar concerns, Wood and Estes (1988) have pointed to the "medicalization" of community services for the elderly that traditionally comprised an array of social and health services. Based on their research, these investigators conclude that the community-based service system is undergoing a restructuring process characterized by:

> (1) the privatization of the most profitable service areas (for example, aspects of home health and nutrition) and the absorption of nonprofit community agencies by for-profit entities; (2) the targeting of services to particular clientele based on ability to pay; (3) the fragmentation of services; (4) the medicalization of social services; and (5) a shift in caregiving functions from the formal delivery system to the informal sector of the home and family (Wood & Estes, 1988, p. 38).

They remind us that government funding spurred the nonprofit health and social service system between the 1960s and 1980, and they suggest that the current changes are exerting great pressure on the nonprofit sector to operate in a competitive mode, shaping their goals by considerations of competitive pricing, profit-making, and market share. Indeed, nonprofit and for-profit hospitals are viewing the elderly as a lucrative market (Kane, 1985). In a similar vein, hospitals and community agencies (including for-profit social work group practices) are marketing health promotion and wellness programs to employees and employers. The question arises as to whether this market mechanism will somehow be more, or even as, effective as population-based nonprofit programs. The answer will probably be mixed, namely, that the needs of those with purchasing power will continue to be met, and in some cases met more effectively, but costs will not be substantially reduced, may even increase, and the needs of some will continue to go unmet. Furthermore, the greatest negative effects of these structural shifts are most likely to fall on those least able to bear them.

Structural Effects on the Poor and Uninsured

By now it is clear that the social environment, as reflected in health policy and in some related family policies, has a pervasive affect on family health-related functions. Unfortunately, these policies also serve to deny to some the social resources that they need to maintain optimal health and to mitigate the negative sequelae of illness. In general, the reshaping of major health care systems exerts a greater negative impact on family health-related functions among the poor than the nonpoor. Indeed, in recent years, we have seen an overarching shift in support for antipoverty programs aimed at the overall health and well-being of the poor toward an expenditure drift for medical care (and for the aged) that fails to address the overall needs of poor families (Starr, 1986).

Furthermore, despite the actual rise in the number of poor (Danziger & Weinberg, 1986), with the greatest rise occurring among children (Burr, 1988), health programs for the poor have been cut back (Starr, 1986). We have already described the overt cutbacks in Medicaid. In addition, a series of more subtle regulatory changes have combined to place the health care, and presumably the health, of the poor in jeopardy. For example, under the 1946 Hill–Burton Act, hospitals that used federal funding for their construction were required to provide a proportion of free care. Very soon, many of these legal obligations will expire; thereafter, many hospitals will no longer be required to provide such service (Starr, 1986). At the same time, the increasingly competitive market in which both for-profit and nonprofit hospitals operate, makes caring for the poor and uncompensated care financially unattractive (Lewin, Eckels, & Miller, 1988). This effect has been exacerbated with the onset of DRGs. Because the poor are more often hospitalized at advanced stages of illness and more often suffer from overlapping illness, their actual cost of care is frequently above that of the standard DRG rate (Starr, 1986).

As a result, there has been a dramatic increase in the practice of "dumping" or transferring of patients to public facilities at a time when these hospitals are experiencing severe funding shortages (Stoesz, 1986). It is clear that, in combination, these structural changes are effectively reducing equitable access to medical care among the poor (Marmor et al., 1986). Moreover, reducing access of the poor to medical care carries the additional risk of depriving the poor of access to other services as well, because so often it is through contacts in the health care system that poor people are informed of other community services (Kulys & Meyer, 1985). Indeed, Marmor and colleagues (1986, p. 347) observe that "it would be perhaps a fitting irony if the spread of for-profit medicine created conditions that prompted massive new governmental interventions into the organization and financing of health care services."

In an era of reduced spending for human services, it is not surprising that little progress has been made in reducing the numbers of Americans without health insurance (Butler, 1988; Davis & Rowland, 1983; Levitan & Shapiro, 1987; Wilensky & Berk, 1982). It is estimated that between 6 and 10 percent of all Americans have no public or private health insurance, including about 25 percent of those below the poverty line (Starr, 1986). A significant proportion of the uninsured are umemployed, and among the unemployed are larger numbers of minority persons (Palley, Feldman, Gallner, & Tysor, 1985). We have already described the negative effects of unemployment on health. In addition, there is evidence that the uninsured forego primary and preventive care and resort to heavy use of emergency rooms (Palley et al., 1985).

The health of poor children is of special concern. Despite the fact that they are more likely to have chronic health problems (Butler, Budetti, MeManus et al., 1985), they are less likely to be cared for by pediatricians, to have a regular source of care, and to receive preventive care (Stein & Jessop, 1985). Not surprisingly, children also are disproportionately represented among the uninsured (NACHRI, 1989), and poor children are least likely to be adequately insured (Task Force Report, 1988; Weeks, 1985).

The special plight of the rural poor with respect to health care has also received attention (Perrin, 1985). For example, there is evidence that up to 40 percent of rural dwellers live in areas lacking adequate health care resources (Lichty & Zuvekas, 1980). Migrant farmworkers and Native Americans are rural minority groups with special needs. The former have been shown to have numerous health problems that go undetected, while service providers demonstrate reluctance to care for this population (Perrin, 1985).

We have alluded to the shift of public resources toward acute medical care. In the case of the poor, however, it can be reasoned that even greater health benefits would accrue from the provision of preventive and primary care (Jones & Rice, 1987; Sardell, 1988). Indeed, there is evidence to support that conclusion. For example, in a recently released report to the House Select Committee on Children, Youth, and Families, it was documented that 1 dollar spent on the Childhood Immunization Program saves the government 10 dollars in medical costs (Kissel, 1986). Similarly, 3 dollars in short-term hospital costs is reported to be saved for every dollar spent for nutrition to reduce the incidence of low birthweight and other problems (Kissel, 1986). Improved birthweight accompanying prenatal medical care among black women is especially noteworthy, in light of the greater infant mortality and morbidity among blacks (Murray & Bernfield, 1988), And finally, substantial savings are found from money spent on prenatal health programs and special Medicaid programs for children (Kissel, 1986). Early evidence also suggests that the health status of Medicaid beneficiaries, who have been terminated by changing eligibility standards, declines over time (Starr, 1986).

Some believe that problems in providing indigent care will reach near-crisis proportions before needed sound action is taken. On the other hand, Starr (1986), a Pulitzer prize-winning sociologist, suggests that the ways to mitigate the health care plight of the poor are already known and are not beyond political or economic reach. What is missing at the moment is a concerted public will toward this goal. Starr concludes:

> Many observers are deeply convinced that the United States cannot afford or agree upon any plan for universal health insurance protection, such as that of most major Western nations. Our world groans under many intractable problems, but I am convinced that this ought not to be one of them. Decent health care for the poor is not a fiscal impossibility, nor a political impossibility, unless we become utterly resigned to a kind of national incompetence in public policy (1986, p. 159).

Undoubtedly, addressing the most glaring gaps in access to health and medical care will be high on the agenda of national and local policymakers throughout the 1990s.

Organizational Effects on Family-Focused Care: Practice Implications

Some organizational environments have traditionally been more receptive to family-focused health care than others. Primary care settings such as public health departments, neighborhood and community health centers, family practices, and schools are foremost among those who routinely incorporate a family approach in their health service models (Ell & Morrisson, 1981). In so doing, these organizations have contributed to documenting the effectiveness and efficiency of family-focused service.

In these organizations, the social goal of the agency as well as the social organization of the care and services provided are compatible and even conducive to incorporating a focus on the family. In many cases, a family approach was deeply rooted in the beginnings of the programs. For example, as early as the end of the nineteenth century, the need to involve parents in preventive health services for children was widely understood, and in 1902, a nurse from the staff of the Henry Street Visiting Nurse Association was loaned to the schools at the request of the public health department (Lesser, 1985). The principle of family-focused health service was established, therein, for schools and for public health departments. Today, a hallmark of Public Law 91-142, the Education for All Handicapped Children Act of 1975, continues to be the requirement of family participation in all aspects of planning the child's educational program (Wiegerink & Comfort, 1987). In recent years, family-centered care has become increasingly visible with the emergence of family practice as a medical specialty, in neighborhood and comprehensive health centers, and most recently in health maintenance organizations.

Inclusion of family-centered services has proven to be more difficult in acute medical care centers. We have already stated that a primary barrier to providing hospital-based services to families results from the lack of adequate financing for family care (Sikes & Rodenhauser, 1987). Additional underpinnings of the reluctance to include family-oriented care can be found in both the mission and social organization of these organizations. First, the primary goal of these institutions is the rapid provision of highly technical life-saving care or highly specialized restorative care to the patient. Second, care is provided in institutions that require highly structured methods of delivering the care that is provided by a multidisciplinary team of specialized professional caregivers. Third, with the advent of DRGs and utilization review, in-patient hospital stays have been shortened, and social work staffs have undergone redeployment from traditional clinical services (Dinerman, Seaton, & Schlesinger, 1986), thereby effectively reducing opportunities for family service. On the other hand, the advent of shortened hospital stays resulting from the DRG legislation demands maximum clinical skill in assisting patients and families in making an effective discharge plan (Holden, 1989), a topic to be discussed in detail in Chapter 9. Finally, structural changes in American health care including increasing centralization of power within hospital administration, emphasis on cost-containment, and a shift to for-profit models of service provision (Califano, 1985; Starr, 1982) challenge practitioners to develop and implement family-oriented care that is consistent with these organizational realities. Family services will be paid for only if it is demonstrated that they are cost-effective.

Examples of organizational effects on attempts to meet the needs of families in hospitals are numerous. Speedling (1982) has vividly illustrated the impact of the professional caregiving structure on the social behavior of the health professionals in relation to family members when a family member is hospitalized for a heart attack. To a great extent, the family was shown to be systematically excluded from effective participation in the management of the patient, but then in a quick reversal of expectations was given primary responsibility at discharge. Others have described problems of staff collaboration when social workers and other family therapists are dependent on the referral process (Anderson, 1984; Block, 1984; Glen, Atkins, & Singer, 1984; Hepworth & Jackson, 1985; Mandelbaum, 1984; McDaniel & Campbell, 1986; Simon, 1983; Sluzki, 1985), and problems in the family's perception of the social worker's role (Mandelbaum, 1984) as having inhibiting effects on attempts to provide family care. Difficulties in training family therapists in medical settings have also been detailed (with remarkable similarities to the field education of social workers in health care) (Ayers, 1985; Hepworth, Gavazzi, Adlin, & Miller, 1988). These barriers to serving families exist despite the extensive research reviewed in Chapter 2. This seeming contradiction illustrates once again that the application of behavioral and social science research findings so often depends on the structure of human service organizations (Chavkin, 1986), as well as on successful "marketing" of a program need or a program design (Pless & Haggerty, 1985). Given the current social context, the organizational barriers to providing family-centered care that impinge on social workers and other health care practitioners in acute care hospitals appear formidable (Baird & Doherty, 1986; Doherty & Burge, 1987).

Despite organizational disincentives and barriers, however, social workers, family therapists, and other health care professionals are demonstrating innovative and creative approaches to extending services to families (Sargent, 1985). These attempts range from systems modifications to maximize the use of social workers in health care to assist families to the establishment of primary family therapy programs in acute medical care settings. For example, a social work department identifies members of its staff as family consultants in an attempt to extend family-oriented therapy (Mandelbaum, 1984). Another recent report details an especially creative use of elderly couple groups within a home health care program (Rosengarten, 1986). Although their numbers are as yet few, family therapists (among whom are social workers) are increasingly employed in hospitals (McCall & Storm, 1985). Other accounts describe increasing involvement of social workers in family practice (Greene, Kruse, & Arthurs, 1985; Greene, Kruse, & Kulper, 1986).

A detailed description of a successful attempt to establish and maintain a family treatment center in a general hospital setting addresses many of the major organizational barriers to family-care (Carter, 1985). The center is administratively and professionally integrated with the general hospital, employs skilled family therapists (including social workers), operates at a profit or break-even point, and sponsors community outreach programs such as family support groups and professional education programs. Family therapy is presumed to enhance family well-being and, thereby, to promote member health. In addition, families coping with a physically ill member are provided a range of supportive services.

In light of short hospital stays, social workers and other health care professionals must expand the provision of community-based family care. Indeed, hospitals are expected to continue to expand their services beyond providing acute medical care to ensure their financial viability (Pettite & Anderson, 1986). Therefore, creative social work departments are also likely to thrive insofar as they are successful in developing and marketing such services (Jansson & Simmons, 1985–1986). Fortunately, evidence already suggests that community service programs effectively mitigate some of the day-to-day burden of caregiving (Quadagno, Sims, Squier, & Walker, 1987). For example, data suggest that supportive residential programs (Hilker, 1987), respite care (Gonyea, Seltzer, Gerstein, & Young, 1988), and, as already mentioned, adult day care (Dilworth-Anderson, 1987) should be expanded in ongoing community-based program planning. There is also convincing evidence that families with a chronically or terminally ill child desire and benefit from an array of community-based services that enable them to maintain quality of life for their child and the entire family (Task Force Report, 1988). Provision of case-management services as well as assisting families to assume case-management activities will be important components in family services (Heagerty, Dunn, & Watson, 1988). Social workers in schools and in the workplace will increasingly encounter opportunities to assist families in their caregiving activities. Indeed, there is evidence that employee assistance programs will be asked to provide services to family caregivers that will assist employees in meeting multiple caregiving responsibilities (Creedon, 1988).

Family Support Programs and Mutual Aid Groups

Up to now, we have emphasized the impact of the social, political, and organizational environment on families' health-related roles. We would be remiss, however, if we failed to observe that families have banded together to collectively advocate to change these environments and to mitigate the negative effects of social and organizational policies. Therefore, in recent years, we have witnessed a rapid growth in specialized family support programs and in family-centered mutual aid groups and organizations (Weissbourd, 1985).

Family support programs are purported to include seemingly disparate programs, such as Head Start, early childhood intervention programs, a parent cooperative day-care center, a comprehensive educational and health program for teen-age mothers, and a national information clearinghouse for parents of handicapped children (Kagan & Shelley, 1987). Family support programs have emerged primarily from grass roots efforts by families and have roots as early as the settlement houses in the late nineteenth century (Kagan & Shelley, 1987). Today, an ecological approach to planning and implementing family support programs underscores the interdependence and interrelatedness of the family system and its similar connections to the community (Weissbourd, 1985; Zigler & Weiss, 1985). From this perspective, a broad range of family support programs will influence family health-related roles.

Parents have also joined forces through support and mutual aid groups (Pizzo, 1987). These groups and organizations have been notably successful in changing pediatric hospital policies, with the result that hospitals today are increasingly more receptive to parental presence and participation in patient care (Azarnoff & Hardgroe, 1981). Today, parent groups are among the leading advocates for shifting manpower and financial resources to assist them in caring for children dependent on technical medical equipment or on health professionals in their homes (Task Force Report, 1988). Family groups have also been very effective not only in obtaining and exposing parents to sources of information about illness and its treatment (Borman, 1985) but in heightening public awareness of specific illnesses. Noteworthy, professional participation in support groups has been shown to be helpful to the success of the group (Cherniss, 1987).

Bioethical Decision Making and Families

We conclude this chapter with a very brief consideration of bioethical decision making, because in our view, this issue illustrates a potential imbalance in family–environment fit. Today, society is confronted with questions that did not concern people until very recently. These include the most basic of all questions: When does human life begin and when does life end (Abramson & Black, 1985; Cassel, 1987)? In the absence of clear cut social norms and community supports, families are increasingly called on to make wrenching bioethical decisions about the care of their loved ones.

Examples of the plight of families are numerous and well-known to social workers in health care. A young couple viewing the fetus during ultrasound imaging may become conflicted in reaching a decision about abortion (Abramson & Black, 1985) or intrauterine treatment (Furlong & Berkowitz, 1985). It is no longer uncommon for a spouse or parent to be faced with a decision about whether to continue the use of life-support technologies. And adult children are distressed by numerous and ongoing decisions related to the medical and long-term care of their elderly parents (Mitrowski, 1985; Nicholson & Matross, 1989; Parsons & Cox, 1989). In some circumstances, families are faced with a decision about whether to donate organs of family members (Batten & Prottas, 1987), while others question whether to tell their child he is dying (Price, 1989). Conflicts arise when the needs of family members are different from those of the patient (Ross, 1982).

Our purpose in reminding the reader of bioethical decision making as it is experienced within families is simply to underscore the plight of families under these circumstances. The task is particularly difficult in light of the lack of community norms. It is important, therefore, that these processes are given ample time and professional information and assistance to ensure that all aspects of the issue are adequately considered.

Conclusion

In this book, we are advocating for social workers and other health care professionals to expand their services to routinely provide family-focused care in the face of illness. At a policy level, the question then arises as to how such care is to be financed and organizationally structured. Indeed, the absence of funding for family services associated with the receipt of acute medical care and limited funding for such care in rehabilitation and long-term care institutions are major deterrents to the routine provision of psychosocial care of families. We are convinced not only that the family service is merited in human terms to alleviate the potential negative effects of illness on families and family members, but also, to and even greater extent, that failure to address "the patient in a family" substantially undermines the psychosocial care of patients and, under many circumstances, reduces the benefits of medical care. Furthermore, we believe that such care will prove to be beneficial to patients and families as well as cost-effective. Indeed, as will be demonstrated in the following chapter, there is already a growing body of evidence to support our contention.

We hope that we have also made a convincing case for the need for family-focused support systems, social policies, and social services to enhance the family's health promotion and prevention activities (Moroney, 1987). Families banding together to meet important needs will continue to be an important component in family support programs. Professionals are advised that targeting high-risk populations appears likely to produce the greatest potential benefits. For example, supportive health and social service programs for pregnant adolescents and minority women would likely result in dramatic reductions in infant morality and birth defects, as well as enhance family well-being (Weatherly, Perlman, Levine, & Klerman, 1985). Such programs must be designed to provide ongoing and comprehensive services (McDonald & Coburn, 1988) and to reduce failures to utilization among high-risk groups (Miller, Margolis, Schwethelm, & Smith, 1989).

Any significant shift in social and organizational policies toward addressing the gaps reviewed in this chapter undoubtedly will require concerted efforts to influence the public will, as well as ongoing demonstration of efficient and effective ways to deliver these services (Sardell, 1988). Failure to meet the health and related social needs of families increases the risk of racial and class inequalities in our society (Bodenheimer, 1989). Social workers and other health care practitioners are challenged to demonstrate effective service delivery toward enhancing family health promotion and family caregiving as well as to continue to document family-related health needs through research.

4
Evaluation of Family Interventions

In Chapter 3, we focused on macro- and meso-interventions directed toward family environments, in the form of social, health, and organizational policies and structures. We also reviewed selected meso-interventions in the form of family support programs and mutual aid groups. In this chapter, we review reported evaluations of interventions pertaining to more narrowly targeted interactions between the family and the health of its members. We pose the question, given the strong justification for family-oriented psychosocial intervention in health care, what recommendations can be made to practitioners, and most important, what is known about the effectiveness of specific intervention strategies?

Existing knowledge indicates that interventions intended to promote health and prevent illness should be based on the assumption that individual health behaviors are strongly influenced by those around us, and that family general well-being can promote the physical health of its members. For example, strategies to enhance the ability and effectiveness of families to promote the health of individual members include family-oriented health education programs and family counseling to reduce family stress and enhance family stress management.

The literature on family response to illness supports two general admonitions to practitioners. First, few families require either extensive psychiatric treatment or long-term family therapy. This conclusion can be drawn in light of clinical and empirical evidence of the courage, strength, and humor displayed by the majority of families as they cope with even the most adverse events. All families will be well-served if they are routinely provided with adequate expert information, with opportunities for safe expression of feelings, fears, and perceptions, with aids in easing immediate stressors, and with support for effective coping responses. A substantial number of families will need additional help in resolving crises, improving communication, changing dysfunctional aspects of family role allocation and functioning, and resolving psychosocial problems precipitated or exacerbated by the illness or disability.

Second, practitioners are advised to routinely incorporate family-oriented psychosocial care into the overall medical management of patients. Developing strategies and designing programs to ensure the *routine* provision of care to families is emphasized because, as already noted, evidence indicates that this aspect of care may be most frequently neglected (Kupst, 1980; Sikes & Rodenhauser, 1987), because family-directed care is assumed to result in direct benefits to patients, and because such care will reduce the negative impact of illness on family relationships and family functioning. At the same time social workers are advised to tailor and target their interventions to family need. This conclusion is based on the evidence that, just as there is great variation in patients' response to illness, so families vary in their responses. The recommendation to match intervention with family coping styles (Jaffe & Jordan-Marsh, 1983) underscores the necessity for skilled family assessment, a subject that will be discussed in detail in subsequent chapters. We now turn to the question: To what extent can the clinician be guided by reported evaluations of health-related interventions with families?

Characteristics of Research on Family Interventions

The literature consists of frequent calls for family-oriented intervention and numerous descriptions of model programs and approaches (Appolone, 1978; Boll, Duvall, & Mercuri, 1983; Bromberg & Donnerstag, 1977; Caroff & Mailick, 1985; Cohen & Wellisch, 1978; Copeland, 1988; Davidson, 1979; Farkas, 1980; Giaquinta, 1977; Leahey & Wright, 1985; Mailick, 1979; Parsonnet & Weinstein, 1987; Piening, 1984; Power & Orto, 1980; Ross, 1979; Shellhase & Shellhase, 1972), to cite only a few examples. These reports usually describe beneficial outcomes for both patients and families. Of clinical interest, studies have been conducted on a rich array of family interventions, thereby highlighting numerous opportunities and avenues to assist families in their health-related activities.

To date, rigorous and systematic evaluation of family interventions is rare. Sample sizes frequently are small, and the intervention is often neither clearly specified nor standardized. The majority of studies are case reports that rely on clinical observation to evaluate the results of the intervention. Although the literature on family practice in health care is relatively small as compared to more general family literature and very small when compared to patient-focused practice, the case study is well-represented. Much of this literature is referred to in later discussions of specific practice approaches.

The case study is well-known to practitioners as an invaluable method to develop and refine practice theory and to initially evaluate the practicality or feasibility of a family intervention. Methodological weaknesses in this design, however, preclude attributing the observed results to the intervention. Recently, more rigorous evaluation designs are being applied to family intervention, in general, and to health-related interventions, specifically. These include case control designs, natural comparison group designs, and controlled designs.

Family interventions vary in the method employed, the outcome that is sought, and the target of the intervention. Family counseling, traditional family therapy, family systems therapy, family groups and groups for individual family members, crisis intervention, educational approaches, and supportive community services, such as early childhood support programs, home care programs, respite and hospice care, rehabilitation programs, and case management services, have all been the subject of evaluation.

Based on a family systems perspective, we assume that the most effective interventions with families will involve at least two family members and include the patient whenever possible. Unfortunately, but consistent with the emphasis on the health-related family literature in general, the family evaluation literature frequently fails to include more than one family member in the intervention. We recognize that, under some circumstances, this emphasis is appropriate or necessary (such as when the patient is unable to participate in the intervention due to the nature of the illness or to its severity). In general, however, we contend that the likelihood of benefiting the patient as well as the family system as a whole will increase when more than one family member participates in the intervention. It is noteworthy, in this regard, that health promotion and prevention interventions are more likely to be focused on whole families or at least on more than one family member. Unfortunately, a family systems focus is far less evident among reported interventions aimed at helping patients and families manage illness and disability.

The studies reviewed here reflect the fact that evaluation of family interventions in health care is in an early stage of development. Few studies have been guided by a theoretical framework. Studies have been conducted on a broad range of interventions, wherein some aspect of family life is addressed. It is premature to compare approaches and conclude that, even under similar conditions, one approach is more effective than another. Despite our firm belief that family interventions should address the family system, we include selected interventions that fail to meet this criteria because we recognize the fact that family-intervention research in health care is still in its infancy, because under some circumstances work with individual family members is appropriate (such as with a single parent or an elderly spouse who is caring for the disabled patient), and because the promising results of even limited family intervention provide confirmation of the potential merits of more extensive family participation.

Combined, the results of evaluations of family interventions in health care provide convincing evidence of its potential benefits. Of greatest import to practitioners, the research to date identifies promising areas for further development and evaluation of family-related practice. Moreover, knowledge already gained in designing measures to assess intervention outcomes and from testing ways to overcome methodological pitfalls common to evaluation research provides a practical base for future clinical demonstration and evaluation.

Family Interventions to Promote Health and Prevent Illness

In this section, we selectively review case studies and more rigorously designed evaluation studies wherein the goal of the intervention is to promote the health maintenance activities of the family. The argument might be made that all psychosocial services for families promote this aspect of family roles, in that if they enhance overall family well-being, they will also promote the physical health of its members. In the interest of parsimony and keeping in mind our specific focus, we review those studies that purport to be specifically health-focused.

Exploratory Studies

Numerous interventions have been developed for parents of newborns (Dooley, Prochaska, & Klibanoff, 1983; Macnab, Sheckter, Hendry et al., 1985) and for high-risk pregnant women. For example, targeting a prenatal information series for women at risk for poor outcomes of pregnancy was designed to reduce social isolation and increase knowledge and use of community resources (Gallivan & Saunders, 1982). Several interventions have been specifically designed to enhance the family's perception and use of its informal social support network (Filinson, 1988). The Family Intervention Project is noteworthy insofar as it was designed as an early intervention aimed at the entire family system (rather than at individual members) of a handicapped child from birth to age 4 (Berger & Fowlkes, 1980). The intervention is based on an ecological framework and uses a case management approach to assist families. Ongoing longitudinal evaluation of the children and their families is in progress.

In a similar model, the Extending Family Resources project was a service model designed to reduce barriers to raising a handicapped child by extending and activating the family's natural support network. Extended social network members and volunteers were provided knowledge and skills related to the handicapped child. The shared background of competence and task orientation was then used to facilitate positive and reciprocal social interactions between the nuclear family and these "extended families" (Moore,

Hamerlynck, Barsh et al., 1982). Evaluations suggested that it is possible to influence primary social network interactions and that this form of intervention is helpful to families with a handicapped child by extending its access to needed social supports.

Controlled Studies

Integrating medical and psychosocial support programs have been shown to be beneficial to families. For example, one study documented the efficacy of comprehensive psychosocial intervention for families of newborns hospitalized in a neonatal intensive care unit (Perrault, Coates, Collinge et al., 1986). The program included: implementing routine care policies that actively encourage and facilitated parental involvement in the infant's care; use of high-risk screening guidelines for referral to the social worker; and providing continuity of medical and psychosocial care through infancy. The effectiveness of the program was evaluated by comparing emergency room and impatient hospital service utilization in 80 patients born before, and 90 patients born after, the institution of the program. The groups had similar medical and social characteristics. During the second year of follow-up, the control group had used the emergency room twice as often as the study group. During the first 2 years, less than one-third of the study group was hospitalized, whereas, one-half of the control group was readmitted. Medical care utilization was presumed to reflect overall psychosocial adjustment of the families; however, psychosocial adjustment was not directly assessed. The results of these data underscore the potential value of comprehensive programs during diagnostic phases.

The Prenatal/Early Infancy Project directs its services toward families in which mothers bearing first children are teen-agers, single, or poor (Olds, Henderson, Tatelbaum, & Chamberlin, 1988). Participating families are randomly assigned into one of four service groups. Group 1 receives the total intervention: (1) a nurse who visits them during the pregnancy and again during the first 2 years of the baby's life, providing educational and general counseling on health and developmental issues; (2) transportation for prenatal and well-child care; and (3) health and developmental screening for the infant at 12 and 24 months of age. The other groups receive progressively fewer combinations of service. Evaluation of the first 4 years of this prevention project indicates substantial benefits during the first 4 years after the birth of a first child, including improved pregnancy outcomes, reduced incidence of child abuse and neglect, and increased likelihood of the mother returning to high school (Olds et al., 1988).

Spurred by evidence of the family's role in maintaining and promoting the health of individual members, investigators have begun to examine the efficacy of family-oriented interventions with the goal of influencing health-related behaviors (see Baranowski & Nader, 1985, for a review). Controlled studies have examined the impact of spouse, partner, or parental involvement in weight reduction programs, in smoking cessation programs, and in school-based programs to change cardiovascular risk behaviors. Unfortunately, study results have been conflicting, in part, due to methodological flaws in design (Baranowski & Nader, 1985). In view of the fact that the behaviors under scrutiny require long-term lifestyle commitments, the greatest weakness in the research to date has been lack of attention to process measures. As a result, the precise mechanisms by which families influence health-related behaviors remain unclear (Baranowski & Nader, 1985). However, educational, behavioral, and supportive intervention strategies directed to families have been demonstrated to merit further study.

One recent controlled study found that parental problem-solving training was associated with child weight loss above that of children whose parents participated in a behavioral or instruction-only weight-loss group (Graves, Meyers, & Clark, 1988). Moreover, differences in weight loss were maintained at 3- and 6-month follow-ups. The potential long-term benefits among children and their natural dependence on family health practices emphasize the need for ongoing evaluation of interventions aimed at parental skill training (Epstein, Wing, Koeske, & Valoski, 1987).

A pretest–posttest factorial design was used to determine whether parental involvement in a school-based health promotion program enhanced its effectiveness (Perry, Luepker, Murray, et al., 1988). Thirty-one schools in four urban school districts in Minnesota and North Dakota were blocked by state and randomly assigned to one of four conditions: the school-based Hearty Heart program, the home-based Home Team program, both programs in sequence, or a no-treatment control group. The Hearty Heart program is a 5-week, 15-session school curriculum taught by third grade classroom teachers. The goal of the program is change in environmental, personal, and behavioral factors. The Home Team program is a 5-week correspondence course involving third graders and their parents. Results indicated that students in the school-based program had gained more knowledge at posttest than students in the other groups, however, students in the home-based program reported more behavior change. These findings lend support to develop family approaches to health promotion among children.

The Family Heart Study is a controlled family-focused study to determine whether an educational and group intervention for families will produce nutritional behavior changes that, over time, will affect physical cardiovascular risk factors (Matararazzo, Connor, Fey et al., 1982). This rigorously designed study is in progress, and the results will extend knowledge about community-based family health promotion.

These studies suggest that social workers are likely to participate in comprehensive family health promotion programs with young families. Social work participation in school-based and workplace programs are less well-represented in the literature. These arenas provide future opportunities for family-focused interventions.

Family Interventions in the Face of Illness or Disability

Exploratory Studies

Several reports are of interest in light of data that family members often experience severe distress during patients' acute hospitalization, especially while patients are in intensive care. For example, family group conferences conducted one evening a week by nursing staff and a psychiatric clinical specialist are reported to be helpful in reducing family members anxiety when the patient is acutely ill (Holub, Ecklund, & Keenan, 1975), and a drop-in-weekly support group for wives of MI patients is reported to be helpful to participants and to provide valuable assessment information to staff (Harding & Morefield, 1976). In a very interesting recent study, a social work department used volunteers in a critical care unit to facilitate communication between family members and staff, lessen the family's sense of isolation during this particularly stressful period, and provide responsive services in a crisis-oriented setting (Parsonnet & Weinstein, 1987). Again, clinical observation was the basis on which program benefits were identified.

In light of evidence that parents frequently seek support from other parents during their child's hospitalization, there is a need to develop and evaluate strategies to maximize this source of support (Lynam, 1987). Groups for patients and families are also reported to enhance adaptation to serious illness and to reduce the isolation accompanying illness (Berger, 1984; Johnson & Stark, 1980) and AIDS (Sheahen, 1984). Case reports suggest that these are indeed beneficial and describe in detail the group format (Gaudet, & Powers, 1989; Gonzales, Steinglass & Reiss, 1989; Mack & Berman, 1988; Ross, 1979; Vandik & Storhaug, 1985). The majority of these groups involve only one family member, although, increasingly, patients and family members are invited to participate, and family groups are conducted. For example, family group therapy conducted by a psychologist–nurse team in a private oncology practice is reported to be helpful to cancer patients and their families (Wellisch, Mosher, & Van Scoy, 1978). Similar reports will be discussed in greater detail in Chapter 10. One group program for siblings of children with cancer is noteworthy because the evaluation component included obtaining feedback through questionnaires completed by both the participants and their parents (Adams-Greenly, Shiminski-Maher,

McGowan, & Meyers, 1986). Of the 124 children who attended day-long educational and support workshops, 88 percent completed the questionnaire, and, of these, the majority reported specific benefits from the program. Parental response was also favorable.

Crisis intervention with families and psychotherapy with spouses is also reported to be helpful to patients. For example, in 7 of 9 cases in which wives of cardiac patients who continued their high-risk behaviors were seen by a family therapist for 3–5 sessions, there was significant improvement in patient's subsequent behaviors (Hoebel, 1976). Nine survivors of myocardial infarction participated in a pilot study using a pretest–posttest design (Brown & Munford, 1983–1984). Patients were having long-term adjustment difficulties, such as dysphoria and work or social dysfunction. The treatment approach consisted of a combination of deep muscle relaxation. imagery-based desensitization, stress and anger management, activity scheduling, and cognitive restructuring. Of special interest, each patient's spouse was trained as a facilitator/co-therapist. Spouses were instructed to ignore depressive behaviors and to positively reinforce desired behavior changes. Social aspects of patient's adjustment improved, although depression as measured by the Zung Depression Scale did not change for most patients. Results underscore the important role of spouses in patient's long-term adaptation to a life-threatening coronary event. Finally, a cognitive therapy approach with psychosomatic children and their parents has been shown to be effective in alleviating the child's symptoms and reducing the use of medical services (Fundingsrud, 1988).

Comprehensive psychosocial intervention programs for cancer are increasingly common and presumably include services to families; however, evidence of the effectiveness of these programs is sparse (Freidenbergs, Hibbard et al., 1981–1982). Two case reports describe such programs and specifically detail their family orientation (Sheldon, Chir, Ryser, & Krant, 1970). In the first study, the beneficial effects of a comprehensive home care program are reported. Special efforts were made by the social workers and medical team members to educate family members and to encourage and support family caregiving roles. Clinical assessment judged the program to be effective. In the second study, the program team included hospital-based social workers, nurses, physicians, including a psychiatrist, and a public health nurse in a case management role (Sheldon et al., 1970). Benefits for both patients and their families were documented by clinical observation; however, it is not clear whether family members were seen individually or together.

A similar comprehensive program was recently designed to prevent recurrent diabetic ketoscidoses among children and adolescent patients in a tertiary diabetes center (Golden, Herrold, & Orr, 1985). Medical, educational, and psychosocial interventions were provided to families based on team members clinical judgment. The rate of recurrence was lower after initiation of the program, even though patients seen during that period were of greater risk because they came from lower socioeconomic and more single-parent families than patients seen prior to the intervention. Again, specific details regarding the intervention with families are lacking. A comprehensive pain treatment program including counseling to improve family relationships was found to be effective in improving patients' psychological status as well as the functioning of the family (Hudgen, 1979).

Controlled Studies

Controlled studies of family interventions to aid patients and families in responding to illness are relatively rare. In general, the existing intervention research should be regarded as heuristic in setting forth a future research agenda. Favorable outcomes have been demonstrated to result from relatively simple educational interventions, counseling, and therapeutic approaches, as well as from comprehensive psychosocial programs. Patients, as well as family members, have been shown to benefit from these family interventions.

Controlled studies of family intervention during acute hospitalization are notably sparse. In a preliminary study, 12 patients hospitalized in a coronary care unit (CCU) were randomly assigned to an experimental or control group (Doerr & Jones, 1979). Family members of patients in the treatment group were given an informational manual concerning the CCU and an opportunity to ask the nurse questions. Control families were given no preparation. Pre- and post- family visitation patient assessments using the State Anxiety Scale found family-prepared patients' anxiety declined, whereas patients exposed to nonprepared families experienced an increase in state anxiety.

In another study, 20 male patients undergoing coronary artery bypass surgery were examined for postcardiotomy psychosis (Chatham, 1978). All patients received preoperative teaching, and all subjects were maintained on cardiopulmonary bypass for at least 60 minutes. The significant other of 10 patients in the experimental group received systematic instruction concerning the functions of the equipment used in the intensive care unit, the postoperative care routine of the patient, and the patients' need for eye contact, frequent touch, and verbal orientation to time, person, and place. Clinical observation by the nursing staff judged the experimental group to be more oriented to time, person, and place, to be more appropriate and less confused, to have fewer delusions and longer sleep periods when compared to controls. Patient alertness, agitation, complaints, depression, activity, and anxiety did not vary between groups.

The use of groups for patients with cancer and for family members is widespread; however, as already noted, the effectiveness of this intervention is rarely evaluated scientifically. Recently two studies have conducted such an examination. In the first, the Exceptional Cancer Patient program in New Haven, Connecticut, was retrospectively studied to assess the impact of a psychosocial support program on survival with breast cancer (Morgenstern, Gellert, Walter et al., 1984). Groups composed of about 8–12 patients plus invited relatives and friends meet weekly for about 90 minutes. The sessions are fairly unstructured and include discussions of patients' problems, meditation, and mental imagery using drawings. Thirty-four white women with breast cancer who participated in the program were compared to a comparable group of women who never participated in the program. Initial analyses indicated a strong beneficial effect of the program on survival. This positive effect remained, although it became statistically nonsignificant when a selection bias in the control group caused by the failure to match on the duration of the lag period between cancer diagnosis and program entry was corrected. Unfortunately, quality of life was not assessed, although the investigators speculate that this type of intervention is most likely to have beneficial effects on social and psychological functioning. Potential direct benefits to family members were also not evaluated.

In the second study, 51 ambulatory patients with commonly occurring cancers and 25 of their spouses participated in a study to evaluate a stress and activity management treatment program in a group (Heinrich & Schag, 1985). Patients had been living with cancer for approximately 2 years before entering the program. Control patients and spouses received current available care from a veterans hospital and a private community hospital. This care included access to psychosocial services and to support groups such as Make Today Count. The treatment intervention was a 6-week, structured, small group program co-led by two psychologists. Components of the treatment included education and information (concerning cancer, cancer therapies, the psychosocial impact of cancer, stress, and adaptive coping), relaxation exercises, cognitive and problem-solving therapy, and activity management (walking and contracting to increase positively valued individual and couple activities). Patients and spouses were evaluated at 4 points in time: pretreatment, posttreatment, 2-month follow-up, and 4-month follow-up.

The treatment group exhibited improvement in knowledge about cancer (noteworthy insofar as patients were not newly diagnosed but had been living with the disease for almost 2 years), in attitudes toward the health care team, and in perceived ability to handle stressful situations. In contrast to these improvements, there were no significant differences between treatment and control subjects on psychosocial adjustment to illness, with both groups improving with the passage of time. The investigators suggested that this lack of difference may be due in part to a placebo effect because the control subjects had numerous contacts with the research team for the extensive data collection. They also raised the question as to whether stress management and problem-solving approaches were the most effective coping techniques for adjusting to certain aspects of living with cancer. We raise a further question as to whether the specific group treatment added a substantial component to the current available psychosocial care received by the control group. It would have been interesting to learn whether benefits differed between spouses and patients, in view of data indicating that husbands of patients with breast cancer may receive fewer psychosocial services than patients.

Several studies have examined components of family intervention in psychosocial programs to enhance the rehabilitation of patients with cardiac illness. Fifty patients with acute myocardial infarction received a planned rehabilitation program from a social worker and occupational therapist team (Thockloth, Ho, Wright, & Seldon, 1973). Adjustment and return to work of treated patients were compared with 50 control patients who received usual care. The patient and family member were seen periodically by the social worker up to 3 months after the patient's return to work. Equal numbers of both groups returned to work, but the time of return to work and well-being varied between groups in the desired direction.

In another study, 258 patients with a documented myocardial infarction were randomly assigned to a control group, an exercise only group, or to a program of exercise plus teaching and counseling (Sivarajan, et al., 1983). Spouses and significant others were invited to attend the classes in the third group, and both patients and family were offered individual counseling as the need arose. Classes covered education and information about coronary artery disease and risk factors, nutrition and diet, exercise and activity, stress and relaxation, work and sexual activity, and emotional reactions to a heart attack. No differences in cigarette smoking or weight loss were found between the three groups. This study raises more questions than it answers, including whether psychological adjustment was affected by the intervention or may have been a factor in the limited effects of the intervention, and to what extent family members were asked to participate in assisting the patient to make behavioral changes.

In a third study, 143 men were randomly assigned to an intensive rehabilitation or a control group (Naismeth, Robinson, Shaw, & MacIntyre, 1979). Treatment patients were seen periodically in the hospital and at home for a period of 6 months. Patients wives were seen on several occasions, sometimes alone and sometimes with the patient. Psychological counseling was conducted by a nurse counselor. Treated patients scored higher on social independence, but no differences were found for return to work, physical functioning, or emotional stability. Especially noteworthy, in that study, patients were classified using the Eysenck Personality Inventory as neurotic introverts and stable extroverts, with neurotic introverts achieving a much better outcome on all three rehabilitation measures than their counterparts in the control group. Although, no evidence was found that rehabilitation exacerbated neurosis, the investigators gained the impression that for the stable extroverts, the program could have negative effects on established coping strategies.

A fourth study of cardiac rehabilitation is of interest because it specifically addressed the potential negative effects of well-intentioned but misguided family support. Eighty-nine postmyocardial infarction patients were assigned randomly to participate in an experimental cardiac rehabilitation program, and 91 patients were controls who received conventional hospital rehabilitation (Burgess, Lerner, Agostino et al., 1987). The intervention was carried out by nurses with masters degrees and was based on a cognitive–behavioral model to alter assumptions and beliefs about heart attack and recovery. Patients, family members, and key people at the patient's workplace were seen. The majority of nurse visits were conducted in patients' homes. The average number of contacts was just over six. Rehabilitation care patients experienced significantly less distress and a more moderate reliance on family support than usual care patients. Moreover, sustaining the patient's independence within the family (a primary goal of the intervention) was reported to be a contributing factor in patients' work resumption.

In a recent pilot study, a cognitive–educational (a combination of health education and rational emotive behavior modification) intervention program aimed at altering coping behavior in asthmatic patients was assessed using a pretest, posttest design (Maes & Schlosser, 1988). Patients and their partners (presumably family members) attended 8 weekly 2–3 hour group sessions. Treated patients reported less emotional distress and used less maintenance medication following the intervention.

Family Therapy Interventions

Controlled studies of family intervention in the treatment of severe childhood asthma attest to the efficacy of this approach. In one study, poor families with an asthmatic child were given a series of educational programs on preventing and managing asthma attacks and on communicating with physicians (Clark, Feldman, Evans et al., 1981). Families receiving the intervention reported being less fearful during an acute attack and more likely to engage in self-care activities following the intervention, although reduction in emergency room visits did not differ significantly.

In a controlled study of family psychotherapy, 33 families with 37 asthmatic children were randomly assigned to experimental or control groups

(Lask & Matthew, 1979). Family therapy consisted of 6, 1-hour sessions focused on improving coping skills in the face of an acute attack. One-year follow-up demonstrated some improvement in asthma control among the children in the experimental group.

In a more recent study, 18 children with severe, chronic, bronchial asthma were randomly divided into two groups, one receiving the family therapy, the other serving as a control group (Gustafsson, Kellman, & Cederblad, 1986). The control families were subsequently offered therapy in a before–after design. The children were followed for 3.5 years. Family therapy was defined as treatment of the entire family, or parts of it, with the aim of changing interpersonal relations as set forth by Minuchin and colleagues (1978). The number of sessions ranged between 2 and 21, with an average of almost 9 sessions. The therapy focused on dysfunctional family interaction, the role of the asthma symptoms in the family system, hidden conflicts, strengthening boundaries between individuals and between parents and children, and enhancing communication about the emotional impact of the disease on the family members. Children of treated families showed significantly greater improvement in clinical symptoms and drug use over controls. The study design precluded distinguishing specific effects of the therapy from possible placebo effects. In another controlled retrospective study using structural family therapy in a pediatric setting, comparisons indicated that treated children had a reduced number of hospitalization days (Gustafsson & Svedin, 1988).

A very interesting study of family therapy in a general medical practice was recently conducted in The Netherlands (Huygen & Smits, 1983). The study was possible because, in recent years, general practitioners are paired with behavioral scientists to provide care to the same population. The practice evaluated in the study consists of 11,000 persons. Patients are referred for family therapy by the general practitioner. The practice defines family therapy broadly as a psychotherapeutic approach that is focused on the immediate social network in which the patient lives. Therefore, the entire family may be seen, part of the family may be seen, or the patient may be seen individually, but with a view to family relationships. Over the past 10 years, referrals to the treating psychologist average about 7 percent of the practice population. Data is reported on the therapy of 138 patients from the same number of families. Nine months after referral, 84 percent of the patients reported that the conditions that had brought about the referral had improved or that they had learned to cope with them. In the opinion of the general practitioners, improvement was seen in almost one-half of the patients, and a decrease in the number of medicines prescribed was established in one-quarter of the cases. Because extensive records are kept on medical care utilization for all patients, including use of care by family members, several interesting observations could be made. First, the data indicated a definite rise in the medical care use by the patient in the 6 months preceding the date of referral to the family therapist and a decline in use shortly after the referral. Some similarity in medical care use among family members was also documented; in general the referred families were high utilizers as compared to the general population. Several other studies also demonstrate that family therapy applied in a family practice setting can lower the frequency of office visits and the use of psychotropic drugs (Candib & Glen, 1983). Social workers in family practice also have found that high users of medical services benefit from family-focused interventions (Roberts & Strange, 1986).

A study of crisis intervention for patients hospitalized following auto accidents is included in this discussion because the design was controlled and because it is an exemplar of an intervention that influences social support provision within families. In the study, patients were randomly assigned to receive intensive psychologically focused crisis intervention while in the hospital, whereas control patients received only a single assessment visit while in the hospital (Porritt, 1979). The treatment was conducted by graduate hospital-based social workers. Treatment patients had significantly better outcomes on a broad range of social and psychological rehabilitation outcomes. Of special interest, patient's receiving the crisis intervention reported higher perceived quality of the social support they received from family and primary network members. The results underscore the importance of family relationships in coping with sudden trauma, but more importantly, they suggest that patient's social support experience is amenable to professional intervention.

Interventions to Enhance Patient Adherence to Treatment Regimens

Adherence to medical treatment regimens frequently requires willingness to give up old lifestyles and/or engage in new behaviors, both of which may be inherently stressful (Leventhal, Zimmerman, & Gutman, 1984). Very often, these behavioral changes should be maintained over long periods of time, even indefinitely, such as in the case of hypertension management. It is not surprising, therefore, that reliable estimates of compliance behavior indicate that lack of adherence is a serious medical problem (DiMatteo & DiNicola, 1982) Recognizing the family's role in many treatment regimens, investigators have begun to examine ways in which family interventions may enhance patient's compliance behavior.

A rural community hypertension control project included an experiment to promote hypertension care utilization and regimen compliance with family involvement as one factor in a factorial design (Baranowski & Nader, 1985). Patients were randomly assigned to one of five groups. The family involvement conditions included spouses or significant others accompanying the patient for hypertension-related clinic visits and being trained in all aspects of the compliance regimen with patients. Modest evidence was found for a positive effect of the family involvement. Further study indicated that there was little family support for compliance behavior, but other data suggested that family involvement may have resulted in a family choice of the particular component of the regimen that was most comfortable to support (Baranowski & Nader, 1985).

A second randomly assigned patients with a diagnosis of essential hypertension to one of three conditions: (1) a routine medical care group; (2) standard medical care plus home visits over a period of 18 months from either public health nurses or specially trained pharmacists; and (3) a group that received the standard medical care and the home visits, but with the additional requirement that a family member or significant other actively participate in the home visits and in the blood pressure monitoring process (Earp, Ory, & Strogatz, 1982). All groups were predominantly black. At the end of 1 year, no group showed a statistically significant advantage. However, during the last 6 months of the second year (after visiting had ended), both intervention groups had better diastolic blood pressure control than the control group. There was no difference between the group involving family and the home visit only group.

A third major intervention study produced the most convincing evidence of a salutary effect of family involvement in hypertension compliance (Morisky, Demuth, Field-Fass et al., 1985). Three different educational interventions, brief individual counseling, instructing the spouse or significant other during a home visit, and patient group sessions were compared. While all groups showed significant improvement in compliance and blood pressure control, the groups with family involvement did best, including having lower overall mortality. All interventions were behaviorally oriented. Long-term effects at 2- and 5-year follow-up periods demonstrated that blood pressure control, appointment keeping, and weight were significantly improved or maintained for only the family support intervention patients (Morisky et al., 1985).

Adherence to medical regimens or lifestyle changes to promote health and reduce one's risk of illness underscores the complexities of human behavior. For example, lack of patient cooperation with doctor's orders may reflect a conscious and knowing choice and may be one way of assuming control in the face of health problems (Doherty & Campbell, 1988). Patients may engage in noncompliance that is perceived to be "logical" from the patient's viewpoint (Trostle, Hauser, & Susser, 1983), or such behavior may be associated with the patient's developmental stage such as in the case of adolescence (Dolgin, Katz, Doctors, & Siegel, 1986; Jamison, Lewis, & Burich, 1986). Problems in practitioner–patient communication and the stress inherent in the medical regimen itself may also deter compliance (Sulway, Tupling, Webb, & Harris, 1980). Further development of family interventions is warranted, however, because a family role in this area is so strikingly and intuitively logical and because even very limited family involvement shows promising results. Furthermore, the value of assessing not only the family context of compliance behavior, but also the broader institutional, community, and cultural context of health-related behavior is dramatically illustrated by ethnographic case studies (Stein & Pontious, 1985).

Interventions for Caregivers

Case studies of interventions for caregivers are numerous, commonly targeted to the caregiver and less frequently include the patient, and include support and educational groups, respite care, adult day care, hospice care, and case management services (Aronson, Levin, & Lipkowitz, 1984; Crossman, London, & Barry, 1981; Glosser & Wexler, 1985; Godkin, Krant, & Dostere, 1983–1984; Gross-Andrew & Zimmer, 1979; Miller, Gulle, & McCue, 1986; Pinkston & Linsk, 1984; Roy, Flynn, & Atcherson, 1982; Schmidt & Keyes, 1985; Selan & Schuenke, 1982; Siegel, 1982; Winogrond, Fisk, Kirsling, & Keyes, 1987).

Two studies are of interest because they examine the benefits of specific family caregiving activities. Spurred by data that the most likely witness of a patient's cardiac arrest will be someone who lives in the home, family members of patients who were at increased risk for sudden death by virtue of their medical diagnosis were trained in cardiopulmonary resuscitation (CPR) techniques (Dracup, Guzy, Taylor, & Barry, 1986). The study design included three groups: a control group in which patients and their families received no intervention, a CPR group, and an education group (patterned after the American Heart Association's Heartsaver Course). Patients did not attend either group. No adverse psychological effects for family members were found, however, neither did family members benefit psychologically from their participation in the intervention as had been hypothesized. Furthermore, patients in the CPR group were more anxious at 3 months' follow-up than patients in the other two groups. Moreover, patients in both CPR and risk factor education groups experienced poorer adjustment to illness at 6 months' follow-up than did control patients. The investigators suggested that the intervention may have weakened the coping strategy of denial and may have exacerbated patients' perceptions of dependency. They underscore that the need for family members to be trained in CPR remains unquestioned, but that future interventions that incorporate methods to moderate the potential negative effects on patients merit exploration. Undoubtedly, a family systems perspective in designing such an intervention would be useful.

The second study examined the effects of a program in which family members of patients with cancer were offered the opportunity to take an active part in the care of the patient (Haggmark, Theorell, & Ek, 1987). Fifty relatives participated in the practical care of the patient in the hospital or at home with close contact with hospital personnel. Forty-five nonparticipating family members formed a comparison group. Twenty-two in the intervention group and 19 in the comparison group were followed 1 and 2 months after the patient's death. Active caregiving family members reported greater social activity at follow-up, while nonparticipants reported greater preoccupation with personal feelings. The study has serious methodological weaknesses including whether the family members' decision to participate in the active care reflected specific coping predispositions. On the other hand, the study highlights an important area for study, in view of the increasing caregiving roles family members are expected to assume.

Other controlled studies suggest that psychosocial interventions that include supportive, educational, and behavioral components aid caregivers and reduce the likelihood that care recipients will be institutionalized. In the first study, 208 individual caregivers, about one-half of whom were giving care to a spouse, enrolled in a support program conducted by a social worker and a community health nurse (Greene & McNahan, 1987). The program consisted of 8 weekly 2-hour group sessions that included emotional support, education, and relaxation training. Participants were compared to 81 individuals who had enrolled but were unable to attend. At the end of the project, significantly fewer care recipients of the participant caregivers had been institutionalized. The investigators noted that, while this was a promising result, the potential costs of caregiving among caregivers was not assessed.

In the second study, 157 family members of elderly persons referred to a Jewish Family and Children's Service were randomly assigned to experimental and control groups (Selzer, Ivry, & Litchfield, 1987). Group member characteristics were remarkably similar on baseline measures. All clients and families received the usual agency services provided by master's level social workers. In addition, the experimental subjects received family-centered training delivered individually by social workers. Results indicated that those receiving the training were more likely to perform case management tasks and to complete more tasks than those in the control group.

Finally, the utility of home care delivered by interdisciplinary teams has been documented. In a methodologically rigorous study, pediatric home care that included a broad range of educational and supportive services was found to reduce psychiatric symptoms of the child's mother, improve the child's psychological adjustment, and improve the satisfaction of the family with the care received (Stein & Jessop, 1984). In a randomized study of a home health care team approach (involving physicians, nurse practitioners, and social workers) for homebound chronically or terminally ill elderly, caretakers expressed significantly higher satisfaction with the care received (Zimmer, Groth-Juncker, & McCusker, 1985).

Bereavement

Little controlled research has been conducted on intervention for bereaved family members (Osterweis, Soloman, & Green, 1984). Several investigators have examined the effects of mutual support groups. One study is of interest insofar as a widow-to-widow program was evaluated. Widows were randomly assigned to either the intervention group (N = 68) or the control group (N = 94) (Vachon, Lyall, Rogers et al., 1980). Widows in the intervention group were paired with a widow contact who provided emotional support and practical assistance. All widows were assessed using a well-validated psychiatric screening instrument at 6, 12 and 24 months after bereavement. Those receiving the intervention followed the same general course of adaptation, but their rate of achieving landmark stages was accelerated in comparison with controls. In another study of widows' groups, a self-help group, a "confidant" group, a consciousness-raising group, and a control group were compared (Barrett, 1978). All treatments demonstrated benefits when participants were compared to controls on various outcome measures.

Anticipatory grief work with families of children with leukemia was evaluated in another study. Sixty-four families were randomly assigned to intensive, moderate, or no support groups (Kupst et al., 1982). The intervention was conducted by social workers and other counselors and focused on anticipatory grief work. Only the intensity of service varied among participants. Ratings by medical, nursing, and psychosocial staff and self-reports indicated that they were no major differences between the intervention and nonintervention groups. In one large-scale survey, level of involvement of bereaved parents in the mutual support group, Compassionate Friends, was not associated with significant differences in depression scores among parents (Videka-Sherman, 1982).

An Agenda for Future Evaluation Research

In general, the studies reviewed reveal several important weaknesses in the family-focused intervention to date. The most obvious weakness is the relative lack of research in the area (Fife, 1980). At the same time, the recent growth of work suggests that this gap will increasingly narrow. Second, in large part, evaluation studies have been atheoretical. Future contributions to our knowledge-base will be enhanced insofar as the intervention is grounded in family theory. Third, studies reviewed vary as to whether the primary target of intervention is the family system or individual family members. Fourth, the interventions are infrequently tailored or targeted on the basis of an a priori assessment of family characteristics and needs. Finally, greater attention to methodological issues in evaluating family interventions is needed.

Need for Conceptual Frameworks

A serious limitation of much of the intervention research, to date, has been its atheoretical nature. This is not surprising given the reality that family work is relatively new in the field of health care. Future clinical research will benefit to the extent that interventions are guided by conceptual frameworks of family functioning and coping. In this way the necessary dialogue between practitioners and theorists will be fostered so as to advance and refine family theory as it pertains to health and illness and, ultimately, to enhance services to families. Historically, social workers have assumed primary responsibility for providing services to families in the community and in health care agencies. The profession is, therefore, strategically and theoretically poised to make significant contributions to the further development and evaluation of family-focused interventions in the health care field, and in so doing, to contribute to the ongoing refinement of family theory. Fortunately, several of the theoretical models pertaining to families are at a stage in their development in which their clinical operationalization is feasible for future intervention research. We will return to this issue in the following chapter.

Targeting Interventions

Assessing family need prior to initiating a planned intervention is a practice axiom. In the following chapters, we will discuss assessment tools and instruments that are available to assist practitioners in this process, as well as methods of family assessment in discharge planning, family therapy, crisis intervention, and family groups. Designing and targeting family interventions for specific populations will go a long way toward reducing ineffective outcomes that arise when families with little need for professional assistance are served. More important, careful planning will reduce the likelihood that families with great need will fail to receive needed services. Moreover, the likelihood of a family being the recipient of a mismatched intervention (an approach that is incompatible with a specific family coping style) will also be decreased. Targeting interventions is also most likely to increase the cost-effectiveness of family interventions.

The Family System

We have already observed that health promotion and prevention interventions are focused in the main, on whole families or at least on more than one family member. This approach is consistent with the underlying assumptions of systems models of family functioning. The fact that several of the interventions demonstrate success in maximizing primary network social support on behalf of families is especially noteworthy. An important professional role in the initiation and ongoing participation in these efforts is also highlighted.

At the same time, we observed that a family system focus is less evident among interventions toward helping patients and families manage illness and disability. More often than not, the interventions are targeted to individual family members, and relatively few interventions are designed to include patients *and* family members. For example, patients *or* family members are provided with education, but few interventions are conducted in the presence of both patients and family members. Similarly, groups for individual family members are far more frequently represented in the literature than family groups. Family therapy approaches are most likely to be conducted from a family systems perspective. Positive outcomes of this method of family work underscore the merits of further evaluation of this approach.

Family Need

Again, despite the extensive literature identifying specific factors that place families at higher risk for poor health outcomes, few interventions have been designed with more than very general risk categories in mind. Thus, interventions are offered to families with a child with cancer, without apparent systematic regard for the sociocultural characteristics of the family, its family structure, and its specific coping style. The question of whether to screen families for need and to tailor an intervention to specified family groups becomes important in view of some research indicating that psychosocial interventions have little effect, if service recipients have little or no need for the specific service offered. Furthermore, other data indicate that families feel underserved, most notably reflected in consistent reports of family dissatisfaction with the extent of information they receive from health professionals, as well as with the manner in which the information is conveyed. Careful assessment of family' need and family' preferences prior to providing psychosocial services to families is likely to reduce the negative perceptions of family members.

In addition, there is a striking gap in research on intervention with the poor and minority populations (London & Devore, 1988). The relative lack of research in this area is especially disturbing in view of the persistent evidence of health disadvantages among these groups. Moreover, we have already documented that the poor and minority groups are less likely to use some psychosocial services. For example, in Chapter 3, we noted that voluntary participation by low-income and/or high-risk populations in prevention-oriented human service programs is minimal, and dropout rates are high (Birkel & Reppucci, 1983). Other evidence suggests that low-income and minority patients and families are least likely to participate in cancer support groups (Taylor et al., 1986; Taylor, Falke, Mazela, & Hilsberg, 1988).

In light of these data, the question must be raised as to what features of an intervention encourage or discourage participation among high-risk families. For example, dense social network structure, commonly found among low-income and minority groups, has been shown to deter the use of prenatal care (McKinlay, 1973) as well as participation in a parent education program (Birkel & Reppucci, 1983). In the latter study, low service utilizers reported friends and kin living within walking distance, suggesting that neighborhood-based services might be more compatible with social network helping styles and thus might encourage participation by some high-risk groups.

The positive effects of neighborhood health centers on health service recipients suggests that increased demonstration and evaluation of community-based family programs are merited. Unfortunately, as we observed in Chapter 3, political support for these health centers is declining despite their documented success. Social workers, therefore, are challenged to advocate such programs. Clearly, an important challenge for future evaluation research concerns the need to design and implement programs in socioculturally sensitive ways (Ell, Mantell, & Hamovitch, 1989; Subramanian & Ell, in press). Equally important, practitioners are encouraged to use their agency practice base to continually document the effects of social and health policies on the family's health-related functions and to identify unmet family needs. These data are critical in attempts to influence policy deliberations.

Family Diversity and the Social Environment

Also disturbing is the failure to design and evaluate family-focused strategies that take into account the varied forms of family structures that prevail in society today. Recent demographic trends irrefutably document the pluralistic nature of families in America. For example, only 7 percent of families consist of an employed father, homemaking mother, and two children (Toffler, 1980). Single-parent, step-families, dual career families, and unmarried couple families are common today. Therefore, family interventions in relation to health-related tasks and functions must take into account family variations in structure, lifestyle, and sociocultural practices.

In addition, the research appears to suffer from a gender gap, insofar as little attention is given to potentially different needs of male and female family members. Moreover, few interventions are targeted to the broader environmental systems of families. Reports of incorporating family health education programs in schools and social agency efforts to reach out to high risk families are noteworthy exceptions.

Evaluation Methods

In general, the evaluation methods employed in family intervention research have been weak. As a result, it is not possible to attribute the reported outcome to the intervention. For example, when multiple interventions are used without appropriate control groups, we do not learn whether one aspect of the intervention is more important than the others or whether the combination of approaches is necessary to achieve the intervention goal. In other cases, the outcome measured is far too global. For example, overall family functioning is assessed following a time-limited intervention focused on a specific stressor or circumstance, rather than a specific family behavior or affective response. Finally, the potential iatrogenic or negative effects of the intervention are ignored in the evaluation. For example, the intervention might result in family members assuming greater caregiving responsibilities, but it might also incur personal costs among family members. Future research will benefit from greater methodological rigor.

Conclusion

A promising beginning in family intervention research has been made. Results should encourage practitioners to expand their attempts to serve families, to carry out their interventions based on theoretical foundations, and to develop ways to evaluate their practice. In a social climate characterized by a desire to keep costs down, social workers will find less than enthusiastic support for extending services to families if there is little evidence that these services will not only aid families, but will also be cost-effective in providing patient care. The evidence reviewed in this book hopefully will encourage social workers and other health care practitioners to expand their work with families and systematically document the results of this service.

5
Assessment Frameworks and Assessment Tools

Having reviewed theories about families and the vast array of research identifying multiple factors in family-health relationships, the social worker faces the formidable task of applying existing knowledge in identifying the health-related needs of families and in planning and implementing family-relevant psychosocial interventions. From the vantage point of the practitioner, the first step in applying what has been learned is to assess family need as it is related to health and illness. The practitioners' task is made easier to the extent that they are guided by applicable conceptual frameworks. Derived from extant knowledge, family assessment frameworks are conceptual lenses that organize, in a systematic way, factors presumed to be relevant to the identification of family need. As conceptual frameworks are increasingly refined, they are more apt to be theoretically grounded and, therefore, of even greater utility to practitioners. In this chapter, assessment tools are examined that might be used in population-based needs assessments, for the purposes of high-risk screening in clinical practice, and for practice-based research.

Population-Based Assessment: The Public Health Model

In an era of limited financial resources and in the context of the overall social climate described in Chapter 3, selecting a target population and a family-focused health promotion or health care intervention requires assessment frameworks that help to prioritize alternative strategies. In this way, decisions can be made to use available resources to produce the greatest benefits (Kaplan, 1985). As recognition of the potential utility of family interventions becomes more widespread, social workers in a broad range of health and nonhealth organizations will be called on to participate in decision-making processes about the development and provision of family-focused health and medical services. Voluntary health agencies, health departments, community centers, wellness centers, schools, industry, unions, hospitals, family service agencies, mental health clinics, and private practitioners are among potential service providers.

Community health needs have traditionally been assessed using the public health framework (Mantell, 1984). The public health model combines an ecological, multicausal, and interactive perspective (Runyan, 1985). Thus, it assumes that health-related events occur as a result of reciprocal and dynamic associations among multiple factors (Runyan, 1985).

The public health model organizes assessment in terms of three categories of interactive influence, the host (the individual), agent (the source of illness or disability), and the social and physical environment. The latter includes not only the physical milieu, but the sociocultural as well. In recent years, the model has increasingly emphasized individual lifestyles as important contributors to health status (Runyan, 1985). The public health field relies heavily on four major sources of assessment data: vital statistics, medical records, health surveys, and epidemiological investigations (Runyan, 1985). To the extent that social work practitioners and administrators develop their skills in amassing and interpreting these data, their contribution to social and organizational policymaking will be advanced.

Vital Statistics

Vital statistics include census data, birthrates, and morbidity and mortality rates. Any one or all of these sources of data might be used to identify a family-focused community health service need. In Chapter 2, we referred to the health disadvantages of persons of lower socioeconomic status as documented by higher morbidity and mortality rates. We also observed that family structure (e.g., single-parent families) is also associated with health disadvantages. Thus, a social agency might combine these data sources in order to describe the community it purports to serve and, in so doing, identify a health service need that might be addressed with agency resources (Rudolf et al., 1985). For example, a statistical mapping procedure (combining income, percentage of female-headed households, percentage of married mothers with children under age 18 in the labor force, and percentage of less-than-1-year residents) has been used to identify high-risk neighborhoods for child maltreatment (Garbarino & Sherman, 1981). Such an approach might also be applied to identifying a neighborhood's need for family-focused health services.

Medical Records

A hospital social work department might examine its medical records and social service records to determine whether families of patients are underserved or to evaluate the appropriateness of a proposed family-focused intervention. For example, a recent review of these records in a large public hospital contributed to identifying potential unmet needs of family members of minority patients with AIDS (Ell et al., 1989). In a similar vein, a review of failed appointments by Hispanic children receiving care from a pediatric communicable disease clinic led to a proposal by one of the authors to provide tailored outreach services to the parents of these children. A review of records of a hospital-based cancer screening program might lead to the recognition that specific segments of that hospital's community are not obtaining these services. In turn, this assessment could be used to design a family-focused wellness program targeted to the underserved population.

Epidemiological Data

Health surveys and epidemiological studies provide both descriptive morbidity and mortality data and analytic or explanatory data that attempt to explicate the relationships between health problems and specific population risk factors (Runyan, 1985). Again we refer to Chapter 2 where findings relevant to family health were reviewed. Epidemiological studies identify sociocultural status as a risk factor in genetic illnesses. In this regard, a human service agency might be presented with an opportunity to promote family health because it already serves a substantial number of persons of a population at risk of Tay–Sachs Syndrome or sickle cell disease or other genetically transmitted illnesses.

In light of the extensive evidence that the family's socioemotional climate is closely related to individual health status, the full range of human service organizations are in a position to initiate interventions with the potential to positively influence family health. Because numerous population risk factors have been identified, agencies can choose to provide services that are compatible with their organization's overarching goals and available resources. For example, a local health department might conduct an assessment that results in identifying substantial numbers of single, working mothers within its community. Recognizing this factor as posing special health risks for the children and the mother's health as well (especially, if the women are also racial or ethnic minorities), a local health department might initiate several interventions to reach out to these women. For example, clinic hours might be extended to accommodate work demands, health educational programs might include supportive services such as childcare, and routine screening to assess overall family health might be initiated.

A child guidance clinic might develop a comprehensive family-focused program for teen-age mothers and their babies (Schmid, 1982) and for teen-age fathers (Hardy & Duggan, 1988). School-based health programs might routinely design interventions so that they are consistent with the documented role of family socialization processes on children's health care practices. Worksite health promotion focused on employees' lifestyles is increasingly recognized as a worthwhile endeavor (Conrad, 1988; Pelletier, 1984). The effectiveness of such programs will undoubtedly be enhanced to the extent that interventions take into account family health roles. To date, however, literature in this area lacks recognition of a family perspective on employee health (Saltzberg & Bryant, 1988). On the other hand, there is growing interest on the part of employers in assessing the service needs of employees caring for children with disabilities (Krauskopf & Akabas, 1988) and elderly parents (Scharlach & Boyd, 1989).

The extensive body of epidemiological research on family sources of life stress, and on the other hand, the equally convincing evidence of the health protective effect of family social support, underscore the necessity to consider these factors when assessing the need for family-focused health interventions. Public health programs, primary medical programs, and family-practice centers are among those that are well-advised to institute screening mechanisms or other assessment techniques (some of which will be discussed in detail later) to identify families at risk because they are experiencing excessive life stress or have inadequate access to social support (Unger & Powell 1980).

Quality of Life Studies

In recent years, a fifth source of data has been added to the public health model. These are commonly called quality of life studies (Caputi, 1982; Kaplan, 1985). Research in this area is still in its infancy; however, interest is growing as advances in medical technology increase the likelihood of survival following serious illness or trauma. Instruments to assess quality of life are only now being developed (Aaronson & Beckman, 1987). To date, the majority of assessment instruments are designed to measure individual patient's experience with a specific illness or with illness in general (Brook, Ware, & Rogers, 1979; Clark & Fallowfield, 1986; Derogatis, 1986; Fletcher, Hunt, & Bulpitt, 1987; Morris & Sherwood, 1987; Selby, Chapman, Etazadi-Amoli et al., 1984; Schipper, Clinch, McMurray, & Levitt, 1984; Schipper & Levitt, 1985). As a result, only inferences can be drawn about the impact of illness on the overall quality of family life. The ability to assess the impact of serious illness and disability on quality of family life will be enhanced as theories of family functioning are refined and operationalized.

Tools to assist in the clinical assessment of the impact of illness on overall family life will be discussed later in greater detail.

Additional Sources of Assessment Data

In some cases, specifically focused assessment tools will be needed for population-based studies. For example, ongoing assessment of the health of populations in communities adjacent to specific environmental hazards require prospective health data, perhaps on a random sample of families. A similar approach might be appropriate for assessment of families of workers in occupational environments known to pose health risks for their employees. Such assessments might track physical indicators as well as measures of overall family functioning and stress. In a different vein, in a population-based study, the Health Family Tree was used to identify young family members who might be at high risk for heart disease or cancer because of familial disease (Williams, Hunt, Barlow et al., 1988). In that study, 24, 332 "trees" were completed by parents and students in 37 high schools in 14 urban and rural communities.

In addition to using statistical and research sources of data, the social worker might employ several other, more subjective, approaches to community needs assessment that are also consistent with the public health model. These include the use of key informants, community meetings, the delphi procedure, and community surveys (Rabkin, 1986; Runyan, 1985). Although some of these methods lack the "objectivity" and generalizability of statistical methods, they can provide valuable information and at the same time enlist community cooperation and enthusiasm for a proposed project. These approaches are especially useful in assessing the adequacy of existing community social services in a particular community or neighborhood.

There is considerable evidence from clinical experience and from early research that the ability of the family system to make linkages to the broader community system is a critical resource in the family's ability to function, especially in the face of stress (Geismar, 1972; 1980; Whittaker et al., 1986). Consistent with this proposition, Geismar and co-workers (1971; 1972) developed tools to assess community support within two categories: the community's primary provisions for survival and maintenance of a minimal level of social functioning, and its services to facilitate social participation, social control, mobility, social and political expression, and adequate living arrangements. In a similar vein, Leighton and colleagues used a case study to assess community integration as it affected a community mental health clinic (Leighton, 1959; Leighton, 1982).

Assessment at the community level (including, in some cases, the community of an agency being the population it serves), almost always involves a question of choice and a corollary assessment of resources. Herein, the spectre of values enters the decision-making process. The role of values in influencing social and organizational policies was discussed in detail in Chapter 3. However, we would be remiss if we failed to underscore the role of values that is inherent even within a public health assessment framework that is so dependent on "objective data." It is important to never lose sight of the role that values play in the interpretation of the data and in the subsequent choice of intervention. For example, a human service agency may perceive its mandate to be compatible with helping families to cope with the stress associated with living near a toxic waste dumpsite, but to be less compatible with efforts to organize multiple families toward a collective political response to the health risk (Bachrach & Zautra, 1985).

Assessing Treatment Environments

Moos and colleagues have recently developed frameworks and tools to assess the characteristics and impact of community-based and hospital-based treatment settings (Moos, 1985). Aspects of interpersonal relationships among patients and staff (involvement, staff support, spontaneity), program goals (autonomy, practical orientation, personal problem orientation, and expression of anger), and program structure (organization, clarity, staff control) are assessed. To date, these instruments have been used to examine the impact on patients; however, the approach might be applied to assessing the impact of programs on families.

Assessment of Family Functioning

Given the fact that family theory is still in a relatively early stage of development, it is not surprising that family assessment tools are also unrefined (Fredman & Sherman, 1987). On the plus side, however, recognition of the need has spurred recent rapid advances in this area by both practitioners and researchers. We have already observed in Chapter 1 that family functioning is a complex phenomenon and that we are currently in a period characterized by the presence of conceptually diverse models of family functioning. We also noted, however, that there is increasing consensus among family theorists, clinicians, and researchers concerning the utility of the general systems paradigm and the ecological perspective as overarching frameworks for observing family functioning (Forman & Hagan, 1983). In general, therefore, although assessment frameworks vary in terms of their specific purpose, the source of information (a single family member versus more than one member), the skills required to conduct the assessment, sensitivity to sociocultural differences, and the degree to which they are based in theory, they are all guided by a dynamic and interactive perspective of family functioning.

To date, the majority of instruments has been developed for research purposes. In some cases, clinical use of these tools for screening and for practice-based evaluation research is feasible and even advisable; however, others may be costly and time consuming to employ. Assessment frameworks developed solely to guide the practitioner commonly include factors known to be relevant to some aspect of family functioning. Check lists, screening tools, family inventories, and tools that assess single or multiple dimensions or relational or transactive family functioning are in various stages of development. The following is a selected review of existing frameworks and tools that have been used to observe relationships between families and health and illness. Practitioners might use these frameworks and tools to establish guidelines for family referral, for purposes of high-risk screening, to evaluate the outcomes of family interventions, and in some cases, to guide clinical assessment.

General Assessment Frameworks

Preassessment Guidelines

We begin by discussing check lists that might better be categorized as preassessment guidelines. One framework was originally developed for physicians, but it is applicable for other health professions. The model outlines an appraisal framework to assist the practitioner in assessing the knowledge base, personal development base, and skills required of the clinician at various levels of practice with a family. The model proposes five levels of clinician's involvement with families in health care: (1) minimal emphasis on the family; (2) providing ongoing medical information and advice; (3) focusing on feelings and support; (4) conducting systematic assessment and planned intervention; (5) and family therapy (Doherty & Burge, 1987). The model, therefore, provides benchmarks as to when to initiate referrals and engage in collaborative practice among different members of the health care team (Doherty & Campbell, 1988).

One check list summarizes medical conditions for which there is a reasonable probability that there will be associated family problems (Schmidt, 1982). The list is not grounded in theory. Medical conditions were selected because existing evidence suggests that either family functioning contributes to the cause of the disease, or because problematic family reactions to the condition have been documented. The list is presented as indications to the physician for convening the family; however, it is also applicable to social workers and other health professionals intending to provide psychosocial services to families. Medical conditions are listed with examples of associated family situation problems and reference to the supporting research. Conditions include pregnancy, failure to thrive, recurrent childhood poisoning, preschool behavior problems, school problems, adolescent maladjustment, major depression, chronic illness, diabetes, cardiac disease and surgery, poor adherence to medical regimes, high inappropriate use of health services, terminal illness, and bereavement (Schmidt, 1982). Barrier and Christie-Seely (1984) propose an expanded list of symptoms, behaviors, and situations that indicate to the physician that there is a need for family assessment. In addition to the conditions already mentioned, they include patients who present with nonspecific symptoms in the absence of organic disease, when one member of a family presents with the same symptoms of another member or when a series of illnesses occur in close sequence within the family, marital and sexual problems, diseases associated with lifestyles and environmental factors, situations calling for advice concerning health promotion, and during developmental stages of family life (e.g., during prenatal care, adolescence, at mid-life).

Assessment Frameworks for Use in Primary Care

Several general psychosocial frameworks are especially applicable for use in primary care. For example, Holman (1983) proposes that family assessment commonly includes four principal areas: the problem, the family as a system, the family and its environment, and the family lifecycle. Holman goes on to pose a series of questions related to each area to be considered by the practitioner. Interviews, use of genograms, ecomaps, family sculpture techniques, and inventories of individual member functioning are suggested as methods to carry out the assessment. Closely akin to the ecomap, the "family circle" has been described as a family assessment tool for physicians (Thrower, Bruce, & Walton, 1982).

In a more recent general assessment formulation, family and individual resources are assessed through the use of a Developmental Assessment Wheel that attempts to organize both social and psychological information (Vigilante & Mailick, 1988). Similarly, Carlton (1984) has adapted Falk's Social Status Examination in Health Care to include a broad range of social and psychological information, some of which is pertinent to family assessment.

The utility of a health-specific family coping index for assessing the need for nursing service was recently examined (Choi, Josten, & Christensen,

1983; Highriter, 1983). Family coping is clinically rated in nine domains: (1) physical independence; (2) therapeutic competence; (3) knowledge of health condition; (4) application of principles of general hygiene; (5) health care attitude; (6) emotional competence; (7) family living patterns; (8) physical environment; and (9) use of community resources. In addition, families are clinically evaluated on: (1) recognition of need for help; (2) clarity of perceptions; (3) supportive exchange; (4) stress level; (5) pattern of coping; (6) fulfillment of roles; (7) energy level; (8) reality orientation; and (9) participative decision making. Whereas, weaknesses in this approach have been observed (Highriter, 1983), the index is purported to be useful in nursing care management and in determining the need for institutional care. Many of the health-specific components examined are also of concern to social workers and other health professionals.

An organized set of questions based on a three-dimensional model for the psychosocial evaluation of family functioning has been reported to be effective as a tool for use by family physicians (Arbogast, Scratton, & Krick, 1978). Developed collaboratively by social workers and a physician, the model is designed to assess the family lifecycle, family process, and the social milieu of the family. Specific questions address household membership, past health problems, current developmental stage, decision-making family alliances, tolerance for difference, extended family relations, community/neighborhood resources, and socioeconomic resources. Again, this framework might be adapted for use by social workers in primary care settings.

A developmental task model sets forth areas to be assessed during pregnancy and the early transition to parenthood (Cohen, 1988). Practitioners are encouraged to assess parents progress through four stages: acceptance of the pregnant state, affiliation with the fetus, preparatory (or nesting) behavior, and the development of a reality-based perception of the neonate. Additional areas to be explored are the parents' previous experience with children, their life apart from parenting, and their social support systems.

A detailed use of the genogram is suggested as one method of obtaining baseline family data in primary medical care practices (Mullins & Christie-Seely, 1984). For each family member represented on the genogram diagram, recording the following data is suggested: (1) baseline demographic and medical history data; (2) family roles, character descriptors, problems; (3) family contact, cohesion, and boundaries; (4) toxic issues (such as family secrets) and nodal events; (4) environmental influence and relationships; and (5) conclusions about family relationship patterns.

Recently, a multidisciplinary task force on the family at the Kellogg Center in Montreal developed guidelines for the assessment of families of primary care physicians. The components of the PRACTICE schema are: (1) *P*resenting problem; (2) *R*oles and structure (included are hierarchical organization, boundaries and individuation, cohesion and control); (3) *A*ffect; (4) Communication; (5) *T*ime in the family lifecycle; (6) *I*llness in the family past and present; (7) Coping with stress; and (8) *E*cology and culture (Barrier, Bybel, Christie-Seely, & Whittaker, 1984). The framework can be used to guide a family-focused interview with one or more family members. Furthermore, the use of ecomaps, the family circle, and other techniques can be incorporated within this framework.

Although not family-focused, a recently developed screening tool is noteworthy because it attempts to assess the well-being of young children. The Pediatric Symptom Checklist (PSC) is a self-report questionnaire designed to be completed by parents of school-aged children (Jellinek, Murphy, Robinson, Feins et al., 1988). The PSC consists of 35 symptoms that can be checked as "often," "sometimes," or "never" present. The instrument yields a psychosocial dysfunction score for which normative data is available; scores of 28 or greater suggest that the child and family receive further evaluation. Preliminary studies indicate that the screening instrument can be used to assess the functioning of lower middle socioeconomic and minority group children (Murphy & Jellinek, 1988).

Family Assessment in the Face of Illness

Christ (1983) has detailed five areas of potential stress for patients with cancer and their families. She suggests that practitioners assess each of the following: (1) the ecological framework of the cancer treatment system; (2) expressions of underlying psychopathology; (3) reactivation of underlying conflict; (4) specific stressor responses; and (5) dissynchrony of coping among patient, family, and health care staff.

In a similar vein, Adams-Greenly (1986) has outlined areas to be assessed among pediatric patients with cancer and their families including: stage of disease, socioeconomic status, family cohesion, and family history. Other disease-specific assessment tools have been developed for the purposes of screening and assessing psychosocial need among hemophilia patients and families (Reiss, Linhart, & Lazerson, 1982) and among families with a child with sickle cell disease (Nishirua, Whitten, & Jenkins, 1980).

Power and Orto (1980) have highlighted psychosocial areas to be assessed when families are faced with serious illness. They suggest that each of the following be examined: (1) how the family has dealt with previous crises; (2) the meaning the illness has to the family; (3) the family lifestyle; (4) coping resources; (5) who is ill and the status and role of the ill family member; and (6) the stage of the family lifecycle. Family physicians have also been advised to incorporate family assessment data into their problem-oriented record (Smilkstein, 1975). Data recommended for inclusion are the social, cultural, religious, economic, educational, and medical resources of the family as well as the functional status of the family. Caroff and Mailick (1985) propose that health care practitioners dichotomize families as high or low functioning following the assessment of family communication, role patterning, family rules, and coping behaviors.

A recently developed framework moves beyond an organized check list as it begins to conceptualize systems interactions between chronic illness and the family lifecycle (Rolland, 1987a,b, 1988a,b). First, a psychosocial typology of chronic or life-threatening illness is proposed. Chronic illnesses are grouped according to key biological parameters, each with different psychosocial demands on the ill individual and his or her family. Thus, the practitioner is advised to consider (1) whether the illness has an acute or gradual onset; (2) whether the illness course is progressive, constant, or relapsing/episodic; and (3) the extent to which the illness will likely shorten one's life span, be a cause of death, and result in incapacitation. Second, the developmental time phases of the illness (i.e., crisis, chronic, terminal) are to be considered. The typology of illness and the phases of illness can be combined to construct a two-dimensional matrix. A family-systems model is then added to form a three-dimensional assessment framework. In this third dimension, key components of the family lifecycle are assessed: periods of transition, life-structure building, and maintaining centripetality and centrifugality. Systematically organizing family assessment data in this way is purported to aid practitioners in planning appropriate family interventions. Empirical data from studies of chronic illness in children support this emphasis on generic features of illness when assessing the impact of illness on families (Jessop & Stein, 1985).

The frameworks presented in this section are obviously broad in scope. They provide the practitioner with a general roadmap for assessing a family's need for psychosocial services. It is clear that these frameworks do not, by themselves, classify or diagnose families, and although systematically organized, they are generally atheoretical. From the perspective of these frameworks, however, individual practitioners can select specific approaches to obtain assessment data and can apply different practice theories to make clinical judgments about which problems require their attention.

Assessment Tools

Self-Report Single Dimensional Family Inventories

Family self-report inventories are a step further along a continuum of generality to specificity. Frequently developed for research purposes, they emphasize specific dimensions of family experience or functioning that are deemed important in family health relationships. In some cases, the selection of dimensions has been based on a specific theoretical perspective. The advantages of such instruments for enhancing the validity and reliability of research findings are obvious. In large part, their clinical application remains to be evaluated; however, they do provide the practitioner with additional sources of data as perceived from the family's subjective viewpoint and, therefore, might be used for high-risk screening.

Before reviewing self-report questionnaires, it is important to provide a context for understanding the nature of this source of family data. In this vein, Fisher and colleagues (1985) have classified family assessment data into three levels: individual relational, and transactional. The individual level of assessment occurs when data from a single family member are utilized without reference to the views, perceptions, or actions of other family members. If individual-level data are collected from two or more family members and then combined in some way, this data is termed *relational*. On the other hand, in the view of these authors, transactional data cannot be obtained from self-report inventories. Rather these data are best obtained from direct observation of family interactions, with or without structured tasks. Distinguishing the source of family assessment data has obvious clinical implications, as is discussed throughout subsequent chapters.

In this section, we review only instruments that, to some extent, have been developed for the purposes of assessing relationships between families and health or illness. Several of these instruments were used in the research reported in Chapter 2. It is important to note, however, that some of the more widely used and standardized instruments to assess single dimensions of family interactions, such as the marital relationship and family communication, also can be used in health-related family assessment (Filsinger, 1983).

Based on the ABCX Model of family stress previously discussed in Chapter 1, McCubbin and his colleagues have developed several instruments to assess separate dimensions assumed to operate in familial response to life stress. The Family Inventory of Life Events (FILE) parallels individual life stress inventories (McCubbin & Patterson, 1987). Parents are asked to indicate whether the family unit has experienced normative and nonnormative stressors, hardships, and prior strains within the past year and to rate the adjustment required by these events. The instrument yields a total weighted stress score for the family and a total demand score and is reported to have adequate validity and reliability. The inventory has been used in studies of families having a child with myelomeningocele (McCubbin, 1988) and cystic fibrosis (Patterson & McCubbin, 1983). In each study, family stress was associated with the child's health status. Clinical use of the inventory has not been reported in the literature; however, it appears that FILE might be a useful screening tool.

A second dimension in most theoretical stress formulations is the potential mediating role of resources. The Family inventory of Resources for Management (FIRM) is a 69-item self-report instrument that assesses: (1) family esteem and communication; (2) family mastery and health; (3) extended family social support; (4) financial well-being; and (5) resource strains (McCubbin & Comeau, 1987). In light of the previously reviewed literature on the moderating role of social support, it is not surprising that scores from this inventory have been associated with the health status of children with myelomeningocele (McCubbin, 1988). The inventory data can be obtained from a single parent or from parents together.

A less detailed instrument has been developed to assess patient's perception of the support from their families. The Family APGAR is a brief questionnaire that is designed to test five areas of family support as perceived by a single family member (Good, Smilkstein, Good, Shaffer, & Arons, 1979; Smilkstein, 1978). The instrument consists of five closed-ended questions to assess a family member's satisfaction with each of five components of family function, such as the help that is received from one's family when the individual perceives a need, the family's expression of affection and emotional support, and family participation. The instrument lends a score that can be used as an indicator of family support. Index scores have been compared to the Family Functioning Index (Pless & Satterwhite, 1973) and to family therapists' assessments and have been shown to be significantly correlated with each, an indication of the validity of the tool (Good et al., 1979). The instrument has also been used in predicting cardiac recovery (Ell & Haywood, 1984) and pregnancy complications (Smilkstein et al., 1984). Numerous instruments have recently been developed to assess individual's perception of the social support they receive from primary and extended network members (Heitzmann & Kaplan, 1988; O'Reilly, 1988; Payne & Jones, 1987; Sarason, Shearin, Pierce & Sarason, 1987). Given the well-documented importance of this resource in coping with illness, assessment of this component in family assessments is recommended (Cooke, Rossmann, McCubbin, & Patterson, 1988).

A third dimension in the stress process is coping. An 80-item check list was developed to assess parents' perceptions of their response to the management of family when they have a child who is seriously and/or chronically ill (McCubbin, McCubbin, Patterson, Cauble et al., 1983). The Coping Health Inventory for Parents (CHIP) is reported to have adequate validity and reliability (McCubbin & McCubbin, 1987) and can be used in a shortened format of 45 items (McCubbin & Comeau 1987). The instrument yields three parental coping patterns: (1) maintaining family integration, cooperation, and an optimistic definition of the situation; (2) maintaining social support, self-esteem, and psychological stability; and (3) understanding the medical situation through communication with other parents and consultation with the medical staff. The clinical utility of the inventory remains to be tested as does its sensitivity to sociocultural differences. Again, the inventory might be a useful screening tool and a measure of outcome following family intervention.

One additional inventory is of interest because it assesses parents' satisfaction with a medical encounter on behalf of their child (Lewis, Scott, Pantell, & Wolf, 1986). Preliminary results from testing the Parent Medical Interview Satisfaction Scale (P-MISS) are consistent with previously reviewed research documenting family's desire for information from and communication with health professionals. In an evaluation of the instrument, parents' distress relief was significantly correlated with the nature of the physician's interpersonal communication with themselves and with their child. This tool might be adapted to obtain parental feedback concerning encounters with social workers. This approach could be used as a quality assurance indicator.

Assessing the Impact of Illness and Quality of Family Life

Tools to assess the impact of general psychological distress on social adjustment are widely used (Weissman, Sholomskas, & John, 1981), however, only recently have efforts been made to tailor assessment to the impact of physical illness. As already noted, in general, these instruments assess individual experience. A well-developed and extensively tested instrument, the Psychosocial Adjustment to Illness Scale (PAIS) (Derogatis, 1986b; Morrow, Chairello, & Derogatis, 1978) examines seven primary domains of adjustment: vocational environment, domestic environment, sexual relationships, extended family relationships, social environment, psychological distress, and health care orientation. Family impact is assessed by an individual member (De-Nour, 1982). The instrument was originally developed to be used in an interview format; however, a self-report version is available as is one designed specifically for spouses (Derogatis, 1978; Derogatis, 1986b). The instrument has been used in a study of parental adjustment to pediatric cancer in which the negative impact was greatest among parents whose child had died when compared to those whose child remained in treatment (Morrow, Carpenter, & Hoagland, 1984).

An early instrument was developed by Pless and Satterwhite (1973) to assess the impact of childhood chronic illness on families and to identify families in need of help. The Family Functioning Index (FFI) consists of 15 questions, yielding six scales (intrafamily communication, cohesiveness, decision making, marital satisfaction, happiness, and closeness) as well as overall functioning. The FFI is intended to be used as a screening tool to assess parental need for service. An inventory to assess family response to chronic childhood illness has been reported (Athreya & McCormick, 1987; Stein & Riessman, 1980). Areas of impact examined are: financial, social/familial, personal strain, and mastery. Clinical application of this framework remains to be explored.

Several instruments have been developed recently to assess the impact of caregiving on family members. In general, these instruments assess stressful or burdensome aspects of caregiving that are assumed to influence an individual family member's social functioning and psychological status. The majority of these assessment instruments have been developed for research purposes, are lengthy, and in some cases presumably too cumbersome for clinical use (Poulshock & Deimling, 1984). We review selected instruments that are relatively brief, with apparent utility as screening tools and for the evaluation of family interventions. It is important to note that these tools are not intended to assess overall family functioning.

The Burden Interview of Zarit, Reeves and Bach-Peterson (1980) assesses caregiver's perception of their own physical health, psychological well-being, finances, social life, and the nature of the relationship between the caregiver and the recipient of care. It has been specifically designed to reflect the stress experiences by caregivers of dementia patients. It can be self-administered or used as part of an interview. It consists of 22 questions about the impact of the patient's disabilities on the life of the caregiver.

The Caregiver Strain Index (CSI) was developed to assess the experience of caregivers of recently hospitalized hip surgery and heart patients aged 65 and over (Robinson, 1983). The CSI consists of 13 dichotomous items that reflect the most common stressors in caring for an elderly family member including: sleep disturbance, inconvenience, confinement, family adjustments, changes in personal plans, competing demands on time, emotional adjustments, upsetting behavior, physical strain, and financial strain. The Cost of Care Index (CCI) has been reported to be a useful case management tool for screening need among informal caregivers (Kosberg & Cairl, 1986). Potential "costs" to caregivers are assessed within 6 dimensions: social disruptions, personal restrictions, economic costs, perceived value of caregiving, care recipient behavior, and physical and emotional health of the caregiver.

One recently developed instrument is noteworthy because it was designed to obtain the family member's assessment of a patient's functional dementia. Therefore, it might be used to enlist the family's participation in assessing family need when providing ongoing services to families with a functionally impaired member. The Functional Dementia Scale (FDS) contains 20 items that assess the family member's perception of the patient's functional status in activities of daily, orientation, and affect (Moore, Bobula, Short, & Mischel, 1983). Face validity suggests that this tool might also be valuable in working with family members of patients with AIDS dementia.

Recognizing that access to coping resources will undoubtedly be a factor in the overall caregiving experience, Goodman (1988) has developed and tested an instrument to assess a caregiver's perception of the social support they receive that is specifically related to their caregiving activities. The instrument was based on categories previously reported to reflect reasons that people join self-help groups. The Perceived Social Supports for Caregivers (PSSC) is a self-administered questionnaire that assesses the following dimensions of caregiving support: modeling, similarity, emotional support, reaction/catharsis, information/guidance, altruism, and linkage to practical assistance.

Family Functioning or Relational Data

The following instruments assess some aspect of family relational data or family functioning. A widely used family assessment instrument in the health care field, the Family Environment Scale (FES), is a 90-item, true–false questionnaire assessing the social climate of families on three dimensions: interpersonal relationships, personal growth, and system maintenance and system change (Moos & Moos, 1982). The instrument was developed from a social–ecological perspective on person–environment transactions, with a view to assess the impact of these transactions on human adaptation (Moos & Moos, 1983). The instrument yields measures on 10 subscales: cohesion, expressiveness, conflict, independence, achievement orientation, intellectual–cultural orientation, active–recreational orientation, moral–religious emphasis, organization, and control. It can be used to measure the family as it currently exists and as members would ideally like it to be. The latter becomes a measure of family satisfaction. A short form of 40 items yields congruence–incongruence scores if administered to more than one family member (Moos & Moos, 1982). Scores on specific dimensions have been associated with adaptation to stressful situations such as coping with illness. Some evidence suggests that it can be used to enhance clinical assessment (Moos & Moos, 1983).

In a preceding chapter, we discussed Olson's Circumplex Model of Family Functioning. The Family Adaptability and Cohesion Evaluation Scale (FACES) is based on the Circumplex Model (Olson, Sprenkle, & Russell, 1979). The most recent version of the instrument, FACES III has undergone extensive validity and reliability testing (Olson, 1986). FACES III is a 20-item, self-report measure to assess family member's perception of the family's adaptability and cohesion. The instrument is administered a second time to obtain member's ideal conceptions of these dimensions of family functioning. A measure of family satisfaction is derived from the perceived–ideal discrepancy scores. The scores on adaptability and cohesion can be plotted onto the Circumplex Model, thereby characterizing families within a matrix of balanced or extreme family types. The instrument was designed to be used with a variety of family structures, including nuclear families and single-parent families. Each of the versions of FACES has been applied in health-related research. Recently, a direct observation method, the Clinical Rating Scale (CRS), has been developed to do clinical assessment on cohesion, change, and communication (Olson, 1988). This assessment tool can be used to evaluate family behavior based on a semistructured interview with one or more family members (Olson & Killorin, 1985). Cross-cultural validity of the instrument is suggested by the results of a recent study of Hispanic families (Vega, Patterson, Sallis, Nader et al., 1986).

Originally developed to evaluate families with adolescents in psychiatric treatment, the Beavers–Timberlawn Family Evaluation Scale (BTFES) uses trained observers to assess family structure, autonomy, affect, perception of reality, and task efficiency from 10-minute videotapes of family interaction (Lewis, Beavers, Gossett, & Phillips, 1976). The instrument is based on family systems models and classifies overall family competence and the style of family interaction as being centripetal or centrifugal. The instrument has been used in a previously reviewed study of dialysis patients (Steidl et al., 1980). In that study, specific areas of family functioning, including strong parental coalition and effective problem-solving skills, were associated with adherence to the medical regimen. The authors suggest that the instrument can be used to identify areas of family functioning that require clinical attention. More recently, a 36-item, self-report instrument has been developed measuring family conflict, family communication, family cohesion, directive leadership, and family health (Beavers, Hampson, & Hulgus, 1985; Corcoran & Fischer, 1987). The self-report instrument is administered to an entire family. The clinical application of this tool in family health-related assessments in clinical practice in health care settings appears worthy of further exploration.

The McMaster Family Assessment Device (FAD) (Epstein, Baldwin, & Bishop, 1983) is a recently designed questionnaire to evaluate families according to the McMaster Model of Family Functioning, a general systems theory model integrating the structure, organization, and transactional patterns of the family (Epstein, Bishop, & Levin, 1978). As previously discussed, this model utilizes a general systems theory approach to describe the structure, organization, and transactional patterns of the family unit. The 53-item questionnaire assesses the overall health and pathology of the family as well as family problem-solving, communication, roles, affective responsiveness, affective involvement, and behavior control. The McMaster Clinical Rating Scale (CRS) is currently being developed. The instrument has been used in studies of families with patients with rheumatoid arthritis, with systemic lupus erythematosus, and who have suffered a stroke (Bishop, Epstein, Keitner et al., 1986).

The Card Sort Procedure (CSP) is based on the Paradigm Model of family functioning presented in Chapter 1 (Reiss, 1981). Its clinical application is questionable because it is costly to administer. The CSP is a behavioral measure of the problem-solving styles of family members as they are presumed to manifest their underlying shared views of social reality (Oliveri & Reiss, 1981). Family members are given a problem to solve individually and then as a group using a card sort procedure. The family is judged by expert observers on their ability to recognize patterns, maintain coordination and agreement, and their sensitivity to new information (Westin & Reiss, 1979). This assessment procedure has been used primarily in relation to families coping with psychiatric disturbance. Its use in assessing families coping with physical illness remains to be evaluated (Reiss, Gonzales, & Kramer, 1986).

Implications for Practice

As we have repeatedly observed, there is no longer doubt that families play vital roles in health and illness, and that family-focused practice is an extremely worthwhile and indeed necessary focus of health practice. At the same time, because we must concern ourselves simultaneously with the well-being of individual family members and well as with the family system, the task before practitioners is formidable and, at times, bewildering. Furthermore, families are complex and ever-changing. As a result, family-focused, health-related assessment must be recognized as requiring assessment frameworks that help us to distinguish complex relationships within and between systems. No single framework will serve all purposes. Therefore, practitioners must choose assessment guidelines and tools that, in their educated judgment, will aid them in working with specific practice populations or in evaluating their practice. In subsequent chapters, we will elaborate on clinical assessment, including important variations related to the specified goal and method of intervention.

To better understand the family-health/illness connection, assessment frameworks are needed for application to family roles in health promotion and maintenance and in the management of illness. On the face of it, existing family assessment frameworks reflect the emerging consensus that an ecosystemic framework is the most comprehensive conceptual framework for understanding family functioning and family health related needs (Forman & Hagan, 1983). In practice, this broad framework is clearly represented in the public health model and can be readily applied to community assessment.

In contrast, an ecosystemic assessment of individual family functioning and of the needs of an individual family is a complex clinical task. The foregoing review has highlighted many of the issues that add to this complexity, including the need to obtain data from more than one family member and to assess systemic transactions within families and between families and their communities (Reiss & Oliveri, 1983). To date, the majority of assessment tools focus on intrafamily relationships, neglecting ecological dimensions of interdependence between the family and its broader social environment and social institutions. Undoubtedly, increasing the dialogue between researchers, theorists, and practitioners would help to improve the theoretical and practical utility of these tools.

On the other hand, as indicated in the foregoing review, preliminary steps toward the refinement of individual family assessment tools have been made. At the same time, the lack of standardized assessment tools underscores the fact that the state of the art in family theory and assessment is still in its early stages of development (Campbell, 1986; Forman & Hagan, 1983). For example, whereas it might appear that many of these instruments are assessing similar family phenomena, one study found no correlations between any of the scales, when comparing the FES, FACES, and the CSP (Oliveri & Reiss, 1984). Failure to find agreement is presumably in large part attributable to differences in the specific assessment procedures employed (i.e., self-report versus outside observation) (Beavers, Hampson, & Hulgus, 1985; Olson, 1985; Sigafoos & Reiss, 1985). Fortunately, other analyses suggest that commonality and convergence among theoretical formulations and their operationalizations are emerging (Bloom, 1985).

Practitioners are encouraged to become increasingly knowledgeable about family theories and their practical application. The intrinsic value of social workers instituting systematic family assessment methods in their practice lies in the likelihood that their efforts will reduce the occurrence of failing to meet the needs of families. The use of screening tools can be an important aid to the practitioner. At the same time, increasing application of these tools by practitioners will enhance the dialogue between practitioners, theoreticians, and researchers that is necessary to advance family theory and to evaluate the outcome of family interventions.

6
Social Work Intervention with Families in Health Care

Earlier chapters provide compelling evidence that the family plays an important role at every stage of a person's illness or disability in either enhancing or retarding the healing process. The capacity of the family to make the adaptive changes that are required by the medical condition is a critical determinant of the outcome for both the patient and the family unit. Hans Falck has reminded us that the illness or disability is always of social significance, since illness influences the relationships of people with each other (Falck, 1978). Just as the family plays an important part in a person's experience as a patient so, too, does the illness play an important part in the welfare of the family system. An illness or disability may seriously influence the functioning of the family unit and the functioning of the family often exerts profound influence on the course of the patient's recovery. The two are reciprocal and intricately interrelated. Social and emotional factors may exert a decisive effect on the ways that somatic illness or injury develops, the degree of recovery, and the ways in which the patient, other members of the family, and the family unit adapt to changes occasioned by the medical condition. The research evidence challenges the social worker to intervene in the family system as well as with the individual patient in order to enable both to cope with the inevitable stress created by illness or disability.

Families are primary social systems consisting of two or more persons bound by ties of blood, marriage, adoption, foster status, or cohabitation and characterized by continuity, mutual commitment, and emotional and economic interdependence. They exist within a broader extended family system and a network of other social systems, resources, and sociocultural environments that strongly influence the ways in which they carry out their emotional and instrumental functions.

It has been suggested that there are as many variations of family life as there are families and that determining who constitutes a family is a practical and empirical question that is contextually determined (Gubrium, 1987). Major variations in family structure influence the ways in which families perform a broad range of health and illness related functions and tasks. The predominant structure continues to be a family consisting of two parents and one or more children. Roles of spouses in these families, however, change over the years so that now in almost one-half of these families, the mother as well as the father is employed outside the home (Rix, 1987). Some families, in which the couples are not married, closely approximate the two married parent household, although ambiguity and unclear expectations are intrinsic to this lifestyle, a state that is most pronounced when children are included (Macklin, 1988). Remarried and step-families are numerous and vary in their degrees of structural complexity: a large majority (70 percent) involve children, most often from the wife's prior marriage (Pasley & Ihinger-Tallman, 1988). Increasingly, homosexual persons are accepting their sexual identity and living in domestic partnerships, sometimes with children in the home (Poverny & Finch, 1988). As in the case of cohabiting heterosexual couples, the extent to which these couples assume the obligations and commitments to family life varies.

Single parent families, usually headed by a woman, are increasingly prevalent (Chilman, 1988; Zimmerman, 1988), owing to no marriage, divorce, or separation. These families tend to be much poorer than two parent families, even though a large proportion of the mothers are employed (Rix, 1987). Although a large majority of these families are white, a disproportion are blacks and Latinos (Berlin, 1988; Chilman, 1988).

The diversity of family structures has implications for the family's health-related functions and tasks. Knowing who belongs to the family is a necessary prelude to determining who should be included in family sessions and who is available for sharing responsibility for the care of patient members. For example, when children of divorced parents are hospitalized, health care professionals are required to take that fact into account (Ahrons & Arnn, 1981). Consent for medical treatments, decisions concerning discharge planning, and bioethical decision making may become more complex as the question of which family members should be informed, consulted, and have legal responsibility. Gay/lesbian families are confronted with similar and additional social and legal problems (Harry, 1988; Poverny & Finch, 1988; Rice & Kelly, 1988). Understanding the family as a social system and variations in structure is essential to effective planning and treatment.

Within each type of family, sociocultural factors influence the family's well-being in terms of health status and access to and use of health care, including ethnicity, socioeconomic states, social mobility, and geography. Some illnesses are more prevalent in particular populations, such as Tay-Sachs disease among Jews of Eastern or Central European origin, sickle-cell anemia among blacks, and acquired immune deficiency syndrome (AIDS) among gay men and intravenous drug users. Poverty is clearly associated with single parenthood and minority ethnic status. Family socialization processes concerning health practices, customs, traditions, and caregiving are also subject to sociocultural influence. For example, definitions of what constitutes illness, expressions of symptoms, and help-seeking behaviors vary among differing sociocultural groups (Mechanic, 1983). Families who are poor seldom have adequate health insurance and money for medicine and other essential health supplies. They may be homeless. Many poor families are headed by a single parent and are underorganized, with a lack of consistency, flexibility, and differentiation in the roles of the members and subgroups that comprise the family system (Aponte, 1976). They are often powerless and excluded from many operations of society, especially when they also experience discrimination owing to their minority ethnic status (Solomon, 1976). The communities in which they live often do not have the kind of institutional resources and community supports necessary for the healthy development of each member and the family.

Values of Family Practice

The interdependency of members of a family, mutually influencing each other, suggests the desirability—indeed often the necessity—for professional help to be given to the family, not just the patient or other members on a one-to-one basis. Family sessions have therapeutic values that benefit both the patient and the family system. Social workers enter into the family as caring, objective, and yet temporary helpers who respect the family's culture, autonomy, and structure. Since all members of the family who participate are simultaneously exposed to the practitioner, there tends to develop mutual understanding of the worker's role. All members can directly experience the practitioner's empathy, concern, and respect for each one as an individual and for the family as a unit. The members develop common knowledge of the medical situation and each other's views and attitudes toward it which enhances motivation and cohesiveness of the family. As the members cope with a problem or participate together in making decisions, they gain self-esteem and increased capacity for facing and solving problems. Learning is facilitated through interaction among the participants. One member may ask a question that did not occur to others but is relevant to them; there is discussion of different as well as similar responses which furthers understanding that differences and conflict can be expressed, weathered, and dealt with. When a person participates in a process of decision making, the decision is often more acceptable and amenable to appropriate implementation.

Trends in Family Practice in Health Settings

Families have been recognized as crucial to the welfare of patients from the beginning of social work practice in the health field. An early pioneer, Ida Cannon, set forth principles of diagnosis and treatment for social workers in hospitals, with an emphasis on people and their environments. She asserted that social workers should give services to individuals, families, and groups of patients (Cannon, 1913, 1923). Leaders in the field of family services agreed with this viewpoint. Mary Richmond, for example, in writing on social diagnosis said that:

> Family caseworkers welcome the opportunity to see at the very beginning of intercourse several of the members of the family assembled in their home environment, acting and reacting on one another, each taking a share in the development of the client's story, each revealing in ways other than words social facts of real significance (Richmond, 1917, p. 137).

That was in the days before social casework and social group work came to be regarded as separate methods and before Richmond had redefined casework as a method of helping people one by one (Richmond, 1922). In the redefinition of casework and group work as distinctive methods, work with family units was almost forgotten (Sherman, 1981).

Renewed interest in work with families gradually occurred in the 1950s. In the classic book on social casework by Gordon Hamilton, it was emphasized that the family might often be the unit of attention, with practitioners utilizing group process as a means of psychosocial treatment with families (Hamilton, 1951). Numerous publications by social workers on family diagnosis and treatment appeared in the 1950s (National Association of Social Workers, 1961, 1965). A major development was a project on developing a framework for practice with families in which social workers from Jewish Family Service in New York City collaborated with a psychiatrist, Nathan Ackerman (see bibliographies in Ackerman, 1958; Ackerman, Beatman, & Sherman, 1961; Ackerman, Beatman, & Sherman, 1967). Since the publication of Ackerman's book, *The Psychodynamics of Family Life* in 1958, numerous theoretical approaches to family therapy have been formulated by psychiatrists, often in collaboration with social workers and members of other professions (Group for the Advancement of Psychiatry, 1970). More recently, social workers have developed models of family therapy, including those referred to as psychosocial (Feldman & Scherz, 1967; Hollis & Woods, 1981; Scherz, 1970; Stamm, 1972; Sherman, 1981); communication (Satir, 1964; behavioral (Gambrill, 1981); problem-solving (Perlman, 1970; Reid, 1981); task-centered (Reid, 1981); adaptive systems (Freeman, 1981); crisis intervention (Parad, 1963; Parad, Selby, & Quinlan, 1976); and ecosystems (Germain, 1977; Hartman & Laird, 1983; Lindenberg, 1980; Meyer, 1983; Northen, 1982).

Among these models of family treatment in social work, there is considerable overlapping of concepts and principles of practice. All models emphasize the interconnectedness between individual behavior and family values, structure, and processes. All view persons as influenced by their families and mental disorders as problems in family functioning. Families are forms of social systems, in which members are interdependent. Interventions tend often to be directed to the structure and interacting processes of the family. Systems theory is used, to some extent, in almost all models of practice.

The family therapy models vary in important ways, although many of the differences are in emphasis rather than kind. Among the major differences are the priority given to assessing and intervening with individuals or the family system; the balance of attention paid to the practitioner's relationships with individuals, subsystems, and the total family; the stance of the practitioner in terms of the amount of control and directiveness as contrasted with family members' participation and self-determination; theories of how people change; the focus of intervention on intrafamily dynamics or broadening the concern to include environmental influences on the family (Hollis & Woods, 1981, pp. 447–488; Tolson & Reid, 1981, pp. 332–333). Tolson and Reid propose that the primary difference among models concerns whether family therapy is viewed as a modality of practice or a theory of behavior. Some writers consider family practice to include treatment with one person if the focus is family-centered. Others regard family therapy as a modality in which the practitioners work with the family unit as a whole or, at least, one of its subsystems. For purposes of this book, family treatment may be defined broadly as a modality of practice that includes work with at least two related persons (Tolson, 1981, p. 346). In health settings, the major purposes refer to the promotion of health, the prevention of problems, and the improvement of the functioning of individuals and families in relation to the illness or disability of one of the members of the family. It includes, but is not limited to family therapy. It is necessary to define the family flexibly to encompass persons with whom the patient is most intimately involved, going beyond the biological or adoptive family.

Family practice or work with the family units or subsystems of a family is not synonymous with family therapy. Therapy implies that the problem is in pathological family functioning. That focus on family dysfunction occurred partially, at least, because the general family therapy movement was developed primarily in psychiatric hospitals and clinics with patients whose diagnosis was schizophrenia and in child guidance clinics. Much work with families in medical settings, schools, neighborhood centers, and industry does not assume that the problem is in the family's structure and communication processes. The problems usually are in the complex interplay of forces within the client and among the client, the family, the organization, other groups, and the social and physical environment. Social workers help families through psychosocial education, supportive counseling, anticipatory guidance, crisis intervention, mediation of conflicts, placement or discharge planning, advocacy, and use of resources as well as through family therapy. They can learn a great deal from understanding family therapy, but there is a crying need for careful selection of models and for modifying them to fit the kind of practice in which they are engaged (Tolson, 1981). Family practice in health settings needs to be appropriate to the services rendered, the particular organizational setting, the types of illness or handicaps of the patients, and the psychosocial needs and problems of both the patients and their families (for a similar idea, see Reid, 1985, pp. 6–7). What is needed is what Tolson refers to as productive eclecticism in which the theory and techniques borrowed are internally consistent and appropriate to the goals of practice (Tolson, 1981, p. 336). What is needed is an ecosystems perspective that views the connection between the person and family and other influential social systems (Meyer, 1983).

Despite reiteration of the need for practice with families, the literature on its use by social workers in health settings is sparse, even though great interest was evident by the 1960s with the publication of two monographs by the National Association of Social Workers (NASW). Although the content of these publications tended to emphasize family diagnosis and work with particular members of the family on behalf of the patient, there were a few excellent formulations of work with family units (NASW, 1961, 1965). The bibliographies in these publications interestingly do not refer to patients in medical settings, but to references on mental illness and children's behavior problems, the concerns about which family therapy was initiated.

The more recent books on social work practice in the field of health tend to give minor attention to work with family units: Indeed, the word family does not even appear in the index of several major books. A growing body of periodical literature, however, does now exist on the subject of family-centered assessment and treatment of patients and families. An examination of the content of these articles, however, reveals that social workers usually take into account certain knowledge about the family situation in planning, assessing, and intervening with the patient or one member of the family and has interviews with one member of the family without the presence of the patient, most frequently with either a mother or a child or a spouse. Work is done with the client and selected members of the family individually. Numerous discussions on work with the family seem to convey the notion that a person who is sick or disabled has forfeited membership in the family. Interviews with only the patient or a member of the family are indeed appropriate for certain purposes at certain times. But there are also times when social work practice should be devoted to conjoint work with the family unit or a subsystem of the family, including participation of the patient as a member of the family. Though still scanty, there is a growing body of literature about work with families as a modality of treatment in health settings.

The social context and structure of the health organization itself create obstacles to the effective use of practice with families. There is often a crisis-oriented milieu in which severe threats to life exist; in which autonomy of social work practice often is circumscribed by medical concerns and threatens the institution's own survival by cost containment policies. One person—not a family—is admitted to a hospital or clinic. That fact, in turn, means that accountability is viewed as being only to the patient and fails to take into account the differential need for attention to families. There is too often inadequate understanding by administrators and other practitioners of the interdependence of the patient–family–social situation gestalt and perhaps, more importantly, how to translate that knowledge into health care programs.

Among some social workers, there is still a preference for working with people one by one, despite evidence that that form of practice is not universally effective. The myth is not dead that help to clients one by one is the treatment of choice, and that anything else is second best. Students still learn much more about the psychosocial development of individuals and personality theory than they do about the development, structure, and processes operating in larger social systems, including the family. The need is to recognize and truly understand that the biological, psychodynamic, interpersonal, and interactional dimensions of human functioning are inseparable. Another obstacle to work with families is owing to the fears and fantasies that some practitioners have about operating within the interactional processes of the family, just as they do in relation to treatment groups. They may fear upsetting the patient or children, losing control of the session, or dealing with overtly expressed conflict. They may not trust the family's own supportive and problem-solving capacities. They may question their competence to use the dynamics of communication among family members as the major source of help. But they can learn. Of course, the limited amount of literature on work with families in health settings is a crucial factor. Although the literature is scattered, as Ruth Ellen Lindenberg said:

> The time is ripe for a model based on an ecological perspective that views the individual within the context of family relationships and broader interactional networks. In such a model, the family would become the target of intervention. The model would also suggest a more egalitarian relationship, with responsibility for decision-making and control of the rehabilitation process shared among clients, families, and rehabilitation workers (Lindenberg, 1980).

Evidence from research reported earlier about the patient–family–social situation interaction and the psychosocial components of illness, disability, and injury provides a rationale for our work with families as do demonstrations of workable approaches to family treatment. Family practice views the family as a system with the potential not only to provide social support to the patient but also mutual support for all the members in facing and weathering the stress that accompanies the medical condition. It is also a system in which changes in norms, communication, roles, conflict, and decision making can benefit both the identified patient and other members of the family. The democratic ethos of the profession reminds us that all people who will be influenced by important decisions should participate in making those decisions, according to their capacities.

Purpose and Goals

The major purposes of family practice in the field of health are to: (1) support the patient and other members of the family in coping with the stress accompanying the illness or injury of one member of the family; and (2) enhance the adaptive capacities of the family to solve its problems and make decisions appropriate to the needs of the patient and the family unit. Within this general purpose, the specific goals will vary, depending upon the assessment of the patient, family, and environmental supports and obstacles. The practitioner may:

1. Develop a supportive socioemotional climate for the family in which the mutual needs and feelings of its members are recognized and acknowledged;
2. Provide the information necessary for the family to understand the physical condition, its treatment demands, and its consequences for individual and family living;
3. Alleviate such feelings as anxiety, guilt, low self-esteem, negative identity, helplessness, and hopelessness;
4. Enhance appropriate participation of family members in the patient's care;
5. Open up and improve the communication process among family members and with significant other people;
6. Assist the family to reestablish and enhance relationships with each other and with significant others in the family's social network;
7. Develop flexibility in making necessary shifts in role responsibilities and develop competence in the performance of the roles;
8. Foster autonomy and differentiation within a cohesive family group;
9. Assist the family to improve its problem-solving capacities in coping with the illness or disability of the patient;
10. Develop awareness of the family's own resources and provide access to essential external resources, including the family's social network and the community's health and welfare resources.

The Ecosystem Orientation to Practice

Social work situations, according to Henry Maas, "involve people's coping with changing environments or with changes in their own capacities to deal with their surrounding. . . . They call for altered patterns of interaction between persons and their context" (Maas, 1984, p. 3). In social work, the changes are brought about in ways that contribute to psychosocial well-being. The nature and extent of change depends on the physical, psychological, and social capacities of persons, and on environmental conditions and resources. The ecosystem approach takes into account the multiple and complex transactions among patients, with their families, the hospital or other medical setting, and their network of social relationships in the community.

A family is a complex, open, goal-directed, and adaptive system, interdependent with other social systems (Freeman, 1981). To help a family, the social worker needs to understand the patient as a complex biopsychosocial organism who is a member of a family and numerous other groups and organizations. The patient is in a family; he is a member even though in a hospital, rehabilitation center, or nursing home (Falck, 1978). As Perlman made clear, the worker is concerned with a patient in a family, not the patient and family (Perlman, 1961). Practitioners need to understand the patient's status and role in the family and the family as a unit—its formation, structure of statuses and roles, communication and decision-making processes, cultural values and norms, and goals. Furthermore, they need to understand the transactions of the patient and family in the health care system and the broader environmental supports and obstacles to goal achievement.

The nature of the need or problem and the client's situation determine the goals and the form of help to be given. Human problems arise from multiple interconnections among biological, psychological, economic, and sociocultural factors, often referred to as a biopsychosocial framework for understanding people in their social contexts (Spiegel, 1981, pp. 121–158). Psychosocial problems encountered in health settings tend to be related to:

1. Lack of knowledge about a specific illness or disability; its treatment, duration, and consequences for the lives of the patient and other members of the family;
2. Cultural attitudes and values that create barriers to the utilization of medical care;
3. Loss and separation, including death;
4. Dysfunctional interpersonal and group relationships;
5. Cognitive or emotional difficulties of the patient or significant other people;

6. Ineffective functioning of the family system;
7. The physical and social environment of the hospital or other health care setting;
8. Inadequate social supports in the family or broader social network;
9. Inadequate housing that does not meet the family's needs and the special requirements of the patient;
10. Lack of sufficient income due to unemployment, low wages, or cost of medical care;
11. Lack of health, educational, or welfare resources in the community.

All illnesses and disabilities pose threats to effective physical and social functioning, but it is also recognized that specific illnesses and disabilities differ in the nature of the stress.

Forms of Treatment in Family Practice

Several forms of family practice contribute to the well-being of the patient and family, the appropriate selection being based on a biopsychosocial assessment. Each form of practice will be described and discussed more fully in subsequent chapters.

Health Promotion

Promotion of good health is carried on through a variety of classes, lectures, and conferences with families. In public health, these activities are regarded as primary prevention (Bloom, 1981; Council on Social Work Education, 1962). Their purpose is to promote a desirable state of affairs and forestall some predictable, unforeseen events. Many hospitals, health maintenance organizations, and public health departments provide educational programs on such topics as nutrition, sex education, weight reduction, pulmonary resuscitation and first aid, forums on cataracts, prevention of low back pain, managing diabetes, stopping smoking, infant care, preparation for childbirth, and management of stress. Physicians or nurses, or other health care professionals, usually are in charge of the sessions, with the social worker serving primarily as either a referral source, consultant, or presenter on the psychosocial aspects of the problem or as a provider of follow-up services to the individual or family.

Conferences or group meetings with families are frequently held to provide knowledge and develop specific skills. They may be single sessions, a series of a few sessions, or several sessions held from time to time during the course of an illness or disability. The focus is often on educating the family, including the patient, about the diagnosis and its significance for the patient and family or changes in the patient's condition; the elements of the treatment plan; and the nature of services and resources available to the patient and family. Particular procedures and skills in self-care or care by others may be taught and demonstrated. A physician or nurse may present the medical information, but it is usually the social worker's responsibility to explore the family's reaction to the information and its potential impact on the members' daily lives.

Family Therapy

Family therapy, as applied to the health field, can be defined as treatment designed to modify or change those elements of the family system that are dysfunctional in that they contribute to the genesis or maintenance of the illness of one or more members of the family. The core of exploration and treatment is to set in motion and encourage the members to recognize the family's process and structure. The therapy aims to bring about shifts in dysfunctional patterns of communication, emotional ties, decision-making processes, roles, interpersonal conflicts, or value conflicts. The therapeutic emphasis is on preserving and enhancing those elements in family functioning that are adaptive and intervening in those aspects that are dysfunctional. The larger goal is to develop competence in coping more effectively with stressful life situations. The particular interventions are based on biopsychosocial assessment that takes into account the needs, capacities, and problems of each member, the family system, and the family's social context. The duration of therapy may be relatively short term or, when the problems in family functioning are numerous and severe, longer term treatment may be indicated.

Crisis Intervention

Crisis intervention is the most frequently mentioned form of practice with families in the health field. It is a process for actively influencing the psychosocial functioning of families as well as of individuals during an acute upset in the steady state or dynamic equilibrium of one or more family members. Sessions with the family may be held to enable its members to support and aid one of its members who is in a state of crisis or to work through the crisis when the family as a whole, or one of its subsystems, is in a crisis state. When a person is in a state of crisis, the steady state is upset as a consequence of exposure to a hazardous event. The state of crisis is temporary, characterized by confusion or other cognitive distortions and by emotional upset which immobilize the ego's problem-solving abilities. The reactions are responses to stress; they are seldom indications of long-term pathology: The major goals of crisis intervention are to reduce the immediate effects of stress and to help the patient and others who are affected by the crisis to mobilize their coping capacities in adaptive ways. The resolution of a crisis involves the family in searching for new ways to cope with the situation and adapt to it. First developed as a service to individuals, crisis intervention is now practiced with family units in which there is a collective crisis or when the crisis of one member is upsetting to others as well.

Discharge Planning and Placement

In the development of practice in the field of health, discharge planning has moved from being considered a chore that social workers do for physicians to one of the most crucial and complex forms of clinical social work. It is a process that almost always involves sessions with other members of the patient's family. The purpose is to facilitate optimum planning for the patient's welfare and the participation of other family members in the movement from medical setting to home or other residence. Both the patient and other members of the family need to be involved in the selection of a residence and prepared for the transition. In instances when return to the family is not feasible, family members still need to be involved with the patient in making decisions from among available alternatives to ensure a proper fit between the patient and the new network of relationships that he or she will enter. Entry into any new group, or return to one after an absence, is a source of anxiety for even physically well and socially effective persons. The appropriate model of social work practice is thus group deliberation and problem-solving.

Group Work with Families

Groups are used in medical settings to help families deal with the problems associated with the illness or disability of one of their members. The groups usually are composed of families or subsystems of families, such as parents or siblings. They are usually composed of families in which the patient members have a common medical condition, which tends toward the development of empathy and understanding among the members, and protection from social ostracism when diseases carry stigmata. In essence, a culture is created that frees family members to disclose and face, in the safety of the group, what they often could not face alone or discuss in the family; for example, the reality of the fatal illness of a young child. The advantages of such groups are that they preserve the wholeness of the family rather than fragmenting it, and, at the same time, they provide for cross-influences and cross-interactions from family to family which can be effective in opening rigid family structures and bringing new inputs of information, perceptions, and problem-solving mechanisms into each family. They stimulate dialogue between generations as well. It is the dynamic force of families helping families—the mutual aid process—that leads to changes in thinking, feeling, and acting in relation to the patient–family situation.

All of these forms of family services fit within the ecosystem perspective for family practice. They are based on biopsychosocial assessments of the family system, its subsystems, and its interactions with a network of other systems within the health organization and in the broader environment. They utilize problem-solving processes and attend to affect, cognition, and behavior—all three—in achieving the primary goals for which each form of family treatment is designed.

Generic Interventive Skills in Family Practice

In entering and serving a family system, the social worker operates from the basis of a theoretical orientation that determines, to some extent, the nature of his particular participation in family sessions. There are commonly recognized clusters of techniques or skills to be used selectively in accordance with the purpose and form of the treatment and of the family-situational context at a given time. The major categories concern the practitioner's relationship with the family and each member; types of predominantly verbal techniques; and skills in problem-solving and task achievement.

Relationship

The social worker initiates, develops, and sustains a positive working relationship with the family and each of its members. Through the relationship, members are free to disclose their feelings, thoughts, and reactions and to experience a sense of acceptance and respect. According to Perlman, "relationship is a catalyst, an enabling dynamism in the support, nurture, and freeing of people's energies and motivations toward problem-solving and the use of help. . . . It is a human being's feeling or sense of emotional bonding with another" (Perlman, 1979, pp. 2, 22). In work with families, from the beginning, the members are emotionally connected to each other—not just to the worker. The ideal client–family–worker relationship is characterized by nonpossessive warmth or acceptance, accurate empathy, genuineness, and respect. Considerable research provides evidence that these qualities positively influence continuance in treatment and practice outcomes. (Bednar & Lawlis, 1971; Carkhuff & Berenson, 1967; Lieberman, Yalom, & Miles, 1973; Rogers, 1975; Truax & Carkhuff, 1967; Truax & Mitchell, 1971).

The development of a working relationship with families is complex and intricate. Members come into a session with a web of experiences and feelings toward each other—a mixture of positive and negative ties. In developing a relationship with families, practitioners are relating to a natural group with a 24-hour daily life outside of the treatment session. They need to understand the web of relationships, taking into account the personalities of the members, the status and role structure of the family, the shared and diverse values and norms, and typical conflicts. Considerable self-awareness and discipline are required. Practitioners initially cannot help being more attracted to some members than to others. It is easy to feel more acceptance and empathy, for example, toward a child with leukemia than to an older brother who is "acting out" from feelings of rejection occasioned by the greater attention bestowed on his sibling. It is easy to label a mother as overprotective, an attitude that interferes with a worker's ability to reach out warmly and sincerely toward her. Self-awareness is needed—a recognition of one's true feelings toward each family member and a striving to overcome negative countertransference reactions. Then, with imaginative consideration of what it would be like to be in each person's situation, practitioners can move toward exemplifying the desired qualities. The major tasks of practitioners are to recognize the strengths and problems in relationships among the family members and work toward improving them. They relate to the flow of communication of emotions among the members—to the family as a unit. The intensity of the relationship between the practitioner and family varies with the purpose of service, the form and duration of treatment, and the particular characteristics and needs of the family members.

Clusters of Techniques

The literature on family practice is sparse in describing the particular interventions used to bring about change in members of the family and the functioning of the family unit in health settings. There is, however, sufficient material to indicate that there are generic procedures or skills in clinical practice that are applied to services for families. These skills are used differentially, according to the assessment and plan of treatment and the particular needs and characteristics of individuals and families.

The techniques of family practice may be characterized as follows: (These authors discuss at least some of these techniques as applied to family practice: Carlton, 1984; Freeman, 1981; Hartman & Laird, 1983; Hollis & Woods, 1981; Nelsen, 1983; Northen, 1982; Reid, 1985; Tolson & Reid, 1981.)

1. *Support or sustainment.* Both the patient and other members of the family need considerable support in order to cope with the issues occasioned by illness or disability. Support means to sustain or hold steady. The specific skills include sensitive listening, expressions of caring, realistic approval, encouragement, and identification and mobilization of social supports in the health care system and in the community. These supportive acts enhance motivation and instill hope.

2. *Ventilation or expression of feelings.* Family members need the opportunity to express and identify the feelings of positive hope, frustration, uncertainty, resentment, anxiety, and guilt that tend to accompany a serious illness or disability of one member. They need to know that it is normal to have these feelings and that they need not remain as obstacles to problem-solving processes. Recognizing and acknowledging the feelings tend to relieve anxiety and to free energy for dealing with them.

3. *Education.* Providing information essential to the family's understanding of the patient's condition, the course of the illness or disability, its potential consequences for the patient's and family's future, and available resources is an important ingredient in all forms of family practice. Educational activities are used not only with the family, but with hospital personnel and selected persons in the patient and family's social network.

4. *Exploration.* The elicitation of necessary information is basic to all forms of social work practice. It is a means for helping the family to examine a situation by bringing facts, feelings, and opinions into the discussion. Through exploratory techniques, the practitioner draws out descriptions of events and problems, possible explanations, and the interconnections between affect and cognition. It is used to open up closed lines of communication, to clarify obstacles to goal achievement, and to identify personal and environmental resources. It is an important step in the problem-solving process.

5. *Direction.* Practitioners use their authority, in the form of professional knowledge and expertise, in offering direction in the form of suggestion and advice. Based on knowledge of the situation, they give direction in order to further the achievement of goals if the information is used or to provide an important source of emotional and cognitive stimulation. The family members have the right to know the reasons for the recommendations made and to express their feelings about and objections to them, when indicated.

6. *Structuring.* Structure is used to create a special environment conducive to fostering effective communication among the participants and to maintain a focus on the tasks to be achieved. The policies, procedures, and

physical setting of the organization provide a framework for practice. Preparation for sessions, arranging space and materials, setting realistic rules or limits, and holding to a clear, yet flexible, focus are means of structuring.

7. *Clarification.* In work with families in health care, clarification is used primarily to develop shared understanding of goals, feelings, and issues relevant to the particular situation. Although sometimes classified as separate techniques, reframing, explanation, evaluative comments, and interpretation are forms of clarification (Reid, 1985). A major means used to clarify behavior and situations is what Hollis and Woods refer to as reflective discussion (Hollis & Woods, 1981). The intent is to change the emotional and conceptual meaning of behavior, relationships, events, or environmental situations. Clarifying comments and questions may be directed toward an individual, subsystem, or family unit within a family perspective that promotes common understanding.

8. *Confrontation.* This set of techniques is used to face one or more members of the family with the reality of an event, emotion, or behavior. Its purpose is to interrupt or reverse a course of thought or action; it disconfirms the acceptability of what is going on, challenging obstacles to the achievement of goals. In work with families, confrontive statements are often directed to the interactional patterns among the participants. Some empirical evidence points to the need to combine a confrontation with support and empathy, if it is to serve a therapeutic aim.

9. *Operant and respondent conditioning.* Conditioning techniques may be used to change the frequency or form of overt behaviors, through such means as positive or negative reinforcement, extinction, token economies, and systematic desensitization. The use of such procedures is based on a thorough assessment. (Gambrill, 1981, has presented the fullest account of behavioral modification with families to date.)

10. *Facilitation of process.* Comments, questions, and actions are used to move forward the interaction among family members. Specific techniques include comments about the functioning of the family in the sessions, encouraging each member to speak through verbal invitations or nonverbal glances, and searching for a common ground by connecting members' concerns. Practitioners guide the process to maximize the value of the family system, engaging the members in a group-centered process, usually exploratory or reflective in nature. They follow several lines of communication simultaneously—the needs and contributions of each member, the interplay between feelings and thoughts, and the patterns of communication. They use a group problem-solving process to help families to resolve conflicts and arrive at decisions that are satisfying to most members. They direct words and actions to different units of attention to achieve particular objectives—to one member, toward the interaction between two or more mem-

bers, or to the family as a whole. When a message is directed to one member, the need is to follow-up to ascertain its meaning to other members. Comments that are directed to the family as a whole or to the relation of one subsystem to the family tend to promote family cohesiveness, common understanding, and effective group problem-solving.

Activity-oriented Interventions

Family treatment, along with service to nonkinship groups, makes extensive use of procedures and skills other than verbal interchange. These activities are used within sessions or as assignments to be performed at home or in the community. Reid (1985) presents an extensive discussion of in-session, home, and environmental tasks; other writers who give considerable attention to such activities are Freeman (1981), Hartman and Laird (1983), Nelsen (1983), and Reid (1985). They are as varied as exercises in communication, role play, family sculpting, video taping and playback, brainstorming, relaxation, preparation of genograms, modeling constructive coping, performing tasks related to role performance, demonstration and rehearsal, and participation in mutually enjoyable activities. The underlying idea is that skills in problem-solving and social competence are developed through purposefully designed activities, along with discussion. There has been less use of such activities in health settings, however, than in family service and mental health clinics.

Professional Use of Self

Underlying the successful use of any procedure or technique is the professional use of self. Practitioners need to be clear about their own values; attitudes toward health, illness, and death; and toward particular types of patients and families. And they need to be clear about their rationale for selecting and using particular models and procedures. They need to take full responsibility for their practice: Self-awareness needs to be translated into expression of feeling and action. They need to be able to examine beliefs, attitudes, and assumptions; to review and evaluate their work; and to use feedback from patients, families, and colleagues. They need to engage in reciprocal learning and teaching and to use consultations from other social workers and members of other professions to further their knowledge and skills.

Interdisciplinary Collaboration

Social workers in the field of health do not operate autonomously, but collaboratively with members of other disciplines—medicine; nursing; physical, occupational, and respiratory therapy; and other specialities. The most frequent form of collaboration occurs when persons from different disciplines share information for assessment and make plans for treatment (Carlton, 1984). In team work, one type of collaboration, people work together in a planned way to provide services to particular patients and families. Much family practice involves the use of a team, for example in providing education or in co-therapy relationships. Successful collaboration requires that social workers be clear about their own profession—its values, purposes, knowledge, skills, and characteristics that differentiate it from other professions and contribute to the medical enterprise. It requires that they subscribe to a holistic approach that integrates biological, psychological, and social knowledge and interventions, with social workers particularly responsible in the psychosocial domain while recognizing the special expertise of colleagues in other disciplines. In collaboration, social workers essentially use their skills in assessment, planning, intervention, and evaluation in participating in a problem-solving process concerning the well-being of patients in their families.

The Social Work Process

Whether a single session, a short-term service, or long-term counseling or therapy, work proceeds from an initial phase, one or more intermediate phases, termination, and follow-up. The content and process will vary with the form of treatment within the generic tasks for the practitioner. In each phase, there are predominant patterns of members' behavior related to socio-emotional issues, typical patterns of family structure and intervention, and tasks to be achieved by the practitioner with the family. What happens in a particular phase influences what happens subsequently.

The Initial Phase

In health settings, the family is brought into the health care system through the illness or physical disability of one of its members. Family treatment thus begins with the first contact with the patient when the practitioner gains an understanding of the client–family–situation gestalt. One or more members of the family may have met the worker casually as they visit the patient. The worker then often reaches out to the family to offer assistance. In other instances, the family may be referred through a colleague who recognizes the need for social work services.

Both the patient and family members may participate eagerly in single session conferences that occur quite informally. But when family sessions are first suggested on a planned basis, the typical feelings are those of uncertainty, anxiety, guilt, hopelessness, and inadequacy to deal with the situation. The members tend to be ambivalent about the value of family sessions, having had little prior experience with psychosocial help in a medical setting. The practitioner is a stranger or newcomer to the family system which is autonomous, self-formed, and with a history of its own and at a particular stage in its development as a family. The family has its set of values and norms, affective ties, a structure of statuses and roles, patterns of communication, and procedures for coping with problems and making decisions. The practitioner needs to understand and respect the family's culture and distribution of roles, including authority aspects, and the ways that the structure and relationships influence the patient's medical condition and the changes that the patient's illness or disability make on family life.

The major tasks to be accomplished during the initial phase are several:

1. The practitioner needs to clarify the purpose of family sessions and the importance of the family's participation.
2. The practitioner assists the family to become oriented to the new helping situation, through offering information about the purpose of family practice, the respective roles of practitioner and members, and mutual expectations; and through responding with acceptance and empathy to the members' concerns and questions.
3. The worker engages the family in determining a purpose and more specific goals, which occurs as the members explore the meaning of the medical condition to them and search for the common ground that underlies varied responses. Often, the worker reframes the goals and problems of individuals into those in the family system.
4. As the family is learning about the services and identifying goals, the worker initiates a working relationship that shows a sincere interest in each member and the family's welfare and that indicates that family sessions can be safe, relatively nonthreatening, and respectful of the family's own desires, characteristics, and lifestyle.
5. In order to enhance motivation and ready the family for work on problems, the worker assists the members in identifying and recognizing some of their feelings about the medical condition and treatment, which tends to reduce anxiety and free the members to begin to work together toward agreed-upon goals.
6. The achievement of the foregoing tasks results in a working agreement

or contract, oral or written, that clarifies the goals and expectation and the service to be rendered.

The major sets of techniques used in this phase are support, exploratior information-giving, and, particularly, facilitation of communication amon family members.

Intermediate Phase

When a family has agreed upon one of more goals to be achieved, wha to expect of each other and of the practitioner, and learned to participat in the communication process, they enter into a work phase. The member generally reflect positive motivation toward the service, with intensificatio of personal involvement, a greater freedom to express their feelings an ideas, and to respect those of others; they tend to participate cooperativel and actively in treatment; conflicts are faced and means found for resolvin or managing them. When the identified patient faces negative changes i his or her condition, there is apt to be a return to the ambivalent feeling experienced in the initial phase, to which the worker must attend.

The major tasks to be achieved during this phase concern working to gether to achieve goals. These may include:

1. Acquiring and using knowledge and skills relevant to the define problems;
2. Identifying and using the members' own capacities and resources a well as outside resources relevant to individual and family needs;
3. Restructuring the distribution of role responsibilities in the family oc casioned by the medical condition of one member;
4. Making decisions concerning the family members' participation in the health care of the patient;
5. Identifying and solving problems in family relationships, communica tion, and structure for the benefit of all concerned.

All of the sets of techniques or professional skills are used in the intermedi ate phase of development, selected according to the nature of the problem and the family's readiness at a given time. Greater use is made of clarifi cation, interpretation, confrontation, and activity-oriented experiences ir reflective discussion and problem-solving. It is important to maintain a bal anced focus between content and process but with a focus on family com munication to enhance the therapeutic potential of family sessions and rela tionships among members.

Termination and Follow-up

Termination may be built in from the beginning of the service, as in sessions dealing primarily with education or crisis intervention. Often, termination takes place when discharge planning has been completed, but it is essential to follow-up with the family to determine the success or failure of the plan. The family group, of course, continues without the practitioner. If treatment has taken place over a number of sessions, the members have become accustomed to participating in working toward agreed-upon goals, have learned to handle the inevitable conflicts that occur from time to time, and now tend to support each other more often; they have learned to solve problems so that they may be expected to be better able to deal with new issues that arise in the course of family living. They may have deep feelings about separation from the practitioner who has helped them to cope with the difficult problems occasioned by the medical condition of one of its members.

The major tasks of this final phase are:

1. To express the combination of positive and negative feelings the members have about ending a particular kind of experience with each other and the practitioner;
2. To review and evaluate the family sessions and the progress that has been made;
3. To complete any important unfinished business;
4. To plan for next steps when the patient still has need for care or the family has special needs to be met; continuity of care must be assured.

Variations in Development

Within the common framework, variations are numerous, especially in relation to the nature and duration of the illness or disability, the purpose and structure of service, the particular needs and characteristics of each member, the family's own structure and ways of operating, and the broad social context that influences the ways that each family moves through the treatment process. Families with patients who are part of an intensive treatment program are influenced by the combination of treatments received by the patient and family at a given time. The members' engagement in the family treatment is affected by what is going on elsewhere. Throughout the process, therefore, collaborative work with colleagues is essential in order to assure consistency and continuity of services to the patient in this family.

7
Family Therapy

he practice of family therapy in the field of health has developed as has nowledge that members of the patient's family and broader social network re affected by the illness or disability and that they, in turn, influence the ature and course of the medical condition. The welfare of the patient and e family unit are inextricably interwoven.

Family therapy is not an entity; practitioners differ concerning the under'ing theory, the unit of service, criteria for assessment, definition of goals, nd the structure and focus of treatment (Hartman & Laird, 1983). Among ocial workers in the health field, however, there is a growing consensus at a biopsychosocial perspective is primary and that the goals, structure, nd focus of treatment will vary with the needs of the patient and family stem. Family therapy is appropriate when a family is unable to cope adapvely to the illness, injury, or disability of one of its members.

Purpose and Goals

he major purpose of family therapy in health care settings is to help the atient and family unit to cope with and adapt to changes brought about by e illness, disability, or hospitalization (Kempler, 1985). Other writers have ated the purpose in similar ways.

Within the general purpose, differential goals are set in collaboration with e family which are related to the nature of the disease or disability and assessment of the patient's and family unit's functioning (Goldenberg & oldenberg, 1980; Group for the Advancement of Psychiatry, 1970; Luthan & Kirschenbaum, 1974; Northen, 1982; Orcutt, 1977; Somers, 1965). ecific goals include helping the family members to:

1. Achieve better understanding of the illness or disability and its effect on the patient and family unit;
2. Reduce anxiety and enhance ability to understand and cope with complex feelings;
3. Accept the reality of the medical condition as it affects the patient and family unit;
4. Enable the patient to comply with the prescribed medical regimen,

assuming the diagnosis is accurate, treatment will do more good than harm, and there is informed consent (Rissman & Rissman, 1987);

5. Enhance positive relationships in the family such as capacity for empathy, mutual aid, and enjoyment of each other and reduce problems that impede the patient's progress, such as enmeshment, isolation, scapegoating, or misuse of power;
6. Resolve interpersonal conflicts among family members and conflicts between the family, the medical system and person or organizations in the community;
7. Enhance the process of communication among members and eliminate barriers to open and clear communication;
8. Facilitate accommodation to shifts in roles and alliances and enhance performance of the new or changed roles;
9. Enhance the family's ability to use a problem-solving process in making decisions that are satisfactory to those who are affected by them;
10. Facilitate the development or maintenance of relationships with significant people beyond the family unit;
11. Secure social supports and material resources to meet the identified needs of the patient or family unit.

The selected goals are the hoped-for outcomes or desires of the family to have something be better. They are most effective as motivators toward achievement if they relate to the results desired by the family that are directly related to the patient's and family's needs and problems relevant to the medical situation. They are most effective also if they are realistic in terms of the family's particular situation and are expressed in terms of positive changes in individual and family functioning. The use of family therapy in health settings does not imply the presence of malfunctioning in the family system prior to the onset of the illness or disability—although that could be the case for some families—but rather that the onset of the medical condition arouses stress or problematic family functioning in both the patient and the other members of the family that extends over a period of time.

In many cases, two or more goals predominate. For example, in working with a family with a deaf child, the goal was to improve communication focusing on the transmission and comprehension of information. But increased competence in communication may threaten the structure of the family, so a second goal was to improve pathological patterns of family structure (Mendelsohn & Rozek, 1983). In situations of noncompliance to the recommended medical regimen, several goals may be indicated such as securing support of family members, reducing psychosocial problems of patient or family members that block effective treatment, or changing dysfunctional patterns of family structure (Doherty & Baird, 1983).

Assessment

Essential to effective practice is an accurate assessment of the patient–family environment interaction. Assessment has been defined as "a differential, individualized, and accurate identification and evaluation of problems, people, and situations and of their interrelations, to serve as a sound basis for differential helping intervention" (Siporin, 1975, p.234). It goes beyond the identification of a problem to an appraisal of the interrelation among biological, psychological, and sociocultural factors and to positive motivations, interests, and capacities.

Process of Assessment

Assessment is a part of a continuous process of interaction between the social worker and the individual or family being served. It involves efforts to engage the family in an exploration of facts and an analysis and interpretation of the facts as they become evident. In accordance with social work values, the search for understanding is reciprocal among practitioner, patient, and family. Members of the family not only react to the practitioner's observations, but they actively contribute information and opinions and respond to the workers' statements about their needs. Their responses serve either as a correction or a reaffirmation of the worker's analysis of the situation at a given time. The preliminary assessment is a tentative one, to be elaborated and modified as the practitioner and family members interact in regard to one or more mutually agreed-upon goals (Northen, 1987).

Content of Assessment

The content of assessment in health care is essentially biopsychosocial in nature because that focus is congruent with the purpose of social work and knowledge about the interacting affects of a medical problem on patient and family. It, therefore, includes four levels of analysis: the patient, the family unit, the family's relationship with the medical care system, and other environmental factors (Berkman & Rehr, 1978; Christ, 1983; Coulton et al. 1982; Mailick, 1979; Northen, 1982, 1988). Comparative analyses of theoretical approaches to practice tend to conclude that, despite some differences, almost all theorists use ecosystem ideas for organizing the data of assessment (Freeman, 1981; Germain, 1979; Meyer 1976; Northen & Roberts, 1976; Turner, 1974). The trend is toward approaching the issue of assessment with full consideration of the multiple and complex transactions that occur among individuals, other people, and environments.

Much of the literature on social work with families in health settings contains presentations of similar content that is essential for making accurate assessments (Carlton, 1984; Christ, 1983; Falck, 1981; Freeman, 1981; Mailick, 1979). Clear guidelines assist practitioners to explore for pertinent data and select appropriate means for obtaining the desired information. Questions that are often appropriate include:

1. Who is the patient in terms of age, gender, occupation, or grade in school, ethnicity, race, stage of development in the life cycle, and the developmental level achieved by the patient?
2. What is the patient's illness or disability—its etiology; onset; whether acute, chronic, or terminal; limitations placed on the patient's physical functioning; its visibility; and attitudes of society toward it?
3. What is the impact of the medical condition on the patient's psychosocial functioning?
4. How do cultural factors influence the patient's and family's response to medical care—ethnic values, religious beliefs, myths, traditions, holidays, and food preferences?
5. How does the medical condition influence the patient's performance of roles in the systems to which he belongs?
6. What is the mental status of the patient? Are there problems in mental and emotional functioning that impede understanding and participation in decision making? Are there earlier traumatic experiences that are related to the current stress?
7. To what extent is the patient motivated to use the help of the practitioner or other resources? What indications are there of positive motivation; and what are the nature of resistances?
8. What are the strengths and abilities that can be supported and developed further?
9. In what ways does the health care system create stress for the patient?
10. What are the goals of the patient in terms of hoped-for outcomes and future plans?

The family is a system in operation that has been disrupted by the introduction of an extraneous force—the illness, injury, or disability of one of its members to which the system must react. Since the purpose of family therapy is to resolve problems in the functioning or the family or between the family and its environment, an accurate assessment of the family is crucial for successful treatment. Although family therapists differ to some extent on the emphasis to be given to certain aspects of family functioning, there is consensus that there is a body of knowledge about the family as a system. The questions to be used to guide the practitioner in evaluating the functioning of families include:

1. What goals do members of the family share, and which ones are not shared?
2. What are the strengths and difficulties in the patterns, quality, and depth of relationships among the members? Consider affective ties, sensitivity to each other's needs, use of power, inclusion and exclusion of which members. How does the illness or disability influence marital, sibling and parent–child relationships?
3. What is the structure and composition of the family? Have there been recent changes such as losses or additions of new members?
4. How does the current and intergenerational family history influence the present situation, particularly its history of illness, disability, and deaths?
5. To what extent is the family flexible and adaptable enough to maintain a dynamic steady state? Which members show the greatest capacity to cope with change, and which ones are least able?
6. How effective or dysfunctional are the patterns of communication, including the extent to which the boundary is open or closed to new information, the presence of double binds, language problems, secrets, clarity of messages, accuracy of perceptions?
7. What are the major subsystems and alliances? How does the family handle the gaps in its roles occasioned by the illness or disability?
8. Who makes what kinds of decisions that affect varied members, what processes are used, and how do these influence the achievement of individual and family goals? Are all members who are capable of participating involved in making decisions that will affect them?
9. What major conflicts occur, around what issues, and what are the means used to solve them?
10. What are the sociocultural influences on the family and its interchange within the larger community as they affect the family?
11. What is the degree of cohesion of the family? How does the family support or interfere with meeting members' needs for dependence–independence–interdependence? How much togetherness and separateness do members want and need? Does the family assure both individual identity (differentiation) and family group identity, with room for difference as well as likeness?

The understanding of the patient-family-situation configuration that is sought cannot encompass all aspects of the individual's or family's functioning. In accordance with the value of the right to privacy and self-determination, the exploration should be limited to the family's informed consent and what is essential for achieving agreed-upon goals. But helpful treatment cannot be given unless the worker has adequate understanding of the nature, interrelated causative factors, and the capacities of family members for coping with the problematic situation. The initial assessment will be greatly enriched as the practitioner observes the members as they participate in family sessions. There is evidence from research (Couch, 1969) that family sessions reveal hidden strengths and positive mutual bonds among members that can become essential therapeutic aids. They illuminate the way in which family members interact with pathological destructiveness, restrictiveness, and mutual pain. They clarify the life situation of the family; provide opportunities for the practitioner to observe the impact of treatment on the patient and other members of the family; and make possible greater speed and accuracy in assessment. An example is taken from a family record presented by Kempler (1985): The T.s are a family consisting of two parents, identical twin boys, age 8, and a girl, age 5.

> Jimmy, one of the twins, had leukemia, was in remission for 1-1/2 years, and had fairly recently had his chemotherapy terminated because he was doing so well. Referral was made to the psychiatry department, not for Jimmy but for his twin brother, Bobby, who was exhibiting learning and behavior problems in school. In the initial interview with the parents alone, it emerged that the children had been told almost nothing about Jimmy's illness, that they never asked questions about it, and that this was the way the parents wanted it to be. . . . Further, the parents worried that discussing Jimmy's illness would unnecessarily arouse anxiety and upset the children. When a family session was scheduled, a striking scene occurred. All three children were totally absorbed in play with the medical toys provided, repeatedly taking each other's temperature and listening to their own and each other's hearts with the stethoscope. This play culminated with Bobby and his sister, Judy, constructing a tomb-like structure with building blocks, chanting that Jimmy was dead and buried in his grave.

Direct observation of the family dramatically revealed information about Judy's and Bobby's feelings about Jimmy's health status and their own health and the distortions in their perceptions of Jimmy's illness. The use of carefully selected play materials provided a means of communicating the feelings that could not be expressed verbally and made it possible for the children to play out the fearful feelings and thoughts about tabooed subjects so they could begin to deal with the reality of the event (Northen, 1988). The parents learned that avoiding the issue of Jimmy's health was anxiety-provoking for the children, rather than protective of them. Observing the children's play shed light on the patterns of interaction among family members and led to a shift in those patterns so that Bobby's symptoms subsided following changes in the parent–child relationship.

Analysis of the Data

When pertinent information has been obtained, the actual assessment consists of the analysis of the individual–family–environment constellation. The purpose is to identify the most critical features and define their interrelationships. The assessment is the practitioner's professional opinion about the facts and their meaning. Perlman (1970) and Somers (1976) have referred to this process as one of problem-solving, done through a process of reflective thinking. Lewis (1982) refers to it as a logical process, which also incorporates intuitive insights. Realistic appraisal involves judgments about what can be changed, supported, or strengthened in the family and its environment. It involves explanations concerning how the situation has come to be the way it is. The worker draws inferences from the information and relates these judgments to the service that can be given.

Explanations, according to Lewis (1982), are most useful when they account for all the known facts and suggest others not previously identified. The explanations that are arrived at through logical thinking are applicable only to a particular case. For example, not everyone who has a diagnosis of cancer exhibits the same responses. The assessment explains how a particular individual or family responds to this event. Strengths as well as difficulties are located. Such an approach tends to deemphasize stereotyping of patients and families by establishing the unique as well as the common responses to factors that contribute to a particular condition.

Accurate assessment requires the ability to consider alternative explanations of difficulties from which a choice is made. For example, in the work of Minuchin and his associates (1975, 1978) with families of children with psychosomatic illnesses, an explanation of causation was developed. On the basis of study and research, they concluded that five characteristics of family interaction were prevalent—enmeshment, overprotection, rigidity, lack of conflict resolution, and involvement of the sick child in parental conflict. These patterns, combined with vulnerability of the child to the illness and somatic expressions of distress, cause children to develop an illness or exacerbate an existing one. Further research may suggest alternative explanations. There is need to determine which alternative is most probable. The product of the analysis is a formulation that integrates the information and draws conclusions about the interrelated factors that contribute to the problematic situation, leading to decisions about intervention.

Planning

Before the first session with a family, considerable planning is essential for a successful outcome. According to Siporin (1975 p. 98), planning is "a deliberate rational process that involves the choice of actions that are calculated to achieve specific objectives at some future time." It is a decision-making process through which the means for achieving the goals are determined. Although planning is an ongoing process, certain decisions need to be made before or after the first session with a family.

Sanction

The health care organization is a complex network of people in interlocking social systems, such as boards of directors, administrators, clerical and paraprofessional personnel, and professional practitioners from medicine and the allied health professions. Within the organization, certain people have the authority to define the services to be given and the conditions under which they are given. The organization sanctions certain forms of practice and has policies concerning such matters as eligibility requirements, payment of services, record-keeping, and resources available. Its structure, policies, and procedures influence matters of access, continuity, equity, and quality of service. Not all health settings have as yet sanctioned the use of family therapy. In order for the service to be sanctioned, key personnel need to be clear about the purpose of family therapy, the means used to achieve the purpose, and ways in which the therapy contributes to the basic mission of the organization. Unless a tentative plan to offer family treatment is carefully made and discussed with appropriate persons, there will be little chance of success. If plans are not made in the best interests of all concerned, the organization does not receive the full benefit of social work expertise.

Offering Service

In health settings, the recommendation to involve a family or some of its members in therapy is made in several ways. Social workers have numerous contacts with patients for purposes of offering a service, making an assessment, or providing help with the patient's concerns. In the course of meeting with the patient, practitioners may learn about problems in the patient's family situation; they may recognize that the seriousness of the patient's condition places him or her at risk which is bound to have repercussions for the family; or the patient may have an illness with strong psychosomatic components that suggests the possibility of malfunctioning in the family's structure that contributes to the illness. In such cases, the practitioner may suggest a family conference through which means it can be ascertained whether or not family therapy is indicated. In other situations, physicians may refer families, in which case the social worker needs to follow through to determine the family's understanding of the referral and its willingness to accept therapy.

Knowledge of which families are best served through family therapy is an important issue, but one about which evidence is inadequate, partially because the practice of family therapy is relatively recent. Using an open systems model, Minuchin and colleagues report success in work with families in which a child is the identified patient with asthma, diabetes, abdominal pain, or anorexia nervosa (Minuchin et al., 1975). Gurman and Kniskern (1981, p. 750) report that structured family therapy is "the most empirically supported psychotherapy approach of any sort for these conditions." Family therapy has also been used successfully with families of adult patients with chronic pain (Boll, DuVall, & Mercuri, 1983). It must be emphasized that family therapy is not a substitute for, but a supplement to, medical treatment.

Selection of Participants

When family therapy is recommended and accepted by at least some family members, one of the most important decisions concerns which family members are to be involved. Usually, the practitioner strives to interest all members of the family in the endeavor, except perhaps very young children. When all of the members attend the first session, they come to sense that each person is important to the task of learning how to work together in dealing with the difficulties relevant to the patient's illness or disability. Since the medical condition of one member often occasions shifts in the roles, alliances, communication patterns, and affective relationships with the patient, the presence of each member can hasten the problem-solving process. The patient, being a member of the family even when hospitalized, needs to be included except when certain circumstances make attendance impossible. In reality, it is not always possible to get all members of the family to attend, so the usual plan is to begin with whatever members can be mobilized.

Structure of Service

Services are offered for various periods of time, depending upon many circumstances. The duration should be related to the goals to be worked toward, the nature and severity of the illness or disability, and the particular needs and capacities of the family members. Some short-term therapy may be at least as effective as long-term treatment of several months or more. Anticipation of time limits may enhance hope that positive outcomes will occur and encourage some members to participate who would be unwilling to commit themselves to an indefinite and prolonged period of time. Because there is some evidence of the effectiveness of well-planned and well-carried out short-term services, there should-be compelling reasons for recommending long-term help (Reid, 1985, p.82).

Frequency, length, and time of sessions are factors to be considered in developing plans for work with families. These issues are dependent to some extent on length of hospital stay or duration of the illness or disability. The length of sessions should be consonant with the capacities of members for sustained work on family matters. Most frequently, sessions last for an hour which allows time for opening comments, a period of work, and a brief summary of what has been accomplished during the session. The time of day and the day of the week that a family meets will influence which members will be able to attend. The schedule of activities for the patient in the hospital or clinic and the school or work schedules of family members need to be considered. Time of meeting and, therefore, working hours of practitioners need to be adapted to the family's situation if they are to meet needs effectively. Accessibility of service should be a primary principle of practice.

The success of family sessions is influenced by the physical and social environment in which the family meets (Hartford, 1971; Seabury, 1971). The adequacy and atmosphere of the room in which the family meets has an important impact on the development of relationships and the ease of communication. Some arrangements of space tend to keep people apart, such as chairs in rows or along walls. Other arrangements draw people together, such as chairs in circles or around a table. A constant location is desirable to provide a sense of continuity for the family. The important point is that practitioners should create and maintain a physical atmosphere that is consistent, supportive, and trustworthy.

Rules that will govern the members' participation in family sessions need to be considered. In addition to organizational policies and procedures, there may be rules about such matters as attendance, smoking or drinking, and use of supplies. Members should, of course, be informed about these rules and the reasons for them and have a right to object to them. Once accepted, they become a part of the contract between the worker and the family. Rules should be established only when they are clearly related to the situation, rather than based on the arbitrary use of power.

Social Work Intervention

The selection of particular procedures and techniques of treatment are influenced by the nature of the illness or disability, the environmental context, the adequacy of individual and family functioning, and the relationships and interactions among family members at a given time. It is the interchange among family members as they learn to help each other that brings about change, with the assistance of the practitioner. The primary task of the social worker is to facilitate the process among the members: "process may be viewed in the dynamic interaction of all the phenomenological aspects of the therapy, encompassing all overt as well as covert interactional expressions of feelings, thoughts, and actions occurring over time" (Group for the Advancement of Psychiatry, 1982). The therapy process occurs over a brief or extended time period. The family's major patterns of behavior are different in the beginning sessions than later and the practitioner's interventions vary accordingly.

The Initial Phase

The social worker often meets a shaky, anxious family in which some of the members doubt that they want to be present. The suggestion of a gathering of the family with a social worker conveys the message that the problems are not with the patient alone, but are mutually shared ones.

If the family came to the session through referral from a physician, the ideal is that physicians make a unique contribution "when they help patients view their somatic problems in a broader biopsychosocial context. Without this agreement on the larger context of the presenting problem, assessment will be sterile, referral be fruitless, and the offer of treatment will be rejected" (Doherty & Baird, 1983, p. 64). But many physicians do not give sufficient time to the referral process, or the patient may not understand the physician's concern and advice. When the family comes to the session through the suggestion of the social worker who has identified the need for the patient to be helped within the family, the worker must give adequate attention to the patient to help him accept the idea and plan how the other family members are to be approached to secure their participation. Because they need to manage their lives adequately under the stress of a medical condition, the family members may suffer from feelings of shame, guilt, fear of self-exposure, or confusion about the purpose and focus of the meetings.

The primary responsibility of social workers during the initial phase is to help the family members to learn to work together so that they can cope more effectively with the difficulties they face that are related to the illness or disability of one member. In working toward this objective, practitioners focus on developing an initial therapeutic relationship, responding to reactions to the medical condition, orienting members to the nature of the service, providing support, and clarifying the problems of individuals and the family unit. Their major roles are to facilitate the family process and engage members in problem-solving. At the same time, they acquire an increased understanding of the family.

Social workers use their understanding of the meaning of the new experience to the members of the family to develop an initial working relationship that will sustain the members through the period of uncertainty and anxiety and serve as a catalyst for improving the relationships among members. In each new situation, a person faces a renewal of the basic conflict of trust versus distrust and the need for synthesizing these polarities (Erikson, 1963). Achievement of trust is relatively easy or hard, depending upon the extent to which people have previously developed a basic sense of trust. The extent to which family members have achieved a basic sense of trust in each other and in the professional helper influences the amount and duration of uncertainty and anxiety that are typical of entry into new situations. Each new experience offers some occasion for mistrust until the unknown becomes familiar. Until members of the family can come to trust the worker and the situation, they cannot participate effectively in a process of helping each other.

Social workers convey trust by modeling, through their own attitudes and behavior, the qualities of acceptance or warmth, empathy, and genuineness, which are components of a professional relationship. They help members to relate to each other in a different way by exhibiting small courtesies that indicate interest in the family's comfort and the members' contributions to the family discussion. They listen sensitively to the members and respond to members' messages with interest and support. They convey an interest in helping members to achieve their goals. In many small ways, they demonstrate that these meetings will be safe and nonthreatening (Freeman, 1981; Northen, 1982; Power & Dell Orto, 1980; Perlman, 1979; Shulman, 1979; Truax & Carkhuff, 1967; Truax & Mitchell, 1971).

In order to develop a relationship characterized by empathy, acceptance, and genuineness, practitioners need to be able to recognize and understand some of their own feelings. Working with families having a member with a serious illness or disability may engender powerful emotions in practitioners, requiring that they cope with unresolved personal issues from the past concerning medical conditions. Unresolved issues may lead to countertransference: workers may overidentify with the family or one of its members, especially a child with a severe chronic illness, be rigid about the structure of sessions, avoid discussion of painful subjects, set unreasonable expectations for change, or support the family's negative views of medical personnel (Piersma, 1985; Wellisch, 1981).

Family members have different emotional reactions to the medical condition and attach different meanings to it. Social workers use the procedure of exploration to uncover and support ventilation of feelings so as to reduce anxiety and stress. They accept these expressions of emotions as natural and valid. They express understanding of the members' uncertainty and ambivalence. As feelings are expressed, they meet them with a feeling response rather than an intellectual one. The principle is to respond to a feeling with a feeling response. Certain interventions facilitate the expression of feelings; others inhibit such expression. One effective technique is to show genuine interest in a member through giving special attention or recognition. Through attending, workers communicate that they are taking in the uniqueness of a person and showing respect for that person. Another type of comment expresses acceptance of feelings, particularly those that convey doubt, hostility, or distrust. A restatement of the feelings expressed by members can be effective if the worker puts into words the feelings she senses the members are trying to express or restates them in a way they are named and hence recognized. To bring a feeling into the common ground of the family's experience, workers may test with the family whether or not the acknowledged feeling is shared by others. An important skill is to be able to respond to the underlying meaning of the members' comments, requests, or challenges. Within a climate that supports the expression of feelings, practitioners try not to activate feelings that cannot be dealt with during the session. They may make a mental note of sensitive areas but hold them for discussion until the individual or family is ready to face them. If practitioners really desire to be helpful to the members and are sensitive to their feelings, their responses are likely to be appropriate. Whether or not the members can yet trust workers responses, they come to feel the acceptance and understanding and begin to grasp what is expected of them.

Orientation

If the members are to make optimum use of the family sessions, they need a common understanding of the situation in which they are becoming involved. They become oriented to the therapy through receiving and seeking information from the practitioner and finding out what they have in common. They need to understand the roles of practitioner and family member, the structure of the service, what is expected of them in the way of attendance, participation, openness, rules, and confidentiality. Workers review the general purpose of the sessions and seek responses to the presentation; responding to questions and comments and giving all members an opportunity to express their ideas about the family meetings. They emphasize that their major role is to facilitate the interactions among members so they become able to help each other.

During the course of early sessions, practitioners convey, in many verbal and nonverbal ways, the norms that facilitate the progress of the family in achieving their desired goals. These norms include the following: (1) mutual support and mutual aid; (2) flexibility in trying out new tasks and adapting old ones; (3) the idea that differences are normal and acceptable, that members can learn from them, and that conflict can be constructive; (4) participation is expected, according to each member's developmental level and capacity; (5) members should take on increasing responsibility for the family's functioning as time goes on, participating in decision making and evaluation processes; (6) procedural rules and policies represent desirable conditions, based on values, through which family therapy can enhance the functioning of the family unit.

Support

If social workers are to contribute to the family's achievement of its goals, they need to give the members sufficient support so that gradually the major support will come from the family itself. Supportive techniques are used to enhance self-esteem and security and encourage the family's efforts to cope with new or difficult situations. What is supported are the strengths and constructive defenses of the members (Frey, 1962; Schmidl, 1950; Selby, 1956, 1979). In systems terms, the steady state needs to be maintained in reasonable balance so that stress is not beyond the members' coping capacities.

The relationship between the practitioner and the family is itself a means through which the members are supported in their efforts to work on family problems. Mutual support is encouraged by the worker's expressions of caring and empathy. Members become supportive of each other as they feel security and trust in the worker and gradually integrate some of the worker's patterns of supportive behavior into their own personalities. In addition to relationships, the primary skills involved in support are the appropriate use of the techniques of attending, encouragement and realistic reassurance, expectation setting, and the use of environmental resources.

Problem Clarification

The purpose of family therapy needs to become explicit if the sessions are to be of optimum benefit to the participants. Practitioners have responsibility to help the members to ascertain what they hope to gain from the therapy in terms of better functioning of the family unit. They communicate what they know about what the family was told about the reason family treatment was suggested, and they explore the responses of each member to that idea. They emphasize, through the questions they ask and comments they make, that no member is to blame for the difficulties, and that each one has something to contribute to bettering the family's functioning. Since it is to be expected that each member will initially define the concern differently, the workers search for the common ground that ties the concerns of one with those of others. From a therapeutic standpoint, the process of goal formulation makes the members aware of the direction in which they want to move.

When asked about what is happening in the family since the patient's illness or disability occurred, most members recognize the connection between the medical condition and changes in the family and are willing to talk about how the illness or disability has affected them (Jaffe, 1978). At times, it is helpful to reframe the family's definition of the problem in a way that clarifies its family relatedness and how it requires new forms of collaborative efforts. An example is of a family consisting of a mother, Mrs. R., Juanita, age 17, and Ramon, age 15, with a recent diagnosis of diabetes. Mrs. R. complained that the problem was Ramon's unwillingness to follow the doctor's orders. Juanita supported her mother, complaining that Ramon was making life miserable for all of them. When the practitioner asked for Ramon's view of the difficulty, he said he was having a hard enough time, without being picked on all the time by his mother and sister, expressing considerable anger at them. Mrs. R. responded with the statement that he would not be picked on if he would do what he was supposed to do. The worker reframed the problem by suggesting that, although Ramon needs to learn to take responsibility for following the medical advice, perhaps the mother and sister can support and help him while he learns to do these things for himself. Reframing allows members to perceive their circumstances in a different and often more constructive light (Freeman, 1981; Reid, 1985).

Facilitation of Family Process

A major task for the social worker in the initial phase is to set in motion a system of communication that involves all members in working toward the agreed-upon goals. Often, other members of the family are hesitant to talk directly with the patient about anything connected with the medical condition. The worker serves as a model, using messages that are clear and congruent, to open up communication between the patient and other members. Members are encouraged to present their ideas, to listen to each other, to ask for clarification, and to respond to each other. As a facilitator, the practitioner helps the family to appreciate the resources that various members bring to the task.

The outcome of the first session or sessions is a working agreement or contract that clarifies the goals toward which members will work together, the expectations that members have for the worker and for each other, the structure of the service, and the major issues to be addressed. Such an agreement provides the members with a sense of involvement and signifies mutual commitment and responsibility. It provides a basis for periodic review of progress (Maluccio & Marlow, 1972; Northen, 1982; 1988; Reid, 1985; Siporin, 1975). When members have had a satisfying experience in the first session, they leave with a sense of hope that family life will be better: Hope is, in turn, a positive motivating force.

The Core Phase

As family treatment moves into the core or work phase, the members recognize that, by working together, both individual and family unit needs are met. In helping the family to work toward achieving its goals, the social worker simultaneously pays attention to the development of the family and to the achievement of new understandings and tasks. Families learn to cope more effectively with their problems in one or more ways: (1) increased understanding of the medical situation and its effects on the family; (2) developing skills to enhance role performance and problem-solving capacities; (3) modifying dysfunctional patterns of relationships and interactions; and (4) utilizing resources and removing environmental obstacles. Which of these issues predominates in discussions and tasks varies with the assessment of each individual and the family unit. During this phase, the practitioner continues to further develop and sustain relationships, provide support, and explore situations to secure more information useful to the members and to the practitioner.

Understanding the Medical Situation

A major focus of the core phase of treatment is to increase common understanding of the medical situation and its meaning for individual and family function (Henry, Knippa, & Golden, 1985; Power & Dell Orto, 1980). To help the family, the practitioner provides accurate information about the illness or disability and its implications for social living, often using a cotherapist or physician to present this material. It is essential, however, to focus on more than the medical problems: equally important is recognition of and emphasis on the remaining capacities of the patient and potential sources of support and healing.

Social workers explore with each member of the family what the medical situation means to him or her and seeks to identify the differences and similarities among the members. They encourage ventilation of emotional reactions, acceptance of them, and ability to manage them. They provide support for members in understanding and coping with their reactions. In clarifying misunderstandings, they may recognize and need to confront denial and other maladaptive defenses that impede understanding, based on an assessment of a family members' readiness to use this information. It needs to be emphasized that there need not be total acceptance of the limitations of the disability or the terminal nature of the illness (Hirschwald, 1982; Shellhase & Shellhase, 1972). The patient must learn to live despite or with the disability and tends not to lose hope that one day he will be better: The family may also be buoyed by such hope. But, severely unrealistic distortions of perceptions and expectations may be modified through correct information and relief of anxiety.

The importance of helping families toward better understanding of the medical situation is illustrated in an example offered by Baptiste (1983) concerning work with families who have experienced the sudden death of an infant. These family members usually have insufficient and inaccurate information about the death. Ignorance, myths, and stereotypes compound and intensify stress. The Sudden Infant Death syndrome (SIDS) seems incomprehensible owing to its suddenness, mysteriousness, and lack of explanations for the event. Parents are bound to feel some responsibility for the death, with feelings of guilt, unvented anger, and sense of inadequacy as parents. They need to become able to realize that they are not responsible for the death; that (with occasional exceptions) they are adequate as parents; that they still can love each other; and that it is highly unlikely that surviving children will die of SIDS. They need to learn to support and reassure each other about the facts of the illness and their part in it. To achieve these outcomes, accurate information is necessary, but insufficient. Practitioners help such families through offering support, encouraging ventilation and understanding of the complex emotions, and helping the family through the mourning process. Understanding is more than cognitive: Affect and problem-solving actions are also involved. Understanding may lead to other adaptive ways of coping with changes in social living occasioned by a medical event.

Development of Skills

Families of patients often need professional help to develop skills that are essential to the resolution of problems connected with the illness or disability. These include skills in communication, problem-solving, and the performance of social roles.

Instrumental to increasing the family's ability to cope with the consequences of the illness or disability is open communication among members and between the family and health care personnel, as repeatedly indicated in the literature (Binger et al., 1969; Cohen, Dizenhuz & Winget 1977; Goldenberg & Goldenberg, 1980; Hollingsworth & Pasnau, 1977; Orcutt, 1977; Oakley & Patterson, 1971; McCollum & Gibson, 1970; Reid, 1985; Satir, 1964; Taksa, 1982). The problems in communication among family members are numerous: lack of common experiences on which to build understanding, the use of double bind messages in which there is a discrepancy between verbal messages or between tone of voice or posture and words, the need to placate others by pretending to agree, blaming others, being exceptionally reasonable, talking about irrelevant topics. On the other hand, in congruent communication, the words relate to the reality of the situation, and the affect is consonant with the words: There is usually little difficulty in understanding the message (Satir, Stokowich, & Taschman, 1975).

Distorted, unclear, and disqualifying messages tend to generate confusion, tension, distance, and even alienation. In health situations, barriers to communication often stem from a desire to protect the patient or others from hurt or sadness or out of accumulated negative feelings toward one or more members of the family (Orcutt, 1977). Closure of communication may signify avoidance as a mode of coping with difficult situations. For example, the patient usually knows or at least suspects the diagnosis. Other family members may also know it but attempt to protect the patient from the truth. The truth is masked with silence, unrelated activity, or cheerful talk that avoids confrontation with reality. When patients seem to be approaching death, family members too often retreat into what has been termed the "conspiracy of silence," isolating themselves from the patient and each other (Hollingsworth & Pasnau, 1977). Even practitioners may combat their own feelings of helplessness by contributing to the avoidance of dealing with the issue.

In efforts to open up communication among family members concerning the diagnosis, course, and prognosis of a severe illness of a child, conflict in goals may occur (Taksa, 1982). Practitioners may want to help the child to express concerns about what is happening and to further the expression of feelings and reactions between parents and with other children. Parents, on the other hand, may desire to protect each other and the children from the reality of the medical situation. In such instances, practitioners need to be strongly supportive of the parents, recognizing that it is natural for them to think that they are protecting the child and family members from further hurt by avoiding discussion, and suggesting that common understanding of the medical situation and its impact on each member of the family can relieve some of the stress that exists.

Social workers, in helping families to communicate more effectively, use varied techniques of treatment. By modeling acceptance, empathy, and genuineness, family members may become more accepting of each other's feelings, fears, and ideas. By listening with attentiveness to their concerns, members may imitate that behavior. Practitioners encourage ventilation of feelings and concerns and invite other members to respond. They identify and call the family's attention to maladaptive patterns of communication, clarifying the meaning of such patterns. They explore with the members their fears of self-disclosure and encourage their efforts to express themselves more freely. To promote learning of skills in communication, they may use action-oriented experiences such as listening games, rehearsal, and role-playing (Nelsen, 1983; Northen, 1988; Reid, 1985).

Problem-solving

Families are often faced with making crucial decisions about the patient's care and treatment or about the distribution of responsibilities for managing daily tasks. The decisions that patients must make, often with the help and support of members of their families, are serious ones, such as whether or not to have elective surgery, remain on dialysis or accept a kidney transplant, have an abortion, seek a consultation from other physicians, inform medical personnel about dissatisfaction with service without negative consequences, plan for family members' participation in caring for a severely disabled person at home, or resolve a family conflict that interferes with the patient's progress toward recovery.

The social worker's emphasis is on the use of a problem-solving process in arriving at and implementing decisions. John Dewey's formulation of problem-solving is widely used in practice (Dewey, 1910). This formulation recognizes that, while there is a logical and rational way for coping with difficulties, emotions influence cognitive processes. Dewey's steps in the problem-solving process are: (1) recognizing the difficulty, (2) defining the problems and goals, (3) considering alternative proposals, (4) choosing one from among the alternatives, (5) planning a course of action for implementing the decision, and (6) carrying out the plan and evaluating the results. A successful experience with solving a particular problem should lead to enhanced ability to cope effectively with other problems.

Essential to problem-solving is the ability to communicate effectively, so practitioners need to help members with their difficulties in sending and receiving clear messages. They lead members through each step of the process and offer support to all members in sharing their ideas, feelings, and proposals. They assist the members to maintain a focus on the reality of their situations so that the resulting decisions are appropriate to the agreed-upon goals and available resources. They use techniques of support, exploration, education, and clarification in order to help the members to maintain focus and deal with the interrelationship among feelings, attitudes, and thought processes that influence decision making.

Competence in Roles

A person is part of a family, having a particular role in it. The role sets of members provide a connectedness between individuals and the family unit. Families have an organization of roles, usually described as those of mother–father, wife–husband, sibling by gender and age, grandparents and other relatives. Within these formal roles, however, the patterns of behavior vary with the family's values, ethnic background, size and composition, economic status, and the physical, psychological, and social characteristics of the members.

It is through the way that roles are assigned that families perform their major functions, including provision of material resources essential to social living, love and affection, companionship, support, socialization, transmission of values, and individual and group identity.

The pattern of roles is disturbed when one or more members are sick or disabled, necessitating shifts in responsibilities connected with particular roles. While patients may lose numerous roles in the family and community, they also must learn the pattern of behaviors expected of the "sick role," which family members need to understand and help the patient to perform. Problems in the family may be the product of temporary or permanent loss of roles caused by the disabled person or the aggravation of dysfunctional role behaviors that preceded the illness or disability. Some families with a flexible role structure will be able to make shifts in roles fairly easily; others will need considerable help when roles have become rigid or when the medical condition is severe. Hospitalization, medical regimens, or death of one member cut off meaningful roles and put too much pressure on the remaining members. To become comfortable and competent with the changes expected of family members requires a "repertoire of skills, knowledge, and qualities that enable each person to interact effectively" (Maluccio, 1979) in the family and wider environment. Patients, to the extent possible, must be included in the discussion, with recognition of what they can still contribute to the family.

Social workers use various sets of techniques, depending upon the nature and severity of the problems in role functioning. In addition to strong doses of support, they explore what has happened in the family since a member became ill or disabled, with particular reference to how family members are coping with the loss of tasks previously performed by the patient. When the nature of the problems are identified, they may engage the family in making decisions about what changes can be made by whom, using the problem-solving process. They may need to help the members work through obstacles that impede the successful performance of the tasks required by shifts in role expectations. One way of doing this is through the use of action-oriented learning by working on specific tasks as part of the content of family sessions or at home, followed by discussion (Reid, 1985). Family members may need to be informed about available health and welfare resources and learn how to use them. As they achieve success in carrying out tasks, their sense of competence and confidence may increase as may family cohesion which, in turn, may enhance capacity to cope with other problems.

Adaptation to changes in roles is not a simple matter. An example of a child with diabetes is given by Freeman (1981) who describes the issues concerning which family members will be responsible for each part of the medical regimen essential to keeping the diabetes under control. If, for example, the mother takes almost full responsibility, a close relationship will develop between mother and sick child, and other members may feel excluded or rejected. The important issue is how the health problem has affected the roles of each member and the network of relationships in the family.

Modifying Patterns of Relationships

One of the major tasks of practitioners in the core phase of family therapy is to enable the members to identify, clarify, and modify patterns of relationships which are obstacles to the family's successful coping with the medical situation (Bateman, 1965; Freeman, 1981; Hartman & Laird, 1983; Henry, Knippa, & Golden, 1985; Reid, 1985). Freeman, particularly, describes the components of the family as an emotional system, giving considerable attention to each of the dynamic forces involved.

The major patterns of relationships that develop in families have tremendous effects on the satisfactions of the member and the family's capacity for coping with stress. These include:

1. *Emotional involvement or affective ties.* (Freeman, 1981; Reid, 1985; Northen, 1982). The degree of emotional connectedness among members is evidenced by their ability to empathize with and support others; the amount of love and affection and how these feelings are shown; the intimacy, closeness, or distance exhibited among members, including enmeshment, disengagement, differentiation, fusion; emotional reactions to the

way power is distributed and the way it is used; and the cohesiveness of the family, that is, the extent to which members are attracted to each other and identified with the family and the nature and effect of their loyalties on the family's ability to interact effectively with the environment.

2. *Subsystems or subgroups within the family.* In every group, subsystems form, based on the common needs and interests of particular members. Certain members of the family form alliances with others with whom they can pursue joint goals, which can be positive in the effect on family functioning or can be maladaptive when they are collusions and coalitions against others. Triangles develop out of dyads, often to reduce anxiety and tension between the members involved in the pair.

3. *Distortions in perception of other people and situations.* Family members may grow up with fantasies about the family and distortions in their perceptions of each other and the family. Family secrets tend to make open communication difficult among members and with persons in the wider environment. In relationships among members, transference and reality elements are intertwined. Members may transfer feelings from earlier experiences to other family members or to the practitioner who often becomes the good and wise parent who is viewed as a source of help and security (Bateman, 1965). Members may vie with each other for the attention and approval of the worker. Practitioners may also distort their perceptions of one or more members. Cross-transferences occur; for example, a wife may be dominating as was her mother; a child's behavior is like that of a grandfather with whom he has been identified by the parents; the husband may react to the oldest daughter as though she were his mother; the practitioner expresses greater empathy with the daughter than with the other members. Experiences that people have in their families of origin affect their expectations for their own children and affects how they will structure sibling roles.

4. *Resistance.* At times, participation in family sessions creates more anxiety than the members are able to handle. The request to examine attitudes and behavior is threatening to people who fear the consequences of knowing more about themselves. Feelings and experiences that have been suppressed may become apparent, creating anxiety. Members may find it difficult to work with other family members toward finding solutions to problems, as they discover that the practitioner cannot do it for them. They may fear rejection if they disclose certain secrets or embarrassing events. Facing things that they find difficult to tolerate upsets the steady state, resulting in resistive behaviors that protect them from more stress than they can tolerate.

Social workers utilize all of the sets of techniques in helping families to resolve their problems in relationships. When, for example, there is rivalry among the members for the worker's attention, they strengthen relationships with the total family rather than with each member. If members react toward them with distrust, hostility, or dependency, they need to analyze and control their own reactions. They may then discuss their observations with the family and elicit their reactions to the statements. They may then move to help members to clarify the meaning of the behavior and responses. When there are conflicts between two or more members, they do not take sides, become a party to secrets or collusions, or judge members as being right or wrong. If workers can avoid these traps, members will be freed to explore new ways of perceiving and relating to each other.

Members can be helped to enhance positive relationships with each other through a technique that Orcutt (1977, p.24) calls "relational awareness with empathy." The practitioner encourages the members' recollections and expressions of feelings around a difficult life experience that relates to the family's stress. The listeners tend to be emotionally moved as they become aware of the meaning of the experience and how it is related to the present situation. With such awareness, empathy and warmth flow, relationships take on a deeper meaning, and reality is perceived more accurately.

Practitioners offer support to relieve too much discomfort and tension by preparing members for what they can expect and providing encouragement and realistic reassurance for efforts and achievements. They provide new information needed by the family to understand what is going on in family interaction. They may teach them concepts of family therapy; for example, Freeman (1981) teaches the family about roles and how they can promote or limit options; how coalitions can create conflict and become barriers to mutual support and help; or how family loyalties can support or impede the effective use of resources. Thus, the family's understanding of how its own structure and process influences its daily living is enhanced. That understanding needs to be followed by making efforts to behave differently.

An example of the treatment of disturbed family relationships is described by Ross, Phipps, and Milligan (1985). A 16-year-old girl with irritable bowel syndrome was referred for family therapy by her physician. The parents had recently been divorced, and the patient suffered from the loss of her father, and there were other disturbed family relationships. It was recognized that the father should be included in the therapy, but the mother refused to consider that. Issues addressed included increasing the family's awareness of the relationship between stress and the medical symptoms; and changing the enmeshed relationship between the girl and her mother and dysfunctional triangles in the nuclear and extended family system. As these problems were worked on, the girl became more able to assume responsibility for the medical problem and deal with the loss of her father.

Exploration of the individual–family–environment situation is an essential basis for reflective discussion used to enhance the members' understanding of the patterns of relationships in the family. Ventilation to reveal the common and different ones is often essential. As feelings and experiences are disclosed, the members can move to considering how they can work together to make things better for the patient and the family unit. Clarification of feelings and patterns of behavior and their consequences for family functioning increases the members' understanding and efforts to make changes that have been agreed upon by all concerned. In reflective discussion, practitioners may introduce hitherto taboo subjects, support the members in staying with the feelings rather than cutting off their expression, and reframe issues to bring new perspectives to the problem-solving efforts. Through making comments that connect events, the worker brings new information for use by the family.

Clarification through linking the problems of one member with those of others is illustrated in an article by Bittner (1984, p. 154):

> For example, Gary L. was a five-year-old boy who protested going to kindergarten complaining bitterly of stomach aches. After obtaining a clean bill of health from the pediatrician, Mr. and Mrs. L. sought family counseling. Mrs. L.'s father had suffered from a chronic illness throughout her childhood, and she had constantly worried about his death. He died when Mrs. L. was nineteen years old. During Gary's infancy, Mr. L. was diagnosed as having a life-threatening illness; however, the illness was in remission, and his prognosis was good. Gary had never been told about his father's illness, although Mrs. L. admitted that she was never free from worry about her husband's health. During the course of family counseling, the worker was able to link Mrs. L.'s worries about loss and separation with Gary's identical concerns; these were symbolically enacted in his refusal to leave home for school. In addition, Mr. L. spoke for the first time about his own fears regarding his illness. Gradually, Mrs. L. began to observe her over-protectiveness toward both her son and her husband. The family ended counseling after five months of weekly sessions. At that time, Gary's symptoms had stopped and Mr. and Mrs. L. were quite pleased with his behavior. . . .

The example illustrates the many skills that are used to illuminate the process that is going on in the family at a given time. The worker asks the family to reflect on what has happened to the family since the illness or disability occurred, and then what can be done to make things better. Clarifying statements may be directed toward a particular member, a subsystem, or the family as a whole. To carry understanding further, interpretations of the meaning of behavior or its roots in the past may be offered for the family's consideration. The worker supplements what the members are able to do for themselves. The focus is on increasing awareness of the feelings and experiences that relate to the current problems in family functioning. Emotional and cognitive understanding go hand in hand and need to be accompanied by action through which family members try out and master different ways of relating and communicating. Reid (1985) provides detailed information about how tasks can be used within sessions, at home, or in the community to help members to develop competence.

Utilization of Resources

Social workers are uniquely qualified to deal with problems in the fit between patient, family, and the environment. A major responsibility is to enable families to make use of resources in the health care system and the community that will aid in the patient's and family's well-being; and to negotiate collaborative relationships with members of other professions and organizations (Carlton, 1984; Northen, 1982, 1988; Power & Dell Orto, 1980; Reid, 1985). Many problems are not reflective of family pathology but of problems in the complexity and maldistribution of health and welfare delivery systems, making knowledge about and access to needed resources difficult for almost anybody.

Health care personnel may have a tendency to ignore the social context in which illness occurs and health is maintained. Norman Cousins (1983) vividly describes how the hospital environment provides not only the essential medical care and treatment, but also creates severe stress for patients and families. He describes how the hospital environment imposes indignity and stress in terms of lack of privacy, separation, encouragement of dependency, disruption of sleep, painfulness of medical procedures, fear of bodily harm, adverse effects of drugs, loss of control, and uncertainty of recovery. These factors may mobilize diverse emotions—anxiety, guilt, shame, depression, and a sense of helplessness and hopelessness. As noted earlier, the social worker can mobilize healing forces through providing support and encouragement, but they go beyond that as they work collaboratively with other staff, contributing their knowledge about the psychosocial effects of hospitalization and how changes in structure and patient–staff relationships can reduce the stress.

Stresses occasioned by lack of adequate resources or unpleasant physical environments, as well as inadequate knowledge and skills, are obstacles to the achievement of their goals by families. Reducing environmental stress is one way to assist families to regain a dynamic equilibrium, and the provision of more adequate opportunities contributes to the psychosocial development of the members, including the patient.

Some patients and other members of their families will reach out to find and use resources when they know what is available and how to make application for material aids or services. But many families need more help than that: They may fear how they will be accepted and received by the persons providing the resource; may not have the anticipated financial resources; or may be too immobilized by stress to take initiative in reaching out to the providers. Perlman (1979) gives examples of patients who have the medicine but also have serious doubts about taking it and of a special training class that was found for a neurologically damaged child whose mother failed to get him there. Such people may need help to express and clarify their feelings, think about the value of the service offered, consider the conditions for the use of the resource, and work through their ambivalence about using the service. For example, a patient may both want and still resist moving from a wheel chair to crutches, and the family may or may not support that move, thus needing considerable help in relation to the decision.

Preceding chapters have provided evidence for the importance of support for families. Family therapy seeks to increase the capacities of family members to support each other, but that may not be sufficient. A frequent task for the practitioner is to help the family to seek support from significant others to alleviate stress and contribute positively to coping efforts. According to Caplan (1974, pp. 216–217), kinship and friendship are the most important types of primary social relationships to be used as support systems. Too often, however, families with a sick or disabled member become isolated and stop participating in social activities with relatives and friends or engaging in other community events. Exploration of this issue and encouragement by the practitioner can have a positive influence on the family's decision to move toward as much normalization of their daily lives as possible.

Self-help groups, which have become ubiquitous in the health field, are alternatives to natural networks for providing support and mutual aid to families with common needs (Gartner & Riesman, 1977; Katz & Bender, 1976; Lieberman, Bowman, & Associates, 1979; Whittaker, Garbarino, & Associates, 1983). Such groups vary in their primary purposes which include controlling undesired behavior such as overeating, smoking, using alcohol and drugs; providing support and aid from peers in coping with stress related to illness, disability, loss, or death; and combating the effects of isolation and stigmatization that accompany certain diseases, such as cancer or AIDS. The practitioner's role consists of referring clients, organizing groups when a need is indicated, and consulting with the group's own leaders at their request (Northen, 1983). At times, there is recognition that the group requires professional leadership, and the self-help group becomes a therapy group.

Termination

Termination, as a vital and important process, is a relatively neglected component of practice in the literature on family therapy. Yet, particularly in health settings, the way a family ends its treatment is often as important to its welfare as is what happened previously, owing to the prevalence of loss and separation that accompany illness and disability. Reid (1985, p. 55) suggests that "the principle is to use termination in a flexible way to help families achieve realistic goals and to end services with a feeling of accomplishment." If members of a family evaluate the meaning of the experience to them and end with a sense of success, they tend to be more able to cope with the other losses and separations they will encounter throughout their lives.

Ideally, termination of family therapy is a planned process that occurs when the agreed-upon goals have been achieved, at least to a satisfactory extent. In planned termination, the practitioner and family agree that sufficient progress has been made for the family to continue to consolidate its gains without the assistance of the practitioner. In some situations, the time of termination was built into the contracting process, with agreement that therapy would continue for an expected period of time, usually with some flexibility to extend the time as needed. Too often, however, families discontinue service before the practitioner judges that they are ready to do so. Unexplored resistance or unexpressed dissatisfaction with some aspect of the service are frequent reasons for early termination, as are changes in the environment of families such as a move to a new community, changes in work or school schedules, or inability to pay fees. Often the unplanned termination results from pressures toward rapid discharge.

During the termination phase, the major responsibilities of the social worker are to prepare for termination, introduce the subject to the family, explore and deal with the reactions of the members, review progress, and focus on unfinished business and plans for the future.

The process of ending a meaningful experience involves the feelings of both family members and the practitioner. In preparing for working with a family in the termination phase, practitioners face the gamut of feelings they have toward ending with each member and the family unit (Nelson, 1983). Typical are some combination of feelings of loss, sadness, guilt, and inadequacy over not having done more, relief, and deep satisfaction. Facing separation from a family with whom one has had a rewarding experience may activate feelings of prior losses and separations. It is the worker who is leaving the family, while the family continues as a unit. Assessment of the meaning of the termination to the practitioner can enhance his ability to help family members face and deal with their reactions. As practitioners anticipate their own reactions and seek control over them, they also engage in anticipatory empathy to understand the possible reactions of the members and their readiness for ending family sessions. As another part of preparation, practitioners make decisions about when and how to introduce the reality of termination.

The decision to terminate is related to the goals agreed upon between the practitioner and the family. The practitioner has followed the family's use of the service, the progress made, and obstacles to further progress. When a time span was set earlier, she reminds the family of that fact. When service is open-ended in duration, she assesses the family's readiness to end and informs the members that they should discuss the issue. Each member will respond somewhat differently to the proposal for termination, but there is almost always some ambivalence that needs to be worked through.

The feelings that are expressed by members vary with such matters as the way they have worked on the difficulties in the preceding phase, the state of the patient's health, the members' coping capacities, and the prior losses and separations that they have encountered. Most endings contain elements of both sadness and gladness. One typical reaction is denial that termination is imminent, a defense against facing the impending separation from the worker and the feelings of anxiety that are stirred up by it. Another typical reaction is anger at what members perceive as lack of acceptance by the worker or even abandonment, rejection, or punishment. To the extent that the worker has become highly valued by the family, the members will feel a sense of loss and need to mourn it (Bowlby, 1960; Bywaters, 1975; Nelsen, 1983). Members may attempt to postpone termination by bringing up new problems, insisting that they cannot get along without the worker, or staying away from sessions. The painful feelings that underlie such reactions are emphasized in the literature, and some research supports the prevalence of such feelings (Lackey, 1982). But there are also feelings of pleasure connected with the final stage of therapy.

Many members of families have predominantly positive reactions about being ready to get along with professional help for the psychosocial problems related to the illness or disability of one member. They have worked on one or more problems that were brought to a satisfactory solution. One example is of a couple whose marriage was threatened by conflict around housing an aged parent with beginning symptoms of Alzheimer's disease. In the course of working on that problem, other conflicts were faced and worked through. The final decision made about the parent was satisfactory to both the couple and the parent. The family expressed deep appreciation for the help given and pride in their own problem-solving capacities. Along with a realistic sense of loss, there was happy anticipation of the ending.

Practitioners have a responsibility to help the family to review and evaluate the progress made by each member and changes in the structure and relationships in the family unit. They support the family's work in this respect, accredit realistic gains, identify any difficulties that still exist, and evaluate the effectiveness of the family therapy. They move the members from prolonged preoccupation with feelings to a focus on what they hoped to gain from the sessions and their progress in achieving the agreed-upon goals. The appraisal of the members' progress has been an ongoing process, but now the family is helped to summarize what has happened during the sessions, what gains each member feels he has made, and how the family unit is operating differently now. The previously agreed-upon goals serve as the criteria against which changes in functioning are evaluated. It is desirable that specific criteria for determining results be formulated and research instruments, such as those presented in Chapter 4, be used to validate or invalidate the practitioner's and members' views of the success of treatment.

In addition to discussion of the possibility of termination, helping families to face and deal with their feelings about it, and reviewing progress, social workers help them to work on unfinished business essential to stabilizing and furthering the gains that have been made. Families need to use the remaining time profitably, and recognition of the brief time left serves as a motivating force in accelerating the work to tie loose ends and to plan ahead for the next steps in normalizing their lives to the greatest extent possible, depending upon whether or not the patient has recovered and, if so, for the re-establishment of his or her roles and social activities. Activities may be used to help members gain confidence in their capacities to move ahead on their own and to identify and use community resources to foster the transition away from professional help. Practitioners support and encourage the members' efforts to reach out to find new ways of using their recently acquired understanding and skills.

In the final act of termination, practitioners inform the family of their availability for additional service if the need becomes apparent. They assure the family that they continue to be interested in their welfare, even though they will no longer be meeting with the family. They express hope that the gains made through the treatment will lead to increased capacity to cope more effectively with new challenges to individual and family functioning.

8
Crisis Intervention

Crisis intervention is an integral part of social work practice in direct work with individuals, families, and groups. In work with families in health settings, it is a process for actively influencing the physical health and psychosocial functioning of the patient and family system when there is an upset in the family's steady state. Being open systems, families "are in a constant state of change, development and restructuring. . . . The process within a system that works to ensure that the degree of change is tolerable is known as a steady state" (Freeman, 1981, p. 42). According to Buckley, the term *steady state* is used "to express not only the structure-maintaining feature, but also the structure-elaborating feature of the inherently unstable system" (Buckley, 1967, p. 15). In family practice, the family may be in a state of collective crisis or it may be mobilized to support and provide aid for one of its members who is in a state of crisis. The state of crisis may be occasioned by a single catastrophic event or a series of lesser stresses that accumulate over time.

The Nature of Crisis Intervention

Crisis intervention is a form of treatment of social and emotional problems, but it is also preventive in that early and successful intervention prevents psychosocial stress from becoming debilitating. Within public health, it is regarded as secondary prevention, the hallmarks of which are early diagnosis and prompt treatment (Bloom, 1981; Caplan, 1951; 1974; Council on Social Work Education, 1962).

A person in a state of crisis is acutely upset. The impact of a hazardous event makes people vulnerable to severe stress. Hazardous events in the field of health tend to be diagnoses of life-threatening or severe chronic illness, the birth of an infant with a deformity, a serious accident, loss of sight, hearing, or a body part, emergency hospitalization, or death of a loved one. Inability to cope effectively with the situation precipitates an individual or family into a state of active crisis (Golan, 1978). "The crisis results when new solutions to problems in living are called for, and habitual coping means do not suffice" (Parad, Selby, & Quinlan, 1986, p. 306).

The crisis is defined by reactions of an individual or family to the stressful situation, not the event itself. People may react very differently to the same hazardous event. For example, in a study of parents of children with leukemia or sarcoma, Hamovitch (1964) found that a majority of parents were able to cope adaptively to the situation, but a substantial minority went into a state of crisis. The state of crisis is a temporary and time-limited threat to the family's life goals. Characteristically, there is considerable emotional upset and cognitive confusion which immobilizes the person's problem-solving capacities and interferes with the performance of social roles. These reactions are normal responses to stress: They are not pathological. The crisis of one member of a family has an impact on the other members and more or less disrupts the functioning of the family unit. Sometimes family members become more upset than does the patient. Members of some families are faced with an increase in stress during the course of the patient's illness or rehabilitation; for example, when there are major changes in treatment procedures, an exacerbation of the difficulty, a crisis in another member of the family, or death. A crisis may be linked to earlier unresolved conflicts, resulting in exaggerated or prolonged stress. And as noted in Chapters 2 and 3, a family crisis may occur in the face of a "pile-up" of general life stressors other than the health event or lack of access to social support.

When people are in a state of crisis, they are especially susceptible to well-timed and well-focused help. The intensification of anxiety may enhance motivation to try new means of coping with the stressful situation. "A small amount of help, appropriately focused, can prove to be considerably more effective than more extensive help at periods of less emotional accessibility" (Golan 1987, p. 365). The resolution of the crisis occurs as the family clarifies its reactions to the event and searches for effective ways of coping with the situation. The total length of time between the initial blow and the final resolution varies widely, depending on the severity of the hazardous event, the capacities of the patient, the tasks that have to be accomplished, and the supports available. The resolution of the crisis may be adaptive or maladaptive.

When a hazardous event occurs, people exhibit a variety of common and specific responses. One of the most frequent initial reactions is shock. In Hamovitch's study of 61 cases of children with leukemia or sarcoma, the most common reaction of the parents was shock. They felt overwhelmed by the diagnosis, followed by prolonged crying spells, inability to work, denial, and anger. Diagnoses of other usually fatal illnesses are responded to with similar symptoms, such as fear, anger, resentment, helplessness, and depression (Cohen, Goldenberg, & Goldenberg, 1977; Gordon & Kutner, 1980; Hubschman, 1983). With epilepsy, the onset of seizures is the event that often overwhelms family members. Seizures are often perceived as life threatening. They terrify observers, and they carry stigma (Ford, 1982). With serious chronic illnesses, in addition to anxiety, there is often unbearable uncertainty and fear of the unknown. Stress and disorganization are inevitable (Fine, 1980).

The birth of a child with a congenital malformation precipitates common responses. In a study of 20 children and their families, Drotar and associates (1980) found that all but two parents suffered shock, with abrupt disruption of their usual feelings, irrational behavior, crying, feelings of helplessness, and being totally unprepared for the event. Every parent used denial as a defense, but the intensity of the reaction varied, depending upon the visibility of the malformation. There were fears that the baby would die, and sadness and anger were directed toward themselves, the hospital staff, and the baby (see also Noble & Hamilton, 1981). Severe injuries, too, create tremendous stress. The first reaction is characterized by anxiety related to fear of death, followed by denial of reality, anger at personnel, depression, turning to religious beliefs for succor, and doubts about living with a serious handicap (Bray, 1980; Phillips, Gorman, & Bordenheimer, 1981). The need for treatment of families of brain-injured patients is described by Blades (1982) and Frye (1982).

In addition to diagnosis, hospitalization—particularly of children—frequently creates unbearable stress. Children may exhibit separation anxiety, fear of strangers, distress at unfamiliar surroundings, fear of painful medical procedures, and physical discomfort. Parents may also suffer from separation anxiety, fear of medical procedures, uncertainty about the outcome, and confusion about juggling their roles with the patient and other family, work, and social roles. Lilliston (1985) describes the disruption of normal psychosocial functioning experienced by victims of traumatic physical disability. The consequences often are an alteration in the sense of body image and identity; shifts in time orientation to the present; grief and depression; and feelings of anxiety, guilt, and rage. Existing coping capacities may be insufficient to manage the stress and the numerous changes necessitated by the disability. The ongoing life of the patient's family is seriously disrupted. Spink (1976) describes similar emotional reactions of parents to a different disability, deafness of a child.

When death occurs, of course, a morass of grief results, with survivors tormented by guilt and self-blame, anger at physicians for not doing enough to save the life, anger at nurses, social workers, and even the dead one. Shock, denial, sadness, anger, and morbid preoccupation are common (Golan, 1987; Kalish, 1982; Simos, 1977). The death of a young child is a particularly difficult event for families. According to Rando (1985), the death of a child contradicts the expectation that children will survive their parents: They frequently express guilt about surviving longer than the child. Parents lose their functional roles in relation to the lost child; they may feel victimized, not only by the actual death but by the loss of the aspirations they invested in the child; and they may experience feelings of isolation from normally supportive social networks. The loss of the child in two-parent families simultaneously affects both partners, who are deeply involved with their own grief and hence less likely to be able to support each other. Siblings also grieve the loss of a young child, the reactions varying with their stage of emotional, cognitive, and social development.

These are a few examples that illustrate the pervasiveness of numerous and mixed emotional reactions of patients and their families to a severe illness, injury, disability, hospitalization, or death. The intense emotional turmoil experienced by many patients and family members corresponds to a state of crisis (Caplan, Mason, & Kaplan, 1965; Hubschman, 1983; Power & Dell Orto, 1980; Rapoport, 1970). Family counseling, based on a crisis intervention model, should result in improvement in the family's adaptation to the threat posed by illness or disability. Crisis intervention is considered appropriate for families with members of all ages, ethnic backgrounds, and socioeconomic status. According to Parad, Selby, and Quinlan (1976), the only requirement is that the clients must be in a state of crisis or affected by persons who are in a crisis.

Crisis-oriented treatment involves the use of several components of service:

1. Early accessibility of help as soon as possible following the hazardous event.
2. Use of time limits, either in the form of a specific or approximate number of sessions or weeks of treatment.
3. Use of a variety of supportive, clarifying, and problem-solving techniques.
4. Focused attention on the crisis and its resolution.

Parad, Selby, and Quinlan (1976, p.311) have said the "essence of crisis is a struggle—a struggle to cope with and master an upsetting situation and regain a state of balance." The practitioner's task is to help the family members with that struggle.

Purpose and Goals of Crisis Intervention

The major broad purpose of crisis intervention is to cushion the immediate impact of the stressful event on the patient and other family members and to help the members to mobilize and use their capacities, interpersonal skills, and social resources for moving toward adaptive coping measures and away from maladaptive coping measures. Within this broad purpose, there are specific goals for each family arrived at through mutual agreement between the practitioner and the family. These may be to help the family to:

1. Reduce anxiety, cognitive confusion, and other symptoms of distress;
2. Understand the details of the hazardous event that led to the state of crisis;
3. Increase understanding of the nature and course of the illness or disability, the feelings associated with it, and its meaning to the patient and family system;
4. Mobilize resources in the environment that will provide support and opportunities to reestablish relationships and activities that were cut off at the time of the precipitating event;
5. Change patterns of affect, cognition, and behavior that hinder efforts to cope adaptively with the crisis;
6. Reduce the impact of dysfunctional patterns of communication, roles, and decision making within the family that contribute to the distress of the members;
7. Identify and implement tasks and make and implement decisions that will alleviate problems related to the crisis.

Such goals are pertinent to the restoration of the upset members to their precrisis level of psychosocial functioning and, in some cases, enable them to move beyond that level to having the capacity for coping with other stressful situations.

Assessment

Since crisis intervention is time-limited, assessment of the patient–family interaction needs to be rapid, pertinent to the crisis, and integrated with the treatment process. The purpose of the assessment is to understand the particular patient's and family's reactions and their ability to cope with the stressful situation, thus individualizing the service to be given. The initial assessment is very tentative: It will change within the process of working with the family. The principle of individualization puts into practice the social work value of the inherent dignity and worth of people. Social workers have the responsibility to understand the situation with which they will deal before taking action. To achieve understanding within a very brief period of time requires expert selection and use of knowledge appropriate to the family's particular situation.

In crisis intervention, the information sought centers around the hazardous event, the patient's and family members' emotional reactions to it, and the members' capacities to understand and find ways to cope with the stress (Golan, 1987; Parad, Selby, & Quinlan, 1976; Power & Dell Orto, 1980; Rapoport, 1970; Smith, 1978). Practitioners use exploratory techniques to identify the hazardous event, the members' common and different emotional responses to it, the meaning of the event to each of them, and the extent of the stress experienced by each member. Likewise, they explore the reactions of the members to the health care system itself. They try to ascertain the family's prior efforts to cope with the situation and discover what adaptive capacities can be used in the problem-solving process. They seek to determine how previous experiences with illness or disability are related to the current situation, and what external sources of support are available to the family.

As practitioners work with the family, they may discover other problems that interfere with the members' abilities to cope effectively with the crisis situation, such as lack of financial resources, unemployment, poor housing, or nonsupportive relatives. Problems in family functioning related to the quality of relationships, communication patterns, decision making, power, and interpersonal conflicts may impede the family's progress in resolving the crisis. The guidelines for assessment of family functioning in the preceding chapter are applicable to assessment of patterns relevant to crisis intervention.

Intervention

Crisis intervention involves problem-solving at the affective, cognitive, and behavioral dimensions. When there are serious disruptions in the steady state, problem-solving efforts are successful when the coping tasks specific to the crisis are accomplished (Kaplan, 1981). In working toward restoring psychosocial functioning to the precrisis level, "treatment thus becomes focused on helping the person or the family engage in the coping tasks that will result in a healthy, positive outcome, free of complications (Golan, 1986, p.24). Three tasks are necessary for crisis resolution: (1) to acquire accurate cognitive perceptions of the crisis situation; (2) to deal with strong emotional reactions to the situation; and (3) to seek and use appropriate interpersonal and institutional resources (Rapoport, 1962).

Families in a state of crisis use numerous coping skills, as described by Moos and Tsu (1977), including:

1. Using defenses, such as denial and rationalization, for self-protection from being overwhelmed;
2. Seeking and using relevant information which relieves anxiety that is due to uncertainty, misinformation, and guilt;

3. Requesting support from significant other people which relieves tension and provides reassurance;
4. Learning skills appropriate to problem-solving;
5. Setting concrete goals which provides hope and a sense of achievement;
6. Rehearsing alternative outcomes which prepares people to deal with expected difficulties and eases fears;
7. Finding purpose or patterns of meaning which provides consolation, encouragement, and restoration of a set of values.

Initial Phase

The major tasks of the practitioner in the initial phase are to orient the members of the family to the purpose and focus of crisis intervention and to reduce the emotional impact of the hazardous event. In addition to the mixed and complex feelings that members bring with them to the first session, there is the additional anxiety and uncertainty that accompanies anyone's entrance into an unknown situation. Practitioners use their understanding of crises and typical reactions to new situations to develop an initial working relationship that conveys the qualities of acceptance, genuineness, and empathy with each member and the family unit. They help the members to relate to them through the many small courtesies that indicate interest in the members comfort. Introductions of each member to the worker and simple statements about the fact that the therapeutic experience may be new for them, that it is natural to feel some uncertainty about what will happen here, and that she has confidence that they will be helped to weather the present difficult period in their lives, helps to develop trust in the worker and enhances motivation. A relaxed atmosphere in which members can choose from among chairs that are arranged informally and can be easily moved is conducive to the development of trust. When there are young children present, the availability of toys and craft materials is essential.

In crisis intervention, the family's goals are usually highly congruent with the purpose for which the service is designed, namely, the relief of stress and the enhancement of capacity for supporting the patient and coping effectively with the consequences of an illness or disability of one member of the family. Early in the session, the social worker discusses the general purpose of the sessions with the family and requests their responses, encouraging each member to comment on it and to offer information about what he hopes will happen in the sessions. Sensitive observation of verbal and nonverbal behavior, listening, and responding with acceptance develops trust and introduces a norm of family members participation in the process.

The social worker also presents clearly the structure of the service—the time, place, frequency of meetings, and the anticipated duration of the treatment. Almost always, families will agree with the practitioner's statement of the general purpose and plan: They may or may not yet be able to elaborate more specific goals and raise questions about structural matters. Their agreement with the general statements, however, constitutes a preliminary informal contract or working agreement between the family and the practitioner.

The major content of the initial session consists of exploration of the crisis configuration (Krause, 1988). The first step is to identify the hazardous event and explore each member's understanding of what happened to the patient and to provide accurate information to correct misunderstandings. Families tend to be preoccupied with the nature and accuracy of the diagnosis or learning about treatment alternatives. The need is to develop cognitive recognition of the situation and common understanding among members of the family. This promotes empathy, not only in relation to the patient but each other as well, and it promotes motivation to cooperate in problem-solving processes. When the patient is too sick or injured to attend the sessions, the members of the family require accurate information about the patient's condition and the medical procedures being used. Knowledge, when presented clearly and at the family's level of understanding, reduces anxiety and prepares members for engaging in other coping efforts.

Once the event itself is clarified, exploration is of the meaning of the event to each member, how it has affected the lives of members, and how the present situation may remind them of previous situations that were extremely upsetting. In exploring the effects of the crisis on the family's life, it is important to seek information about practical problems caused by the crisis, such as unemployment, financial pressures, lack of transporation, or day care. Expression of feelings may center around these practical needs. When there are practical needs, priority is given to helping the family to find and use appropriate resources.

Along with cognitive understanding, the major focus is on the members' emotional reactions to the hazardous event and its impact on their lives. Expressions of feelings often occur simultaneously with efforts to achieve cognitive understanding. Social workers not only observe the members for clues as to their affect but also listen to their verbal expressions of feelings. High anxiety is characterized by such indicators as physical agitation, a high-pitched voice, tight neck and shoulder muscles, and other bodily reactions—even at times in emergency rooms by such physical symptoms as nausea, fainting, and diarrhea (Epperson, 1977). Practitioners encourage ventilation of feelings, letting the members know that it is natural to experience anxiety at this time. At the same time, they need to control the amount of material that is revealed. Premature expressions by one member may result in other members pulling back and challenging defenses, when they are still essential (Krause, 1988).

In the use of exploration, social workers encourage the participation of members in the discussion. They attempt to encourage a pattern of communication that gives recognition to each member's efforts, according to each one's readiness to contribute to the discussion. They may ask if a feeling expressed by one member is similar to or different from those of others. They may request, either through words or gestures, that the members respond to each other's messages. They may make comments that connect the contribution of one member to that of another or point out the common and different perceptions. In such ways, they demonstrate that one important means of help is mutual aid—members helping each other and each contributing to the family's welfare.

As they are provided with knowledge about the illness, disability, or injury, denial is one of the primary early coping devices used for self-protection, preventing members from becoming overwhelmed. Denial is considered to be adaptive when a medical condition occurs that overwhelms a person's coping capacities. A person may need to deny the impact of the event, the nature and seriousness of the medical condition, and its consequences. Denial is useful in preventing the patient and other family members from becoming overwhelmed, and it permits a more gradual transition to facing the reality of the situation. Successful coping requires motivation and hope, and denial of the seriousness of the event is a means of keeping hope alive. Although practitioners provide accurate information, they recognize the need for the defense and do not confront it directly in the earliest stage of treatment. They also recognize the need to deal with the reality, by making statements about what the situation is and conveying understanding that it can be hard for persons to believe what really happened.

Denial is a phase in the process of resolving the crisis. An example is given by Epperson (1977). Mr. and Mrs. Smith, the middle-aged parents of a 19-year-old son, John, were awakened by a telephone call from the police who reported that John had been in a serious accident. Mr. and Mrs. Smith and their 17-year-old daughter, Lisa, were rushed to the emergency center. They were under great stress, exhibiting many symptoms of extreme anxiety. This was followed by denial. The record states:

> John was severely damaged in the car accident. He had multiple fractures and several lacerations that would heal over time. But a spinal cord injury would leave him permanently paralyzed from the waist down. After a lengthy discussion with the family, the doctor left and Mrs. Smith began to cry. Her husband tried to comfort her, saying: "Everything will be all right. You know John: he's

> a tough kid. He'll be walking again, you'll see." He repeated this statement to Lisa and to the social worker. Later he told the nurse about spinal cord-injured army buddies who had leaned to walk again and that there was no reason why John couldn't do the same (p. 268).

Along with anxiety and denial, early expressions of feeling may reflect anger toward self, another family member, medical personnel, or the practitioner. In the initial phase, practitioners listen and accept the angry expressions and wait to discuss their source until a little later in the helping process. They need to maintain a balance between instilling hope and holding to the reality of the situation.

The primary sets of procedures and skills used in the early stage are support, ventilation of feelings, exploration, education, and facilitation of communication among the members. Just before ending the first session, workers often give a brief summary of what has happened in the session, pointing out that the members have accomplished a great deal in enhancing their understanding of the patient's and family's situation and in expressing their feelings, concerns, and ideas to each other. When true, they note that they are now ready to work together to reduce the stress and to make plans for their parts in assisting the patient and working on difficulties resulting from the illness or disability. They engage them in making a decision to continue in family counseling and remind them of the time and place for the next session and the anticipated duration of the service.

Core Phase

The major focus of the mid-phase of crisis intervention entails finding ways to cope with the difficulties related to the crisis and helping the family move from a state of disorganization to one of reasonable balance. Germain and Gitterman (1980), pp. 113–14) point out that many people, particularly those who are poor or discriminated against, have had little in their lives to encourage a positive outlook toward attempting new ways of coping. The practitioner's responsibility is to provide the conditions that make coping possible, as mentioned earlier.

One important factor in the successful resolution of a crisis is the nature and quality of the information received by the patient and family. The intensity of a crisis is reduced through education. Frye (1982) notes that "the basic, underlying principle is that families cope better when they understand events and are encouraged to channel anxiety into positive, participating activities." Through teaching the necessary knowledge and skills, practitioners enable families to participate in the patient's care or rehabilitation which contributes to the resolution of the crisis.

In this stage, work needs to continue on ventilation and understanding of feelings engendered by the crisis event. There may be further expressions of anxiety and continued need to deny the reality of the medical condition or its disrupting influences on the family. The practitioner moves beyond ventilation to clarifying the nature of the emotional reactions and finding their source, which tends to reduce their intensity. Anger is now more openly expressed. It may take the form of blaming self or others and be directed toward the physician or other personnel who have not done enough to cure the patient. Eventually, the anger is directed toward the patient, who is often the real source of anger. The patient is blamed for disrupting family routines and causing stress and disorganization within the family. An illustration is from Epperson (1977, p.269).

> Lisa was the first to articulate her angry feelings. In response to her father's statements of denial, she began to accuse him of always having to be in control, of telling everyone what they could or could not do: "You're always telling everyone what they're going to do. Just because you say he is going to walk again doesn't mean he's going to." She began to blame him for the accident. "You're the one who told him to get out. This wouldn't have happened if he was at home." . . . Mrs. Smith lashed out at Lisa for being disrespectful to her father. There was further blaming of the inefficiency of the police and criticism of society in general. Family members need to be reassured that they are not bad for expressing anger, but that such expression can lead to the reduction of stress when feelings are directed toward the real object. Validation of angry feelings, when appropriate, also helps. Simple statements that convey understanding validate the feelings, e.g. "I understand why you wish that the ambulance could have arrived earlier."

Often, after expressing anger, the members move toward expressions of remorse, feeling guilty for blaming the patient and for what they perceive as their part in provoking the crisis. Gradually, although they regret that the incident occurred, they realize that they could not have prevented it. Gradually, these emotions are integrated as the members become reconciled to what happened and develop a sense of hope that the family will survive the stress. The family is now ready to mobilize its own and external resources to develop a viable plan of action for coping with the situation.

Affect, cognition, and action are interrelated. As the family members express their feelings, they come to understand and master them and simultaneously to work on selected problems that were created by the hazardous event.

Through exploration and decision making, the family decides upon particular goals related to the crisis that they wish to pursue to restore the family's steady state. Among the most common goals are:

1. deciding about changes in roles necessitated by the patient's medical condition;
2. enhancing the members' ability to communicate their concerns and hopes;
3. changing dysfunctional relationships among family members that have occurred in response to the crisis;
4. mobilizing internal and external resources to provide support and aid to the patient and family system; and
5. making plans for the future related to the patient's full recovery or living within the limits imposed by the illness or disability and at times the anticipated death of the patient.

The illness, disability, or death of one member of the family shifts the expectations for role performance of all family members, including the patient, of course. Someone must fulfill the responsibilities formerly carried by the patient, and, in addition, decisions must be made about who will be responsible for what part of the care of the patient, with encouragement of the patient to do as much as possible for herself. The family can engage in a problem-solving process to assess what the realistic capacities of each member are and to make decisions about task assignments. Rational planning can result in better service to the patient and, simultaneously, enhance the competence of other family members. At the same time that new role assignments are being made, there may also be a need to normalize relationships with other people. Members need to continue to find satisfaction from their other roles in the family, at work or school, and in the community.

Problems in communication within the family often become obstacles to successful coping with the crisis. Fear of discussing subjects that have been taboo make open communication impossible, accelerating the stress. A typical example taken from a record of practice follows:

> The case is one of Mr. T., age 76, who was hospitalized with an unknown illness which later was diagnosed as terminal cancer. Since Mr. T. was quite depressed, the physician had not told him about the diagnosis, but had informed the concerned family members—his daughter and her husband with whom he lived and a twenty-five year old granddaughter. Being in the hospital, deepened Mr. T.'s depression. Thus, when the family visited Mr. T., any discussion of the illness was avoided. The members talked about events in the community and in their lives which they thought would cheer him up. But his mood only worsened and the interaction between Mr. T. and the other members was extremely limited. The family dreaded seeing him and felt guilty for having these feelings. The oldest daughter had requested a meeting with the social worker to get suggestions for dealing with the problem. The social worker recommended that a way be found to discuss the diagnosis with Mr. T., but they were unwilling to go

against the physician's recommendation. With the permission of the doctor, the worker suggested a family meeting in Mr. T.'s room. After a brief transition, she opened the discussion with comments about how many patients and family members feel better if they talk about the illness. She asked if Mr. T. would be willing to say what he knew about his illness. He looked startled, paused for a minute, and then said that no one had bothered to tell him what was wrong but he knew he was going to die and that he thought he had cancer. He said he did not tell these folks about it because he did not want to worry them. Once out in the open, there were expressions of relief and both the patient and other family members could begin to find adaptive ways of coping with this dreadful situation.

In response to conditions occasioned by the crisis, dysfunctional patterns of relationships may develop among family members. When problems in relationships follow the precipitating event, it is assumed that they are not rigid and can be modified within the focus and duration of crisis intervention. Examples are one or more members of the family acting in overprotective ways toward the patient, an unrealistic dependence of the patient on other family members, withdrawal of family members from maintaining relationships with friends, relatives, and colleagues, and scapegoating of the patient or another family member who is blamed for the disruption of the family's usual patterns of living.

Many families need help to discover and use resources that can provide emotional support or health and welfare resources to the sick or disabled person and other family members. The family may be helped to engage in problem-solving concerning what other people can do to help and what material aids and medical and social services are necessary.

Planning for the future should give family members a sense of more control over their lives. Discussions about the future may range from specific tasks to be performed to coping with the terror around the prospect of losing a loved one. Effective planning is based upon clarity about the patient's prognosis and the family's strengths, and it may need to include anticipatory planning for the survival of the family in the event of death.

Skills of the Social Worker

Social workers help the family members to handle their feelings, accept the reality of the illness, and reorganize their roles, communication processes, and relationships through following a number of principles of practice. The literature, however, gives little attention to an elaboration of the principles that apply to crisis intervention with families (Golan, 1987;

Parad, Selby, & Quinlan, 1976). Based on generic principles (Northen, 1982, pp. 300–310) and a review of the literature, we propose that competent practice is guided by these principles.

1. Social workers develop and sustain an accepting, empathic, and genuine relationship with each member of the family, facilitate relationships among the members, and are aware of and able to control their own emotional reactions toward members and their medical conditions.
2. They offer considerable support to the members in their self-disclosures, providing necessary reassurance and encouragement.
3. They are able to modify the initial assessment of individual needs as they become apparent, the structure and operating processes of the family, and the family's needs for social networks and health and welfare resources. They are able to differentiate between precrisis dysfunction and temporary upset of individuals and disruptions of family living owing to the crisis.
4. They maintain a focus on the crisis configuration and on the members' capacities, rather than on limitations and pathology.
5. They use the group problem-solving process to assist members in the solution of a limited number of realistic goals toward which to direct their efforts, in making decisions from among available alternatives, and in translating the decision into action.
6. They use educational techniques in contributing knowledge, making suggestions, offering advice, and teaching skills in communication, problem-solving, and resource utilization, according to the needs of the family.
7. They engage members in reflective discussion of their different and common emotional reactions and perceptions of situations, appropriately clarifying and interpreting their meaning so affective and cognitive mastery of the stressful situation is gained.
8. When necessary, they confront individuals or the family unit with their irrational thinking, destructive use of defenses, or malfunctional behavior to enable members to face and come to grips with obstacles to effective functioning. The confrontation must be accompanied with expressions of empathy and support.
9. They are able to project an aura of optimism and hope, expressing confidence in the family's abilities to master current difficulties.
10. They facilitate communication of feelings, attitudes, and cognitions among the members and with personnel in the health setting and significant others in the community, and they facilitate optimal participation of members in the family sessions to the extent of the members' capacities.

11. They collaborate with physicians, nurses, and other personnel in assuring accessibility and continuity of services needed by the patient and family.
12. They work within the agreed-upon time limit and use time dynamically to heighten the family's motivation and ability to focus on the selected goals. But they may also extend the time when there is clear indication of need for it.
13. They respect the members' needs to protect themselves against further stress and do not arouse more anxiety than can be dealt with at a given time.
14. They use skills differentially, according to the major goals and the needs of members, thus implementing the principle of individualization of individuals and family systems.
15. They engage in a self-examination process to identify and correct the errors made in facilitating the family process.

The key factor in social work practice with families is the practitioner's direct intervention in an operating social system that has existed and continues to exist outside the treatment sessions. It consists of persons who are integral to each other's lives and are critically important to each other. The worker enters the system, "hoping not only to influence it directly, but also to teach its participants, through direct experience, how to modify it and how to maintain its resilience in the face of further threat" (Couch, 1969, p. 93). In addition to the achievement of the particular goals, the family unit develops increased cohesiveness and becomes able to cope more effectively with whatever new crises occur.

Termination

In crisis intervention, termination is a brief process, owing to the time-limited nature of crises and the service that was built into the working agreement. Ideally, the members have become able to come to terms with the reality of the medical condition and its consequences for their lives and have reestablished a fairly balanced steady state. The resolution of the crisis provides a natural time for termination: nevertheless, as Rapoport (1970) notes, "termination needs to be dealt with explicitly."

The limited duration of the service relates to the fact that crises are of limited duration, estimated to be up to 6 weeks until some adaptive or maladaptive solution is found (Golan, 1987). The short time span does not mean that the service has been less meaningful to the members than if it had been of longer duration. The nature of crisis situations and the specificity of the goals may indeed have resulted in the family's development of intensive relationships with the practitioner, probably more so for some members than for others. The members are bound to have ambivalent feelings about separating from the worker. Unlike service given to one person or to people in groups, it is the practitioner who is leaving the family.

Just as the members brought complex and ambivalent emotions to the initial sessions, so, too, are similar feelings aroused by the realization that the family's experience is ending. After all, the members have disclosed intimate feelings and shared difficult experiences with the practitioner as well as with each other, so they will need help in dealing with their feelings about ending. It is natural to feel some degree of sadness when one has completed a meaningful experience and is separating from the provider of that experience. The sadness is aggravated by the fact that the awareness of the ending may reactivate feelings of loss from the crisis situation and earlier experiences. The members may resist termination in numerous ways—denial, anger at the worker for leaving them, feelings of inadequacy to go it alone, or apparent regression. The major theme is separation and loss, with anxiety about managing without professional help and being able to sustain the gains. When members face the reality of their feelings about the loss that is inherent in termination, they react with expressions of anxiety and sadness and engage in reflective thinking about the situation. Ability to accept the separation can be a major source of therapeutic gain. The fact that they have dealt constructively with their feelings around the crisis situation tends to make it possible to accept the ending in a short period of time. If they can cope with separation from the worker, the result may be increased capacity to deal effectively with later losses in their lives.

Almost simultaneously with their concerns about separation, the members display positive feelings toward ending the family sessions. Feeling competent to cope more effectively with traumatic situations is accompanied by feelings of satisfaction and hope for the future. Usually one result of crisis intervention is an enhanced sense of family identity and competence to deal with stress.

In order to use the ending period for therapeutic gains, practitioners perform several tasks. It is their responsibility to: (1) request that members discuss their perceptions of the experience in coming together around the medical condition; (2) explore and clarify feelings about termination and resolve whatever ambivalence there may be about separating from the worker; (3) engage the members in a review and evaluation of gains and losses and support the progress made; (4) identify needs that can be met through referral to other services or through informal natural networks or self-help groups; (5) respond to final concerns expressed by members and, if appropriate, make plans for follow-up sessions which often prevent further problems; and (6) end the session with a brief summary of the experience and say good-by. In the words of Golan (1978, p. 29), the family is left with the basic message that it "has engaged in a constructive experience and has learned certain coping patterns that can be used during future stressful situations."

9

Discharge Planning, Placement, and Follow-up

Discharge planning is a process of transition that prepares a family unit, including the patient, for securing adequate home care or community services or arranging transfer of the patient from one residential setting to another. A transition is defined by Golan (1986, p. 3) as "a process of change, moving an individual from one relatively stable state through an interval of strangeness and uncertainty on the way to a new stable state." It is not only an individual but the total family, however, that must adapt to the life transition of relocation of one of its members.

Relocation is one of life's typical and severe sources of stress (Holmes & Rahe, 1967). Such stressful situations, according to Maas (1984, p. 3) "call for altered patterns of interaction between persons and their social contexts." Such stressful events tax people's coping capacities. Numerous types of problems are associated with transitions (Golan, 1986). Some families have trouble in coping with the feelings of loss and anxiety that are associated with an uncertain future. The family's steady state is disrupted by the need to reincorporate the patient into the family or to adjust to his separation from daily living with the family or in the case of a high-risk infant to incorporate a new family member who is likely to be dependent on technical medical care provided by parents in the home. Patients and family members have difficulty separating themselves from the past or relinquishing and changing roles that are no longer appropriate. There may be difficulties in making decisions or coping with the new conditions imposed by the choices. Some families have difficulties in sustaining their efforts in adapting to the new setting and role demands until the changes become somewhat stabilized and the family members have developed an adequate network of social supports. Deteriorating medical conditions or changing family circumstances may also precipitate a new crisis after discharge. Families with a chronically ill or handicapped child may also face new crises in conjunction with developmental changes of the child and the family over time (Brissette, Zinman, Fielding, & Reidy, 1987). Therefore, discharge should include anticipatory guidance and planned opportunity for follow-up.

Purposes and Goals

The goals of discharge or placement planning are stated in different ways. Coulton (1979, p. 5) sets the purpose within a broad perspective which is to achieve a good fit between person–environment "to promote and restore a mutually beneficial interaction between individuals and society. . . . Person–environment fit refers to the degree of congruence or correspondence between the individual's needs, capabilities, and aspirations, and the resources, demands, and opportunities characteristic of the environment." Achieving a good fit includes the coping behaviors of people and the qualities of the social and physical environment. Zelinka (1982) states that the goal is "discharge to the most suitable environment for continued good health care as soon as the patient's medical condition stabilizes."

At a more specific level, the Health Care Financing Administration (1981), clarified long-term care policies for elderly people with the following goals:

1. High quality of the care provided
   (a) Maximize each individual's chances of survival and, to the extent possible, the opportunity for physical, mental, social, and interpersonal functioning
2. Equitable access to needed services
   (a) Promote care in the least restrictive environment, subject to individual preferences and capabilities
   (b) Minimize gaps and coverage, particularly among the most indigent and impaired elderly
   (c) Equalize the geographic availability of health and social services
3. Cost control and service delivery
   (a) Assure that services are targeted to individuals who have demonstrated need for care
   (b) Reinforce, rather than erode, self-help and informal support from family and friends
   (c) Reduce the cost of inflation of long-term care services by more appropriate use of existing resources

In a similar vein, recent statements by study groups have set forth guidelines for the long-term care of children with chronic illness or disability (Ad Hoc Task Forces on Home Care of Chronically Ill Infants and Children, 1984; Butler, Rosenbaum, & Palfrey, 1987; Task Force Report on Technology Dependent Children, 1988). In recent years, medical technology has advanced with the result that many more infants and children are surviving birth-related disorders, life-threatening illness, and accidents. At the same time, trends in the delivery of medical care emphasize short hospital stays and increased provision of ambulatory and home-based care. Families, including very young and even first-time parents, therefore are, called on to assume major responsibilities for the ongoing care and coordination of comprehensive medical and social services for their child. Some families must juggle the sometimes conflicting needs of the ill or handicapped child with the needs of healthy siblings (Craft, Wyatt, & Sandell, 1985). Many of these families require ongoing case management services following discharge and in addition may require access to respite care (Los Angeles Children's Roundtable, 1989).

Most of the literature on discharge planning deals with populations of older people, but the goals are equally pertinent to work with families of infants, children, adolescents, and younger adults.

Discharge: An Essential Service

Effective discharge planning is critical to the patient's health and the family's welfare. It is also important to the hospital from a fiscal point of view: practitioners face pressures of time limits, in expediting the earliest possible discharge (Berkman, 1984; Caputi & Heiss, 1984). If the planning process is not adequate, the length of stay may increase when that is not desirable. The patient may be released to an inappropriate level of care, require readmission to the hospital, or suffer the loss of gains made during the period of hospitalization. In addition, the hospital may increase its risk of liability if discharge planning is inappropriate to the needs of the patient.

A report by a social work intern provides an example of an inappropriate discharge concerning an 84-year-old patient with terminal cancer. She had lived alone since the death of her husband 2 years prior. She was too ill to return home and refused to move to a nursing home; she felt she still needed hospital care. When the case was presented at a team meeting, the social worker recommended that the patient be allowed to remain in the hospital, at least until a conference could be held with the daughter and son who, along with the patient, could be involved in planning for the patient's discharge from the hospital. The physician, supported by the nurse, insisted that a nursing home placement be found immediately because the patient could not go home and could not remain in the hospital. The worker tried to help the patient to choose between two nursing homes, but the patient did not want to go to either of them. In desperation, she selected what she considered to be the best of the two placements and told the patient there simply was no alternative. Under protest, the patient was transferred to the nursing home. The next day, the social worker at the nursing home called to say the patient was too ill for the level of care provided in the nursing home: Two days later, the patient was sent back to the hospital and died a few days later. The daughter and son expressed much anger that they had not been involved in the shift from the hospital. Due to relative lack of experience and pressure from the physician and nurse, the social worker had compromised her own professional values and judgment.

How different the foregoing situation was from another one reported by Simmons (1986). Following hospitalization, a 68-year-old woman was discharged on a routine basis, without adequate assessment of the suitability of her return home to live with her son. After a period of time, the son called the hospital's case management program requesting the names of convalescent hospitals in order to place his mother. Her need for care was so great that it required the son to come home from work to assist her four times daily, threatening his employment and disrupting his personal life, which was hard on both of them. The social worker suggested a home visit to identify the problems and help mother and son consider the best solution to the problem. Assessment identified an extremely low income, lack of knowledge of eligibility for in-home health care, hazards to good nutrition, an untreated gout condition, and a lack of transporation to the physician's offices. But there was also a good relationship between mother and son and a desire to find out what was best for both of them. A planning session resulted in a decision, supported by the physician, to attempt in-home care. A variety of services were mobilized including personal care, Meals on Wheels, a lifeline emergency response system, physical therapy, and transporation to the physician's office. Along with stabilization of medications and treatment of gout, the enrichment of social support also proved stimulating. As a result, what seemed like a hopeless case transformed itself into a predictably safe in-home care arrangement with which both mother and son were extremely satisfied.

Discharge planning has high priority in assuring quality of care in social work departments in hospitals. This position is supported by a survey of 55 departmental directors (Patti & Ezell, 1988). Ninety-six percent of the respondents gave this service the second highest priority. The question, however, related to discharge planning within the time limits set by the policy of Diagnostic-Related Groups. Although the need to complete planning within a limited time period may indicate some reduction of quality, the third highest priority, selected by 93 percent of the directors, was that social work services should be provided in accord with quality of care standards. A concern is that the implementation of the plans had much lower priority than the planning itself—only 45 percent of the respondents gave this service high priority. A good plan can result in negative consequences unless it is implemented. There still tends to be over simplification of the discharge process, particularly for high risk patients and lack of conviction about the dangers posed by lack of adequate follow-up services for patients and family members.

In efforts to control rising costs, reimbursement agencies have initiated restrictive mechanisms, creating dilemmas for social workers (Berkman et al., 1988). Social workers must be held responsible for practicing within the values and standards of their profession. Fiscal requirements are not always in harmony with social work's humanistic value system. Discharge planning, a traditional task for social workers, still bears the stigma associated with the provision of concrete services, with inadequate understanding of the complexity of the service and its therapeutic aspects (Blazyk & Canavan, 1985). It is not a simple service. It is one of the most complex of all social work services, involving a collaborative effort among the patient, family members, appropriate professional staff, and often persons representing community resources. Involvement of the family is crucial to the success of the endeavor.

Effective discharge planning and follow-up requires a clinical social work framework (Caroff & Mailick, 1985). It requires a biopsychosocial assessment, efficient identification of patients and families in need of help, skilled supportive treatment of patient and/or family, knowledge about and ability to make effective referrals, linkage, case advocacy, and evaluation of the planning and follow-up process. Ideally, it begins with the patient's admission, and, once survival is assured, one of the central concerns of patients and their families is successful transition back to home and community when possible or to the best possible alternative living arrangement. Discharge planning, according to Caroff and Mailick, is a point of entry for the social worker and an ongoing theme which can be a focus for clinical work between the worker and the family, of which the patient is a member. The ecosystems approach to practice requires that the social worker take into account the biopsychosocial aspects of human behavior and development and the complex and multiple transactions that occur among people in their families, the health care system, social networks, and organizations. The intersystem approach is relevant because discharge planning and placement interventions involve the patient's and family members' coping with changing environments and the members' capacities to deal with the new surroundings. In the case of children, there is ample evidence that family members benefit from early participation in the care of their child and in preparation for their caretaking roles in the home (Algren, 1985; Tamlyn & Arklie, 1986).

Screening and Assessment

The complexity of discharge planning and follow-up makes it essential to identify families who are apt to require it as early as possible. Early screening for high-risk cases is one means of preparing for discharge from the beginning, even prior to admission to the hospital in some cases (Peterson et al., 1987). The need is for a valid system of determining which patients need social work help. One proposal is for a system of screening to identify patients with high social risk. Earlier screening and assessment may give practitioners more adequate time to use their skills, making more possible a thorough psychosocial assessment and the securing of essential resources. In one effective system, "preadmission screening combines an early psychosocial assessment with a needs assessment which emphasizes that effective social work practice combines a psychodynamic and environmental perspective" (Berkman et al., 1988, p. 49).

Efforts have been made to identify high-risk patients who need special discharge planning (Berkman et al., 1988; Wolock & Schlesinger, 1986). In a research project, Berkman and associates (1988) found that high-risk indicators are: no known method of payment; Asian patients or non-English speaking ones; living alone; age 75 or older; admitted to hospital from an institution, nursing home, chronic rehabilitation hospital, detoxification center, half-way house, or state school. The other important criterion is high-risk medical diagnoses or medical procedures—predominantly those that are life -threatening or physically dysfunctional illnesses or disabilities. The study demonstrated the value of preadmission screening, but it must be recognized that such screening cannot be done in emergencies. Other factors might also be important that were not covered in the survey but are known to influence posthospital adjustment, such as the level of functioning of the patients's family and environmental supports. Peterson and associates (1987) notes that high-risk screening may fail to identify many patients who need service. In a review of research on screening, Coulton (1988) noted lack of full agreement about the effectiveness of such procedures, partly because of failure to distinguish between screening, assessment, and early intervention (Rehr, Berkman, & Rosenberg, 1980).

As an alternative to case finding by social workers, some social work departments rely on referrals from other health professionals, usually physicians. The effectiveness of this source in identifying needy patients depends upon the referral agent's knowledge about the goals, values, and principles of modern discharge planning and follow-up. In the present climate of cost containment, the danger is ever present that staff involved in discharge planning will focus on the fiscal implications of the discharge plan and lose sight of the complex needs of the patient and family system. As Blumenfield (1986) says "discharge planning must not be allowed to become a euphuism for cost containment" (p. 52). Physicians may not be competent to identify appropriate cases. Peterson (1987) recommends that when social workers receive referrals, they should accept the referral as a starting point from which to do their own assessment and engage with the patient and family in a problem-solving process, rather than simply carrying out the orders of the referring person.

General guidelines for assessment apply to discharge planning as well as to other forms of treatment, but some information is particularly important (Caroff & Mailick, 1985; Zelinka, 1982). The focus of assessment is on the health status, needs, problems, and capacities of the patient, the needs of individuals in the family, family structure, processes, and resources; the nature and demands of the transition itself; and the resources, supports, and limitations of the environment.

In assessment of the patient, it is important to be clear about the affects of age, gender, race, ethnicity, and marital status on the planning process. These characteristics help to determine the fit between the person and the living environments into which he might move. The patient's physical and mental status partially determine his opportunities for having a reasonable quality of life. Among these health issues are mobility, vision and hearing capacities, depression, incontinence, medications, alcohol and drug abuse, and risk of suicide (Simmons, 1986).

Since the family has the potential for being the primary support and/or care group for the patient, discharge planning takes into account the adequacy of the family's functioning and resources. Guidelines for the assessment of families have been proposed by Caroff and Mailick, (1985), Coyle (1962), Northen (1982), Somers (1965), and Wilson and Ryland (1964). The content of the assessment includes:

1. Life stage of family and age and position of the ill or disabled member;
2. Family values within the context of culture, attitudes toward responsibility, dependence, and independence;
3. Commonly held goals and goals of individuals that are different;
4. The meaning of the illness or disability to the family, particularly when it offers secondary gains, encapsulates the system, or maintains a dysfunctional system;
5. The quality of relationships within the family;
6. How family members communicate information, opinions, and feelings.
7. How family members resolve both instrumental and affective problems associated with the illness or disability;
8. Rigidity or permeability of family boundaries;
9. Role-patterning and rule-making that influence the division of labor and the distribution of authority;
10. The resources of the family, including the degree to which it has a supportive network and its financial circumstances;

11. The nature and severity of stressful situations, in addition to those occasioned by the illness or disability of a member; some families are so overwhelmed by stress that they are already at-risk and unable to take much responsibility for the after-care of the patient.

In addition to understanding the patient and family, it is necessary to assess the nature of the particular transition and its meaning to the patient and family. Although the person may still be sick or disabled, once discharged from the hospital, he assumes a new role of former patient, with its own special characteristics. When in the hospital the patient grants a large degree of control to the hospital with the expectation that the power will be used appropriately to cure or ease the medical problem. Discharge planning demands a sudden reversal of the patient role in that the former patient, family members, or others need to quickly resume responsibility for activities that were suspended during hospitalization. It is a transition state that suggests the need for substantial life reorganization and changes in identity. Usually, the hospital staff's responsibility to the patient and family ends. "When the person leaving the hospital is impaired, chronically ill, or in need of rehabilitation, placement, or intensive after-care, however, there may be more difficulty in coping with the change of status" (Blazyk & Canavan, 1985, p. 491). Family members may fear the unknown, have difficulty in facing the reality of taking home a member with medical difficulties, who also may feel depressed and have impaired capacities for independence. Blazyk and Canavan go on to say that "as long as the family member is safely cared for by hospital personnel, the family need not directly face the reality of discharge. The denial of any long term deficiencies in the patient's functioning can be maintained as long as hospital care and treatment are continued and hope is fostered. Once discharge becomes imminent, the new homeostasis is threatened, as is the denial that has aided the family or patient thus far and the stage is set for a discharge crisis" (p. 491). Good discharge planning and follow-up can prevent that crisis from occurring.

Assessment of supports, opportunities, and obstacles in the environment are important, including evaluation of the home as an environment when returning home is a viable alternative or evaluation of other living facilities that may be considered in the decision-making process. The environment surrounding the place of residence also needs to be assessed. In assessing living environments, it is necessary to consider whether they provide adequate opportunities for interchange with other people to prevent isolation of the former patient. There is need to consider the cultural milieu in relation to the former patient's values and traditions and the opportunities for social activities and the pursuit of hobbies. "Effective biopsychosocial functioning requires environments that are responsive to individual needs, place realistic demands on persons, and provide opportunities to master developmental tasks and to secure the resources essential for effective living" (Northen, 1988, p. 21).

The data secured from the assessment are essential to determine the maximum feasible level of independence possible for the patient. There is a risk that patients may be placed unnecessarily in an institution who would be able to return home or live in another, less restrictive, environment. The opposite risk is the placement of the patient at home or in a setting that requires considerable independence when the patient needs more safeguards and supports. Within a general level of dependence–independence, it is essential to find the best possible solution for a particular person, taking into account patient–family needs and interests.

Intervention

Social workers' interventions consist of all of the sets of techniques used in clinical social work, with a focus on relocation of patients from the medical facility to their own home or to an alternative residence or from their own home to another setting. The major tasks for the social worker are both socioemotional and instrumental in nature. The tasks are to:

1. Analyze the implications of the assessment for making and implementing a plan and explore for additional information when indicated.
2. Facilitate the participation of the family, including the patient, to the fullest extent possible in deciding upon and implementing a postdischarge plan.
3. Clarify the feelings and attitudes of family members toward the patient's medical condition and discharge.
4. Involve appropriate medical personnel in providing adequate, appropriate information about the medical situation and the purpose and rationale for discharge at a given time.
5. Use a family problem-solving process to make decisions about the patient's relocation.
6. Assist the family in implementing the plan, making use of specialized instruction, skill-training, and community resources.
7. Terminate the patient's and family's contacts within the health care facility and make a transition to the new setting.
8. Assure the patient and family that there will be adequate follow-up in monitoring, evaluating, and, when indicated, changing the plan.

Planning

The assessment of patient, family, transition, and environment guides the practitioner in carrying out the other tasks. For example, the degree of mobility and the specific needs for health care are factors in deciding where the patient can relocate. The family's ability to reorganize its role structure in flexible ways, the health of other family members, and the family's financial situation influence whether or not the patient should return home or what external resources will be necessary to make at-home care possible. Assessment of the positive and negative characteristics of available out-of-home care is crucial to determine the fit between the patient and the possible site of relocation.

Discharge plans are apt to be suitable and effective if the patient and other members of the family participate actively in the family sessions. One important key to the success of effective discharge is involving the patient, other members of their families, and persons in the resource system in planning and decision-making processes so as to assure that their unique perspectives are included (Simmons, 1986). Active participation enhances the likelihood of compliance with and successful implementation of plans and makes more possible retention or restoration of maximum independence and avoidance of needless institutionalization. The social worker serves as a link to the patient, family, and community resources (Shulman and Tuzman, 1980).

A number of factors can erode the patient's participation in the planning process. Clearly, reduced length of stay and increasing pressure to move the patient out swiftly point to a need for early initiation of discharge planning (Berkman, 1984; Caputi & Heiss, 1984). Lack of family, conflicts among family members, lack of knowledge of resources and modes of payment, financial problems, extremely poor health, and misperceptions of the patient's ability to make decisions contribute to a dangerous tendency to minimal involvement of patients and families in the planning process. Simmons (1986, p. 12) reminds social workers that "it is all too easy to view discharge planning as a service provided by professionals rather than a collaborative effort between professionals, patients, and families." Full involvement of the patient and other family members is critical to the successful implementation of the plan, since the successful carrying out of the plan often involves their approval and cooperative efforts. Not only is there a tendency to plan for, rather than with, the family, but too often the choice is made to work only with the patient or a family member instead of with the family unit to which the patient belongs.

A study by Abramson (1988) found that most elderly patients do participate in planning for discharge from acute care hospitals and that they often control the decision. When the family controls the decision, even patients who are competent to participate have very little influence on the plan for their futures. In almost all situations, family members or significant other persons participated in the planning process. Workers spent substantially more time with family members than they did with patients. Abramson reports that these findings are consistent with those of other studies (Coulton el al., 1982; Gambel, Heilbron, & Reamer, 1980; Levey, 1980; Townsend, 1986, York & Caslyn, 1977). In Abramson's study, the connection between high levels of family activity and low levels of patient activity was frequently due to the poor physical condition of the patient and priority given to the interests of the family over those of the patient. As reported in Chapter 2, loss of control over the physical and social environment is associated with impaired physical and mental health, decreased personal and social well-being, and increased mortality rates, especially among those elderly persons who are forced to relocate.

The studies on patient participation in discharge planning fail to take into account the inextricable connection between patient and other family members. Patients are members of families even when hospitalized and needing to be relocated away from the family. Self-determination is an important value, but so, too, is the right of people to participate in making decisions that affect their lives. What happens to one member of the family—the patient—also influences the other members.

Describing the role of the administrator, Simmons (1987, p. 10) notes that "a cornerstone of effective leadership is the development of consensus building skills to mobilize existing human resources on behalf of a common goal. True power rests on the ability to build consensus about shared values and goals and to build agreement about methods for achieving them." At the microlevel of intervention in discharge planning, the intent is to achieve a true consensus among patient, other family members, social worker, and physician concerning the values, goals of relocation, and ways of achieving a good fit between the patient-family unit needs, and the resources to be selected. The patient's and family's welfare are inextricably interwoven.

The social worker enables family members to participate in many ways. People participate in meetings when they are clear about the purpose and feel that they have something to contribute. Hence, the practitioner should clarify the purpose and explain how each member of the family can influence the plan to be made. As in other forms of service previously presented, the practitioner develops a relationship of trust and conveys, through nonverbal as well as verbal comments, acceptance, genuineness, and empathy. She may open the meeting by commenting, so as to reduce anxiety, that people often hesitate to speak at first, suggest that perhaps the patient might begin by giving his ideas about what he would like to happen when he leaves the hospital or other residence, and ask other members to comment on that, showing acceptance of what each has to say. By beginning with the patient, it is clear to everyone that his own opinions are important. She may offer support in the form of realistic reassurance and encouragement. She provides whatever information the members need to explore an issue or suggest solutions to problems. She structures the room so that there is ease of communication among the members. There are times when she may need to regulate the conversation by reminding members of the purpose and focus of the session, limiting a member who tries to control or dominate the discussion so as to provide opportunity for others to participate. She involves the members in the process through giving active encouragement, attending to each member's message, and making nonverbal gestures of support. Through comments and questions, she requests verbalization of information, feelings, and ideas and seek responses from other members to the comments and questions of one.

Family members are apt to come into the planning session with considerable anxiety and uncertainly about the patient's future and what is expected of them in dealing with the issues of relocation. Knowledge that the patient is no longer to remain in the hospital or other living place may arouse feelings about the illness or disability and its consequences for daily living; the nature and quality of care that has been given; and a spirit of hopefulness or despair about the prognosis. The practitioner opens up discussion of these doubts and feelings through some appropriate comment to convey the information that preparing for discharge often seems difficult for the patient and other family members, that people often feel somewhat upset about the patient's condition, or they may have quite different feelings and ideas about the best plan for the patient and family. Through her own accepting behavior, she encourages ventilation of feelings and comments on those that are shared and those that might be unique to a particular person. As anxiety and concerns become understandable, the members may be freed to engage in a problem-solving process to develop a postdischarge plan for the patient and family members.

Anxiety, uncertainty, and lack of hope are partially reduced through their expression and clarification, but accurate knowledge is essential to change people's perceptions of the transitional situation. Discharge planning is a team effort, involving physicians in making and explaining diagnoses, prognoses, and complications in daily living stemming from the illness or disability. Patients and family members need to have a common understanding of these medical matters. Nurses may need to be involved in providing knowledge and skills necessary for self-care or for family members to care for the patient. If reasons for recommending or requiring discharge at a particular time are made clear to the family, such information might dispel fears of too early discharge and enhance motivation to work toward a viable plan.

The heart of the discharge planning process is the use of a group problem-solving approach to making decisions about a postdischarge plan for the patient. The steps in the process were described in Chapter 7: recognizing the difficulty; defining the problems and goals; considering alternative proposals; choosing one from among the proposals made; planning a course of action for implementing the decision; and carrying out the plan and evaluating the results. The difficulty is clearly that of making a transition from living in one place to moving to another place and usually also includes relinquishing the hospitalized patient role to become a former patient. The patient may need to relocate in his own home, a relative's home, a board and care home, a rehabilitation center, a retirement community that has medical and health services, or a nursing home. The problems in achieving a good plan will vary with the data secured during the process of assessment. Of particular importance is the severity of the remaining medical problems.

Golan (1986) has suggested a number of typical problems associated with life transitions. As adapted to discharge planning, they include the need to cope with the threat to the sense of security that came from the structure and familiar routines of the hospitalization; anxieties and frustrations involved in pressures to make decisions within a brief period of time; lack of communication between and among family members; lack of family cohesiveness; ambivalence about the choices that are available and the one that is made; the need to develop new standards of well-being, often including coming to terms with lessened gratifications; dealing with loss and separation from significant persons in the situation being left; coping with feelings of inadequacy and loss of self-esteem occasioned by loss or changes in roles and interpersonal relationships held prior to the illness or disability; and lack of adequate money, medical supplies, and other material resources.

In achieving the goals of discharge planning, practitioners intervene to lessen or resolve the problems that interfere with making and implementing a satisfactory postdischarge plan. Simultaneously, with a focus on the cognitive tasks involved in problem-solving, practitioners attend to the affective and relationship aspects of individual and family behavior.

Adequate consideration of alternate proposals is crucial in the decision-making process. Studies provide considerable evidence that having choices has a significant impact on the health and satisfaction of former patients (Beaver, 1979; Ferrari, 1963; Jones & Manor, 1977;). These studies support the conclusion of Coulton et al. (1982) that "careful consideration of alternatives for long term care and the environment each would provide may lead more often to the selection of an environment that is congruent with a patient's perceptions of his or her own needs and desires. Closer fit between person and environment has been shown to have a positive effect on the physical and mental health of the elderly individual and long term care." These authors were writing about elderly patients, but the conclusion is also pertinent to work with children and younger adults.

A challenge to social workers is to involve the family even when the time available is short. Not all patients have family members with whom they regularly interact. Hubschman (1983) reports a case in which the business office of a hospital called the social worker to state that a patient in his late 1970s needed to be discharged very soon. After meeting with the patient, the worker learned he had a sister and a brother living in the city whom he had not seen for a number of years, but he did not object to the worker's suggestion that she contact them. The siblings were startled to get the call, said they had a poor relationship with the patient, and did not want to be burdened with him. When the worker reassured them that there would be no obligation on their part, they agreed to come to a meeting to help make a decision about discharge. They made it very clear that they were unwilling, however, to take care of him or to pay for the cost of care. When the family session began, the atmosphere was cold. The worker restated the purpose of the meeting and commented that it was good that they had all expressed enough interest to explore a plan together. The patient said he was not sure of their interest and said "they would be glad when he was dead." Brother and sister reacted with silence. The worker made clear that they were not there to bring up the past but to make the best plan for the patient. After considerable discussion, they all agreed that since the patient could not return to independent living, he would sell his home and get the care he needed in a nursing home. His brother and sister agreed to help him sell his home and distribute its contents. At the conclusion of the meeting, they agreed they would keep in closer touch and might even look forward to a better relationship.

Following the meeting, the social worker met with the patient to assure him that she would meet with him before the final discharge. She also met with the brother and sister, who talked about the positive changes in their brother. The worker had made clear that the final decision was the patient's, thus enhancing his sense of control over his destiny; but she also involved family members in the planning process. As in this case, it is important not to work around the patient or to form alliances with family members that exclude the patient. Important decisions to be made in the problem-solving process include the selection of a residence for the patient; family members' roles in caring for, supporting, or engaging in activities with the patient; the kind and amount of self-care by the patient; and the human and material resources to be sought and used.

Whatever the setting to which the patient goes, he is required to make rapid changes from a hospitalized patient role, which encourages dependency and relieves him temporarily from obligations, to a discharged patient role in which the physical environment is far different as are expectations for his behavior. The patient needs to learn new roles and family members need to learn to adapt to those roles. "Discharge demands a sudden reversal of the patient role in that the individual, family, or society must quickly resume responsibility for activities and burdens suspended during hospitalization" (Blazyk & Canavan, 1985, p.491). As noted earlier, discharge is a transition that may require substantial changes in expectations for the patient and the family. Realistic goal setting requires knowledge about what the patient's needs are and assessment of anticipated changes in family functioning.

Return home is often the choice that is made by families, particularly with the increased emphasis in health care on preventing institutionalization and the increased availability of home health care. Basic to the success of this plan is a thorough assessment of the family unit in its broader physical and social environment and changes in family functioning that are bound to occur with the return of the patient. When a patient returns home and still needs some assistance with the tasks of daily living, the burden of care and concern for the patient falls largely on the family. The social worker may need to work with the family to renegotiate roles and deal with the feelings and attitudes about them. Before making the decision final, the family needs to acquire understanding of the impact of the illness or disability and any long-term consequences on family life. Blazyk and Canavan (1985) have identified two extreme attitudes of family members that effect the patient's readjustment to family living. One pattern is exclusion of the patient from many family activities; the family has closed ranks without the absent member and continues to maintain minimal communication with him. The other pattern is overinvolvement, in which the family is unable to recognize positive changes in the patient's condition, and family activities are focused around the patient. When such patterns are identified, therapeutic techniques, as elaborated in Chapter 7, are used in short-term treatment.

Adequate attention to the roles of family members in taking care of a patient is an important facet of planning. When many tasks are involved, different members may assume responsibility for them, according to their interests and abilities. Too often, caretaking becomes centralized in one member and becomes a tremendous burden for that person (Cox, Parsons, & Kimboko, 1988). Many caretakers are worn out from the time and difficult responsibilities of caring for another family member, with the result that their own mental and physical health is impaired. The need is to plan for adequate external resources and for respite care for the primary caretaker (Scharlach, 1988). With renewed interest in families as natural helping systems has come recognition that family resources must not be overextended (Brody, 1979; Cantor, Rehr, & Trotz, 1981; Simmons, 1986; Simmons, Ivry, & Seltzer, 1985). Many adults have other demands from children, marriage, parents, and careers concurrent with the care of a patient.

As part of the planning and after relocation, social workers become resource consultants. They direct their attention to family members' capacities to use their personal resources and skills in order to achieve their agreed-upon goals. The provision of services—financial assistance, medicaid, house-keeping, and health care—is necessary, but the need is to provide them in such a way that they do not reinforce dependency and powerlessness. Solomon (1976, p. 347) says that "the resource consultant role is defined here much more broadly than that of resource dispenser or resource provider; it involves linking clients to resources in a manner that enhances their self-esteem as well as their problem-solving capacities." The consultant offers his knowledge and expertise to the family, whose members participate extensively in the process. The consultant needs to assess the family's positive motivation or resistance to the use of community resources that are available. Some services may be rejected because of pride, insistence on independence, or unwillingness to spend available money. When that happens, exploration of feelings and attitudes is essential, followed by information about the need and consideration of the consequences of refusal to use resources that are thought to be necessary to the patient's health.

When home care is the preferred choice of the patient and family system, the social worker's task is not completed. There is need to monitor the plan to assure its continued suitability. As situations change, the original decision needs to be renegotiated. In one situation, for example, as the patient became able to do more for herself, the family members encouraged this, but the patient interpreted the change as rejection and angrily complained that the family was no longer providing care. A family conference was held with the goal of reestablishing a coordinated care plan. It became clear to the social worker and other staff present that the type of care given had changed because the patient's needs had changed. The patient had enjoyed having people wait on her: What she viewed as rejection was the family's reaction to her being more able to become independent. The changes, however, were not discussed with the patient. When reassured about the fact that she was still loved and the reasons for the changes explained, a new plan was worked out with the participation of the nurse and home health aide concerning the distribution of responsibilities between the patient and other family members. After trying out the new plan for a week, all agreed that it was realistic and workable (Lotz, 1982). The social worker, using an ecosystems approach, is often the most appropriate person to coordinate the services provided to the patient and family (Kirschner & Rosengarten, 1982).

Alternatives to Home Care

Alternatives to home care are numerous and may be more appropriate fo the patient than efforts to maintain the patient in a home setting. Dependin upon the patient's goals and the medical–social situation, the decision may be placement in some type of residential facility. In addition to assessment of the patient–family–community interaction, careful attention needs to be given to the proposed residence itself in order to assure a good fit of the patient/family with the new environment. Among the many factors to be considered are the religious or sectarian auspice; standards of sanitation and safety; arrangement for cooking or meal service; the attractiveness of the physical surroundings; opportunities for socialization; arrangements concerning furnished rooms or provision of one's own furniture and supplies; the size of units; schedules that must be followed; the program of activities; opportunities for participation in the community; and the ease with which family members can visit or the patient can visit them and travel elsewhere if the physical condition permits it. Finally, the values and norms of the institution, as they support or conflict with those of the patient, are important determinants of the suitability of a particular place for a given person.

An example is from the case of Mrs. N., age 82, who came to live with her daughter, Mrs. A., son-in-law, Mr. A., and their three children 3 years ago, following the sudden death of her husband. Mrs. N. fell and broke her hip a year ago and was returned home upon discharge from the hospital. She also had a congestive heart problem. Mr. A.'s work kept him away from home two or three nights a week. Until the incident of the broken hip, the plan for having Mrs. N. in the home had worked well because Mrs. N. helped with the care of the home and the children so Mrs. A. could work part-time. During the past 3 months, conflict between Mrs. N. and her daughter and son-in-law accelerated. Mr. and Mrs. A. became frustrated by the amount of care demanded by Mrs. N., who seemed to enjoy being waited upon. Mrs. N. also became upset because the children, now ages 16, 15, and 12, were spending more time with their friends and behaving in ways that were disapproved of by their grandmother. After an intense argument, Mr. A. said he could not stand the quarreling any longer, so his mother-in-law would have to go to a rest home. She could no longer remain with them. Mrs. N. was shocked, hurt, and angry, protesting that whatever was the source of tension was not her fault. She called her social worker in the home health care center, who arranged for a family conference.

Mrs. N. and Mr. and Mrs. A. were present when the worker arrived for the conference. When the worker asked if the children would be coming to the meeting, Mr. A. said this was not their business—that the adults had to settle matters first. The worker opened the session by saying she thought they all knew that Mrs. N. had called her because she felt she was no longer wanted here, and this matter was something the family should talk about. Mrs. N. said she did not know what had happened—things were going all right so far as she was concerned. Mrs. A. then said calmly, "Mother, you have been living with us, and it is not easy to say this, but we feel it would be better for you to live somewhere else, at least for awhile." Mrs. N. said, "Awhile—I'll be dead in a while—I'm an old lady with a weak heart." Mr. A. said, "but, much as we love you, we cannot go on as we are now, and we'll be glad to pay for your care in a home where you can make friends and we can visit you." Mrs. N. cried and, after a while, said that she had long dreaded such a day. Mr. and Mrs. A. were both upset by this and said they just didn't know what to do now. The worker commented that it was natural for them all to feel sad about the situation. Mrs. A. said, "It makes me want to change my mind," and then, after a silence, "but it just won't work." The worker said she realized it would be hard to make such an important decision. They might change their minds, but, if they were adamant about Mrs. N.'s leaving, there were many other things to consider. . . .

At the next session, the worker had some time alone with Mrs. N., who said she'd been wanting to talk to her. She said she had decided that she wants to leave—"they keep me penned up here now that I'm old—and, to tell you the truth, I am old. I'm not much good at doing useful things anymore, but I can visit, crochet, take care of my room, and even cook some favorite things." At this time, Mr. and Mrs. A. arrived. The worker opened the session by saying we had a big job to do—to find out what plan for living is best for Mrs. N. and also best for the A. family. She suggested that Mrs. N. begin by trying to say what she thought would be the best living situation for her. She said that since she couldn't live here, she'd like to find a place where she could make some friends "since you all reject me." Mr. and Mrs. A. looked sad, but Mrs A. said they still loved her—they did not reject her—but they thought she'd be happier elsewhere. Mrs. N. then started to talk about the kind of living situation she would like. She wants to live where she can get whatever health care she needs now or later; she doesn't want to live with too many strangers or with only old women; she wanted a place where she could make friends and go places, like the movies. She didn't want to sit in a rocking chair all day. . . .

Three days later, the daughter called to say that she had told the children about the plan to have Mrs. N. move out. The two older children, particularly, had reacted with anger and resentment against the parents, accusing them of turning out someone who had helped them and whom they loved. The daughter had been hysterical about it all evening. The children felt they must be to blame for it and promised to do anything to keep their grandmother here. Mrs. A. said she was not sure they could go through with the placement, and the worker agreed they should take time to reconsider it. She suggested the children attend the next family session.

Mrs. A. opened the session by saying that the family was agreed that they could work out their problems without placing Mrs. N. somewhere else. The oldest boy said he certainly would do anything not to lose his grandmother, and the other children agreed with him. Mrs. N. said, "Now they don't want me to leave, but I want to go. We won't be losing each other. I'll visit them, but I won't be a burden anymore." The other members insisted she would not be a burden, but Mrs. N. said she had never planned to live with them forever. It was nice coming here when her husband died, and then she had to stay because of the broken hip, but now she can get along all right with her walker. Later she said, "I know that you care about me, but you're like all the other young folks, you think you have to look after an old lady like a child." The worker suggested that the decision had to be one that Mrs. N. could accept, but that before the final decision, she should consider the family's wishes. Maybe they should find out what alternative living arrangements would be possible before the final decision. Mrs. N. said her mind was made up, but she certainly needed help in finding a place to live. Mrs. A. was crying during this time. Then she put her arm around her mother and said, "You know that we all love you. I don't know what we were thinking to ever ask that you leave." Mrs. N. said, "I do know. If you hadn't loved me, I'd have left long ago." Mrs. A. turned to the worker and said, "Tell her that she should give up her notion of ever leaving us." The worker said she couldn't do this: Mrs. N. could not be forced to stay here. It would be important for everyone to think more about this matter.

Mrs. N. thanked the worker for coming. The daughter and son-in-law followed the worker out of the house to say they couldn't understand it and didn't know what to do. The worker suggested they talk more about this with each other and the children, reviewing the times when they were not happy together and whether they could really change those things that bothered them then. They explained that their friends and relatives would criticize them for placing their mother somewhere else, and Mrs. A. thought maybe her mother was determined to leave just to spite them for asking her to leave. The worker said that these things might be true, but Mrs. N. seemed to really want to try to find a place where she could make friends and be more independent.

At the next session, Mr. A. said that things were going along just fine here, and Mrs. N. seemed to be her old, cheerful self again, but she was still determined to leave. Mrs. N. said, "That's right." The worker asked if everyone would be willing to let Mrs. N. go if she could find a place that would be suitable for her and where they could visit back and forth. Mrs. A. said they really have no choice, and they would all do whatever they could to help Mrs. N. do whatever would make her happy. Mrs. N. asked if the worker had gotten any information about places where she might live. The worker described several options, including a board and care home, a foster family home, and a retirement home. She said she did not think that Mrs. N. would want a rest home or a nursing home—she was too active for that. Mrs. N. agreed. The family participated in asking questions about the different types of facilities. The children insisted it be a place where they could visit and be close enough that Mrs. N. could come to stay with them at times. Mrs. N. said she thought that two of the places seemed very nice and asked further questions about them, asking if she could visit them. Mr. A. said he'd be glad to take Mrs. N. to visit those two places along with the worker.

When Mr. A. and Mrs. N. arrived at the agency, Mr. A. asked if he should go along with the worker and Mrs. N. to see the places. Mrs. N. said she'd rather just go alone with the worker because she really wanted to make up her own mind. As they drove to the first place, Mrs. N. told the worker that she really wanted to be where she could go places when she felt well enough—to movies and concerts: She felt her family had been too fearful of letting her do things. Mrs. N. thought the first place, a group home, would be suitable, but the worker said she thought she should also look at the other place—a retirement home in which there were health facilities, such as the physical therapy that Mrs. N. needed, and a small kitchen in the studio apartments where residents could fix a cup of tea or other snacks. Mrs. N. was driven all around the retirement place in a wheelchair so she could see it faster. When she returned to the office where the worker was waiting, she said "this is where I want to be." She asked more questions of the manager and learned that she could bring her own furniture, if she wished, and that they had activities that she could attend, and a bus to take residents to events in the community. She commented that it took her a long time to make up her mind to live independently of her daughter's family, but once she made up her mind, she was a sticker. When they reached the daughter's home, the entire family greeted them, full of questions. Mrs. N. told them of her decision and said that now that she knew what she really wanted to do, she'd like for them all to come and see the place before she moves in. That was easily arranged.

This case illustrates the use of clinical social work knowledge and skills in helping a family to make an appropriate decision concerning a plan for one of its members. Within a process of working with the family, the practitioner assessed the patient's needs, capacities, and resources; the patterns of communication and relationships among the members; the relative merits of varied living arrangements; and the suitability of alternative plans for the patient and other members of the family. She supported the expression of feelings and acknowledged the conflicts among the members. She did not minimize the importance of the conflicts, but she engaged the members in evaluating the importance of them in terms of interpersonal and family relationships. She engaged the family in a problem-solving process that led to a decision that was acceptable to the patient and the rest of the family. She met separately, for brief periods of time, with the patient and with the daughter and son-in-law, making flexible use of individual, couple, and family sessions. She asserted the value that the ultimate decision was to be made by the patient, but with a concern also for the family's well-being. She used all of the major categories of interventive skills that were elaborated in Chapter 6.

Although nursing homes were not seriously considered for Mrs. N., even though that was the initial plan of Mr. and Mrs. A., they are suitable and necessary in many instances. When it is necessary to move to a nursing home, stress tends to increase for both the patient and the family. A considerable amount of stigma is attached to placement in nursing homes, and families often feel guilty and frustrated in not being able to take adequate care of a family member. The high cost also creates serious problems for families; most insurance does not cover nursing home care. In a study of the perceived stressfulness of becoming a nursing home resident, Gordon (1985) tested and validated this new item for the scale of Holmes and Rahe (1967) on stressful life events. The findings were that this event was perceived as being more stressful than marriage, personal injury, and illness, and about equally as stressful as a jail term or the death of a close family member, other than a spouse.

There is some reality to resistance to entering nursing homes. Indeed, a recent report from the Health Care Financing Administration states that approximately 43 percent of nursing homes nationwide did not meet standards for food safety, and 30 percent did not meet standards for the personal care needs of patients (*Seattle Times,* December 4, 1988). The report gives information about all the nation's long-term care facilities that accept residents served by Medicare or Medicaid. But, despite these situations, the study also showed that the quality of care is better than ever, and that there are some excellent facilities. The implication for practice is that social workers carefully assess the quality of particular nursing homes before presenting them as alternatives.

Pilsuk and Parks (1988) provide evidence that home care is not necessarily better or cheaper than nursing homes. The important point, however, is that the concern of social work is the welfare of the patient and family. Most persons being cared for at home are not candidates for nursing homes. Most nursing home residents are older, single, have major medical or mental disorders, and are highly dependent. Many are not long-term residents (Lewis, Cretin, & Kane, 1985). What is needed is a policy that provides for continuity of care from independent living to institutionalization and back to home care, when possible. In a good nursing home, there is not only attention to medical needs, but also to the psychosocial needs of the residents.

Research by Retsinas and Garrity (1985) challenges the prevalent view that residents in nursing homes are unable to form meaningful relationships with other residents. They point out that "not withstanding the popular image of residents who wait only for visitors from 'outside,' the nursing home contains a lively social world with its own friendship patterns. Intimacy remains a human need (Lowenthal and Haven, 1968) and residents who can no longer fill roles of worker, spouse, or parent can still be friends—a role central to the residents' morale" (p. 376). There may be serious barriers to social participation, such as severe medical problems, arrangement of physical space that discourages movement, or inadequate or unattractive central areas. In their study of nursing home residents, Retsinas and Garrity concluded that "within a nursing home, residents do make friends, and the key determinants of sociability are the residents' lucidity, ability to speak, and ability to see. . . . For residents who are able to communicate, the nursing home may offer new friendships. Indeed, withdrawing from the larger world may enable residents to enter a new social world" (pp. 379, 384). It is important to recognize that the study did not consider the issue of the extent to which the staff offers a program of activities and counseling to help residents develop skills in relationships and participate in available activities.

In analyzing alternatives to institutionalization of the frail elderly, Knight and Walker (1985, p. 361) point out that for some individuals, institutional care may be necessary and appropriate. Families may be able and willing to provide care, or they may not. Some families lack capacity to perform skilled nursing care; indeed, they may engage in behavior toward the patient that is clearly harmful to physical health and social well-being. When institutionalization is clearly necessary, the responsibility is to select the least restrictive and most life-enhancing environment.

Discharge from a hospital or rehabilitation center is a process of termination from a place that provides a network of health and social services. To be helpful to the client in leaving the medical facility, the practitioner needs a perspective on human development that incorporates the concepts of loss and separation related to the significance of social relationships to people and that explains the ways people defend themselves against, cope with, and master the experience of separation and loss (Erikson, 1963; Maas, 1984; Shapiro, 1980). The nature and intensity of the feelings depend upon numerous factors: the health status of the patient, the length of hospitalization, the available network of social supports, the persons from whom the patient will be separated, the environment that he is leaving and the one into which he is moving, and past experiences with separation. Patients and family members often have developed a network of meaningful relationships with personnel and other patients in the health care facility and have derived a sense of security from the schedule and routines, even though they may be eager to leave. Discharge may also mean separating from a social worker in situations when the social worker is not able to do the follow through work.

Examples of some of the feelings that patients have about leaving the medical setting are indicated by the following statements:

Mrs. G. I don't care when they set the date for me to leave. If I have to leave, I'll just go on and leave. If the doctors are through with me here, and there's nothing else they can do for me, and if they don't want me here, then I'll just go ahead and leave.
Mrs. T. I don't want to go. I want to stay here, but they won't let me.
Mr. B. You've been so helpful. How in the world will I manage without you, and without my nurse?

In a poignant excerpt from a family interview with a patient with metastic disease, her husband, and daughter, the patient describes the impact that leaving the hospital had on her. Worby and Babineau (1974) assert that the presence of a physician and social worker enables the family members to disclose the feelings they had been fearful of discussing among one another, facilitating the grieving process.

Patient: I came home from the hospital and I wasn't myself.
Daughter: No. Well, I stayed with her. In fact, I think I handled her more than Dad did. So, she seemed to be pretty good when she was with me.
Patient: I was terribly depressed when I went home from the hospital. I didn't want to go home.
Husband: No, she fought going home.
Patient: Oh, I didn't want to go home, Doctor. Why was that? When they told me I was going home, I just—I didn't think I was ready to go home.
Daughter: That's all she'd say.
Husband: I think it was the fear of leaving the hospital and the care she'd been receiving, knowing she wouldn't be able to get that same care at home. However, the doctors told me the care was not needed and there was *no* reason she couldn't go home.
Patient: I felt like I'd lost my last friend when they sent me home.
Social worker: The hospital being kind of a friend, so to speak?
Patient: Uh huh. Having what I have.
Husband: That first night at home was like a nightmare. I sat up all night long with her. The next morning I called her doctor and explained the situation, and he immediately prescribed a sleeping capsule.
Doctor: You must have been scared.
Patient: I was.
Doctor: You must have been panicked.
Husband: She was. She had some rather bad moments all night long.
Patient: I was just petrified. I was frightened, afraid of being alone. And, as I say, I got all that attention in the hospital. I had all that care

and then to just be sent home on my own . . . I was just petrified. And then when they said they were going to send me home. . . . [laughs]
Doctor: You figured they gave up on you.
Patient: Yes, I just figured they would send me home to die, see? Now I can talk about it. I couldn't talk about it before. I was so scared, I couldn't even talk about it.
Husband: This is the first I actually heard her talk about it.
Daughter: Uh huh.
Social worker: Is this new to you, too, talking freely like this?
Husband: Yes.

The transition from hospital to home or another type of residence is often difficult for patient and family. Social workers need to recognize these feelings, permit their expression, clarify their nature, and move toward a focus on the future. As doubts and concerns become understandable, people are freed to act on the positive side of the ambivalence and move ahead to next steps.

The selection of a particular plan for the care of the patient is a complicated decision that takes into account the patient's needs, not just for adequate nursing and other health care, but also for opportunities to participate in family and community activities to the extent possible within the limitations of the medical condition; the family's availability, willingness, and capacity to provide the essential care; and the informal social and material resources that are available and to which the family has access. The best interests of the patient guide the problem-solving process, but that is insufficient: The welfare of the family must also be considered. In the long run, these go together.

Once a choice has been made, further decisions need to be made concerning which family members will do what to carry out the plan and then to prepare them to assume the accepted responsibilities. For example, in a home care plan, considerable education may be needed to teach the specific skills required to care for the patient, to enhance the ability of the patient to care for himself as much as possible, and to learn what the necessary resources are and how to apply for them. When interpersonal conflict emerges, the practitioner helps the family to face and resolve it. In addition to cognitive teaching, the practitioner may engage the family in demonstrations, rehearsal, and role-playing to prepare them for carrying out their tasks in a competent manner. When the patient is to move to a new setting, decisions need to be made and enacted concerning such matters as completing admission procedures, moving possessions, preparing the new room or apartment, always with the fullest possible participation of the patient. Follow through is as essential as is planning and carrying out the plan.

The problem-solving process moves from decision to action: The plan must be implemented. Ideally, there is continuity of service through action and follow-up. Follow-up activities are often referred to as case management, but that term indicates that the practitioner is the one who manages, rather than the person who helps the family to coordinate needed services to the extent of its ability. The practitioner bears the responsibility to help the patient/family adapt to the patient's return home or to maximize the potential benefits of placement outside the home.

Ensuring accessibility and continuity of services after discharge is often essential. Families may need counseling as difficulties in reintegrating the patient into family life occur or as a patient is adapting to a new living environment. When a hazardous event occurs, they may need crisis intervention. They may need help in mobilizing their social network of extended family members and friends in order to combat isolation and enhance competence or to join support groups in a medical organization or community, usually consisting of patients and families with a common illness or disability. They may need to connect with appropriate health, educational, employment, or social resources in the community and learn how to apply for and use the resources. One problem in achieving accessibility and continuity of services is that social workers in hospitals are often not authorized to continue their work with families in the postdischarge phase. Early in their work with patients and their families, therefore, practitioners need to develop liaisons with community organizations that can take responsibility for the proper coordination of postdischarge activities. These may be case management agencies, visiting nurse services, home health care centers, or family service associations. They need to carefully prepare the patient and family for the transfer from the worker and hospital to the new resource center. The situations of patients and families change, and this requires new solutions to whatever problems emerge.

10
Group Work with Families

Groups have become an important modality of practice in health care settings as evidenced by the burgeoning of literature, particularly since 1975 (Northen, 1989). A large majority of the groups are therapy or support groups for patients, but there is increasing emphasis on groups for relatives and caretakers and a relatively small number that are composed of patients and one or more family members. When patients are young children who cannot participate in groups, some groups are designed for both parents and occasionally also older siblings. The groups provide support and opportunities to find means to cope effectively with the psychosocial problems associated with illness and disability.

Multiple family or patient–family groups are used in medical and rehabilitation settings to help families deal with the problems occasioned by a medical condition of one of the members. The groups are occasionally composed of family units, but more often they are composed of subsystems of families, such as parents or spouses. They are usually composed of members of families in which the patients share a common illness or disability, which tends to develop empathy and understanding among the members. They also provide protection from social ostracism when a disease carries a stigma, as in epilepsy and AIDS. In essence, a culture is created that frees family members to disclose their feelings and concerns within the safety of the group, which they often could not face alone or discuss with other members of the family. A particularly tragic example is the reality of a dying child.

The advantages of family groups is that they preserve the wholeness of the family rather than fragmenting it, and, at the same time, they provide for cross-influences and cross-interactions from family to family which can be effective in bringing new inputs of information, perceptions, and problem-solving mechanisms into each family (Leichter & Schulman, 1968). They stimulate dialogue between generations as well. It is the dynamic of families helping families that primarily leads to changes in thinking, feeling, and acting in relation to the patients' medical conditions.

Rationale for Use of Groups

The family plays an important part in the patient's experiences with illness or disability, and the patient's role is integral to the welfare of the family system. The illness or disability seriously influences the functioning of the family and the functioning of the family seriously influences the course of the patient's rehabilitation. As Huberty (1980, p. 434) says: "The process of adapting to illness is not one that takes place within each patient in isolation but rather is an interactional process of adjustment between the patient and his spouse, his children, his parents, as well as among those significant others as they form a network of emotional and social supports." The welfare of patient and family are intricately interrelated.

The absence or disruption of social supports is a major risk factor, both in the patient's becoming ill and in slowing the course of recovery or rehabilitation. As has been indicated in earlier chapters, the absence of adequate social ties results in higher morbidity and mortality rates, and the presence of supportive relationships facilitates both recovery and emotional adaptation. The family is expected to be a major natural support system, but many families are not able to provide the support needed by the patient, and many families also need support to cope with changes in their lifestyles occasioned by the patient's condition. Rubin (1985) reports that a "slim body of existing research tells us that, even where supportive and solid family relationships exist, friends count in any number or ways—from playmates to soulmates" (p. 10). Whether child or adult, peers provide a reference outside the family against which to measure and judge ourselves; they support us as we adapt to new rules and new roles; and they reduce feelings of isolation and loneliness.

For successful rehabilitation, effective participation of family members is essential. Compliance with medical recommendations is impeded or facilitated by members of the patient's family. Families who are supportive, understanding, organized, and neither overinvolved nor disengaged are more helpful in securing the patient's appropriate compliance. Based on preliminary findings of a large research project, Westin and Reiss (1979) state that:

> The multiple family group is one technique which can be used now by rehabilitation practitioners to involve family members early in the rehabilitation process. Group sessions can make the family more aware of the patient's difficulties, involve the family to a greater extent in his/her rehabilitation, and insure a family-oriented rehabilitation plan. These sessions permit families to learn from one another and to know that they are not alone. The multiple family group emphasizes that the family is part of the treatment program of the patient from beginning to end.

A sense of some control over the lives of patients and family members is associated with progress. Persons who believe that they can influence outcomes in some way perceive situations as less stressful and employ more effective problem-solving strategies. When they lack a sense of control, they employ more defensive means of coping with stress. Patients and families who participate in activities that give them some sense of control over their lives have better psychosocial outcomes. Groups of families potentially provide additional support for families, peer pressures toward conformity with desirable treatment regimens, and emphasize active participation which lessens the sense of lack of control.

Groups are often the most useful means for coping with the psychosocial problems associated with illness and disability. They possess motivational forces, often referred to as therapeutic factors or change mechanisms, that explain why groups may be the preferred modality of practice for certain purposes and persons. Primary research on these mechanisms has been conducted by Corsini and Rosenberg (1955) and Yalom (1970, 1980, 1985). Numerous social workers have also contributed to knowledge about the operation of these forces in groups (Couch, 1969; Goldstein, 1981; Lonergan, 1982; Marks, 1956; National Association of Social Workers, 1960; Northen, 1988; Shulman, 1979). The change mechanisms are support, ventilation, universalization, instillation of hope, altruism, acquisition of knowledge and skills, self-understanding, reality testing, and existential awareness. These factors are particularly pertinent to the situations faced by patients and their families (Boyd, 1977; Dell Orto & Power, 1980; Huberty, 1980; Johnson & Stark, 1980; Kurland, 1984; Mack & Berman, 1988; Mailick, 1984; Mervis, 1983; Northen, 1983, 1989; Roback, 1984; Valancy, 1981; Walwork, 1984). These dynamic forces may be summarized as follows:

1. *Peer support.* Support from peers, in addition to support from professional helpers, reduces isolation and anxiety and facilitates self-expression and willingness to try out new ideas and behaviors. The absence or disruption of social supports are major risk factors in the patient's becoming ill and in slowing the course of recovery. Social support is a mediator of stress, enhancing immunity and facilitating recovery.

2. *Universality.* One of the most powerful insights that emerges in family groups is the awareness that a person is not alone. The realization that similar feelings and difficulties are common among the members lessens the sense of being unique and alone. Self-esteem and mutual esteem often are enhanced by recognizing that others have difficulties, too, and yet are likeable people. Members discover the reassuring fact that they are not the only ones with troublesome feelings, which makes such feelings less frightening and controlling of their behavior.

3. *Catharsis/ventilation.* Free and appropriate expression of emotions and concerns, when these are accepted by others, lessens anxiety and frees energies for work toward the achievement of other desired goals. Many patients and their families lack supportive sanction for ventilating the flow of

feelings and painful experiences. The group provides a safe and supportive milieu for doing this, an important step toward channeling affect constructively.

4. *Instillation of hope.* By identifying with the group and unconsciously perceiving other members' expectations that some things can be better, members come to accept the optimistic goals of the group and move toward their achievement. They see how others have endured similar problems and coped with them successfully. Realistic optimism is in itself a healing factor.

5. *Acquisition of knowledge and skills.* As accurate information is provided by practitioners or knowledgeable group members, erroneous beliefs and myths are extinguished. The group provides a safe place to acquire needed knowledge; to risk new ideas, efforts, and behaviors; and to master new or changed social roles in the family and community. Most patients and family members have unmet needs for information about the medical situation and how to cope with it.

6. *Altruism.* As members interact with each other, the group becomes a mutual aid system. Personal identity and self-esteem are enhanced as members learn that they can extend help to others as well as receive help. Each member carries a contributing as well as a receiving role. The experience of helping others is therapeutically valuable. People relate better to others who appreciate and use what they can contribute: Contributing to others reduces morbid self-absorption and enhances self-esteem and optimism.

7. *Reality testing.* By sharing and comparing one's feelings and cognitions with those of others, distortions of perceptions about self, other persons, and situations are reduced as members reevaluate their behavior and receive feedback from peers. Responses from peers are often more readily accepted and dealt with than those that are offered by a practitioner.

8. *Insight.* Through observing other members, reflective thinking, and feedback from other members, persons may develop understanding not only of their patterns of feeling, thinking, and behaving, but also of the impact of these patterns on relationships with others and on their competence in performing their vital roles. Such understanding is a step toward changes in self-defeating attitudes and behaviors.

9. *Existential awareness.* In some groups, being able to face the basic issues of living and dying and the meaning of living with a serious handicap has special psychological significance for patients and family members.

10. *Cohesiveness.* The mutual acceptance of members by each other makes the group attractive to its members: Mutual acceptance and empathy fulfill the basic human need to belong. When members feel that they belong to a group that has meaning for them, they are influenced by other members and by the norms of the group. The sense of belonging counteracts many feelings of stigma and deviancy. The quality of relationships provides a

blend of support and challenge: There develops the sense of "relative safety of controlled intimacy" (Goldstein, 1981, p. 102).

The presence of these forces in multiple family groups in health settings has not been tested through research, but writers have observed their impact on members of their groups. Research on a wide variety of groups, however, has been conducted on the subject (Block, Crouch, & Reibstein, 1981; Dickoff & Lakin, 1963; Hill, 1975; Lieberman, Yalom, & Miles, 1973; Maxmen, 1973; Rohrbaugh & Bartels, 1975; Yalom, 1985). The research findings that do exist indicate that some factors are more important than others for some types of groups and some types of members and even for different members of the same group. "Furthermore, these dynamic forces need to be viewed as potential benefits; they are not present automatically in groups, but need to be fostered by the practitioner" (Northen, 1988).

Planning for the Formation of Groups

Adequate planning is perhaps the most important procedure to assure the formation and success of a group. Planning is a complex process, particularly so when more than one member of a family is to participate in the group experience. Necessary to adequate planning is knowledge of the health care system, the psychosocial aspects of illnesses and handicaps, and an accurate assessment of the needs and problems of patients and their families that accompany the physical disability or illness. Kurland's research (1980) identified the major decisions to be made in planning for the organization of a group. These are decisions concerning the social context, including the policies and sponsorship of the agency or organization; the needs and problems of the prospective members; the group's purpose and its composition, structure, and anticipated content.

Institutional supports are necessary to make it possible for a practitioner to carry out the appropriate services. Health care centers need to develop proper procedures for identifying prospective members, making staff assignments, and systems of accounting and fee schedules that assure the appropriate use of groups. Securing sanction for the operation of groups is crucial to their success. Attitudes of personnel, wittingly or unwittingly, may create barriers for practitioners' efforts to meet clients' needs through membership in a group. Procedures for securing sanction include securing the approval of appropriate administrators for a specific plan, presenting the purpose and tentative plan for the group at staff meetings, and seeking staff's suggestions for its improvement and implementation (D'Affliti & Weitz, 1974; Karp & Getzel, 1986; Lonergan, 1982). Sanction is usually secured when administrators and other staff have a clear understanding of the needs to be met through a patient/family group and how that service will supplement or complement, rather than compete with, other services.

Purpose and Goals

The major purpose of patient/family groups is to provide support to patients and their families in coping with the stress and psychosocial problems associated with the illness or physical disability of one of the family members. The literature sets forth numerous goals related to the general purpose which vary with particular groups. They include helping patients and family members to:

1. Reduce isolation and anxiety by providing a supportive social network for members.
2. Express, share, and clarify feelings connected with the illness or disability.
3. Improve communication within families, among families, and with medical personnel.
4. Involve family members in participating appropriately in the care of the patient and in helping the patient to take as much responsibility for self-care as possible.
5. Clarify role expectations and make necessary changes in roles.
6. Resolve problems in interpersonal, intrafamily, and intragroup relationships.
7. Foster the members' sense of trust in the availability of medical and nursing personnel.
8. Acquire accurate information about the hospital program, the illness or physical disability, and the psychosocial consequences for the patient and family.
9. Acquire insight into internal, interpersonal, and family conflicts aroused by the medical condition of a member of the family.
10. When there is a fatal illness, "work toward an appropriate death . . . in terms of the psychological state of the terminal patient" (Wellisch, Mosher, & Van Scoy, 1978, p. 226).
11. Contribute to the staff's understanding of family issues.
12. Gain a sense of accomplishment and power or control over the situation.
13. Enhance the use of appropriate hospital and community resources.
14. Ease the transition from hospital to home or from acute care to rehabilitation.
15. Anticipate and plan for needs and potential problems upon discharge from the medical facility.

Goals develop out of an assessment of the needs of patients and family members as evidenced through staff observations and clients' verbalized concerns. Eastman and Saur (1979), for example, conducted a survey of needs as expressed by parents of patients. The parents of handicapped children stated that their needs were for support and understanding, improvement of child care skills, learning to accept their children's handicaps, use of community resources, and improvement of social relationships with respect to the impact of the disability on marriage, parent–child relationships, and relationships among siblings. They concluded that these needs could be met most effectively through a time-limited group with a planned structure that would provide support and include education and counseling.

Composition

The particular combination of persons who are members of a group is one important determinant of the participants' satisfaction and the degree to which the goals will be achieved (Bertcher & Maple, 1985; Boer & Lantz, 1974; Hartford, 1971; Levine, 1979; Northen, 1988; Redl, 1953; Yalom, 1985).

In mental health and family–children's services, groups are typically composed of parents or guardians and their children. In health settings, groups of couples tend to predominate, either parents of sick children or spouses, one of whom is ill or disabled. In health settings, young children are not often included in family sessions, owing to the parents' desires to protect them from anxiety or to policies that discourage hospital visits by children. Some practitioners view young children as being unable to contribute to family problem-solving: Others assert that children's behavior can reveal emotional patterns or relationship sequences that might otherwise not be noticed (Janzen & Harris, 1980), thus enhancing treatment.

In health settings two means for determining the composition of a group predominate. In some groups, the membership is self-selected, consisting of persons who respond to notices sent by physicians, nurses, social workers, or other health personnel. Notices are received both by patients having a common illness or disability and by members of their families. With the exception of the common medical condition, most groups are heterogeneous in terms of such factors as age, gender, race, ethnicity, and economic status. Access to such groups is controlled by the health practitioners who decide to whom notices are sent. Social workers may or may not have an opportunity to influence the initial composition of such groups. But, it they meet with such groups, they have a responsibility to review the purpose of the group with the members and, if it becomes apparent that some members cannot benefit from the group, discuss the issue with them and help them find a more suitable form of help or a different group.

In the other type of group formation, there is selective intake and placement of families, according to criteria that are relevant to the group's purpose, which is the most important consideration. The specific goals and needs of the couples or families should be those that can be met through the group's purpose. Some common need or problematic situation is essential to provide a focus for the group's work, usually an illness or disability of a family member. Some balance between homogeneity and heterogeneity of member characteristics tends to make for an effective working group. These factors include age range, gender, socioeconomic status, ethnicity, family structure, major problems and capacities in coping with the illness or disability, and the stage in the life cycle of the different families. Due to a limited population from which to select families, it is not always possible to take into account a full range of factors that influence group participation. The suitability of the purpose of the group, combined with a common medical condition, may make considerable heterogeneity workable. One example is of a group of couples in which the husband had epilepsy that could not be controlled through the use of medication. Among the five couples, the ages ranged from 24 to 69; all were Anglo except for one Puerto Rican couple; there were large variations in incomes and occupations; and the family composition varied considerably. But the commonality of epilepsy, which tends to isolate and stigmatize persons, was so important that the group became very cohesive despite the wide differences among the members (Northen, 1988).

The literature seldom describes the criteria that were employed in determining group composition, but there are some exceptions. Eisenberg (1984), for example, organized groups for families of patients with congenital spinal cord injuries or similar neurological disorders with comparable symptoms. The criteria were: Members were to be at least 13 years old; patients needed medical clearance to participate; members were to have no behavior symptomatic of severe emotional disturbance that might be disruptive to group process; and members of nuclear or extended families of patients must participate. In another situation, D'Afflitti and Weitz (1974) formed a group for patients with strokes and their families. The criteria were: The patient had a stroke; members were to be mentally and verbally competent to participate; there must be at least one family member willing to participate; and the final destination for the patient was to be home. In order to assure that members of families attend the group sessions, it is essential to clarify this expectation from the beginning.

Structure

Numerous decisions need to be made about the structure of a group that includes the general organization of the group, its anticipated duration, place, time, and frequency of meetings, necessary supplies and equipment, leadership, size of group, fees, and whether the group is open-ended or closed to new members. Great variations occur in the structure of groups.

One modification of patient/family groups is a program consisting of a group for patients with Alzheimer's disease, a group for family members of patients, and a time when patients and family members come together. Sessions begin with a meeting of patients and their families, followed by separate meetings, and then a final coming together for a brief time. Family members rotate through the patient group to enhance their understanding of the realistic level of patients' capacities and provide a demonstration of suitable activities for patients. The need for such a program was identified because patients progressively decline in cognitive and behavioral abilities, which diminishes the quality of life for patients and their families. The care needed by the patient has a serious impact on the family. With the progression of the illness, the caretaker members become more and more preoccupied in providing for the patient's needs, shared activities decrease, and little peer support is available (Aronson, Levin, & Lipkowitz, 1984).

Other modifications of multiple family groups occur. For example, regular meetings of parents of children with spina bifida were held, but parents also participated in the children's play program (Bergofsky, Forgash, & Glassel, 1979). In another time-limited group primarily for parents of asthmatic children, the children participated in some meetings to help them facilitate communication (Barmettler & Fields, 1975–1976).

Groups generally meet weekly for 1.5–2 hours. Size of groups vary usually from three to six patients and their families. The use of coleaders clearly predominates, most often a social worker–nurse team but often with physicians coming to present medical information. Usually, the social worker directs the group discussion, and the nurse or physician takes responsibility for medical information and responds to questions and comments about hospitalization and medical concerns.

An important decision to be made is whether or not to permit members to join after the group has started—that is, to have an open group—or to close it to new members after an initial period of time. Some groups are semiclosed with the entry of new members when an old one has terminated the group on a planned basis. Closed or semiclosed groups have characteristics that make them appropriate for numerous purposes of therapy, counseling, ongoing support, and psychosocial education. There is an expectation that attendance will be regular which tends to enhance commitment to the group; the dynamic therapeutic forces operate more fully; and a sense of stability and cohesiveness develops. Members move more rapidly into the later intermediate stages, making it possible for them to go further in the work of facing and living with the stress and changes in life style produced by the medical condition of a family member (e.g., D'Afflitti & Weitz, 1974; Barmettler & Fields, 1975–1976; Eastman & Saur, 1979; Leff, 1975; Mailick, 1984; Pueschel & Yeatman, 1977; Steinglass et al., 1982; Walwork, 1984).

Two kinds of open-ended groups may be formed (Schopler & Galinsky, 1985). In some groups, the members enter at any time in the group's development and are expected to come until they no longer need the group (e.g., Abramson, 1975; Bergofsky, Forgash, & Glassel, 1979; Karp & Getzel, 1986). In other groups, the membership is transient; members come and go according to their sense of need (e.g., Johnson & Stark, 1980; Wellisch, Mosher, & Van Scoy, 1978).

In open groups with transient membership, the composition shifts from meeting to meeting, upsetting the group's steady state as new families enter the group and others are no longer there. Members tend to perceive their relationships with each other as transitory. Mutuality is based more on the need for substantive content and group support than on interpersonal and family relationships. If such groups are to be effective, according to Yalom (1983), each session needs to be regarded as a group experience in itself. Each session needs a clear beginning, work phase, and ending. Open groups can be used for meeting certain needs of families provided they have limited and specific goals, appropriate expectations for members' participation, ways of dealing with changes in membership, and plans that motivate some members to attend regularly for a period of time (Galinsky & Schopler, 1987). In a review of the literature on open-ended groups, Schopler and Galinsky, (1985, p. 87) state that:

> The unique feature of open-ended groups is their provision for ongoing membership change. New members are accepted on a continuing basis and can attend as long as their needs warrant. . . . When groups are open, clients do not have to wait for service, and group attendance can be tailored to the individual requirements of members.

The important point is that practitioners be clear about the purpose and hoped-for outcomes of the group experience and plan accordingly.

Owing to the reality that many groups in health settings are short-term, practitioners need to adapt their knowledge and skills to work with aggregates of families who come together for even a brief time. Short-term family groups are used most often for educational purposes, as in providing necessary information to families about the nature of the illness or disability, its consequences for family life, or teaching skills necessary for the in-home care of patients. The shorter the duration of the group, the more likely it is to be highly structured, with one or more practitioners who take a central role. Structure provides support. Yet, at the same time, practitioners need to remain sensitive and flexibly responsive to the needs of each patient and family. In multiple family counseling and therapy groups, many families need service beyond a few sessions in order to be helped to cope with strong emotions, improve their patterns of communication, modify dysfunctional roles, and/or reintegrate the patient into life in the family and community. It is clear that the duration of the group should vary with the needs of the families.

Content Themes

The content of the group develops from the particular goals agreed upon by the members from discussions with prospective members in pregroup interviews. Pregroup interviews are often used to orient the prospective members to the group, clarify the group's purpose and focus, ascertain the positive motivation and potential resistance to membership, explain the rationale for family participation, help to make a decision about becoming a member, and determine the particular interests and concerns that can be addressed in the group.

The decisions that are made in the planning process are interrelated: For example, identified needs are translated into goals that, in turn, influence the composition, structure, and content of the group.

One example of the planning process concerns groups for patients who had strokes and their families (D'Afflitti & Weitz, 1974). The groups were organized in a rehabilitation setting. Support from the director and staff of the services was secured through contact with the director, who approved of a presentation of the plan for the group at a staff meeting. The need for the group emerged as staff noticed that many patients and their family members were having difficulty with the emotional acceptance of the patients' disabilities. Families have great impact on the patient's motivations and expectations. Stroke patients improve more rapidly when there is mutual empathy among family members and when there is adequate physical and psychological stimulation. In groups, patients can influence each other toward working on problems and provide mutual support as well. Two major goals were set: to encourage families and patients to share their feelings about the stroke, leading to a constructive adjustment to the disabilities; and to encourage the use of appropriate supports and resources in the community. Criteria for membership included at least one member of a patient's family who was willing to attend meetings. A nurse and social worker coled the group which met for 1.5 hours weekly for 3 months. The size of groups ranged from three to five patients and their family members, including spouses, children, and siblings. In pregroup contacts, the patient was interviewed first, giving permission to contact the family, followed by a meeting with the patient and his family to discuss the group contract. Some groups were open, others closed. Closed groups were found to be more comfortable and productive: Cohesion developed that allowed the group to go further in the work of facing and living with the losses produced by the stroke.

Another example is a plan for a group of parents of young children who were born with serious physical handicaps. It became clear to the staff that parents needed support, understanding of their feelings and concerns, and practical help. One mother suggested the need for a group for parents whose children had neurological problems. A small, closed, discussion–educational group was formed to provide mutual assistance to its members who share a stressful life situation. The goals were to improve caretaking skills, learn about community resources, understand the roles of health professionals, reduce feelings of isolation and stigma, enhance parental comfort with and gain satisfactions from the child, and improve communication skills between parents, parents and children, and other persons. The criteria for membership included having a preschool child with a diagnosis of brain damage, willingness of both parents to attend the group, and parents without severe psychopathology. Pregroup interviews were held with couples to assess the appropriateness of the group for them, to orient them to the group's purpose and structure, and to solicit their ideas and concerns out of which developed the goals for the group. Decisions were made to have a closed group in order to keep participation high, a short-term structured group lasting for 2 months and meeting weekly for 1–2 hours, and coleadership. The content of the group consisted of information and discussion of themes related to the goals of the group.

Assessment

As members come together and discuss their feelings, ideas, and experiences, patterns of interaction develop that either further or hinder operation of the potentially therapeutic forces. Assessment of the group as well as of individuals is essential so that the practitioner can work toward supporting or modifying what is occurring at a given time. The major properties of groups to be assessed include communication, socioemotional ties, role, subgroup formation, values and norms, and cohesion (e.g., Deutsch, 1973; Hartford, 1971; Northen, 1988; Schein, 1985; Seabury, 1980; Shaw, 1981).

Communication, verbal and nonverbal, is the basic process through which members relate to each other and accomplish their goals. As members exchange feelings, thoughts, and experiences, they reciprocally influence each other. They vary in their abilities to send clear messages to others, to perceive accurately those sent by others, and to respond to the messages received. Messages sent may be unclear, ambiguous, or contradictory. Messages received may be distorted through language barriers, selective inattention, hearing losses, environmental disturbances, transferences or countertransference reactions, dysfunctional mental processes, or attitudes toward the sender. The pattern of communication that tends to be most effective is group centered, rather than worker directed, in which there is reciprocal interaction among the members.

Socioemotional ties develop among the members. In every human relationship, according to Phillips, there are "emotional reactions to oneself, to the other person, and to the specific content of the material expressed" (Phillips, 1957, p. 93). Mutual acceptance involves the ability to accept and show empathy toward other members, based on identifications and common interests and needs. Some members may stereotype others negatively owing to false perceptions based on transference reactions in which feelings, attitudes, and patterns of response are transferred from other earlier relationships. The present relationship with the practitioner, other member, or medical personnel is misunderstood in terms of the past. Mutual acceptance in which members accept others and feel accepted by others is a powerful therapeutic force.

Members of groups bring their roles as patient and/or family members—spouse, parent, sibling, child—each with its own set of expectations for behavior. They also hold other roles at work, school, club, and in the community. All of these roles are altered when one member of the family is seriously ill or disabled. But in the group, they are all in the role of member; it is an active role of participating in a give and take process with others. As they interact with each other, the group becomes a system of mutual aid. The emphasis on mutual aid does not detract from the importance of the role of professional leader who has special responsibilities in forming and maintaining the group and in contributing knowledge and insights beyond what the members are able to do for themselves.

In multiple family or couple groups, subgroups are present from the beginning. Each family is a subsystem of the group, having its own unique history and set of shared values, traditions, patterns of communication, and lifestyle. Within the family, the subsystems of spouses, parents, siblings, and special parent–sibling alliances exist. The patient has a special sick role within the family, at least temporarily, and may be part of an alliance with a primary caretaker. In addition to individual family groups, cross-family subgroups will develop out of the interchange among members as they identify those with whom they have the most in common. Parents often identify with other parents, patients with other patients, and children with other children of similar age. These subgroups are normal, but the practitioner needs to assess their impact on the group and work toward finding and building on the underlying commonalties. In assessing the subgroup structure, the basic questions concern the way subsystems relate to the group as a whole, whether there is cooperation or conflict among them, and whether they serve as strengths or obstacles to the work of the group at a particular time.

Each person and each family brings a set of cultural beliefs, traditions, and behaviors into the group, based on family history, ethnicity, and religion which influences attitudes toward illness, treatment, and life and death issues. These factors need to be taken into account in helping the members to understand and accept some of their differences, as well as their common interests and concerns, and to understand their reactions to diagnosis, treatment, and the culture of the medical setting. While understanding and accepting the cultures of the members, a major task for the practitioner is to help the group create a set of norms to guide their behavior and mobilize the therapeutic forces (Schein, 1985; Yalom, 1985). Boyd (1977) describes a group for parents of children thought to be fatally ill showing how the usual community norms include a taboo against discussion of death, tending to result in withdrawal or avoidance of the sick person and family. She reports that the major therapeutic effort was "to create a sub-culture, a new social reality, that frees parents of fatally ill children from some of the constraints of 'acceptable' behavior required of them by the broader society and offered them a substitute support system" (Boyd, 1977, p. 252). The leaders introduced and sanctioned norms that permitted the parents to face what they often could not face alone, with each other, or with families and friends. The new norms fostered open communication including permission to raise questions about medical issues and medical personnel; ventilate, explore, and find acceptance for intense feelings; and face death and mourn their impending loss, and still maintain appropriate hope. In groups generally, the norms of members are maintained when appropriate to the members' needs, and new ones are developed that further the pursuit of the group's goals. These norms are those that promote mutual aid, conformity to medical regimens, acceptance of the reality of changes necessitated by the medical condition, and efforts to cope effectively with the medically related problems.

A cohesive group develops when the patterns of communication, relationships, and norms meet the needs of the members. The members are mutually attracted to the group. Research indicates that the more cohesive the group, the greater its meaning to the members. Groups with high degrees of cohesion are more effective in achieving their goals than those with lower cohesion (Garvin, Reid, & Epstein, 1976, p. 264; Levy, 1984, pp. 80–97; Lieberman, Yalom, & Miles, 1973, pp. 302–313; Shaw, 1981, pp. 200–300; Yalom, 1985, pp. 52–56). In cohesive groups, regularity of attendance and punctuality predominate; there are frequent expressions of "we" feelings; and relationships among members are generally accepting, interdependent, and intimate. Members are committed to participation in the group's discussions and activities, and they express verbally their sense of satisfaction with the group. The group's norms provide appropriate guidelines for behavior and promote an atmosphere characterized by informality, spontaneity, and appropriate self-disclosure. The members have strong feelings of belonging to a group that is clearly distinguished from other groups and social networks (Levy, 1984, pp. 37–50).

Intervention

The primary task of the practitioner is to facilitate the group process so that members are helped through mutual support and aid. Facilitating the process involves motivating and assisting members to participate actively and collaboratively in the group. In fulfilling this task, practitioners use all of the major sets of interventive skills: (1) developing relationships between the worker and each member, within families, and among families; (2) providing support through demonstrating acceptance and empathy, attending to each member while maintaining a focus on the group, giving encouragement and realistic reassurance, defining realistic expectations, and articulating the feelings, concerns and ideas that members have in common; (3) structuring the situation to create an optimal milieu for work through such means as flexible use of policies, preparation for sessions, use of space and time, defined limits, and focused discussion and activities; (4) using exploratory techniques to elicit information, feelings, and beliefs about each member's circumstances and going beyond ventilation to seek understanding of diverse and common concerns and capacities; (5) offering education and advice for the purpose of securing the knowledge and skills required for coping with and gaining some control over the difficult situations occasioned by the illness or disability; (6) using confrontation at times when it is necessary to challenge dysfunctional attitudes, behaviors, and group interactions; (7) clarifying the members' understanding of themselves and others in relation to the impact of the illness or disability on daily living and in reference to required changes in social roles, including interpretation of the meaning of behavior.

These skills are used to support give and take among the members. The therapeutic potential of the group is enhanced when the object of the intervention is interactions among the parts or the group as a whole, as differentiated from communications between the practitioner and one member at a time. The members engage in a problem-solving process that includes affect, cognition, and action. It integrates feelings with reflective thinking about means for coping with stress and results in some decision to be implemented through action.

Initial Stage of Group Development

In the first stage of group development, the members enter the first session with considerable uncertainty about what to expect in terms of leadership, content, and their own participation. Although generally positively motivated, they usually have some ambivalence about becoming members of the group. Each family unit or subsystem of a family that is present is concerned about what, if anything, it has in common with other families and whether or not it will be accepted by others. There is little basis for trusting the practitioners, except as pregroup interviews have built a beginning relationship. When combined with the strong emotions that members usually have in reference to the illness or disability of one member of the family, it is clear that members need considerable support and acceptance from the practitioner before they become able to support and accept each other. Early discussion, therefore, tends to be superficial and scattered and centered on the medical situations.

Understanding the difficulties that members have in entering a group provides guidance for practitioners. Members feel supported when they have accurate knowledge about the group's purpose, structure, and expectations. Orientation of members to the group is the primary task for leaders in the initial meeting. Clarifying the general purpose of the group and exploring how that fits in with the members' particular goals; sharing the information about what were the criteria for inclusion of persons in the group; engaging the group in responding to the suitability of the time and frequency of meetings; clarifying what members can expect of the leader and the leader of them; dealing with matters of confidentiality—all of these topics tend to reduce anxiety and uncertainty and begin to engage the members in the group process. Introducing members to each other and asking each family to say whatever it wished about the medical condition and the feelings about it tends to bring out common concerns from which topics for discussion emerge. As members take part in the discussion, they become familiar to each other, and a friendly and accepting milieu develops.

When members enter into discussion, the tendency is to go over the history of the medical problem and the restrictions it has placed on the patient and family members. The tendency is to externalize their problems with queries about the medical aspects of care (Boyd, 1977; Huberty, 1980; Karp & Getzel, 1986; Kurland, 1984; Wellisch, Mosher, & Van Scoy, 1978). Examples are parents who ask how one can know whether certain medical interventions are necessary; another asks why the nurses assigned to the baby are continually changed; still another complains that it took too long to get a diagnosis. Patients and their relatives need to have their concerns addressed early in the group's development. Having accurate information reduces feelings of anxiety and helplessness. For these reasons, groups are frequently attended by physicians or nurses who make presentations about the medical condition, its treatment, and some of the psychosocial consequences, and who respond to the patients' concerns. Films may also be useful in providing education: For example, Eisenberg (1984) used films on the goals of rehabilitation, on medical aspects of spinal cord injuries, and on the emotional responses to disability and the role of the family in the adjustment process. Care is taken to prepare members for such films after assessing their readiness to benefit from them and to follow through with discussion of questions and concerns raised by the film or other activity.

In a group of parents of children with severe illnesses, by the end of the first session the members were able to begin to express their feelings more directly.

> Mrs. H. said that the hospitalization was very hard on her; sometimes she does not know what to do. Mr. F. responded, "yes, it is hard, and it's even harder when the baby is hospitalized for a lengthy stay." He said their baby has had many surgeries and faces still more. During one very stressful weekend, his wife fell apart. She said it was horrible. The practitioner acknowledged their pain and explored ways the members might do things to relieve the stress.

Hope is a powerful motivating force. Toward the end of the first session, group leaders often give very brief summaries of what has happened thus far. They request that members consider whether they understand the purpose of the group, the practical arrangement, the ways members will work together with the leader, and share their views about how the group can benefit them. When the members respond positively, a tentative working agreement or contract has been achieved, and it is likely that members will return for the next meeting.

Intermediate Stages

Skill in helping families cope with their problems in groups is based on in-depth understanding of the illness or disability, the psychological and social components of typical stresses and problems that occur, the means for coping with stress and solving problems, and environmental supports and obstacles to problem-solving. Equally important is understanding directed toward relationships and communication within and between families. The group is a special kind of environment for its members, but it is also the primary instrument for helping the members. The group itself is the primary agent of change. These are the major ingredients of a psychosocial approach to which practitioners with groups are committed (Roback, 1984).

Groups move at different paces from a primary focus on ventilation of feelings to exploration of the meaning of the medical conditions and to enhanced coping with or resolution of family problems. D'Afflitti and Weitz (1974) describe, for example, how this shift occurred in a group of stroke patients and their families. The members reminisced about what life was like before the stroke; then gradually worked toward reconciling the past with the present, with a focus on what can be done now to make living better. One patient said, "I know we won't be able to go out as much, but do you think we could go out to dinner sometimes?" And another one said, "I can't fish any more, but the boys could put me in the boat and take me with them anyway." In the early stage, prolonged reminiscence may be a way of denying or avoiding the reality of the present, but now it becomes a way of adapting to the loss of body function (Wellisch, Mosher, & Van Scoy, 1978). Another major theme was discussion of solutions to problems connected with the patient's return home. The focus on concrete details decreased anxiety, increased a sense of control over the situation, and allowed families to begin to restructure their lives.

Major Themes

The content of the group experience beyond the first one or two sessions consists of discussion of themes that very with the members' situation and concern with the nature of the illness or disability and its impact on psychosocial functioning. Most groups deal with several themes:

1. *Emotional responses to the illness or disability.* Ventilation of intense emotions predominates in the early phases of group life. They cover a range of feelings—anger, guilt, helplessness, hopelessness, depression, stigma, loneliness, isolation, fears of doing things wrong. Beginning with a chance to ventilate in a safe environment, the members often move toward recognition of the universality of feelings connected with illness or disability as well as their unique meaning to a particular person. Once feelings are expressed and accepted by others, they lose some of their intensity and hold on a person and the members then may turn toward active problem-solving.

2. *Education.* In order to cope realistically with the consequences of an illness or physical disability, the members seek information concerning the diagnosis, treatment, prognosis, and consequences for the patient's and family members' futures. They attempt to understand the situation by reviewing the history of the medical condition, raising many questions of the practitioners, and receiving appropriate information from physicians and nurses who colead groups or are used as resources as the need arises. Skills in caring for patients at home and helping patients care for themselves comprise a substantial amount of the content of some groups.

3. *Supports.* The group is an important source of support for its members, but the need for supports within the medical setting, at home, and in the community is a frequent topic of discussion. The members consider how they can reach out to relatives or neighbors, often develop contacts with

each other outside the group sessions, and deal with the availability and accessibility of health and welfare resources. Upon termination of some groups, members join self-help groups in the community.

4. *Problems in social relationships.* A serious illness or physical handicap disrupts existing relationships within the family and community and requires skills in relating to a complex network of personnel in the medical setting and referral sources. Group members often discuss how the illness has had an impact on their relationship with the ill person, spouse, or sibling. Relationships with nurses, physicians, physical and occupational therapists, and various technicians are of concern to members of most groups. Among spouses, the impact of the medical condition on the marital relationship concerns the members, including threats to the survival of the marriage. Coping with the reactions of relatives, friends, and acquaintances to the illness or disability, especially when a disability is visual or when an illness is a stigmatized one, comprises a substantial part of the content of some groups.

5. *Existential issues and religion.* Especially in situations when the illness is a life-threatening one or when physical disabilities place serious limitations on mobility, a considerable amount of content deals with anticipatory mourning or responses to death.

Early Threats to the Group

Following the initial orientation to the group and acceptance of a working agreement, groups move more or less rapidly into a stage of work that focuses on coping with the problems that are relevant to the illness or disability. Ambivalence and uncertainty about being a member and about the benefits to be derived from the group, however, continue beyond the first session. Groups often go through a period—brief or prolonged—of testing the practitioner's attitudes, concerns, and competence. Often feeling that they have little control over the course and treatment of the medical condition, they need to assure themselves that they have some freedom and control within the group. Testing of practitioners may occur in dramatic or subtle ways.

An example of a dramatic incident is described by Boyd (1977), writing about a group for parents of fatally ill children.

> Of necessity the group tested if certain behavior was allowed and considered acceptable, primarily by testing the leaders and then the members. For example, the first testing was regarding honesty in expression of feeling. At the second meeting, when the leader was attempting to summarize the previous meeting as a way of beginning the session, the "provocateur" in the group

> booed him, interrupting the worker; other members looked stunned and embarrassed. The worker acknowledged that it was a "slap" and an expression of anger. The parent denied real anger but said she needed some comic relief. The group leader asserted, while members shuddered, "that she was saying something very important, that others were likely feeling the same, that while their anxiety was building, we were droning on and they were getting angry." This released laughter and sighs of relief and a flood of discussion about how ambivalent people felt about engaging in the group and about the pain experienced when they come to the meeting, because it reminded them of their child's illness. . . . The leader acknowledged this as an understandable reaction and said "we were glad they had the courage to return to share their reactions in spite of this" (p. 258).

In a similar incident, the social worker (Akner, 1983 p. 12) reports that:

> Following a great deal of time in ventilating, she decided the time had come to have members make decisions about what they wanted to work on next. With too much intellectualizing and for too long a time, she presented her summary of what the group had been doing and their need to make a decision. Not one person had anything to say and there was a long silence. Finally, one of the men turned toward her slowly and said," I have no idea what you just said." Everyone laughed and the worker, recognizing that she had talked too much and over intellectualized, said, "Thank you for being able to say that. What I wanted to say was really simple—why do you come here?" The members were then able to focus on the concerns that could be met in the group.

These incidents both reflect the need for practitioners to become aware of their own unhelpful behaviors, such as a tendency to talk too much, and to be able to respond to members in nondefensive ways.

More subtle questioning of the leader's power and attitude may take the form of comments or questions about the benefits of medical treatment, whether anything additional can be done, or comments about the lack of caring on the part of nurses or physicians. They project their concerns about the group's leader externally on to other persons or things when their underlying questions are whether or not the group will benefit them or whether the worker accepts and understands them. Sensitive listening and self-awareness can alert the worker to these concerns so that discussion of them can occur in the group. A simple "maybe you wonder if I care," "perhaps you're not sure this group can help either," or "it's natural that you can't trust me yet" can lead to more in-depth exploration of the members' ambivalence, the groups' purpose and expectations, and the worker's relationship and role than had occurred in earlier sessions.

When these concerns are articulated and discussed, the members develop into a mutual aid system for working toward the accomplishment of agreed-upon goals. The members become more willing and able to disclose their real feelings and suggestions to the other members, to accept differences as well as commonalties among them, and to support and stimulate each other toward more effective ways of coping with stress. In a group, there had been avoidance of facing the diagnosis of a life-threatening illness, but some members were now able to do that. One woman began to cry and said she just could not say the word cancer without crying. One of the men said he could understand that because he had cried for a long time. Another woman said that it was all right to cry here. Some members said that they held their feelings in all week because they could not cry around their young children and friends. The first woman who was still crying, said that she felt better already, knowing that here she could say how she really was feeling.

Obstacles to Progress

Obstacles to the group's progress occur from time to time and need to be addressed by the practitioner and the group members.

One obstacle is resistance, a trend of forces against using the help that is offered, which reduces positive motivation and serves as a means to avoid further anxiety and protect oneself from hurt. The members may resist by such means as staying away or coming late, monopolizing the discussion, remaining silent, engaging in repetitive comments or behavior, changing the subject, or telling about the past to avoid dealing with the present. Resistance is often a response to anxiety about the content or progress of the group. Members may fear disclosing certain highly charged experiences or family secrets or become aware of emotions and ideas that have been suppressed. When anxiety increases beyond a tolerable level, people resist. Some resistance is a reasonable response to the practitioners' behaviors, as when they confront members directly in a judgmental way without empathy or when they make interpretations about meanings that are too threatening to the members. Some resistance may also be occasioned by the behavior of some members toward others, as when confrontations and interpretations offered by members are inappropriate. The members need strong support from the practitioner in recognizing that their behavior has prevented them from working toward the goals, and the practitioners need to respond by encouraging members to respond, giving realistic reassurance to reduce the threat, universalizing the problem, and encouraging a refocusing of the discussion.

Another obstacle to progress consists of patterns of roles that are disruptive to the group, although the members benefit a great deal from learning how to deal with this problem (Hartford, 1971, pp. 208–218; Merton, 1949, pp. 281–326; Northen, 1988, pp. 28–31; Shaw, 1981, pp. 241–247). In order to understand these roles, the practitioner needs to assess what there is in the person in the role and what there is in the other members and the group process that accounts for the situation. A monopolizer feels compelled to hold the center of the stage, becoming anxious when someone else becomes the center of the group's attention. The help-rejecting complainer is a variant of the monopolizer (Yalom, 1985). Such persons are self-centered, present many problems and complaints in an exaggerated manner, reject help that is offered, and blame others for their problems, often authority figures on whom they are dependent. A scapegoat is another role that causes distress to the person in the role and threatens the group's morale. The members have turned their aggression onto a member who symbolizes something they dislike in themselves and on whom they project their hostility, thus channeling group tensions and avoiding dealing with real conflicts. The scapegoat is usually a member from whom the others do not fear retaliation. Other roles of concern to the practitioner include the rejected member, the silent one, the clown, and the provocateur.

What practitioners do in influencing a change in such roles depends upon their assessment of the meaning of the role to the person and the group. With the monopolizer or the help-rejecting complainer, early efforts may be directed toward encouraging spread of participation among all the members through stating this as an expectation, requesting that members take turns, giving nonverbal encouragement to all members to enter into the discussion, or making brief summaries to encourage others to enter into the conversation. The worker also needs to show empathy toward the person in the role. If the worker can convey interest in the person and suggest how he or she can participate effectively, the cycle might be broken. Limits may need to be set through requests to give others a chance to participate or to wait until others have finished speaking. When these efforts fail, the worker may then use more direct means to clarify the nature of the problem, its meaning to the group, what members do to perpetuate the situations, and how they might work it out together. He engages the group in discussion to, in Yalom's words, "illuminate the process" (Yalom, 1985, pp. 143–80).

With a scapegoat, leaders use themselves in similar ways, first using indirect means to prevent stereotyping; then working directly to identify the problem and its impact on the group, clarifying the conditions that led to scapegoating; analyzing the stresses on the group that result in the projection of hostilities onto a particular member; identifying the behaviors the scapegoat performs to provoke scapegoating; and restructuring patterns of relationships (Schutz & David, 1981). Workers need to be able to accept and empathize with all members and to focus on the common feelings and underlying problems. In any dysfunctional role, the problem is a result of the interaction between the person in the role and the needs of the group.

Another obstacle to progress concerns the stress experienced by practitioners who are working with families in which a member has a serious illness or physical disability. The wish is often to be able to solve the problems quickly in a concrete way. D'Afflitti and Weitz (1974) describe how they tried to compensate for patient's problems by becoming active and directive. They tended to interrupt silences and focused on one individual at a time, instead of fostering group involvement. They often responded to questions for which there were no answers such as the specific cause of a stroke, instead of seeking and dealing with such real questions as "why me? What did I do to deserve this?" Practitioners tend to try to understand and trust the group process. Enhanced self-awareness of one's attitudes and competence in practice increases professional competence.

Facilitating Group Process

The skillful practitioner facilitates the process of mutual aid through his relationships with the members and appropriate use of therapeutic techniques, with strong emphasis on quietly supporting the group process, rather than directing or dominating it. An example is taken from an article about a group of parents who were coping with the death of infants (Walwork, 1984). One theme concerned the attitudes and reactions of friends and relatives to the death. One mother expressed anger at a relative who told her that she now had a little angel in heaven. The mother recounted that she did not want an angel in heaven and how cruel and insensitive that comment was. Members gave her much support and validated her feelings and suggested how she might respond to such comments, such as: "This isn't the way I feel about it" or "it doesn't help me to think about my baby's death that way." The practitioner simply gave nonverbal support to these helpful suggestions, enhancing the group's sense of being able to help each other.

Another example of a practitioner's quiet support of the group process occurred when a patient in the group was scheduled to receive a leg brace (Huberty, 1980). Her husband said that this was proof that his wife would never recover. Another patient, who had recently received a brace, challenged this belief. Saying that this is what his wife will be able to do, he stood up and began walking around the group. This well-timed demonstration achieved more than would be possible through a practitioner's reassurance and challenge, convincing the couple and other members of the group that securing braces and other aids to mobility represents progress.

At other times, the social worker needs to intervene actively to interrupt and refocus the discussion, as in working with resistance or dysfunctional roles, in helping the members toward greater understanding, and in making changes in behavior. In a group for parents of children with asthma (Barmettler & Fields, 1975–1976), there was child-focused review of the painful past, with growing awareness not only of a tendency for family life to revolve around the child with asthma, but also that the parents felt controlled by the child. In a brief excerpt, Mr. J. said, "This is what I meant. I have to control what I do for fear he will have an attack." The social worker, requesting greater understanding, asked, "Can you tell us how that makes you feel?" Mrs. J. "frustrated and a little mad." Mr. J. "more than a little mad—I actually resent Judy." Such sharing between husbands and wives strengthens the relationship between them and stimulates other members to examine more deeply the impact of the patient on their lives. Issues between spouses often arise, as, for example, when there is a child patient, the men may feel left out and the women feel the men have put the burden on them.

In a group of spouses in which the husband had uncontrollable epileptic seizures, a major theme became the impact of the seizures on the marital relationship (Akner, 1983). The wives expressed fears of losing their husbands, anger at not having a reliable partner, and lack of sexual activity for fear of precipitating a seizure. Husbands, on the other hand, said their wives were over protective, prevented them from trying to do as much as possible, and felt dependent. Members felt isolated from family and friends because of people's misunderstanding of seizures and discomfort in being with the patients.

The major agent of change is the group, but the worker needs considerable knowledge and skill to help the members to help each other, and he often needs to add his own understanding of the issues under discussion. In a group of parents of infants with serious handicaps, one mother, Mrs. T., expressed extreme fear of holding her baby, saying that she thought that touching the baby would cause more pain than the baby already had. Mrs. Y. said she had that trouble, too. Mrs. A. said she disagreed. Although her baby had surgery, she held her because she understood that it is important for babies to be held and cuddled from the very beginning of life. Mr. T. said that he was as concerned about hurting the baby as was his wife. He's sure that their baby must be in great pain. Mr. Y. said that some babies may be in more pain than others. The members continued to discuss their ideas about holding their babies and how much pain infants feel. The worker commented that it might help them to sort out what some of the issues are and what is known about them. The members all agreed that this would be helpful.

The worker noted their concerns about the amount of pain felt, which varies with each baby; much of the pain is controlled by medicine. She thought the doctors and nurses could tell them about how much pain their child was in, and there was discussion of this matter. The second issue they discussed was whether or not physical contact with the child is desirable, and she noted that early bonding between parent and infant promotes healthy development, adding that there are, of course, times when that is not possible. The third issue they discussed concerned how painful it is for them to have handicapped infants. Holding infants may give the babies a sense of security and comfort rather than increase their pain. Parents are often afraid to cuddle the baby because it reminds them of the baby's condition and their disappointment in having a child who starts life with a serious handicap. She requested that the members respond to these ideas. The practitioner, in an accepting way, has given the members accurate information, suggested they communicate their concerns about pain to their nurses or doctors, universalized the fears, and offered an interpretation of the meaning of the reluctance to hold the baby. The interpretation is offered in a tentative manner, followed up by seeking the group's responses to it.

These problems in relationships require the use of all the sets of interventions. Within an atmosphere of mutual support and acceptance, the movement tends to be from ventilation and exploration of feelings, to identification of problems, and, finally, to efforts to cope with and resolve the problems. There is increased use of such interventions as confrontation, clarification, and interpretation by the practitioner when the members are unable to help each other. The worker may offer confrontive statements that face members with the reality of a feeling, behavior, or situation; they may make comments that clarify patterns of behavior or connect one experience to another one; they may make interpretations that deal with the meaning of behavior. Through these types of interventions, the members may gain new perceptions of the connections among affect, knowledge, and experience, which understanding is used in the process of decision making concerning the care and treatment of the patient, the distribution of roles and expectations for behavior in family and community roles, the means for enhancing communication and strengthening relationships within and outside of the family, and ways to normalize living as much as possible within the limits of the illness or handicap.

Termination

Terminating from a group in health settings may or may not occur simultaneously with discharge from a hospital or the end of a course of treatment in an outpatient department. For some patients and family members, termination is perceived not only as separation from the group worker and the other members of the group, but also as the end of medical assistance, caring relationships with medical personnel, and lessening of hope for further progress. Many patients have suffered serious losses in physical capacity and vital social roles: Their families' roles and relationships have been disrupted by the illness or disability of one of their members. Leaving the group and also often the hospital adds one more stressful experience.

When faced with loss or separation from persons who have been important to them, the steady state is upset and anxiety increases. Even when the reason for termination is a highly positive one, it can create difficulties for the family. For example, families may feel they have not had time either to prepare the home for the return of the patient or to learn adequate skills in home care. Recognizing that the end is imminent, members of groups react with a variety of emotional and behavior responses. Research indicates that typical reactions are sadness, denial, anger, apparent regression to earlier behaviors, flight, and feelings of rejection and abandonment (Lackey, 1982; Northen, 1988). Ambivalence about ending has two sides—the sad and painful feelings and the satisfying, positive reactions that come with the realization that some gains have been made and things are better now. But there is probably always some sense of loss in leaving an experience that has been beneficial and, in groups, leaving the members who have been a source of support and stimulation.

To help a family leave a continuing group or to help the group itself to end in a way that promotes the enhancement of psychosocial functioning, the practitioner carries out several tasks. Just as members needed help to resolve their ambivalence about joining a group, they now need help to acknowledge, ventilate, and explore their feelings about termination. They need to have help to review their experiences in the group and to appraise the progress they have made or the obstacles still to surmount. They need to anticipate and make realistic plans for transitions to life without the group, including the use of social networks and community resources. If the termination process is properly understood and handled, it serves as an important means for integrating changes in affect, cognition, and action. If successful, the practitioner has prepared the members for alleviating stress and for finding adaptive ways of coping with medical situations and the losses and separations that they will face in the future.

References

Aaronson, N. K., & Beckmann, J. (Eds.). (1987). *The quality of life of cancer patients.* New York: Raven Press.

Abbey, A., Abramis, D. J., & Caplan, R. D. (1985). Effects of different sources of social support and social conflict on emotional well-being. *Basic and Applied Psychology, 6,* 111–130.

Abramson, J. S. (1988). Participation of elderly patients in discharge planning: Is self-determination a reality? *Social Work, 33,* 443–447.

Abramson, M. (1975). Group treatment of families of brain-injured patients. *Social Casework, 56,* 235–241.

Abramson, M., & Black, R. B. (1985). Extending the boundaries of life: Implications for practice. *Health and Social Work, 10,* 165–173.

Ackerman, N. (1958). *The psychodynamics of family life.* New York: Basic Books.

Ackerman, N., Beatman, F.L. & Sherman S.N. (1967). *Expanding theory and practice in family therapy.* New York: Family Service Association of America.

Adams-Greenly, M. (1986). Psychological staging of pediatric cancer patients and their families. *Cancer, 58,* 449–453.

Adams-Greenly, M. Shiminiski-Maher, T., McGowan, N., & Meyers, P. A. (1986). A group program for helping siblings of children with cancer. *Journal of Psychosocial Oncology, 4,* 55–67.

Ad Hoc Task Forces on Home Care of Chronically ill Infants and Children (1984). Guidelines for home care of infants, children, and adolescents with chronic disease. *Pediatrics, 75,* 434–436.

Ahern, D. K., & Follick, M. J. (1985). Distress in spouses of chronic pain patients. *International Journal of Family Therapy, 7,* 247–256.

Ahrons, C. R., & Arnn, S. (1981). When children from divorced families are hospitalized: Issues for staff. *Health and Social Work, 6,* 21–28.

Akner, L. (1983). *A group for individuals with epilepsy and their spouses. Paper presented at the Fifth Annual Symposium.* Association for the Advancement of Social Work with Groups.

Alderman, M. H., & Schoenbaum, E. E. (1975). Detection and treatment of hypertension at the work site. *New England Journal of Medicine, 293,* 65–68.

Alexander, C. S., & Markowitz, S. (1986). Maternal employment and use of pediatric clinic services. *Medical Care, 24,* 134–147.

Algren, C. L. (1985). Role perception of mothers who have hospitalized children. *Children's Health Care, 14,* 6–9.

Allen-Meares, P., & Lane, B. A. (1987). Grounding social work practice in theory: Ecosystems. *Social Casework, 68,* 515–521.

Alonzo, A. (1986). The impact of the family and lay others on care-seeking during life-threatening episodes of suspected coronary artery disease. *Social Science and Medicine, 22,* 1297–1311.

American Cancer Society. (1981). *A Study of Black Americans' Attitudes Toward Cancer and Cancer Tests.* (ACS Report No. 0520).

American Cancer Society. (1985a). *A Study of Hispanics Attitudes Concerning Cancer and Cancer Prevention.*

American Cancer Society. (1985b). *Cancer Statistics.* Author.

American Cancer Society. (1986). *Cancer in the Economically Disadvantaged: A Special Report.*

Ammerman, R. T., Van Hasselt, V. B., & Hersen, M. (1988). Maltreatment of handicapped children: A critical view. *Journal of Family Violence, 3,* 53–72.

Anderson, B. L., & Hacker, N. F. (1983). Psychosexual adjustment following pelvic exenteration. *Obstetrics and Gynocology, 61,* 331–338.

Anderson, B. L., & Jochimsen, P. R. (1985). Sexual functioning among breast cancer, gynecological cancer, and healthy women. *Journal of Consulting and Clinical Psychology, 53,* 25–32.

Anderson, T. (1984). Consultation: Would you like co-evolution instead of referral? *Family Systems Medicine, 2,* 370–379.

Angel, R., & Worobey, J. L. (1988). Single motherhood and children's health, *Journal of Health and Social Behavior, 29,* 38–52.

Antonovsky, A. (1979). *Health, stress, and coping.* San Francisco: Jossey-Bass.

Antonovsky, A., & Sourani, T. (1988). Family sense of coherence and family adaptation. *Journal of Marriage and the Family, 50,* 79–92.

Antonucci, T. C. (1985). Personal characteristics, social support and social behavior. In E. Shanas & R. H. Binstock (Eds.), *Handbook of aging and the social sciences,* (2nd ed.). New York: Van Nostrand.

Aponte, H. J. (1976). Underorganization of the poor family. In P. J. Guerin (Ed.), *Family therapy: Theory and practice* (pp. 432–444). New York: Gardner Press.

Appolone, C. (1978). Preventive social work intervention with families of children with epilepsy. *Social Work in Health Care, 4,* 139–148.

Arbogast, R. C., Scratton, J. M., & Krick, J. P. (1978). The family as patient : Preliminary experience with a recorded assessment schema. *The Journal of Family Practice, 7,* 1151–1157.

Aronson, M. K., Levin, G., & Lipkowitz, R. (1984). A community-based family/patient group program for Alzheimer's disease. *The Gerontologist, 24,* 339–342.

Athreya, B. H., & McCormick, M. C. (1987). Impact of chronic illness on families. *Rheumatic Disease Clinics of North America, 13* 123–131.

Auslander, G. K., & Litwin, H. (1988). Social networks and the poor: Toward effective policy and practice. *Social Work, 33,* 234–238.

Austin, C. D. (1986). Positive potential. *Health and Social Work, 11,* 69–70.

Axtell, L. M., & Meyers, M. H. (1974). *Recent Trends In Survival of Cancer Patients 1960–71.* (Department of Health, Education, and Welfare Publication No. 76–767) Washington, DC: U.S. Government Printing Office.

Axtell, L. M., & Meyers, M. W. (1978). Contrasts in survival of Black and White cancer patients, 1960–1973, *Journal of National Cancer Institute, 60,* 1209–1215.

Ayers, J. (1985). Training of family therapists in health. In J. R. Springer & R. H. Woody (Eds.), *Health promotion in family therapy* (pp. 117–129). Rockville, MD: Aspen Publications.

Azarnoff, P., & Hardgrove, C. (1981). *The family in child health care*. New York: John Wiley and Sons.

Bachrach, K. M., & Zautra, A. J. (1985). Coping with a community stressor: The threat of a hazardous waste facility. *Journal of Health and Social Behavior, 26,* 127–141.

Bailey, E. J. (1987). Sociocultural factors and health care-seeking behavior among Black Americans. *Journal of the American Medical Association, 79,* 389–392.

Baillie, V., Norbeck, J. S., & Barnes, L. E. A. (1988). Stress, social support, and psychological distress of family caregivers of the elderly. *Nursing Research, 37,* 217–222.

Bain, R. P., Greenberg, R. S., & Whitaker, J. P. (1986). Racial differences in survival of women with breast cancer. *Journal of Chronic Diseases, 39,* 631–642.

Baird, N. A., & Doherty, W. J. (1986). Family resources in coping with serious illness. In M. A. Karpel (Ed.), *Family resources: The hidden partner in family therapy*. New York: The Guilford Press.

Baldwin, S., & Glendinning, C. (1983). Employment, women and their disabled children. In J. Finch & D. Groves (Eds.), *A labour of love: Women, work, and caring*. London: Routledge & Kegan Paul.

Baltrusch, H. J. F., & Waltz, M. (1986). Early family attitudes and the stress process: A life-span and personological model of host-tumor relationships. In S. Day (Ed.), *Cancer, stress and death* (2nd ed.). New York: Plenum Medical.

Baptiste, C. A. Jr. (1983). Time-elapsed marital and family therapy with sudden-infant-death-syndrome families. *Family Systems Medicine, 1,* 47–59.

Baranowski, T. & Nader, P. R. (1985). Family health behavior. In D. C. Turk and R. D. Kerns (Eds.), *Health, illness and families: A life-span perspective* (pp. 51–80). New York: John Wiley & Sons.

Barbarin, O. A. (1983). Coping with ecological transitions by Black families: A psychosocial model. *Journal of Community Psychology, 11,* 308–322.

Barbarin, O. A. (1988). Psychological risks and invulnerability: A review of the theoretical and empirical basis of preventive family-focused services for survivors of childhood cancer. *Journal of Psychosocial Oncology, 5,* 25–41.

Barbarin, O. A., & Chesler, M. A. (1984). Coping as interpersonal strategy: Families with childhood cancer. *Family Systems Medicine, 2,* 279–288.

Barbarin, O. A., Hughes, D., & Chesler M. A. (1985). Stress, coping and marital functioning among parents of children with cancer. *Journal of Marriage and the Family, 47,* 473–481.

Barker, R. G. (1978) *Habitats, Environments, and Human Behavior.* San Francisco: Jossey-Bass.

Barmettler, D., & Fields, G. M. (1975–1976). Using the group method to study and treat parents of asthmatic children. *Social Work in Health Care, 1,* 167–76.

Bar-on, D., & Dreman, S. (1987). When spouses disagree: A predictor of cardiac rehabilitation. *Family Systems Medicine, 5,* 228–237.

Barrett, C. (1978). Effectiveness of widows' groups in facilitating change. *Journal of Consulting and Clinical Psychology, 46,* 20–31.

Barrier, D., Bybel, M., Christie-Seely, J. & Whittaker, Y. (1984). PRACTICE—A family assessment tool for family medicine. In J. Christie-Seely (Ed.), *Working with the family in primary care* (pp. 214–234). New York: Praeger.

Barrier, D., & Christie-Seely, J. (1984). The presenting problems of families and family assessment. In J. Christie-Seely (Ed.), *Working with the family in primary care* (pp. 201–213). New York: Praeger.

Barusch, A. S. (1988). Problems and coping strategies of elderly spouse caregivers. *The Gerontologist, 28,* 677–685.

Bass, D. M., Tausig, M. B., Noelker, L. S. (1988–1989). Elder impairment, social support and caregiver strain: A framework for understanding support's effects. *The Journal of Applied Social Sciences, 13,* 80–117.

Bateman, E. L. (1965). The worker's use of self in family interviewing. In National Association of Social Workers (Eds.), *The family is the patient: The group approach to treatment of family health problems* (pp. 66–69). New York: National Association of Social Workers.

Batten, H. L., & Prottas, J. M. (1987). Kind strangers: The families of organ donors. *Health Affairs, 6,* 35–47.

Beautrais, A. L., Fergusson, D. M., & Shannon, F. T. (1982). Life events and childhood morbidity: A prospective study. *Pediatrics, 70,* 935–940.

Beaver, M. (1979). The decision-making process and its relationship to relocation adjustment in older people. *The Gerontologist, 19,* 567–574.

Beavers, W. R. (1983). Hierarchical issues in a systems approach to illness and health. *Family Systems Medicine, 1,* 47–55.

Beavers, W. R., Hampson, R. B., & Hulgus, Y. F. (1985). Commentary: The Beavers Systems approach to family assessment. *Family Process, 24,* 398–405.

Beavers, W. R., & Voeller, M. N. (1983). Family models: Comparing and contrasting the Olson Circumplex Model with the Beavers Systems Model. *Family Process, 22,* 85–98.

Becerra, R. M., & De Anda, D. (1984). Pregnancy and motherhood among Mexican American adolescents. *Health and Social Work, 9,* 106–123.

Becker, M. H., & Green, L. W. (1975). A family approach to compliance with medical treatment. *International Journal of Health Education, 18,* 173–182.

Bednar, R. L., & Lawlis, G. F. (1971). Empirical research in group psychotherapy. In A. E. Bergin & S. L. Garfield (Eds.), *Handbook of psychotherapy and behavior change* (pp. 812–838). New York: Wiley.

Bedsworth, J. A., & Molen, M. T. (1982). Psychological stress in spouses of patients with myocardial infarction. *Heart and Lung, 11,* 450–456.

Belle, D. (1982). The stress of caring: Women as providers of social support. In P. Goldberger and S. Breznitz (Eds.), *Handbook of Stress: Theoretical and Clinical Aspects* (pp. 496–505 New York: Free Press.

Belle, D. E. (1983). The impact of poverty on social networks and supports. *Marriage and Family Review, 5,* 37–58.

Berg, J. W., Ross, R., & Lotourette, H. B. (1977). Economic status and survival of cancer patients. *Cancer, 39,* 467–477.

Berger, J. M. (1984). Crisis intervention: A drop-in support group for cancer patients and their families. *Social Work in Health Care, 10,* 81–92.

Berger, M., & Fowlkes, M. A. (1980). Family intervention project: A family network model for serving young handicapped children. *Young Children, 35,* 22–32.

Bergofsky, R. E., Forgash, C. S., & Glassel, A. F. (1979). Establishing therapeutic groups with the families of spina bifida children in a hospital setting. *Social Work with Groups, 2,* 45–54.

Berkanovic, E., & Telesky, C. (1982). Social networks, beliefs and the decision to seek medical care: An analysis of congruent and incongruent patterns. *Medical Care, 20,* 1018–1026.

Berkanovic, E., Telesky, C. & Reeder, S. (1979). Structural and social psychological factors in the decision to seek medical care. *Medical Care, 19,* 693–709.

Berkman, B. (1984). Social work and the challenge of DRG's. *Health and Social Work, 9,* 2–3.

Berkman, B., Bedell, D., Parker, E., McCarthy, L., & Rosenbaum, C. (1988). Preadmission screening: An efficiency study. *Social Work in Health Care, 13,* 35–50.

Berkman, B., & Rehr, H. (1978). Social work undertakes its own audit. *Social Work in Health Care, 3,* 273–286.

Berkman, L., & Syme, L. (1979). Social networks, host resistance and mortality: A nine-year follow-up study of Alameda County residents. *American Journal of Epidemiology, 109,* 187–204.

Berlin, G. (1988). The new permanence of poverty. *The Ford Foundation Letter, 19,* 1–3, 8–9.

Bertalanffy, L. V. (1974). General system theory and psychiatry. In S. Arieti (Ed.), *American handbook of psychiatry* (pp. 1095–1117). New York: Basic Books.

Bertcher, H. J., & Maple, F. (1978). *Creating groups.* Beverley Hills, CA: Sage Publications.

Bertcher, H. J., & Maple, F. (1985). Elements and issues in group composition. In M. Sundel, P. Glasser, R. Sarri, & R. Vinter (Eds.), *Individual change through small groups.* New York: Free Press.

Binger, C. M., Ablin, A. R., Feuerstein, R. C., Kusher, J. H., Zoger, S., & Mikkelsen, C. (1969). Childhood leukemia: Emotional impact on patient and family. *The New England Journal of Medicine, 280,* 414–418.

Birkel, R., & Reppucci, D. (1983). Social networks, information-seeking, and the utilization of services. *American Journal of Community Psychology, 11,* 185–205.

Bishop, D. S., Epstein, N. B., & Baldwin, L. M. (1981). Disability: A family affair. In D. S. Freeman & B. Trute (Eds.), *Treating families with special needs* (pp. 3–14). Ottawa, Ontario, Canada: Alberta Association of Social Workers.

Bishop, D. S., Epstein, N., Keitner, G. I., Miller, I. W., & Srinivasan, S. V. (1986). Stroke: Morale, family functioning, health status, and functional capacity. *Archives of Physical Medicine and Rehabilitation, 67,* 84–87.

Bittner, R. (1984). Therapeutic mother-child groups: A developmental approach. *Social Casework, 65,* 154–161.

Black, R. B. (1980). Support for genetic services: A survey. *Health and Social Work, 5,* 27–34.

Black, R. B., Dornan, D. H., & Allegrante, J. P. (1986). Challenge in developing health promotion services for the chronically ill. *Social Work, 31,* 287–293.

Black, R. B., & Furlong, R. (1984). Impact of prenatal diagnosis in families. *Social Work in Health Care, 9,* 37–50.

Black, L., Hersher, L., & Steinschneider, A. (1978, November) Impact of Apnea Monitor on family life. *Pediatrics, 62,* 681–685.

Blades, B. C. (1982). Psychological recovery from burn surgery. In T. S. Kerson (Ed.), *Social work in health settings* (pp. 50–70). New York: Longman.

Blazer, D.G. (1982). Social support and mortality in an elderly community population. *American Journal of Epidemiology, 115,* 684–690.

Blazyk, S., & Canavan, M. M. (1985) Therapeutic aspects of discharge planning. *Social Work, 30,* 489–496.

Bloch, D. A. (1983). Family Systems Medicine: The field and the journal. *Family Systems Medicine, 1,* 4–11.

Bloch, D. A. (1984). The family as a psychosocial system. *Family Systems Medicine, 2,* 387–396.

Bloch, S., Crouch, E., & Reibstein, J. (1981). Therapeutic factors in group pychotherapy. *Archives of General Psychiatry, 38,* 516–526.

Block, A. R., Boyer, S. L. & Imes, C. (1984). Personal impact of myocardial infarction: A model for coping with physical disability in middle-age. In M. G. Eisenberg & M. A. Jansen (Eds.), *Chronic illness and disability through the life-span: Effects on self and family* (pp. 209–221). New York: Springer.

Bloom, B. L. (1985). A factor analysis of self-report measures of family functioning. *Family Process, 24,* 225–239.

Bloom, J. A., et al. (1987). Psychological response to mastectomy. *Cancer, 59* (Suppl.), 189–196.

Bloom, J. A. (1982). Social support, accommodation to stress and adjustment to breast cancer. *Social Science and Medicine, 16,* 1329–1338.

Bloom, J. A., & Spiegel, D. (1984). The relationship of two dimensions of social support to the psychological well-being and social functioning of women with advanced breast cancer. *Social Science and Medicine, 19,* 831–837.

Bloom, M. (1981). *Primary prevention.* Englewood Cliffs, NJ: Prentice-Hall.

Blotcky, A. D., Raczynski, J. M., Gurwitch, R., & Smith, K. (1985). Family influences on hopelessness among children early in the cancer experience. *Journal of Pediatric Psychology, 10,* 479–493.

Blugrass, K. (1986). Caring for the family. In B. A. Stoll & A. D. Weisman (Eds.), *Coping with Cancer Stress* (pp. 149–154). Boston: Martinas Nijholt Publications.

Blumenfield, S. (1986). Discharge planning: Changes for hospital social work in a new health care climate. *Quality Review Bulletin, 12,* 51–54.

Bodenheimer, T. S. (1989). The fruits of empire rot on the vine: United States health policy in the austerity era. *Social Science and Medicine, 28,* 531–538.

Boer, A. K., & Lantz, J. E. (1974). Adolescent group therapy membership selection. *Clinical Social Work Journal, 2,* 172–181.

Boll, P. G., DuVall, M. L., & Mercuri, L. G. (1983). Structural family therapy in a multidisciplinary facial pain center: A case report. *Family Systems Medicine, 1,* 78–91.

Borman, L. D. (1985). Self-help and mutual aid groups. In N. Hobbs & J. M. Perrin (Eds.), *Issues in the Care of Children with Chronic Illness* (pp. 771–789). San Francisco: Jossey Bass.

Boss, P. (1988). *Family stress management.* Newbury Park: Sage Publications.

Bostrom, D. (1965). Some points for the practitioner. *The family is the patient: The group approach to treatment of family health problems* (pp. 61–69). New York: National Association of Social Workers.

Boukydis, C. F. Z., Lester, B. M., & Hoffman, J. (1987). Parenting and social support networks in families of term and preterm infants. In C. F. Z. Boukydis (Ed.), *Research on support for parents & infants in the postnatal period* (pp. 61–83). Norwood, N.J.: Ablex Publishing.

Boulding, K. E. (1956). General systems theory: The skeleton of science. *Management Science, 2,* 197–208.

Bowlby, J. (1960). Separation anxiety. *International Journal of Psychoanalysis, 41,* 85–113.

Bowling, A. (1987). Mortality after bereavement: A review of the literature on survival periods and factors affecting survival. *Social Science and Medicine, 24,* 117–124.

Boyd, R. A. (1977). Developing new norms for parents of fatally ill children to facilitate coping. In Prichard, E. P. et al. (Eds.), *Social work with the dying patient and the family* (pp. 251–265). New York: Columbia University Press.

Boyle, I. R., di Sant'Agnese, P. A., Sack, S., Millican, F., & Kulczychi, L. L. (1976). Emotional adjustment of adolescents and young adults with cystic fibrosis. *Journal of Pediatrics, 88,* 318–326.

Bracht, N. F. (1978). The scope and historical development of social work, 1900–1975. In N. F. Bracht (Ed.), *Social work in health care: A guide to professional practice* (pp. 3–18). New York: The Haworth Press.

Bramwell, L. (1986). Wives' experiences in the support role after husbands' first myocardial infarction. *Heart & Lung, 15,* 578–584.

Branch, L. G. Friedman, D. J., Cohen, M. A., Smith, N., & Socholitzky, E. (1988). Impoverishing the elderly: A case study of the financial risk of spend-down among Massachusetts elderly people. *The Gerontologist, 28,* 648–652.

Brantley, P. J. (1988). Convergence between the daily stress inventory and endocrine measures of stress. *Journal of Consulting and Clinical Psychology, 4,* 549–551.

Bray, G. B. (1980). Reactive patterns in families of the severely disabled. In P. W. Power & A. E. Dell Orto (Eds.), *Role of the family in the rehabilitation of the phyically disabled* (pp. 161–164). Baltimore: University Park Press.

Brenner, M. H. (1984). Estimating the effects of economic change on national health and social well-being. A study prepared for use of the Subcommittee on Economic Goals and Intergovernmental Policy, Joint Economic Committee, U.S. Congress, Washington, D.C.: U.S. Government Printing office.

Brenner, M. H. (1985). Economic change and the suicide rate: A population model circulating loss, separation, illness, and alcohol consumption. In M. Zales (Ed.), *Stress in Health and Disease* (pp. 24–41). New York: Brunner/Mazel.

Breslau, N., Salkever, D., & Staruch, K. S. (1982). Women's labor force activity and responsibilities for disabled dependents: A study of families with disabled children. *Journal of Health and Social Behavior, 23,* 169–183.

Breslau, N., Staruch, K., & Mortimer, E. (1982). Psychological distress in mothers of disabled children. *American Journal of Diseases of childhood, 136:* 682–686.

Breslau, N., Weitzman, M., & Messenger, K. (1981). Psychological functioning of siblings of disabled children. *Pediatrics, 67,* 344–353.

Brissette, S., Zinman, R., Fielding, M., & Reidy, M. (1987). Nursing care plan for adolescents and young adults with advanced cystic fibrosis. *Issues in Comprehensive Pediatric Nursing, 10,* 87–97.

Broadhead, W. E. Kaplan, B. H., James, S. A., Wagner, E. H., Schoenback, V. J., Grimson, P. H., Siegfried, T. C. & Gehlback, S. S. (1983). The epidemiological evidence for a relationship between social support and health. *American Journal of Epidemiology, 117,* 521–537.

Brody, E. M. (1979). Message from the president. *The Gerontologist, 19,* 516.

Brody, E. M. (1985). Parent care as a normative family stress. *The Gerontologist, 25,* 19–29.

Brody, E. M., Johnsen, P. T., & Fulcomer, M. C. (1984). What should adult children do for elderly parents? Opinions and preferences of three generations of women. *Journal of Gerontology. 39,* 736–746.

Brody, E. M., Kleban, M. H., Johnson, P. T., Hoffman, C., & Schooner, C. B. (1987). Work status and parent care: A comparison of focus groups of women. *The Gerontologist, 27,* 201–208.

Bromberg, H., & Donnerstag, E. (1977). Counseling heart patients and their families. *Health and Social Work, 2,* 159–172.

Bronfenbrenner, U. (1979). *The ecology of human development: Experiments by nature and design*. Cambridge, MA: Harvard University Press.

Brook, R. H., Ware, J. E., & Rogers, W. H. (1979). Overview of adult health status measures fielded in Rand's Health Insurance Study. *Medical Care, 17,* (Suppl.) 1–131.

Brown, B. W., & McCormick, T. (1988). Family coping following traumatic head injury: An exploratory analysis with recommendations for treatment. *Family Relations, 37,* 12–16.

Brown, J., & Fitzpatrick, R. (1988). Factors influencing compliance with dietary restrictions in dialysis patients. *Journal of Psychosomatic Research, 2,* 191–196

Brown, M. A., & Munford, A. (1983–84). Rehabilitation of post MI depression and psychological invalidism: A pilot study. *International Journal of Psychiatry in Medicine, 1,* 291–297.

Bruhn, J. G. (1988). Life-style and health behavior. In D. S. Gochman (Ed.), *Health Behavior: Emerging Research Perspectives* (pp. 71–86). New York: Plenum Press.

Bruhn, J. G. (1977). Effects of chronic illness on the family. *Journal of Family Practice, 4,* 1057–1061.

Bruhn, J. G., Chandler, B., Miller, M. C., Wolf, S., & Lynn, T. N. (1966). Social aspects of coronary heart disease in two adjacent, ethnically different communities. *American Journal of Public Health, 56,* 1493–1506.

Bruhn, J. G., Philips, B. U., Levine, P. L., & Mendes de Leon, C. (1987). *Social support and health: An annotated bibliography*. New York: Garland Publishing.

Bruhn, J. G., Philips, B. U., & Wolf, S. (1982). Lessons from Roseto 20 years later: A community study of heart disease. *Southern Medical Journal, 75,* 575–580.

Bryan, F. A., & Evans, R. W. (1980). Hemodialysis partners. *Kidney International, 17,* 350–356.

Buck, F. M., & Holmann, G. W. (1981). Personality, behavior, values and family relations of children of fathers with spinal cord injury. *Archives of Physical Medicine and Rehabilitation, 62,* 432–438.

Buckley, W. (1967). *Sociology and modern systems theory.* Englewood Cliffs, NJ: Prentice-Hall.

Buckley, W. (Ed.). (1968). Society as a complex adaptive system. *Modern systems research for the behavioral scientist* (pp. 490–513). Chicago: Aldine Publishing.

Bucquet, D., & Curtis, S. (1986). Socio-demographic variation in perceived illness and the use of primary care: The value of community survey data for primary care service planning. *Social Science and Medicine, 23,* 737–744.

Burgess, A. W., Lerner, D. J., D'Agostino R. B., Vokonas, P. S, Hartman, C. R., & Gaccione, P. (1987). A randomized controlled trial of cardiac rehabilitation. *Social Science and Medicine, 24,* 359–370.

Burke, R. J., & Weir, T. (1971). Marital helping relationships: The moderators between stress and well-being. *Journal of Psychology, 95,* 121–130.

Burke, R. J., & Weir, T. (1982). Husband-wife helping relationships as moderators of experienced stress: The "mental hygiene" function in marriage. In H. I. McCubbin, A. E. Cauble & J. M. Patterson (Eds.), *Family stress, coping, and social support* (pp. 221–238). Springfield, IL: Charles C. Thomas.

Burr, C. K. (1985). Impact on the family of a chronically ill child. In N. Hobbs & J. M. Perrin (Eds.). *Issues in the care of children with chronic illness.* (pp. 24–40). San Francisco: Jossey- Bass.

Burr, W. (1973). *Theory construction and the sociology of the family.* New York: John Wiley & Sons.

Burr, B. H., Guyer, B., Todres, I. D., Abrahams, B., & Ciodo, T. (1983). Home care for children on respirators. *New England Journal of Medicine, 309,* 1319–1323.

Bush, M. (1988). *Families in distress: Public, private, and civic responses.* Los Angeles: University of California Press.

Butler, J. A., Budetti, P., McManus, M. A., Stenmark, S., & Newacheck, P. W. (1985). Health care expenditures for children with chronic illnesses. In N. Hobbs & J. M. Perrin (Eds.), *Issues in the care of children with chronic illness* (pp. 827–863). San Francisco: Jossey-Bass.

Butler, J. A., Rosenbaum, S., & Palfrey, J. S. (1987). Sounding Board: Ensuring access to healthcare for children with disabilities. *The New England Journal of Medicine, 317,* 162–164.

Butler, P. A. (1988). *Too poor to be sick.* Washington, D.C.: American Public Health Association.

Bywaters, P. (1975). Ending casework relationships. *Social Work Today, 6,* 336–338.

Cafferata, G. L., & Kasper, J. D. (1985). Family structure and children's use of ambulatory physician services. *Medical Care, 23,* 350–360.

Cain, L. P., Kelly, D. H., & Shannon, D. C. (1980). Parents' perceptions of the psychological and social impact of home monitoring. *Pediatrics, 66,* 37–41.

Cairns, N. U., Clark, G. M., Smith, S. D., & Lansky, S. B. (1979). Adaptation of siblings to childhood malignancy. *Journal of Pediatrics, 95,* 484–487.

Califano, J. A. (1985). *America's health care revolution: Who lives? Who dies? Who pays?* New York: Random House.

Camasso, M. J., & Camasso, A. E. (1986). Social supports, undesirable life events, and psychological distress in a disadvantaged population. *Social Service Review, 60,* 378–394.

Campbell, T. L. (1986). Family's impact on health: A critical review. *Family Systems Medicine, 4,* 135–332.

Candib, L., & Glenn, M. (1983). Family medicine and family therapy: Comparative development, methods, and roles. *Journal of Family Practice, 16,* 773–779.

Cannon, I. M. (1913, 1923). *Social work in hospitals.* New York: Russell Sage Foundation.

Cantor, M. (1983). Strain among caregivers: A study of experience in the United States. *The Gerontologist, 23,* 597–604.

Cantor, M., Rehr, H., & Trotz, V. (1981). Workshop II: Case management of family involvement. *The Mt. Sinai Journal of Medicine, 48,* 566–568.

Caplan, G. (1951). A public Health approach to child psychiatry. *Mental health, 35,* 235–249.

Caplan, G. (1974). *Support systems and community mental health.* New York: Behavioral Publications.

Caplan, G. (1976). The family as a support system. In G. Caplan & M. Killileu (Eds.), *Support systems and mutual help: Multidisciplinary Explorations* (pp. 200–220). New York: Grune and Stratton.

Caplan, G., Mason, E. A., & Kaplan, D. M. (1965). Four studies of crisis in parents of prematures. *Community Mental Health Journal, 2,* 149–161.

Caplan, R. D., Van Harrison, R., Wellons, R. O., & French, J. R. P. (1980). *Social support and patient adherence: Experimental and survey findings.* Ann Arbor: The University of Michigan.

Caputi, M. A. (1982). A 'quality of life' model for social work practice in health care. *Health and Social Work, 7,* 103–110.

Caputi, M. A., & Heiss, W. A. (1984). The DRG revolution. *Health and Social Work, 9,* 5–12.

Carkhuff, R. R., & Berenson, B. (1967). *Beyond counseling and therapy.* New York: Holt, Rinehart, and Winston.

Carlton, T. O. (1984). *Clinical social work in health settings: A guide to professional practice with exemplars.* New York: Springer Publishing Co.

Carmichael, L. P. (1976). The family in medicine: Process or entity? *Journal of Family Practice, 3,* 562–571.

Caroff, P., & Mailick, M. D. (1985). The patient has a family: Reaffirming social work's domain. *Social Work in Health Care, 10,* 17–34.

Carpenter, J. O., & Davis, L. J. (1976). Medical recommendations-followed or ignored? Factors influencing compliance in arthritis. *Archives of Physical Medicine and Rehabilitation, 57* 241–246.

Carter, B., & McGoldrick, M. (Eds.). (1988). *The changing family life cycle: A framework for family therapy.* New York: Gardner Press.

Carter, R. E. (1984). Family reactions and reorganization patterns in myocardial infarction. *Family Systems Medicine, 2,* 55–65.

Carter, R. E. (1985). Establishing and maintaining a family treatment center in a general hospital setting. *Family Systems Medicine, 3,* 133–142.

Cassel, C. K. (1987). Decisions to forgo life-sustaining therapy: The limits of ethics. *Social Service Review, 61,* 553–564.

Cassel, J. (1976). An epidemiological perspective of psychosocial factors in disease etiology. *American Journal of Public Health, 64,* 1040–1043.

Cassserta, M. S., Lund, D. A., Wright, S. D., Redburn, D. E. (1987). Caregivers to dementia patients: The utilization of community services. *The Gerontologist, 27,* 209–214.

Cassileth, B. R., & Hamilton, J. N. (1979). The family with cancer. In B. R. Cassileth (Eds.). *The cancer patient* (pp. 233–247). Philadelphia: Lea & Febiger.

Cassileth, B. R., Lusk, E. J., Strouse, T. B., Miller, D. S., Brown, L. L., & Cross, P. A. (1985). A psychological analysis of cancer patients and their next-of-kin. *Cancer, 55,* 72–76.

Catalano, R. (1979). *Health, behavior and the community: An ecological perspective.* New York: Pergamon Press.

Catalano, R., & Dooley, C. D. (1977). Economic predictors of depressed mood and stressful life events in a metropolition community. *Journal of Health and Social Behavior, 18,* 292–306.

Catalano, R. A., Dooley, D., & Jackson, R. L. (1985). Economic antecedents of help seeking: Reformulation of time-series test. *Journal of Health and Social Behavior, 26,* 141–152.

Catalano, R., Rook, K., & Dooley, D. (1986). Labor markets and help-seeking: a test of the employment security hypothesis. *Journal of Health and Social Behavior, 27,* 277–287.

Cella, D. F., Perry, S. W., Kulchycky, S., & Goodwin, C. (1988). Stress and coping in relatives of burn patients: A longitudinal study *Hospital and Community Psychiatry, 39,* 159–166.

Centers for Disease Control. (1986). Report of the Secretary's Task Force on Black and Minority Health. *Morbidity and Mortality Weekly Report, 33,* 109–112.

Chandra, V., Szklo, M., Goldberg, R., & Tonascia, J. (1983). The impact of marital status on survival after an acute myocardial infarction: A population-based study. *American Journal of Epidemiology, 117,* 320–325.

Chatham, M. A. (1978). The effects of family involvement on patients manifestations of post- cardiotomy psychosis. *Heart and Lung, 7,* 995–999.

Chavkin, N. F. (1986). The practice-research relationship: An organizational link. *Social Service Review, 60,* 241–250.

Chekryn, J. (1984). Cancer recurrence: Personal meaning, communication, and marital adjustment. *Cancer Nursing, 7,* 491–496.

Chenoweth, B., Spencer, B. (1986). Dementia: The experience of family caregivers. *The Gerontologist, 26,* 267–272.

Cherlin, A. J. (Ed.) (1988). *The changing American family and public policy.* Washington, D.C.: The Urban Institute Press.

Cherniss, D. P. (1987). Stability and growth in parent-support services: A national survey of peer support for parents of premature and high-risk infants. In C. F. Z. Boukydis (Ed.), *Research on support for parents & infants in the postnatal period* (pp. 161–196). Norwood, N.J.: Ablex Publishing Corporation.

Chesler, N. A., & Barbarin, O. A. (1984). Relating to the medical staff: How parents of children with cancer see the issues. *Health and Social Work, 9,* 49–65.

Chesney, A. P., Chavira, J. A., Hall, R. P., & Gary, H. E. (1982). Barriers to medical care of Mexican-Americans: The role of social class, acculturation, and social isolation. *Medical Care, 20,* 883–891.

Childrens' Defense Fund (1986). *Childrens' defense budget: An analysis of F. Y. 1987 federal budget and children.* Washington D.C. 1986.

Chilman, C. S. (1988a). Never-married, single, adolescent parents. In C. S. Chilman, F. M. Cox & E. W. Nunnaly (Eds.), *Variant family forms: Families in trouble series, volume 5* (pp. 17–38). Newbury Park: Sage Publications.

Chilman, C. S. (1988b). Public policies and families. In C. S. Chilman, E. W. Nunnaly & F. M. Cox (Eds.), *Chronic illness and disability: Families in trouble series, volume 2* (pp. 211–219). Newbury Park: Sage Publications.

Chirakos, T. N., Reiches, N. A., & Moeschberger, M. L. (1984). Economic differentials in cancer survival: A multivariate analysis. *Journal of Chronic Diseases, 37,* 183–193.

Choi, T., Josten, L. V., & Christensen, M. L. (1983). Health-specific family coping index for noninstitutional care. *American Journal of Public Health, 73,* 1275–1277.

Christ, G. H. (1983). A psychosocial assessment framework for cancer patients and their families. *Health and Social Work, 8,* 57–64.

Clark, A., & Fallowfield, L. J. (1986). Quality of life measurements in patients with malignant disease: A review. *Journal of the Royal Society of Medicine, 79,* 165–169.

Clarke, N. M., Feldman, C. H., Evans, D., Millman, E. J., Wailewski, Y. & Valle, I. (1981). The effectiveness of education for family management of asthma in children: A preliminary report. *Health Education Quarterly, 8,* 166–174.

Cleveland, P., Walters, L. H., Skeen, P., & Robinson, B. E. (1988). If your child had Aids . . .: Responses of parents with homosexual children. *Family Relations, 7,* 150–153.

Cobb, S. (1976). Social support as a moderator of life stress. *Psychosomatic Medicine, 38,* 300–314.

Cobb, S. (1979). Social support and health through the life course. In *Family stress, coping and social support* (pp. 189–199). Springfield, IL: Charles Thomas

Coe, R. M., Wolinsky, F. D., Miller, D. K., & Prendergast, J. M. (1985). Elderly persons without family support networks and use of health services. *Research on Aging, 7,* 617–222.

Coffman, S. P. (1983). Parents' perceptions of needs for themselves and their children in a cerebral palsy clinic. *Issues in Comprehensive Pediatric Nursing, 6,* 67–77.

Cohen, F. (1982). Personality, stress, and the development of physical illness. In G. C. Stone, F. Cohen & N. E. Alder (Eds.). *Health psychology: A handbook* (pp. 561–571). San Francisco: Jossey-Bass.

Cohen, M., Goldenberg, I., & Goldenberg, H. (1977). Treating families of bone marrow recipients and donors. *Journal of Marriage and Family Counseling, 3,* 45–51.

Cohen, M. M., & Wellish, D. K. (1978). Living in limbo: Psychological intervention in families with a cancer patient. *American Journal of Family Therapy, 32,* 561–571.

Cohen, P., Dizenhuz, I. M., & Winget, C. (1977). Family adaptation to terminal illness and death of a parent. *Social Casework, 58,* 223–228.

Cohen, R. L. (1988). Developmental tasks of pregnancy and transition to parenthood: An approach to assessment. In R. L. Cohen (Ed.). *Psychiatric consultation in childbirth settings: Parent-and child-oriented approaches.* (pp. 38–51). New York: Plenum Medical Book Co.

Cohen, S. (1988). Psychological models of the role of social support in the etiology of physical disease. *Health Psychology, 7,* 269–297.

Cohen, S., Sherrod, D. R., & Clark, M. S. (1986). Social skills and the stress-protective role of social support. *Journal of Personality and Social Psychology, 50,* 963–973.

Cohen, S., & Syme, S. L. (Eds.). (1985). *Social support and health.* New York: Academic Press.

Collins, A. H., & Pancoast, D. L. (1976). *Natural helping networks.* Washington D.C.: National Association of Social Workers.

Combs-Orme, T. (1987). Infant mortality: Priority for social work. *Social Work, 32,* 507–511.

Conrad, P. (1988). Worksite health promotion: The social context. *Social Science and Medicine, 26,* 485–489.

Cooke, B. D., Rossmann, M. M., McCubbin, H. I., & Patterson, J. M. (1988). Examining the definition and assessment of social support: A resource for individuals and families. *Family Relations, 37,* 211–216.

Cooper, E. T. (1984). A pilot study of the effects of the diagnosis of lung cancer on family relationships. *Cancer Nursing, 7,* 301–308.

Cooper, R. S., Simmons, B., Castaner, A., Prasad, R., Franklin, C., & Ferlinz, J. (1986). Survival rates and prehospital delay during myocardial infarction among Black persons. *The American Journal of Cardiology, 57,* 208–211.

Copeland, D. R. (1988). Stress and the patient's family. In M. L. Russell (Ed.). *Stress management for chronic disease* (pp. 30–48). New York: Pergamon Press.

Coppotelli, H. C., & Orleans C. T. (1985). Partner support and other determinants of smoking cessation maintenance among women. *Journal of Consulting and Clinical Psychology, 53,* 455–460.

Copstick, S. M., Taylor, K. E., Hayes, R., & Morris, N. (1986). Partner support and the use of coping techniques in labour. *Journal of Psychosomatic Research, 30,* 497–503.

Corcoran, K., & Fischer, J. (1987). *Measures for clinical practice: A sourcebook.* New York: The Free Press.

Corsini, R. J., & Rosenberg, B. (1955). Mechanisms of group psychotherapy: Process and dynamics. *Journal of Abnormal and Social Psychology, 51,* 406–411.

Couch, E. (1969). *Joint and family interviews: In the treatment of marital problems.* New York: Family Service Association of America.

Couglan, G. W., & Humphrey, M. (1982). Presenile stroke: Long-term outcome for patients and their families. *Rheumatology and Rehabilitation, 1,* 115–122.

Coulton, C. (1979). A study of person-environment fit among the critically ill. *Social Work in Health Care, 5,* 5–17.

Coulton, C. J. (1981). Person-environment fit as the focus in health care. *Social Work, 26,* 26–35.

Coulton, C. J. (1984). Confronting prospective payment: Requirements for an information system. *Health and Social Work, 9,* 13–24.

Coulton, C. (1988). Evaluating screening and early intervention: A puzzle with many faces. *Social Work in Health Care, 13,* 65–72.

Coulton, C. J., Dunkle, R. E., Goode, R. A., & Mac Intosh, J. (1982). Discharge planning and decision making. *Health and Social Work, 7,* 253–261.

Council on Social Work Education (1962). *Public health concepts in social work education.* New York: Council on Social Work Education.

Cousins, N. (1983). *The healing heart: Antidotes to pain and helplessness.* New York: Norton

Cox, C. (1986). Physician utilization by three groups of ethnic elderly. *Medical Care, 24,* 667–676.

Cox, E. O., Parsons, R. J., & Kimboko, P. J. (1988). Social services and intergenerational caregivers: Issues for social work. *Social Work, 33,* 430–434.

Coyle, G. (1962). Concepts relevant to helping the family as a group. *Social Casework, 42,* 347–354.

Coyne, J. C., & Anderson, B. J. (1988). The psychosomatic family reconsidered: Diabetes in context. *Journal of Marital and Family Therapy, 14,* 113–123.

Coyne, J. C., & Delongis, A. (1986). Going beyond social support: The role of social relationships in adaptation. *Journal of Consulting and Clinical Psychology, 54,* 454–460.

Coyne, J. C., Wortman, C. B., & Lehman, D. R. (1988). The other side of support: Emotional overinvolvement and miscarried helping. In B. H. Gottlieb (Ed.), *Marshalling social support: Formats, processes, and effects* (pp. 305–330). Newbury Park, CA: Sage Publications.

Craft, M. J., Wyatt, N., & Sandell, B. (1985). Behavior and feeling changes in siblings of hospitalized children. *Clinical Pediatrics, 24,* 374–378.

Craig, T. K. J., & Brown, G. W. (1984). Life events, meaning and physical illness: A review. In A. Steptoe & A. Mathews (Eds.), *Health Care and Human Behavior.* (pp. 7–40). New York: Academic Press.

Creedon, M. A. (1988). The corporate response to the working caregiver. *Aging, 358,* 16–19, 44–45.

Crnic, K. A., Greenberg, M. T., Ragozin, A. S., Robinson, N. M., & Bashman, R. B. (1983). Effects on stress and social support on mothers and premature and full-term infants. *Child Development, 54,* 209–217.

Croog, S. H., & Fitzgerald, E. F. (1978). Subjectives stress and serious illness of a spouse: Wives of heart patients. *Journal of Health and Social Behavior, 19,* 166–178.

Croog, S., Lipson, A., & Levine, S. (1972). Help patterns in severe illnesses: The role of kin network, non-family resources and institutions. *Journal of Marriage and the Family, 34,* 32–41.

Crossman, L., London, C., & Barry, C. (1981). Older women caring for disabled spouses: A model for supportive services. *The Gerontologist, 21,* 464–470.

Cunliffe, M., & Caldwell, O. (1965). Dramatization of family interview. *The family is the patient: The group approach to treatment of family health problems* (pp. 48–60). New York: National Association of Social Workers.

D'Afflitti, J. D., & Weitz, G. W. (1974). Rehabilitating the stroke patient through patient-family groups. *International Journal of Group Psychotherapy, 25,* 327–332.

Dansiger, S. H. & Weinberg, D. H. (1986). (Eds.). *Fighting poverty: What works and what doesn't.* Cambridge, MA.: Harvard University Press.

Davidson, D. M. (1979). The family and cardiac rehabilitation. *The Journal of Family Practice, 8,* 253–261.

Davidson, D. M. (1983). Recovery after cardiac events. In J. S. Spittell, Jr., (Ed.). *Clinical Medicine* (pp. 1–20). Philadelphia: Harper & Row.

Davis, K., & Rowland, D. (1983). Uninsured and underserved: Inequities in health care in the United States. *Quarterly/Health and Society, 61,* 149–176.

Dayal, H., Polissar, L., Yang, C. Y., & Dahlberg, S. (1987). Race, socioeconomic status and other prognostic factors for survival from colo-rectal cancer. *Journal of Chronic Diseases, 40,* 857–864.

Dayal, H. H., Power, R. N., & Chiu, C. (1982). Race and socioeconomic status in survival from breast cancer. *Journal of Chronic Disease, 35,* 675–683.

Dean, C. (1987). Psychiatric morbidity following mastectomy: Preoperative predictors and types of illness. *Journal of Psychosomatic Research, 31,* 385–392.

Dell Orto, A. E., & Power, P. W. (Eds). (1980). Physical disabilities and group counseling: A proactive alternative for families of the disabled. *Role of the family in the rehabilitation of the physically disabled* (p. 419–432). Baltimore: University Park Press.

Del Vecchio-Good, M. J., Smilkstein, G., Good, B. J., Shaffer, T., & Arons, T. (1979). The family APGAR Index: A study of construct validity. *The Journal of Family Practice, 8,* 577–582.

Demers, R. Y., Altamore, R., Mustin, H., Kleinman, A., & Leonardi, D. (1980). An exploration of the dimensions of illness behavior. *Journal of Family Practice, 11,* 1085–1092.

Dempsey, G. M., Buchsbaum, H. J., & Morrison, J. (1975). Psychosocial adjustment to pelvic exenteration. *Gynecologic Oncology, 3,* 325–334.

Denniston, R. W. (1981). Cancer knowledge attitudes and practice among Black Americans. In C. Medlin & G. P. Murphy (Eds.), *Cancer among Black populations,* (pp. 69–78). New York: Alan R. Liss.

De-Nour, A. K. (1982) Social adjustment of chronic dialysis patients. *American Journal of Psychiatry, 139,* 97–99.

Department of Health, Education and Welfare. (1982). *Health of the disadvantaged: A chart book,* Washington, DC: U.S. Government Printing Office.

Derogatis, L. R. (1986a). Psychology in cancer medicine: A prospective overview. *Journal of Consulting and Clinical Psychology, 54,* 632–638.

Derogatis, L. R. (1986b). The psychosocial adjustment to illness scale (PAIS). *Journal of Psychosomatic Research, 30, 77*–91.

Derogatis, L. R., Morrow, G. R., Fetting, J., Penman, D. P., Sheryl, S., Arthur M., Henrichs, M., & Carnicke, C. L. M. Jr. (1983). The prevalence of psychiatric disorders among cancer patients. *Journal of the American Medical Association, 249,* 751–757.

De Rosnay, J. (1975). *The macroscope: A new world scientific system.* New York: Harper & Row Publishers.

Deutsch, K. W. (1968). Toward a cybernetic model of man and society. In W. Buckley (Ed.), *Modern systems research for the behavioral scientist* (pp. 387–400). Chicago: Aldine Publishing Company.

Deutsch, M. (1973). *The resolution of conflict*. New Haven, CT: Yale University Press.

Dew, M. A., Bromet, E. J., & Schulberg, H. C. (1987). A comparative analysis of two community stressors' long-term mental health effects. *American Journal of Community Psychology, 15,* 167–184.

Dewey, J. (1910). *How we think*. Boston: Heath.

Dhooper, S. S. (1983). Family coping with the crisis of heart attack. *Social Work in Health Care, 9,* 15–30.

Dickoff, H., & Lakin, M. (1963). Patients' views of group psychotherapy: Retrospections and interpretations. *International Journal of Group Psychotherapy, 13,* 61–73.

Dill, D., Feld, E., Martin, J., Beukema, S., & Belle, D. (1986). The impact of the environment on the coping efforts of low-income mothers. *Family Relations, 29,* 503–509.

Dillon, C. (1985). Families, transitions, and health: Another look. *Social Work in Health Care, 10,* 35–44.

Dilworth-Anderson, P. (1987). Supporting family caregiving through adult day-care services. In T. H. Brubaker (Ed), *Aging, Health, and Family: Long-Term Care* (pp. 129–142). Newbury Park: Sage Publications.

Di Matteo, M. R., & Di Nicola, D. D. (1982). *Achieving patient compliance: The psychology of the medical practitioners role*. New York: Pergamon Press.

Di Matteo, M. R., & Friedman, H. S. (1982). *Social psychology and medicine*. Cambridge, Mass.: Oelgeschlager, Gunn and Hain.

Dinerman, M., Seaton, R., & Schlesinger, E. G. (1986). Surviving DRG's: New Jersey's social work experience with prospective payments. *Social Work in Health Care, 12,* 103–113.

Doerr, B., & Jones, J. W. (1979). Effects of family preparation on the state anxiety level of the CCV patient. *Nursing Research, 28,* 315–316.

Doherty, W. J., & Baird, M. A. (1983). Forming a therapeutic contract that involves the family. In W. J. Doherty & M. A. Baird (Eds.), *Family therapy and family medicine* (pp. 64–75). New York: Guilford Press.

Doherty, W. J., & Burge, S. K. (1987). Attending to the context of family treatment: Pitfalls and prospects. *Journal of Marital and Family therapy, 13,* 37–47.

Doherty, W. J., & Campbell, T. L. (1988). *Families and health*. Newbury Park: Sage Publications.

Doherty, W. J., & McCubbin, H. I. (1985). Families and health care: An emerging arena of theory, research, and clinical intervention. *Family Relations, 34,* 5–11.

Doherty, W. J., Schrott, H. G., Metcalf, L., & Iasiello-Vailas, L. (1983). Effect of spouse support and health beliefs on medication adherence. *Journal of Family Practice, 17,* 837–841.

Dohrenwend, B. S., & Dohrenwend, B. P. (Eds.). (1981). *Stressful life events and their contexts*. New York: Prodist.

Dolgin, M. J., Katz, E., Doctors, S. R., & Siegal, S. E. (1986). Caregivers' perceptions of medical compliance in adolescents with cancer. *Journal of Adolescent Health Care, 7,* 22–27.

Dooley, B., Prochaska, J. M., & Klibanoff, P. (1983). What next? An educational program for parents of newborns. *Social Work in Health Care, 8,* 95–103.

Doty, P. (1986). Family care of the elderly: The role of public policy. *The Milbank Quarterly, 64,* 34–75.

Dracup, K., Guzy, P. M., Taylor, S. E., & Barry, J. (1986). Cardiopulmonary resuscitation training: Consequences for family members of high-risk cardiac patients. *Archives of Internal Medicine, 146,* 1757–1761.

Drotar, D., Baskiewicz, Irvin, N., Kennel, J., & Klaus, M. (1980). The adaptation of parents to the birth of an infant with a congenital malformation: A hypothetical model. In P. W. Power & A. E. Dell Orto (Eds.), *Role of the family in the rehabilitation of the physically disabled* (pp. 195–207). Baltimore: University Park Press.

Drotar, D., & Crawford, P. (1985). Psychological adaptation of siblings of chronically ill children: Research and practice implications. *Developmental and Behavioral Pediatrics, 6,* 355–362.

Dubos, R. (1959). *Mirage of health.* New York: Harper and Row.

Dunkel-Schetter, C. (1984). Social support and cancer: Findings based on patient interviews and their implications. *Journal of Social Issues, 40,* 77–98.

Dunkel-Schetter, C., & Wortman, C. B. (1982). The interpersonal dynamics of cancer: Problems in social relationships and their impact on the patient. In H. S. Friedman & M. R. DiMatteo (Eds.), *Interpersonal issues in health care,* (pp. 69–100). New York: Academic Press.

Dunst C. J., Cooper, C. S., & Bolick, F. A. (1987). Supporting families of handicapped children. In J. Garbarino, P. E. Brookhouser, K. J. Authier and Associates (Eds.). *Special children—special risks: The maltreatment of children with disabilities* (pp. 17–46). New York: Aldine de Gruyter.

Durkheim, E. (1951). *Suicide: A study in sociology.* In G. Simpson (Ed.). Glencoe, Ill.: Free Press.

Dutton, D. B. (1985). Socioeconomic status and children's health. *Medical Care, 23,* 142–154.

Eakes, E. D., Hayes, S. G., & Feinleib, M. (1983). Spouse behavior and coronary heart disease in men: Prospective results from the Framingham Heart Study: II: Modification of risk in Type A husbands according to the social and psychological status of their wives. *American Journal of Epidemiology, 118,* 23–41.

Earp, J., Ory, M. G., & Strogatz, D. S. (1982). The effects of family involvement and practitioner home visits on the control of hypertension. *American Journal of Public Health, 72,* 1146–1154.

Eastman, J. N., & Saur, W. G. (1979). A group model for building strengths in families with disabled children. In N. Stinnett, B. Chesser & J. Defrain (Eds.), *Building family strengths: Blue prints for action* (pp. 301–310). Lincoln: University of Nebraska Press.

Edelstein, J., & Linn, M. W. (1985). The influence of the family on control of diabetes. *Social Science and Medicine, 21,* 541–544.

Egan, K. J., & Beaton, R. (1987). Response to symptoms in healthy, low utilizer of the health care system. *Journal of Psychosomatic Research, 31,* 11–21.

Egbuonu, L., & Starfield, B. S. (1982). Child health and social status. *Pediatrics, 69,* 550–557.

Eggert, L. L. (1987). Support in family ties: Stress, coping, and adaptation. In T. L. Albrecht & M. B. Adelman & Associates. *Communicating Social Support* (pp. 80–104). Beverly Hills, CA.: Sage Publications.

Eisdorfer, C. (1985). The conceptualization of stress and a model for further study. In M. R. Zales (Ed.), *Stress in health and disease* (pp. 5–23). New York: Brunner/ Mazel.

Eisdorfer, C. (1981). Introduction to the stress and coping paradigm. In C. Eisdorfer, D. Cohen, A. Kleinman & P. Maxim. *Model for clinical psychopathology* (pp. 175–222). New York: SP Medical and Scientific Books.

Eisenberg, M. G. (1984). Spinal cord injuries. In H. B. Roback (Ed.), *Helping patients and their families with medical problems* (pp. 107–129). San Francisco: Jossey-Bass.

Ell, K. (1984). Social networks, social support and health status: A review. *Social Service Review, 58,* 133–149.

Ell, K. (1985-1986) Coping with serious illness: On integrating constructs to enhance clinical research, assessment and intervention. *International Journal of Psychiatry in Medicine, 15,* 335–355.

Ell, K. (1985). The role of social work in rehabilitating people with disabilities. In E. Pan, S. Newman, T. Backer & C. Vash (Eds.), *Annual Review of Rehabilitation, 4* (pp. 145–179). New York: Springer Publishing Company.

Ell, K., & Dunkel-Schetter, C. (in press). Social support and adjustment to myocardial infarction, angioplasty and coronary artery bypass surgery. In S. A. Shumaker & S. M. Czajkowski (Eds.), *Social support and cardiovascular disease.*

Ell, K. O., & Haywood, L. J. (1984). Social Support and recovery from myocardial infarction: A panel study. *Journal of Social Service Research, 4,* 1–9.

Ell, K., Larson, D., Finch, W., Sattler, F., & Nishimoto, R. (1989). Mental health services among ambulatory patients with human immunodeficiency syndrome infections. *Journal of Health and Social Policy.*

Ell, K., Mantell, J., & Hamovitch, M. (1988). Socioculturally–sensitive intervention for patients with cancer. *Journal of Psychosocial Oncology,* 6, 141–155.

Ell, K., & Morrison, D. R. (1981). Primary care. *Health and Social Work, 6,* (Suppl.), 353–435.

Ell, K., Nishimoto, R., Mantell, J., & Hamovitch, M. (1988a). Longitudinal analysis of psychological adaptation among members of patients with cancer. *Journal of Psychosomatic Research, 32,* 429–438.

Ell, K., Nishimoto, R., Mantell, J., & Hamovitch, M. (1988b). Psychological adaptation to cancer: A comparison among patients, spouses, and non-spouses. *Family Systems Medicine, 6,* 335–348.

Elliot, S. A., Sanjack, M., & Leverton, T. J. (1988). Parents groups in pregnancy. In B. H. Gottlieb (Ed.), *Marshaling social support: Formats, processes, and effects* (pp. 87–110). Beverly Hills, CA: Sage Publications.

Engel, G. L. (1977). The need for a new medical model: A challenge for biomedicine. *Science, 196,* 130–136.

Engel, G. L. (1980). The clinical application of the biopsychosocial model. *American Journal of Psychiatry, 137,* 535–541.

Epperson, M. M. (1977). Families in sudden crisis: Process and intervention in the critical care center. *Social Work in Health Care, 2,* 265–273.

Epstein, A. M., Stern, R. M., Tognetti, J., Begg, C. B., Hartley, R. M., Cumella, E., & Ayanian, J. Z. (1988). The association of patients' socioeconomic characteristics with the length of hospital stay and hospital charges within diagnosis–related groups. *New England Journal of Medicine, 318,* 1579–1585.

Epstein, N. B., Baldwin, L. M., & Bishop, D. S. (1983). McMaster family assessment device. *Journal of Marital and Family Therapy, 9,* 171–180.

Epstein, N. B., Bishop, D. S., & Levin, S. (1978). The McMaster model of family functioning. *Journal of Marriage and Family Counseling, 4,* 19–31.

Epstein, L. H., Wing, R. R., Koeske, R., & Valoski, A. (1987). Long-term effects of family-based treatment of childhood obesity. *Journal of Consulting and Clinical Psychology, 55,* 91–95.

Erikson, E. H. (1963). *Childhood and society, 2d ed.* New York: Norton.

Estes, R. J. (Ed.). (1984). *Health care and the social services.* St. Louis: Warren H. Green, Inc.

Evans, R. C., Burlew, A. K., & Oler, C. H. (1988). Children with sickle-cell anemia: Parental relations, parent-child relations, and child behavior. *Social Work, 33,* 127–130.

Falck, H. (1978). Social work in health settings. *Social Work in Health Care, 3,* 395–403.

Falck, H. (1981). *The social status examination in health care.* Richmond, VA: School of Social Work, Virginia Commonwealth University.

Farkas, S. W. (1980). Impact of chronic illness on the patients' spouse. *Health and Social Work, 5,* 39–46.

Feinberg, E. A. (1985). Family stress in pediatric home care. *Caring, 4,* 38–41.

Feldman, F. L. (1987). Female cancer patients and caregivers: Experiences in the workplace. *Women and Health, 2,* 137–154.

Feldman, F. L., & Scherz, F. (1967). *Family social welfare: Helping troubled families.* New York: Atherton Press.

Ferrari, M., Matthews, W. S., & Barabas, G. (1983). The family and the child with epilepsy. *Family Process, 22,* 53–59.

Ferrari, N. A. (1963). Freedom of choice. *Social Work, 8,* 8–13.

Fielding, D., Moore B., Dewey, M., Ashley, P., McKendrick, T., & Pinkerton, P. (1985). Children with end-stage renal failure: Psychological effects on patients, siblings and parents. *Journal of Psychosomatic Research, 29,* 457–465.

Fife, B. L. (1980). Childhood cancer is a family crisis: A review. *Journal of Psychosocial Nursing and Medical Health Services, 18,* 29–34.

Fife, B., Norton, J., & Groom, G. (1987). The family's adaptation to childhood leukemia. *Social Science and Medicine, 24,* 159–168.

Figley, C. R. & McCubbin, H. I. (1983). *Stress and the family Volume II: Coping with catastrophe.* New York: Brunner/Mazel.

Filinson, R. (1988). A model for church-based services for frail elderly persons and their families. *The Gerontologist, 28,* 483–486.

Filsinger, E. E. (1983). Choices among marital observation coding systems. *Family Process, 24,* 317–335.

Finch, J., & Groves, D. (Eds.). (1983). *A labour of love: Women, work, and caring.* London: Routledge & Kegan Paul.

Fine, J. (1980). Family treatment in a medical hospital setting. In C. Janzen & O. Harris (Eds.). *Family treatment in social work practice* (pp. 200–258). Atasca, IL: F. E. Peacock.

Finlayson, A. & McEwen, J. (1977). *Coronary heart disease and patterns of living.* New York: Croom Helm.

Finley, N. J., Roberts, M. D., & Banahan, B. F. (1988). Motivators and inhibitors of attitudes of filial obligations toward aging parents. *The Gerontologist, 28,* 73–83.

Fisher, L., Kokes, R. F., Ransom, D. C., Phillips, S. L., & Rudd, P. (1985). Alternative strategies for creating "relational" family data. *Family Process, 24,* 213–224.

Fitting, M., Robins, P., Lucas, M. J., & Eastham, J. (1986). Caregivers for dementia patients: A comparison of husbands and wives. *The Gerontologist, 26,* 248–252.

Fleming, R., Baum, A., & Singer, J. E. (1984). Toward an integrative approach to the study of stress. *Journal of Personality and Social Psychology, 46,* 939–949.

Fletcher, A. E., Hunt, B. M., & Bulpitt, C. J. (1987). Evaluation of quality of life in clinical trials of cardiovascular disease. *Journal of Chronic Disease, 40,* 557–566.

Flor, H., Turk, D. C., & Scholz, B. O. (1987). Impact of chronic pain on the spouse: Marital, emotional and physical consequences. *Journal of Psychosomatic Research, 31,* 63–71.

Folkman, S. (1984). Personal control and stress and coping processes: A theoretical analysis. *Journal of Personality and Social Psychology, 46,* 839–852.

Ford, C. A. (1982). Epilepsy in childhood: Pediatric neurology clinic. In T. S. Kerson (Ed.), *Social work in health settings* (pp. 144–160). New York: Longman.

Forman, B. D., & Hagan, B. J. (1983). A comparative review of total family functioning measures. *The American Journal of Family Therapy, 11,* 25–40.

Foster, M., & Berger M. (1985). Research with families with handicapped children: A multilevel systemic perspective. In L. L. Abate (Ed.). *The handbook of family psychology and therapy* (pp. 741–780). Homewood, IL: The Dorsey Press.

Framo, J. (Ed.). (1971). *Conference on systematic research on family interaction: A Dialogue between family researchers and family therapists.* New York: Springer.

Frank, D., Dornbush, R. L., Webster, S. K., & Kolony, R. C. (1978). Mastectomy and sexual behavior. A pilot study. *Sexuality and Disability, 1,* 16–26.

Franklin, D. L. (1988). Race, class, and adolescent pregnancy: An ecological analysis. *American Journal of Orthopsychiatry, 58,* 339–354.

Fredman, N., & Sherman, R. (1987). *Handbook for measurements for marriage and family therapy.* New York: Brunner/Mazel.

Freedman, S. A., Pierce, P. M., & Reiss, J. G. (1987). Model program outreach: A family-centered community-based case management model for children with special health care needs. *Children's Health Care, 16,* 114–117.

Freeman, D. S. (1981). *Techniques of family therapy.* New York: Aronson.

Frey, L. A. (1962). Support and the group: Generic treatment form. *Social Work, 7,* 35–42.

Friedenbergs, I., Gordon, W., Hibbard, M., Levine, L., Wolf, C., & Diller, L. (1981-

1982). Psychosocial aspects of living with cancer: A review of the literature. *International Journal of Psychiatry in Medicine, 11,* 303–329.

Friedlander, R. J., & Viederman, M. (1982). Children of dialysis patients. *American Journal of Psychiatry, 139,* 100–103.

Friedman, L. C., Nelson, D. V., Smith, F. E., & Dworkin, R. J. (in press). Women with breast cancer: Perception of family functioning and adjustment to illness. *Psychosomatic Medicine.*

Friedrich, W. N., & Friedrich, W. L. (1981). Psychosocial assets of parents of handicapped and nonhandicapped children. *American Journal of Mental Deficiency, 85,* 551–553.

Frierson, R. L., Lippmann, S. B., & Johnson, J. (1987). AIDS psychological stresses on the family. *Psychosomatics, 28,* 65–68.

Frye, B. A. (1982). Brain injury and family education needs. Rehabilitation Nursing, 7, 27–29.

Fuchs, V. (1975). *Who shall live?* New York: Basic Books.

Fuchs, V. R. (1986a). Has cost containment gone too far? *The Milbank Quarterly, 64,* 479–488.

Fuchs, V. R. (1986b). *The health economy.* Cambridge, MA.: Harvard University Press.

Fulmer, R. (1988). Lower-income and professional families: A comparison of structure and life cycle process. In B. Carter and M. McGoldrick (Eds.), *The changing family life cycle: A framework for family therapy.* New York: Gardner Press.

Funch, D. P., & Marshall, J. (1983). The role of stress, social support, and age in survival from breast cancer. *Journal of Pychosomatic Reasearch, 27,* 77–83.

Fundingsrud, H. P. (1988). A consultation model in a pediatric outpatient clinic: Conversations with psychosomatic children and their parents. *Family Systems Medicine,* 6, 188–200.

Furlong, R. M., & Berkowitz, R. L. (1985). Intrauterine treatment: Meeting the psychosocial needs of the family. *Health and Social Work, 10,* 55–62.

Galinsky, M. J., & Schoppler, J. H. (1987). Practitioners' views of assets and liabilities of of open-ended groups. In J. Lassner, K., K. Powell, & E. Finnegan (Eds.), *Social group work: Competence and values in practice.* New York: Haworth Press.

Gallivan, L. P., & Saunders, J. (1982). Prenatal information series for women at risk. *Health and Social Work, 7,* 134–139.

Gambel, J. A., Heilbron, M., & Reamer, F. (1980). Hospital social workers become "decision makers" in nursing home placement. *Journal of American Health Care Association,* 6, 19–23.

Gambrill, E. (1981). A behavioral perspective of families. In E. R. Tolson & W. J. Reid (Eds.). *Models of family treatment.* New York: Columbia University Press.

Garbarino, J., Brookhouser, P. E., Authier, K. J., & Associates. (1987). *Special children—special risks: The maltreatment of children with disabilities.* New York: Aldine de Gruyter.

Garborino, J., & Sherman, D. (1981). Identifying high-risk neighborhoods. In J. Garborino, S. H. Stocking & Associates. *Protecting children from abuse and neglect: Developing and maintaining effective support systems for families*. San Francisco: Jossey-Bass.

Garfinkel, I., & McLanahan, S. S. (1986). *Single mothers and their children: A new American dilemma*. Washington, D.C.: Urban Institute Press.

Garn, S. M., Bailey, S. M., & Higgins, T. T. (1980). Effects of socioeconomic status, family line and living together on fatness and obesity. In R. M. Lauer & R. B. Sheklle (Eds.), *Childhood prevention of atherosclerosis and hypertension* (pp. 187–204). New York: Raven Press.

Garner, J. D. (1986). Social Darwinism to the face? *Health and Social Work, 11,* 70–72.

Garrity, T. F. (1973). Vocational adjustment after first myocardial infarction: Comparative assessment of several variables suggested in the literature. *Social Science and Medicine, 7,* 705–717.

Gartner, A. S., & Riessman, F. (1977). *Self help in the human services*. San Francisco: Jossey- Bass.

Garvin, C., Reid, W. J., & Epstein, L. (1976). A task-centerd approach. In R. W. Roberts & H. Northen (Eds.). *Theories of social work with groups*. New York: Columbia University Press.

Gates, C. C. (1980). Husbands of mastectomy patients. *Patient Counselling and Health Education, 3,* 38–41.

Gath, A., Smith, M. A., & Baum, J. D. (1980). Emotional behavioral and educational disorders in diabetic children. *Archives of Disease in Childhood, 55,* 371–375.

Gaudet, L. M., & Powers, G. M. (1989). Systems treatment in pediatric chronic illness: A parent group program. *Family Systems Medicine, 7,* 90–99.

Geersten, H. R., Klauber, M. R., Rindflesh, M., Kane, R. L., & Gray, R. (1978) A re-examination of Suchman's views on social factors in health care utilization. *Journal of Health and Social Behavior, 16,* 226–237.

Geismar, L. L. (1972). *Early supports for family life: A social work experiment*. Metuchen, N.J.: Scarecrow Press.

Geismar, L. L. (1980). *Family and community functioning: A manual of measurement for social work practice and policy*. Second, revised and expanded edition. Metuchen, N.J.: Scarecrow Press.

Geismar, L. L., Lagay, B., Wolock, I., Gerhart, U. C., Fink, H. (1979). *Early supports for family life: A social work experiment*. Metuchen, N. J.: Scarecrow Press.

Gentry, W. D. (1984). Behavioral medicine: A new research paradigm. In Gentry, W. D. (Ed.) *Handbook of behavioral medicine* (1–8). New York: The Guilford Press.

George, L. K., & Gwyther, L. P. (1986). Caregiver well-being: A multidimensional examination of family caregivers of demented adults. *The Gerontologist, 26,* 253–259.

Germain, C. B. (1977). An ecological perspective on social work practice in health care. *Social Work in Health Care, 3,* 67–76.

Germain, C. B. (1978). General-systems theory and ego psychology: An ecological perspective. *Social Service Review, 52,* 535–550.

Germain, C. B. (1987). Human development in contemporary environments. *Social Service Review, 61,* 565–579.

Germain, C. B., & Gitterman, A. (1980). *The life model of social work practice.* New York: Columbia University Press.

Geyman, J. P. (1977). The family as the object of care in family practice. *Journal of Family Practice, 5,* 571–575.

Giacquinta, B. (1977). Helping families face the crisis of cancer. *American Journal of Nursing, 77,* 1585–1588.

Gillis, C. L. (1984). Reducing family stress during and after coronary artery bypass surgery. *Nursing Clinics of North America, 19,* 103–111.

Glenn, M. L., Atkins, L., & Singer, R. (1984). Integrating a family therapist into a family medical practice. *Family Systems Medicine, 2,* 137–145.

Glosser, G., & Wexler, D. (1985). Participants' evaluation of educational support groups for families of patients with Alzheimers' disease and other dementias. *The Gerontologist, 25,* 232–236.

Gochman, D. S. (1985). Family determinants of children's concepts of health and illness. In D. C. Turk & R. D. Kerns (Eds.). *Health, illness and families: A life-span perspective* (pp. 23–50). New York: John Wiley & Sons.

Godkin, M. A., Krant, M. J., & Doster, N. J. (1983–84). The impact of hospice on families. *International Journal of Psychiatry in Medicine, 13,* 153–165.

Golan, N. (1978). *Treatment in crisis situations.* New York: Free Press.

Golan, N. (1986). *The perilous bridge.* New York: Free Press.

Goldberg, R. J., Wool, M. S., Glicksman, A., & Tull, R. (1984). Relationship of the social environment and patients' physical status to depression in lung cancer patients and their spouses. *Journal of Psychosocial Oncology, 12,* 73–80.

Goldberg, S. B. (1973). Family tasks and reactions in the crisis of death. *Social Casework, 54,* 421–433.

Golden, M. P., Herrold, A. J., & Orr, D. P. (1985). An approach to prevention of recurrent diabetic ketoacidosis in the pediatric population. *Journal of Pediatrics, 107,* 195–200.

Goldenberg, I., & Goldenberg, H. (1980). *Family therapy: An overview.* Monterey, CA: Brooks/Cole Publishing Co.

Goldson, E., Millon, P. J., & Bentovim, A. (1985). Failure to thrive: A transactional issue. *Family Systems and Medicine, 3,* 205–213.

Goldstein, H. (1981). *Social learning and change.* Columbia, SC: University of South Carolina Press.

Gonyea, J. G., Seltzer, G. B., Gerstein, C., & Young, M. (1988). Acceptance of hospital-based respite care by families and elders. *Health and social Work, 13,* 201–208.

Gonzales, S., Steinglass, P., Reiss, D. (1989). Putting the illness in its place: Discussion groups for families with chronic medical illnesses. *Family Process, 28,* 69–87.

Good, M. J. D. V., Smilkstein, G., Good, B. J., Shaffer, T. & Arons, T. (1979). The family APGAR Index: A study of construct validity. *The Journal of Family Practice, 8,* 577–582.

Goodman, C. (1988). Personal communication on the Perceived Social Supports for Caregivers Scale.

Goodwin, J. S., Hunt, W. C., Key, C. R., & Samet, J. M. (1987). The effect of marital status on stage, treatment, and survival of cancer patients. *Journal of the American Medical Society, 258* 3125–3130.

Gordon, G. K. (1985). The social readjustment value of becoming a nursing home resident. *The Gerontologist, 25,* 382–388.

Gordon, N. B., & Kutner, B. (1980). Long term and fatal illness in the family. In P. W. Power & A. E. Dell Orto (Eds.), *Role of the family in rehabilitation of the physically disabled* (pp. 208–219). Baltimore: University Park Press.

Gorlick, C. A. (1988). Economic stress, social support, and female single parents. *Canadian Social Work Review, 5,* 194–205.

Gorton, T. A., Doerfler, D. L., Hulka, B. S., & Tyroler, H. A. (1979). Intrafamilial patterns of illness reports and physician visits in a community sample. *Journal of Health and Social Behavior, 20,* 37–44.

Gotay, C. C. (1984). The experience of cancer during early and advanced stages: The views of patients and their mates. *Social Science and Medicine, 18,* 605–613.

Graham, H. (1987). Women's smoking and family health. *Social Science and Medicine, 25,* 47–56.

Grandstaff, N. W. (1976). The impact of breast cancer on the family. *Frontiers of Radiation Therapy Oncology, 11,* 146–156.

Grassi, L., & Molinari, S. (1987). Family affective climate during the childhood of adult cancer patients. *Journal of Psychosocial Oncology, 4,* 53–62.

Graves, T., Meyers, A. W., & Clarke, L. (1988). An evaluation of parental problem-solving: Training in the behavioral treatment of childhood obesity. *Journal of Consulting and Clinical Psychology, 56,* 246–250.

Gray, R. (1978). A re-examination of Suchman's views on social factors in health care utilization. *Journal of Health and Social Behavior, 16,* 226–237.

Gray, E. B. (1982). Perinatal support programs: A strategy for the primary prevention of child abuse. *Journal of Primary Prevention, 2,* 139–152.

Gray, B. H. (1986). *For-profit enterprise in health care.* Washington, D.C.: National Academy Press.

Greene, G., Kruse, K., & Arthurs, R. J. (1985). Family practice social work: A new area of specialization. *Social Work in Health Care, 10,* 53–73.

Greene, G. J., Kruse, K. A., & Kulper, T. (1986). Identifying potential family practice social work opportunites. *Social Work in Health Care, 11,* 89–97.

Greene, V. L. (1983). Substitution between formally and informally provided care for the impaired elderly in the community. *Medical Care, 21,* 609–619.

Greene, V. L., & McNahan, D. J. (1987). The effect of a professionally guided caregiver support and education group on institutionalization of care receivers. *The Gerontologist, 27,* 716–721.

Greenley, J. R., & Davidson, R. E. (1988). Organizational influences on patient health behaviors. In D. S. Gochman (Ed.). *Health behaviors: Emerging research perspectives* (pp. 215–230). New York: Plenum Press.

Grey, M. J., Genel, M., & Tamborlane, W. V. (1980). Psychosocial adjustment of latency-aged diabetics: Determinants and relationships to control. *Pediatrics, 65,* 69–72.

Gross-Andrew, S., & Zimmer, A. H. (1979). Incentives to families caring for disabled elderly: Research and demonstration project to strengthen the natural supports system. *Journal of Gerontological Social Work, 1,* 19–133.

Group for the Advancement of Psychiatry (1970). *The field of family therapy* (Report No. 78). New York: Brunner/Mazel.

Group for the Advancement of Psychiatry (1982). *The process of child therapy.* New York: Brunner/Mazel.

Gubrium, J. F. (1987). Organizational embeddedness and family life. In T. H. Brubaker (Ed.). *Aging, health, and family* (pp. 23–41). Newbury Park, CA: Sage.

Guendelman, S. (1985). At risk: Health needs of Hispanic children. *Health and Social Work, 10,* 183–190.

Guendelman, S., & Schwalbe, J. (1986) Medical care utilization by Hispanic children: How does it differ from Black and White peers? *Medical Care, 24,* 925–937.

Gunderson, E. K. E., & Rahe, R. H. (Eds.). (1974). *Life stress and illness.* Philadelphia: Charles C. Thomas.

Gurman, A. S. & Kniskern, D. P. (1981). *Handbook of family therapy.* New York: Brunner/Mazel.

Gustafsson, P. A., & Goran-Svedin, C. G., (1988). Cost effectiveness: Family therapy in a pediatric setting. *Family Systems Medicine, 6,* 162–175.

Gustafsson, P. A., Kjellman, N. I. M., & Cederblad, M. (1986). Family therapy in the treatment of severe childhood asthma. *Journal of Psychosomatic Research, 30,* 369–374.

Haan, M., Kaplan, G. A., & Camacho, T. (1987). Poverty and health: Prospective evidence from the Alameda County Study. *American Journal of Epidemiology, 125,* 989–998.

Haggerty, R. J. (1980). Life stress, illness and social supports. *Development of Medical Child Neurology, 22,* 391–400.

Hale, J. A., & Hunter, M. M. (1988). *From HMO movement to managed care industry; The future of HMOs in a volatile healthcare market.* InterStudy Center for Managed Care Research.

Hall, A. D., & Fagen, R. E. (1968). Definition of system. In W. Buckley (Ed.), *Modern systems research for the behavioral scientist* (pp. 81–92). Chicago: Aldine Publishing Company.

Hall, L. A., & Farel, A. M. (1988). Maternal stress and depressive symptoms: Correlates of behavior problems in young children. *Nursing Research, 37,* 156–161.

Hallowitz, D. (1970). The problem-solving component in family therapy. *Social Casework, 51,* 62–75.

Hamilton, G. (1951). *Theory and practice of social case work.* New York: Columbia University Press.

Hamovitch, M. B. (1964). *The parent and the fatally ill child.* Duarte, CA: City of Hope Medical Center.

Hansen, D. A., & Johnson, V. A. (1980). Rethinking family stress theory: Definitional aspects. In W. Burr, R. Hill, I. Reiss & I. Nye (Eds.), *Contemporary theories about the family.* (pp. 582–603). New York: Free Press.

Hanson, C. L., & Henggeler, S. W. (1987). Social competence and parental support as mediators of the link between stress and metabolic control in adolescents with insulin-dependent diabetes mellitus. *Journal of Consulting and Clinical Psychology, 55,* 529–533.

Harder, W. P., Gornick, J. C., & Burt, M. R. (1986). Adult day care: Substitute or supplement? *The Milbank Quarterly, 64,* 414–441.

Harding, L., & Morefield, M-A. (1976). Group intervention for wives of myocardial infarction patients. *Nursing Clinics of North America, 11,* 339–347.

Harding, R. K., Heller, J. R., & Kesler, R. W. (1979). The chronically ill child in the primary care setting. *Primary Care, 6,* 311–324.

Hardy, J. B., & Duggan, A. K. (1988) Teenage Fathers and the Fathers of Infants of Urban, Teenage Mothers. *American Journal of Public Health, 78,* 919–922.

Harry, J. (1988). Some problems of gay/lesbian families. In C. S. Chilman, F. M. Cox. & E. W. Nunnally (Eds.). *Variant family forms: Families in trouble series.* Vol. 5 (pp. 95–113). Newbury Park, CA: Sage

Hartford, M. E. (1971). *Groups in social work.* New York: Columbia University Press.

Hartman, A., & Laird, J. (1983). *Family-centered social work practice.* New York: The Free Press.

Harwood, A. (1981). *Ethnicity and Medical Care.* Cambridge, MA: Harvard University Press.

Havighurst, C. C. (1986). The changing locus of decision making in the health care sector. *Journal of Health Politics, Policy and the Law, 11,* 697–735.

Haynes, S. G., Eakes, E. D., & Feinleib, M. (1983). Spouse behavior and coronary health disease in men: Prospective results from the Framingham Heart Study. I. Concordance. *American Journal of Epidemiology, 118,* 23–41.

Hayward, R. A., Shapiro, M. F., Freeman, H. E., & Corey, C. R. (1988). Inequities in health services among insured Americans. *New England Journal of Medicine, 318,* 1507–1512.

Hazuda, H. P., Stern, M. P., Gaskill, S. P., Haffner, S. M., & Gardner, L. I. (1983). Ethnic differences in health knowledge and behaviors related to the prevention and treatment of coronary heart disease. *American Journal of Epidemiology, 117,* 717–728.

Heagerty, B., Dunn, L., Watson, M. A. (1988). Helping caregivers care; Oregon hospital offers support groups, classes, respite care, and a resource center. *Aging, 358,* 7–10.

Hearn, G. (1969). *The general systems approach: Contributions toward a holistic conception of social work.* New York: Council on Social Work Education.

Heinrich, R. L., & Schag, C. C. (1985). Stress and activity management: Group treatment for cancer patients and spouses. *Journal of Counseling and Clinical Psychology, 53,* 439–446.

Heitzmann, C. A., & Kaplan, R. M. (1988). Assessment of methods for measuring social support. *Health Psychology, 7,* 75–109.

Henry, P. W., Knippe, J., & Golden, C. J. (1985). A system model for therapy of brain-injured adults and their families. *Family Systems Medicine, 3,* 427–439.

Hepworth, J., Gavazzi, S. M., Adlin, M. S., & Miller, W. L. (1988). Training for collaboration: Internships for family-therapy students in a medical setting. *Family Systems Medicine, 6,* 69–79.

Hepworth, J., & Jackson, M. (1985). Health care for families: Models of collaboration between family therapist and family physicians. *Family Relations, 34,* 123–127.

Herrenkohl, L. (1988). The impact of prenatal stress on the developing fetus and child. In R. L. Cohen (Ed.), *Psychiatric consultation in childbirth settings: Parent-and-child-oriented approaches.* New York: Plenum Medical.

Hewett, S. (1976). Research on families with handicapped children—an aid or an impediment to understanding? *Birth Defects: Original Article Series, 12,* 35–46.

Hibbard, J. H. (1985). Social ties and health status: An examination of moderating factors. *Health Education Quarterly, 12,* 23–34.

Highriter, M. E. (1983). Measurements of family progress in coping with health problems. *American Journal of Public Health, 73,* 1248–1250.

Hilker, M. A. (1987). Families and supportive residential settings as long-term care options. In T. H. Brubaker (Ed.). *Aging, health, and family: Long-term care* (pp. 234–246). Newbury Park: Sage Publications.

Hill, R. (1949). *Families under stress: Adjustment to the crisis of war separation and reunion.* Westport, CT: Greenwood Press.

Hill, R. (1958). Social stresses on the family: Generic features of families under stress. *Social Casework, 39,* 139–150.

Hill, R. (1971). Modern systems theory and the family: A confrontation. *Social Science Information, 10,* 7–26.

Hill, R. (1981). Whither family research in the 1980's: Continuities, emergents, constraints, and new horizons. *Journal of Marriage and the Family, 43,* 255–257.

Hill, W. F. (1975). Further consideration of therapeutic mechanisms in group therapy. *Small Group Behavior, 6,* 421–429.

Hill, W. G. (1966). The family as a treatment unit: Differential techniques and procedures. *Social Work, 11,* 62–68.

Hines, P. M. (1988). The family life cycle of poor black families. In B. Carter & M. McGoldrick (Eds.), *The changing family life cycle: A framework for family therapy.* New York: Gardner Press.

Hinton, J. (1981). Sharing or withholding awareness of dying between husband and wife. *Journal of Psychosomatic Research, 25,* 337–343.

Hirschwald, J. F. (1982). Rehabilitation of a quadraplegic adolescent: Regional spinal cord injury center. In T. S. Kerson (Ed.). *Social work in health settings* (pp. 126–143). New York: Longman.

Hirst, M. (1985). Young adults with disablities: Health employment and financial costs for family carers. *Child: Care, Health and Development, 11,* 291–307.

Hobbs, N., & Perrin, J. M. (1985). Issues in the care of children with chronic illness. San Francisco: Jossey-Bass.

Hobfall, S. E., & Lerman, M. (1989). Predicting receipt of Social Support: A longitudinal study of parents' reactions to their child's illness. *Health Psychology, 8,* 61–77.

Hoch, C., & Hemmens, G. C. (1987). Linking informal and formal help: Conflict along the continuum of care. *Social Service Review, 61,* 432–446.

Hoebel, F. C. (1976). Brief family-interactional therapy in the management of cardiac-related high-risk behaviors. *Journal of Family Practice, 3,* 613–618.

Holahan, C. J., Wilcox, B. L., Spearly, J. L., & Campbell, M. D. (1979). The ecological perspective in community mental health. *Community Mental Health Review, 4,* 1–9.

Hollingsworth, C. E. & Pasnau, R. O. (1977). *A family in mourning: A guide for health professionals.* New York: Grune & Stratton.

Holden, M. O. (1989). Meeting diagnostic related group goals for elderly patients. *Health and Social Work, 14,* 13–21.

Hollis, F., & Woods, M. E. (1981). *Casework: A psychosocial therapy, 3rd ed.* New York: Random House.

Holman, A. M. (1983). *Family assessment: Tools for understanding and intervention.* Beverly Hills: Sage Publications.

Holmes, T. W., & Rahe, H. (1967). The social readjustment rating scale. *Journal of Psychosomatic Research, 11,* 213–218.

Hooyman, N., Gonyea, J. & Montgomery, R. (1985). The impact of in-home services termination on family caregivers. *The Gerontologist, 25,* 141–145.

Holub, N., Eklund, P., & Keenan, P. (1975). Family conferences as an adjunct to total coronary care. *Heart and Lung, 24,* 767–769.

Horner, M. M., Rawlins, P., & Giles, K. (1987). How parents of children with chronic conditions perceive their own needs. *Maternal and Child Nursing, 12,* 40–43.

Horowitz, A. (1985). Family caregiving to the frail elderly. In C. Eisendorfer (Eds.). *Annual Review of Gerontology and Geriatrics, 5,* 194–246.

Horowitz, M. J., Krupnick, J., Kaltreider, N., Wilner, N., Leong, A., & Marmar, C. (1981). Initial psychological response to parental death. *Archives of General Psychiatry, 38,* 316–322.

Horowitz, S. M., Morgenstern, H., & Berkman, L. F. (1985). The impact of social stressors and social networks on pediatric medical care use. *Medical Care, 23,* 946–959.

House, J. S., Landis K. R., & Umberson, D. (1988). Social relationships and health. *Science, 241,* 540–545.

House, J. S., Robbins, L. & Metzner, H. L. (1983). The association of social relationships and activities with mortality: Prospective evidence from Tecumseh. *American Journal of Epidemiology, 116,* 123–140.

Hubbard, P., Muhlenkamp, A. F., & Brown, N. (1984). The relationships between social support and self-care practices. *Nursing Research, 33,* 266–269.

Huberty, D. (1980). Adapting to illness through family groups. In P. W. Power & A. E. Dell Orto (Eds.), *Role of the family in the rehabilitation fo the physically disabled.* Baltimore: University Park Press.

Hubschman, L. (Ed.).(1983). Family involvement: Working with the family. In L. Hubschman (Ed.), *Hospital social work practice* (pp. 78–104). New York: Praeger Publishers.

Hudgen, A. J. (1979). Family-oriented treatment of chronic pain. *Journal of Marriage and Family Therapy, 5,* 67–78.

Hulka, B. S., Kupper, L. L., & Cassel, J. C. (1972). Determinants of physician utilization. *Medical Care, 10,* 300–309.

Huygen, F. J. A., & Smith, A. J. A. (1983). Family therapy, family somatics, and family medicine. *Family Systems Medicine, 1,* 23–32.

Hyman, M. D. (1972). Social isolation and peer performance in rehabilitation. *Journal of Chronic Diseases, 25,* 85–97.

Jacobs, P. & McDermott, S. (1989). Family caregiver costs of chronically ill and handicapped children: Method and literature review. *Public Health Reports, 104,* 158–163.

Jacobs, S., & Ostfeld, A. (1977). An epidemiological review of the mortality of bereavement. *Psychosomatic Medicine, 39,* 344–357.

Jaffe, D. T. (1978). The role of family therapy in treating physical illnesses. *Hospital and Community Psychiatry, 29,* 169–174.

Jaffe, D. T., & Jordan-Marsh, M. (1983). Styles of couple response to a health behavior change program. *Family Systems Medicine, 1,* 37–46.

Jamison, R. N., Lewis, S., & Burish, T. G. (1986). Cooperation with treatment in adolescent cancer patients. *Journal of Adolescent Health Care, 7,* 162–167.

Jansson, B. S., & Simmons, J. (1985–1986). The ecology of social work departments: Empirical findings and strategy implications. *Social Work in Health Care, 11,* 1–16.

Janzen, C., & Harris, O. (1980). *Family treatment in social work practice*. Itasca, IL: F. E. Peacock.

Jellinek, M., Murphy, J. M., Robinson, J., Feins, A., Lamb, S. & Fenton, T. (1988). The Pediatric Symptom Checklist: Screening school age children for psychosocial dysfunction. *Journal of Pediatrics, 112,* 201–209.

Jennings, J. (1987). Elderly parents as caregivers for their adult dependent children. *Social Work, 32,* 430–433.

Jessop, D. J., & Stein, R. E. (1985). Uncertainty and its relation to the psychological and social correlates of chronic illness in children. *Social Science & Medicine, 20,* 993–999.

Jeter, K., (1983). Analytic Essay: Family stress and bereavement. In H. I. McCubbin & C. R. Figley (Eds.), *Stress and the family, Vol I: Coping with normative transitions* (pp. 219–225). New York: Brunner/Mazel.

Johnson, E. M., & Stark, D. E. (1980). A group program for cancer patients and their family members in an acute care teaching hospital. *Social Work in Health Care, 5,* 335–349.

Johnson, S. B. (1985). The family and the child with chronic illness. In D. C. Turk & R. D. Kerns (Eds.). *Health, illness and families: A life-span perspective* (pp. 220–254). New York: John Wiley and Sons.

Jones, D. E. & Vetter, N. J. (1984). A survey of those who care for the elderly at home: Their problems and their needs. *Social Science and Medicine, 19,* 511–514.

Jones, I., & Manor, L. (1977). *Decision making: A psychological analysis of conflict, choice, and commitment*. New York: Free Press.

Jones, W., & Rice, M. F. (1987). *Health care issues in Black America: Policies, problems, and prospects*. Westport, CT: Greenwood Press.

Joseph, M. V., & Conrad, A. P. (1989). Social work influence on interdisciplinary ethical decision making in health care settings. *Health and Social Work, 14,* 22–30.

Kagan, S. L., & Shelly, A. (1987). The promise and problems of family support programs. In S. L. Kagan (Ed.), *America's family support programs: Perspective and prospects* (pp. 3–18). New Haven, CT: Yale University Press.

Kalish, R. A. (1982). Death and survivorship: The final transition. In F. M. Berardo (Ed.), *Middle and late life transitions*. New York: American Academy of Political and Social Science.

Kane, R. A. (1985). Health policy and social workers in health: Past, present, and future. *Health and Social Work, 10,* 258–270.

Kane, R. A., & Kane, R. L. (1987). *Long-term care: Principles, programs and policies*. New York: Springer Publishing Co.

Kanner, A. D., Coyne, J. C., Schaefer, C. & Lazarus, R. S. (1981). Comparison of two modes of stress measurement: Daily hassles and uplifts versus major life events. *Journal of Behavioral Medicine, 4,* 1–20.

Kaplan, D. M. (1981). Interventions for acute stress. In J. Spinetta & P. Deasy-Spinetta (Eds.), *Living with children*. St. Louis: C. V. Mosby.

Kaplan, H. B. (1983). *Psychosocial issues: Trends in theory and research*. New York: Academic Press.

Kaplan, R. M. (1985). Quality-of-life measurement. In P. Karoly (Ed.). *Measurement strategies in health psychology* (pp. New York: John Wiley and Sons.

Karp, J. A., & Getzel, G. S. (1986). Group work with parents of infants in a neonatal intensive care unit. Unpublished paper. Association for the Advancement of Social Work with Groups.

Kasl, S. V. (1984). Chronic life stress and health. In A. Steptoe & A. Mathews (Eds.). *Health care and human behavior* (pp. 41–66). New York: Academic Press.

Kasl, S. V., & Cooper, C. L. (Eds.). (1987). *Stress and health: Issues in research methodology*. New York: John Wiley.

Katz, A. H. (1980). Genetic counseling in chronic disease. *Health and Social Work, 5,* 14–19.

Katz, A. H., & Bender, E. (1976). *The strengths in us: Self-help groups in the modern world*. New York: New Viewpoints.

Kazak, A. E. (1986). Families with physically handicapped children: Social ecology and family systems. *Family Process, 25,* 265–281.

Kazak, A., & Clark, Williams, N. (1986). Stress in families of children with Myelomeningocele. *Developmental Medicine and Child Neurology, 28,* 220–228.

Kazak, A. E., & Marvin, R. (1984). Differences, difficulties, and adaptation: Stress and social networks in families with a handicapped child. *Family Relations, 33,* 67–77.

Kazak, A. E., & Wilcox, B. L. (1984). The structure and function of social support networks in families with handicapped children. *American Journal of Community Psychology, 12,* 645–661.

Kempler, B. (1985). Family treatment in the health setting: The need for innovation. *Social Work in Health Care, 10,* 45–53.

Kendall, K. A. (1988). The evolving family: An international perspective. *International Social Work, 31,* 81–93.

Kerner, J., Harvey, B., & Lewiston, N. (1979). The impact of grief: A retrospective study of family function following loss of a child with cystic fibrosis. *Journal of Chronic Diseases, 32,* 221–225.

Kerns, R. D. & Turk, D. C. (1985). Behavioral medicine and the family: Historical perspective and future directions. In D. C. Turk and R. D. Kerns *Health, illness and families* (pp. 338–354). New York: John Wiley and Sons.

Kerr, M. E. (1981). Family systems theory and therapy. In A. S. Gurman & D. P. Kniskern (Eds.), *Handbook of family therapy* (pp. 226–255). New York: Brunner/Mazel.

Kessler, R. C., House, J. S., & Turner, J. B. (1987). Unemployment and health in a community sample. *Journal of Health and Social Behavior, 28,* 51–59.

Kessler, R. C., McLeod, J. & Wethington, E. (1985). The cost of caring: A perspective on the relationship between sex and psychological distress. In I. G. Sarason & B. Sarason (Eds.) *Social support: Theory, Research and Applications.* The Hague, Holland: Martinus Nijhoff.

Kester, B. L., Rothblum, E. D., Lobato, D., & Milhous, R. L. (1988). Spouse adjustment to spinal cord injury: Long-term medical and psychosocial factors. *Rehabilitation Counseling Bulletin, 32,* 4–21.

Khaw, K. T., & Barrett-Connor, E. (1986). Family history of heart attack: A modifiable risk factor? *Circulation, 74,* 239–244.

Kiesler, C. A. & Morton, T. L. (1988). Psychology and public policy in the "health care revolution." *American Psychologist, 43,* 993–1003.

King, N. (1980). The behavioral management of asthma-related problems in children: A critical review of the literature. *Journal of Behavioral Medicine, 3,* 169–189.

Kirschner, C., & Rosengarten, L. (1982). The skilled social work role in homecare. *Social Work, 29,* 527–530.

Kissel, S. J. (1986). State aid for the poor. *Health and Social Work, 11,* 67–68.

Kitagawa, E. W., & Hauser, P. M. (1973). *Differential mortality in the United States: A study of socioeconomic epidemiology.* Cambridge, MA.: Harvard University Press.

Klein, D. M. (1983). Family problem-solving and family stress. In H. I. McCubbin, M. B. Sussman & J. M. Patterson (Eds.), *Social stress and the family* (pp. 85–112). New York: Haworth Press.

Klein, R. F., Dean, A., & Bogdonoff, M. D. (1967). The impact of illness upon the spouse. *Journal of Chronic Disease, 20,* 241–248.

Klerman, G. L., & Clayton, P. (1984). Epidemiologic perspective on the health consequences of bereavement. In M. Osterweis, F. Soloman & M. Green (Eds.). *Bereavement: Reactions, consequences and care* (pp. 15–46). Washington, D. C.: National Academy Press.

Knight, B., & Walker, D. L. (1985). Towards a definition of alternatives to institutionalization for the frail elderly. *The Gerontologist, 25,* 358–363.

Knowles, J. H. (1977). The responsibility of the individual. *Daedalus, 106,* 57–80.

Kobrin, F. E., & Hendershot, G. E. (1977). Do family ties reduce mortality? Evidence from the United States, 1966–1968. *Journal of Marriage and the Family, 39,* 737–745.

Koch, A. (1985a). A strategy for prevention: Role flexibility and affective reactivity as factors in family coping. *Family System Medicine, 3,* 70–81.

Koch, A. (1985b). "If only it could be me": The families of pediatric cancer patients. *Family Relations, 34,* 63–70.

Koch-Hattem, A. (1986). Siblings experience of pediatric cancer: Interviews with children. *Health and Social Work, 11,* 107–117.

Koch-Hattem, A., Hattem, D. M., & Plummer, L. P. (1987). The role of mental-health resources in explaining family adaptation to stress: A preliminary analysis. *Family Systems Medicine, 5,* 206–219.

Korsch, B. M., Fine, R. N., & Negrete, V. F. (1977). Noncompliance in children with renal transplants. *Pediatrics, 61,* 872–876.

Kosberg, J. I., & Cairl, R. E. (1986). The cost of care index: A case management tool for screening informal care providers. *The Gerontologist, 26,* 273–278.

Koski, M., & Kumento, A. (1975). Adolescent development and behavior: A psychosomatic follow-up study of childhood diabetics. *Modern Problems in Pediatrics, 12,* 348–353.

Kramer, R. M., & Grossman, B. (1987). Contracting for social services: Process management and resource dependencies. *Social Service Review, 61,* 32–55.

Krant, M. J., & Johnson, L. (1977–78). Family members' perceptions of communication in late stage cancer. *International Journal of Psychiatry in Medicine, 8,* 203–216.

Kratochvil, M. S., & Devereux, S. A. (1988). Counseling needs of parents of handicapped children. *Social Work, 69,* 420–426.

Krause, N. (1988). Positive life events and depressive symptoms in older adults. *Behavioral Medicine, 14,* 101–112.

Krauskopf, M. S. & Akabas, S. H. (1988). Children with disabilities: A family/workplace partnership in problem resolution. *Social Work Papers, 21,* 28–35.

Kremer, E. F., Sieber, W., & Atkinson, J. H. (1985). Spousal perpetuation of chronic pain behavior. *International Journal of Family Therapy, 7,* 258–269.

Kucia, C., Drotar, D., Doershuk, C., Stern, R., Boat, T., & Matthews, L. (1979). Home observation of family interaction and childhood adjustment to cystic fibrosis. *Journal of Pediatric Psychology, 4,* 189–195.

Kuhn, T. S. (1970). *The structure of scientific revolutions.* Chicago: University of Chicago Press.

Kulys, R., & Meyer, R. (1985). Good health: Whose responsibility? *Social Work in Health Care, 11,* 63–84.

Kupst, M. J. (1980). Continuing involvement with families after the death of a child from cancer. In J. L. Schulman & M. J. Kupst (Eds.), *The child with cancer* (pp. 56–62). Illinois: Charles C. Thomas.

Kupst, M. O., & Schulman, J. L. (Eds.). (1980). Family coping with leukemia in a child: Initial reactions. *The child with cancer* (pp. 111–128). Springfield, Ill.: Charles C. Thomas Publisher.

Kupst, M. J., Tylke, L., Thomas, L., Mudd, M. E., Richardson, D., & Schulman J. L. (1982). Strategies of intervention with families of pediatric leukemia patients: A longitudinal perspective. *Social Work in Health Care, 8,* 31–47.

Kurland, R. (1978). Planning: The neglected component of group development. *Social Work with Groups, 1,* 173–178.

Kurland, R. (1980). A model for planning for social work with groups. Ph.D. dissertation, University of Southern California.

Kurland, R. (1984). Characteristics and issues generic to the use of groups in chronic illness. Unpublished paper. Symposium for the Advancement of Social Work with Groups.

Lackey, M. B. (1982). The termination phase in social work with groups. Ph.D. dissertation. University of Southern California.

Lansky, S. B., Cairns, N. U., Hassanein, R., Wehr, J., & Lowman, J. T. (1978). Childhood cancer: Parental discord and divorce. *Pediatrics, 62,* 184–188.

Lask, B., & Matthew, D. (1979). Childhood asthma: A controlled trial of family psychotherapy. *Archives of Disease in Childhood, 54,* 116–119.

Lau, R. R., & Klepper, S. (1988). The development of illness orientations in children aged 6 through 12. *Journal of Health and Social Behavior, 29,* 149–168.

Lavigne, J. V. (1980). The siblings of childhood cancer patients: Psychosocial aspects. In J. L. Schulman & M. J. Kupst M. J. (Eds.), *The child with cancer* (pp. 37–47). Springfield, IL: Charles C. Thomas Publisher.

Lavigne, J. V., & Ryan, M. (1979). Psychologic adjustment of siblings of children with chronic illness. *Pediatrics, 63,* 616–627.

La Voie, J. C. (1985). Health in the family life cycle. In J. C. Hansen (Ed.), *Health promotion in family therapy.* Maryland: Aspen Publications.

Lazarus, R. S. (1966). *Psychological stress and the coping process.* New York: McGraw-Hill.

Lazarus, R. S. (1981). The stress and coping paradigm. In C. Eisdorfer, A. Kleinman, & P. Maxim (Eds.) *Models for clinical psychopathology* (pp. 177–214) New York: Spectrum Publications.

Lazarus, R. S., & Folkman, S. (1984). *Stress appraisal, and coping.* New York: Springer.

Leahy, M., & Wright, L. (1985). Intervening with families with chronic illness. *Family Systems Medicine, 3,* 60–69.

Leff, B. (975), A club approach to social work treatment within a home dialysis program. *Social Work in Health Care, 1,* 33–40.

Lehman, D. R., Ellard, J. H., & Wortman, C. B. (1986). Social support for the bereaved: Recipients' and providers' perspectives on what is helpful. *Journal of Consulting and Clinical Psychology, 54,* 438–446.

Lehman, D. R., Wortman, C. B., & Williams A. F. (1987). Long-term effects of losing a spouse or child in a motor vehicle crash. *Journal of Personality and Social Psychology, 52,* 218–231.

Leiber, L., Plumb, M. M., Gerstenzang, M. L., & Holland, J. (1979). The communication of affection between cancer patients and their spouses. *Psychosomatic Medicine, 38,* 379–389.

Leichter, E., & Schulman, G. L. (1968). Emerging phenomena in multifamily group treatment. *International Journal of Group Psychotherapy, 18,* 59–69.

Leigh, H., & Reiser, M. F., (1980). *The patient: Biological, psychological, and social dimensions of medical practice.* New York: Plenum Press.

Leighton, A. H. (1959). *My name is legion.* New York: Basic Books.

Leighton, A. H. (1974). Social disintegration and mental disorders. In S. Arieti (Ed.), *American handbook of psychiatry* (2nd ed.). (pp. 411–422). New York: Basic Books.

Leighton, A. H. (1982). *Caring for mentally ill people.* Cambridge, MA: Cambridge University Press.

Lesser, A. J. (1985). Public programs for crippled children. In N. Hobbs & J. M. Perrin (Eds.). *Issues in the care of children with chronic illness,* (pp. 733–756). San Francisco: Jossey-Bass.

Leventhal, H., Leventhal, E. A., & Nguyen, T. V. (1985). Reactions of families to illness: Theoretical models and perspectives. In D. C. Turk & R. D. Kerns. *Health, illness, and families: A life-span perspective* (pp. 108–145). New York: John Wiley & Sons.

Leventhal, H., Zimmerman, R., & Gutman, M. (1984). Compliance: A self- regulation perspective. In W. D. Gentry (Ed.). *Handbook of behavioral medicine.* New York: Guildford Press.

Levey, S. (1980). *Study of hospital discharge for patients 65 and over.* New York: Greater New York Hospital Association.

Levine, B. (1979). *Group pychotherapy: practice and development.* Englewood Cliffs, NJ: Prentice-Hall.

Levitan, S. A., & Shapiro, I. (1987). *Working but poor: America's contradiction.* Baltimore: The Johns Hopkins University Press.

Levy, A. (1984). Group cohesion. Ph.D. dissertation, University of Southern California.

Levy, J. M. (1988). Family response and adaptation to a handicap. In J. P. Gerring & L. P. McCarthy (Eds.). *The psychiatry of handicapped children and Adolescents: Managing emotional and behavioral problems* (pp. 215–246). Boston: Little, Brown & Co.

Levy, R. L. (1983). Social support and compliance: A selective review and critique of treatment integrity and outcome measurement. *Social Science and Medicine, 17,* 1329–1338.

Levy, S. M. (1985). *Behavior and cancer.* San Francisco: Jossey-Bass.

Lewin, L. S., Eckels, T. J., & Miller, L. B. (1988). Setting the record straight: The provision of uncompensated care by not-for-profit hospitals. *New England Journal of Medicine, 318,* 1212–1215.

Lewis, C. C., Scott, D. E., Pantell, R. H., & Wolf, M. H. (1986). Parent satisfaction with children's medical care. *Medical Care, 24,* 209–215.

Lewis, H. (1982). *The intellectual base for social work practice.* New York: Haworth Press.

Lewis, J. M., Beaver, W. R., Gossett, J. T., & Phillips, V. A. (1976). *No single thread: Psychological health in family systems.* New York: Brunner/Mazel.

Lewis, M. A., Cretin, S., & Kane, R. L. (1985). The natural history of nursing home patients. *The Gerontologist, 25,* 382–388.

Lezak, M. D. (1978). Living with the characterologically altered brain injured patient. *Journal of Clinical Psychiatry, 39,* 592–598.

Lichtman, R. R., & Taylor, S. E. (1986). Close relationships and the female cancer patient. In B. L. Anderson (Ed.), *Psychological perspectives women with cancer* (pp.233–256). New York: Springer-Verlag.

Lichtman, R. R., Taylor, S. E., & Wood, J. V. (1987). Social support and marital adjustment after breast cancer. *Journal of Psychosocial Oncology, 5,* 47–74.

Lichtman, R. R., Taylor, S. E., Wood, J. V., Bluming, A. Z., Dosik, G. M., & Leibowitz, R. L. (1985). Relations with children after breast cancer: The mother-daughter relationship at risk. *Journal of Psychosocial Oncology, 2,* 1–19.

Lichty, S. S., & Zuvekas, A. (1980). Rural health: Policies, progress and challenges. *Urban Health, 9,* 26–29.

Lieberman, M. A., Bowman, L. D., & Associates (1979). *Self help groups for coping with crisis Origins, members, processes.* San Francisco: Jossey-Bass.

Lieberman, M. A., Yalom, I. D., & Miles, M. B. (1973). *Encounter groups: First facts.* New York: Basic Books.

Lilliston, B. A. (1985). Psychosocial responses to traumatic physical disability. *Social Work in Health Care, 1,* 33–40.

Lindenberg, R. E. (1980). Work with families in rehabilitation. In P. W. Power & A. E. DellOrto (Eds.), *Role of the family in the rehabilitation of the physically disabled* (pp. 516–525). Baltimore: University Park press.

Linsk, N. L., Keighter, S. M., & Osterbusch, S. E. (1988). States' policies regarding paid family caregiving. *The Gerontologist, 28,* 204–212.

Linsk, N. L., Osterbusch, S. E., Simon-Rusinowitz, & Keigher, S. M. (1988). Community agency support of family caregiving. *Health and Social Work, 13,* 209–218.

Litwak, E. (1985). *Helping the elderly: The complementary roles of informal networks and formal systems.* New York: Guilford Press.

Lloyd, G. G. & Cawley, R. H. (1983). Distress or illness? A study of psychological symptoms after myocardial infarction. *British Journal of Psychiatry, 142,* 120–125.

Lobato, D., Faust, D. & Spirito, A. (1988). Examining the effects of chronic disease and disability on children's sibling relationships. *Journal of Pediatric Psychology, 13,* 389–407.

London, H., & Devore, W. (1988). Layers of understanding: Counseling ethnic minority families. *Family Relations, 37,* 310–314.

Lonergan, E. C. (1982). *Group intervention: How to begin and maintain groups in medical and psychiatric settings.* New York: Jason Aronson.

Lotz, N. L. (1982). Reestablishing a coordinated care program: Home health services. In T. S. Kerson (Ed.). *Social work in health settings* (pp. 226–283). New York: Longman.

Lowenthal, M. F. & Haven, C. (1968). Interaction and adapatation: Intimacy as a critical variable. *American Sociological Review, 33,* 20–30.

Luthman, S., & Kirschbaum, M. (1974). *The dynamic family.* Palo Alto: Science and Behavior Books.

Lynam, M. J. (1987). The parent network in pediatric oncology. *Cancer Nursing, 10,* 207–216.

Maas, H. (1984). *People and contexts: Social development from birth to old age.* Englewood Cliffs, NJ: Prentice-Hall.

Mack, S. A., & Berman, L. C. (1988). A group for parents of children with fatal genetic illness. *American Journal of Orthopsychiatry, 58,* 397–404.

Macklin, E. D. (1980). Nontraditional family forms: A decade of research. *Journal of Marriage and the Family, 42,* 175–192.

Macklin, E. D. (1988). AIDS: Implications for families. *Family Relations, 37,* 141–149.

Macnab, A. J., Sheckter, L. A., Hendry, N.J., Pendray, M. R., & Macnab, G. (1985). Group support for parents of high risk neonates: An interdisciplinary approach. *Social Work in Health Care, 10,* 63–71.

Maddocks, I. (1980). The impoverishment of community life and the need for community health. In N. F. Stanley & R. A. Joske (Eds.). *Changing disease patterns and human behavior* (pp. 48–62). London: Academic Press.

Maes, S., & Schlosser, M. (1988). Changing health behavior outcomes in asthmatic patients: A pilot intervention study. *Social Science and Medicine, 26,* 359–364.

Maguire, G. P., Lee, E. G., Bevington, D. J., Suchemann, C. S., Crabtree, R. J., & Cornell, C. E. (1978). Psychiatric problems in the first year after mastectomy. *British Medical Journal, 15,* 963–965.

Mailick, M. (1979). The impact of severe illness on the individual and family: An overview. *Social Work in Health Care, 5,* 117–128.

Mailick, M. D. (1984). The short-term treatment of depression of physically ill hospitalized patients. *Social Work in Health Care, 9,* 51–61.

Malinak, D. P., Hoyt, M. F., & Patterson, V. (1979). Adults' reactions to the death of a parent: A preliminary study. *American Journal of Psychiatry, 136,* 1152–1156.

Maloney, B. D. (1988). The legacy of aids: Challenge for the next century. *Journal of Marital and Family Therapy, 14,* 143–150.

Maluccio, A. N. (1979). Promoting competence through life experiences. In C. B. Germain (Ed.). *Social work practice, people, and environments.* New York: Columbia University Press.

Maluccio, A. N., & Marlow, W. D. (1974). The case for the contract. *Social Work, 19,* 28–36.

Mandelbaum, E. K. (1984). The family medicine consultant: Reframing the contribution of medical social work. *Family Systems Medicine, 2,* 309–319.

Mantell, J. E. (1984). Social work and public health. In R. J. Estes (Ed.). *Health care & the social services* (pp. 207–259). St. Louis: Warren H. Green, Inc.

Margolis, L. H., McLeroy, K. R., Runyan, C. W., & Kaplan, B. H. (1983). Type A behavior: An ecological approach. *Journal of Behavioral Medicine, 6,* 245–258.

Marks, M. (1956). Group psychotherapy for emotionally disturbed children. In National Conference of Social Work, Group Work and Community Organization 1956. New York: Columbia University Press.

Marmor, T. R., Schlesinger, M., & Smithey, R. W. (1986). A new look at nonprofits: Health care policy in a competitive age. *The Yale Journal on Regulation, 3,* 313–349.

Marshall, J. R., Rice, D. G., O'Mera, M., & Shelp, W. D. (1975). Characterisitics of couples with poor outcome in dialysis home training. *Journal of Chronic Diseases, 28,* 375–381.

Martin, P. (1975). Mental breakdown in families of patients with Spina Bifida Cystica, *Developmental Medicine and Child Neurology, 17,* 757–764.

Masnick, G., & Bane, M. J. (1980). *The nation's families: 1960–1990.* Boston, Mass.: Auburn House Publishing Co.

Masters, J. C., Cerreto, M. C., & Mendlowitz, D. R. (1983). The role of the family in coping with childhood chronic illness. In T. G. Burish & L. A. Bradley (Eds.), *Coping with chronic disease: Research and applications* (pp. 381–407). New York: Academic Press.

Metarazzo, J. D., Connor, W. E., Fey, S. G, Carmody, T. P, Pierce, D. K, Brischetto, C. S, Baker, L. H, Connor, S. L. & Sexton, G. (1982). Behavioral cardiology with emphasis on the family heart study. In T. Million, C. Green & R. Meagher (Eds.), *Handbook of clinical psychology* (pp. 301–336). New York: Plenum Press.

Matthews, K. A., & Rakaczky, C. J. (1986). Familial aspects of the Type A behavior pattern and physiologic reactivity to stress. In T. H. Schmudt, T. M. Dembroski & G. Bluumchen (Eds.). *Biological and psychological factors in cardiovascular disease* (pp. 228–245). New York: Springer-Verlag.

Matthews, K. A., Siegel, J. M., Kuller, L. H., Thompson, M. & Varat, M. (1983). Determinants of decisions to seek medical treatments by patients with acute myocardial infarction symptoms. *Journal of Personality and Social Psychology, 44,* 1144–1156.

Maurin, J., & Schenkel, J. (1976). A study of the family unit's response to hemodialysis. *Journal of Psychosomatic Research, 20,* 163–168.

Maxmen, J. S. (1973). Group therapy as viewed by hospitalized patients. *Archives of General Psychiatry, 28,* 404–408.

Mayou, R. L. (1981). Effectiveness of cardiac rehabilitation. *Journal of Psychosomatic Research, 25,* 423–427.

Mayou, R. L., Foster, A., & Wiliamson, B. (1978). The psychological and social effects of myocardial infarction on wives. *British Medical Journal, 1,* 699–701.

McAdoo, H. P. (1982). Levels of stress and family support in Black families. In H. I. McCubbin, A. E. Cauble & J. M. Patterson (Eds.). *Family stress, coping, and social support* (pp. 239–252). Illinois: Charles C. Thomas.

McAndrews, I. (1976). Children with a handicap and their families. *Child: Care, Health and Development, 2,* 213–237.

McCall, C., & Storm, C. L. (1985). Family therapists and family therapy programs in hospital settings: A survey. *Family Systems Medicine, 3,* 143–150.

McCarthy, R., Horwat, K., & Konarska, M. (1988). Chronic stress and sympathetic-adrenal medullary responsiveness. *Social Science and Medicine, 26,* 333–341.

McCollum, A,., & Gibson, L. (1970). Family adaptation to the child with cystic fibrosis. *The Journal of Pediatrics, 77,* 571–578.

McCubbin, H. I. (1979). Integrating coping behavior in family stress theory. *Journal of Marriage and the Family, 41,* 237–244.

McCubbin, M. A. (1988). Family stress, resources, and family types: Chronic illness in children. *Family Relations, 37,* 203–210.

McCubbin, H. I., & Comeau, J. K. (1987). FIRM: Family Inventory of Resources for Management. In H. I. McCubbin & A. I. Thompson (Eds.). *Family assessment inventories for research and practice* (pp. 145–160). Madison: University of Wisconsin.

McCubbin, H. I. & Figley, C. R. (Eds.). (1983). *Stress and the family, Vol I: Coping with normative transitions.* New York: Brunner/Mazel.

McCubbin, H. I., Joy, C. B, Cauble, A. E., Comeau, J. K., Patterson, J. M., & Needle, R. H. (1980). Family stress and coping: A decade review. *Journal of Marriage and the Family, 42,* 855–871.

McCubbin, H. I., & McCubbin, M. A. (1987). Family systems assessment in health care. In H. I. McCubbin & A. I. Thompson (Eds.). *Family assessment inventories for research and practice* (pp. 165–174). Madison: The University of Wisconsin.

McCubbin, H. I., & McCubbin, M. A. (1988). Typologies of resilient families: Emerging roles of social class and ethinicity. *Family Relations, 37,* 247–254.

McCubbin, H. I., McCubbin, M. A., Patterson, J. M., Cauble, A. E., Wilson, L. R., & Warwick, W. (1983). CHIP—Coping Health Iventory for Parents: An assessment of parental coping patterns in the care of the chronically ill child. *Journal of Marriage and the Family, 45,* 359–370.

McCubbin, H. I., Nevin, R. S., Cauble, A. E., Larsen, A., Comeau, J. K., & Patterson, J. M. (1982). Family coping with chronic illness: The cause of cerebral palsy. In H. I. McCubbin, A. E. Cauble & J. M. Patterson (Eds.) *Family stress, coping and social support* (pp. 48–61). Springfield, IL: Charles C. Thomas.

McCubbin, H. I., & Patterson J. M. (1982). Family adaptation to crisis. In H. I. McCubbin, A. E. Cauble & J. M. Patterson (Eds.). *Family stress, coping, and social support* (pp. 26–47). Springfield, IL: Charles C. Thomas.

McCubbin, H. I., & Patterson, J. M. (1983). The family stress process: The double ABCX model of adjustment and adaptation. In H. I. McCubbin, M. B. Sussman & J. M. Patterson (Eds.) (7–37). *Social stress and the family: Advances and developments in family stress theory and research.* New York: Haworth Press.

McCubbin, H., & Patterson, J. (1987). FILE: Family Inventory of Life Events and Changes. In H. McCubbin & A. Thompson (Eds.) *Family assessment inventories for research and practice* (pp. 81–98). Madison: University of Wisconsin.

McDaniel, S., & Campbell, T. L. (1986). Physicians and family therapist: The risks of collaboration. *Family Systems Medicine, 4,* 4–8.

McDonald, T. P., & Coburn, A. F. (1988). Predictors of prenatal care utilization. *Social Science & Medicine, 27,* 167–172.

McGoldrick, M. (1988). Ethnicity and the family life cycle. In B. Carter & M. McGoldrick (Eds). *The changing family life cycle: A framework for family therapy.* New York: Gardner Press.

McHugh, S., & Vallis, M. (1985). Illness behaviour: Operationalization of the biopsychosocial model. In S. McHugh & M. Vallis (Eds.). *Illness behavior: A multidisciplinary model* (pp. 1–31). New York: Plenum Press.

McKeever, P. (1983). Siblings of chronically ill children: A literature review with implications for research and practice. *American Journal of Orthopsychiatry, 53,* 209–218.

McKinlay, J. B. (1972). Some approaches and problems in the study of the use services: An overview. *Journal of Health and Social Behavior, 13,* 115–152.

McKinlay, J. B. (1973). Social networks, lay consultation and help-seeking behavior. *Social Forces, 51,* 275–292.

McNett, S. C. (1987). Social support, treatment and coping responses and effectiveness in the functionally disabled. *Nursing Research, 36,* 98–103.

Medalie, J. H. (1980). The development and transmission of health and disease with particular emphasis on the family. In H. R. Leavill, A. Clark (Eds.), *Textbook of Preventive Medicine,* New York: Mcgraw-Hill.

Medalie, J. H., Synder, M., Groen, J. J., Newfeld, N. H., Goldbourt, U., & Riss, E. (1973). Angina Pectoris among 10,000 men: Five year incidence and univariate analysis. *American Journal of Medicine, 55,* 583–594.

Meddin, J., & Brelje, N. (1983). Unexpected positive effects of myocardial infarction on couples. *Health and Social Work, 8,* 143–146.

Mendelsohn, M., & Rozek, F. (1983). Denying disability: The case of deafness. *Family Systems Medicine, 1,* 37–47.

Mermelstein, R., Cohen, S., Lichtenstein, E., Baer, J., & Kamarck, T. (1986). Social support and smoking cessation and maintenance. *Journal of Consulting and Clinical Psychology, 54,* 447–453.

Merton, R. K. (1949). *Social theory and social structure*. Glencoe, IL: Free Press.

Mervis, P. (1983). Commentary. In G. Rosenberg & H. Rehr (Eds.). *Advancing social work practice in the health care field* (pp. 125–128). New York: Haworth Press.

Meyer, C. H. (1976). *Social work practice: The changing landscape*. New York: Free Press.

Meyer, C. H. (Ed.). (1983a). *Clinical social work in the eco-systems perspective*. New York: Columbia University Press.

Meyer, C. H. (1983b). Selecting appropriate practice models. In A. Rosenblatt & D. Waldfogel (Eds.). *Handbook of clinical social work* (pp. 731–749). San Francisco: Jossey-Bass.

Meyer, R. J., & Haggerty, R. J. (1962). Streptococcal infections in families: Factors altering individual susceptibility. *Pediatrics, 29,* 539–549.

Michielutte, R., & Diseker, R. A. (1982). Racial differences in knowledge of cancer: A pilot study. *Social Science and Medicine, 16,* 245–252.

Micklin, M., & Choldin, H. M. (Eds.). (1984). *Sociological human ecology: Contemporary issues and applications*. London: Westview Press.

Miller, C. L., Margolis, L. H., Schwethelm, B., & Smith, S. (1989). Barriers to implementation of a prenatal care program for low income women. *American Journal of Public Health, 79,* 62–64.

Miller, D. B., Gulle, N., & McCue, F. (1986). The realities of respite for families, elements and sponsors. *The Gerontologist, 26,* 467–470.

Miller, J. G., & Miller, J. L. (1980). The family as a system. In C. K. Hofling & J. M. Lewis (Eds.), *The family: Evaluation and treatment*. New York: Brunner/Mazzel.

Miller, M., & Diao, J. (1987). Family Friends: New resources for psychological care of chronically ill children in families. *Child Health Care, 15,* 259–264.

Mindel, C. H., Wright, R., & Starrett, R. A. (1986). Informal and formal health and social support systems of Black and White elderly: A comparative cost approach. *The Gerontologist, 26,* 279–287.

Minuchin, S. (1974). *Families and family therapy*. Cambridge, MA: Harvard University Press.

Minuchin, S., Baker, L., Roseman, B., Liebman, T., & Todd, T. (1975). A conceptual model of psychosomatic illness in children. *Archives of General Psychiatry, 32,* 1031–1038.

Minuchin, S., Rosman, B., & Baker, L. (1978). *Psychosomatic families*. Cambridge, MA: Harvard University Press.

Mishel, M. H., & Murdaugh, C. L. (1987). Family adjustment to heart transplantation: Redesigning the dream. *Nursing Research, 36*, 332–338.

Mitrowski, C. A. (1985). Social work intervention with geriatric cancer patients and their children. *Social Casework, 66*, 242–245.

Moore, I. M., Gillis, C. L., & Martinson, I. (1987). Psychosomatic symptoms in parents 2 years after the death of a child with cancer. *Nursing Research, 36*, 104–108.

Moore, J. A., Hamerlynck, L. A., Barsh, E. T., Spieker, S., & Jones, R. R. (1982). *Extending family resources*. Seattle, Washington: Children's Clinic and Preschool Spastic Aid Council, Inc.

Moore, J. T., Bobula, J. A., Short, T. B. & Mischel, M. (1983). A functional dementia scale. *The Journal of Family Practice, 16*, 499–503.

Moos, R. H. (1979). Social-ecological perspective on health. In G. C. Stone, F. Cohen, N. E., Adler & Associates (Eds.), *Health psychology: A handbook*. San Francisco: Jossey-Bass Publishers.

Moos, R. H. (1985). Evaluating social resources in community and health care contexts. In P. Karoly (Ed.), *Measurement strategies in health psychology*. New York: John-Wiley & Sons.

Moos, R. H., & Moos, B. S. (1976). A typology of family social environments. *Family Process, 15*, 357–371.

Moos, R. H., & Moos, B. S. (1977). The crisis of illness: An overview. In R. H. Moos (Ed.), *Coping with physical illness*. New York: Plenum Medical Book Co.

Moos, R. H., & Moos, B. S. (1982). *Family environment scale manual*, Palo Alto, Ca.: Consulting Psychologists Press.

Moos, R. H., & Moos, B. S. (1983). Adaptation and the quality of life in work and family settings. *Journal of Community Psychology, 11*, 158–168.

Moos, R. H., Insel, P. M. (Eds.). (1974). *Issues in social ecology: Human milieus*. Palo Alto, CA: National Press Books.

Moos, R. H. & Tsu, V. D. (Eds.). (1977). *Coping with physical illness*. New York: Plenum Medical Books.

Morgenstern, H., Gellert, G. A., Walter, S. D., Ostfeld, A. M., & Siegel, B. S. (1984). The impact of a psychological support program on survival with breast cancer: The importance of selection bias in program evaluation. *Journal of Chronic Diseases, 37*, 273–282.

Morisky, D. E., Demuth, N. M., Field-Fass, M., Green, L. W., & Levine, D. M. (1985). Evaluation of family health education to build social support for long-term control of high blood pressure. *Health Education Quarterly, 12*, 35–50.

Moroney, R. M. (1983). *Families, care of the handicapped, and public policy*. New York: Haworth Press.

Moroney, R. M. (1987). Social support systems: Families and social policy. In S. L. Kagan (Ed.). *America's family support programs: Perspectives and prospects* (pp. 21–37). New Haven, CT: Yale University Press.

Morris, J., & Royle, G. T. (1988). Offering patients a choice of surgery for early breast cancer: A reduction in anxiety and depression in patients and their husbands. *Social Science and Medicine, 26*, 583–585.

Morris, J. N., & Sherwood, S. (1987). Quality of life of cancer patients at different stages in the disease trajectory. *Journal of Chronic Diseases, 40,* 545–553.

Morris, T., Greer, H. S., & White, P. (1977). Psychological and social adjustment to mastectomy. *Cancer, 40,* 2381–2387.

Morrow, G. R., Carpenter, P. J., & Hoagland, A. C. (1984). The role of social support in parental adjustment to pediatric cancer. *Journal of Pediatric Psychology, 9,* 317–329.

Morrow, G. R., Chairello, R. J., & Derogatis, L. R. (1978). A new scale for assessing patient's psychosocial adjustment to medical illness. *Psychological Medicine, 8,* 605–610.

Morycz, R. K., Malloy, J., Bozich, M., & Martz, P. (1987). Racial differences in family burden: Clinical implications for social work. *Gerontological Social Work with Families, 10,* 133–154.

Motwani, J. K., & Herring, G. M. (1988). Home care for ventilator dependent persons: A cost-effective, humane public policy. *Health and Social Work, 13,* 20–24.

Mullins, H. C. & Christie-Seeley, J. (1984). Collecting and recording family data. In J. Christie-Seely (Ed.), *Working with the family in primary care* (pp. 179–191). New York: Praeger.

Murphy, J. M., & Jellinek, M. (1988). Screening for psychosocial dysfunction in economically disadvantaged and minority group children: Further validation of the pediatric symptom checklist. *American Journal of Orthopsychiatry, 58,* 450–456.

Murray, J. L., & Bernfield, M. (1988). The differential effect of prenatal care on the incidence of low birth weight among Blacks and Whites in a prepaid health care plan. *New England Journal of Medicine, 319,* 1385–1391.

Myrdal, A. (1968). *Nation and Family*. Cambridge. MA: M.I.T. Press.

Naismith, L. D., Robinson, J., Shaw, G. B., & Macintyre, M. J. (1979). Psychological rehabilitation after myocardial infarction. *British Medical Journal, 1,* 439–446.

National Association of Children's Hospitals and Related Institutions, Inc. (NACHRI) (1989). *Profile of child health in the United States,* Alexandria, VA: Author.

National Association of Social Workers (NASW) (1960). *Use of groups in the psychiatric setting*. New York: Author.

National Association of Social Workers (1961). *Family centered social work in illness and disability: A preventive approach*. New York: Author.

National Association of Social Workers (1965). *The family is the patient: The group approach to the treatment of family health problems*. New York: Author.

Navarro, V. (1975). Health and the corporate society. *Social Policy , 5,* 41–49.

Neal-Cooper, F., & Scott, R. B. (1988). Genetic counseling in sickle cell anemia: Experiences with couples at risk. *Public Health Reports, 103,* 174–178.

Nelsen, J. C. (1983). *Family treatment: An integrative approach*. Englewood Cliffs, NJ: Prentice-Hall.

Nersesian, W. S., Petit, M. R., Shaper, R., Lemieux, D., & Naor, E. (1985). Childhood death and poverty: A study of all childhood deaths in Maine, 1976 to 1980. *Pediatrics, 75,* 41–50.

Nevin, N. C., Johnston, W. P., & Merrett, J. D. (1981). Influence of social class on the risk of recurrence of anencepholus and spina bifida. *Development Medicine and Child Neurology, 23,* 155–159.

New, P. K. M., Ruscio, A. T., Priest, R. P., Petritsi, D., & George, L. A. (1968). The support structure of heart and stroke patients: A study of the role of significant others in patient rehabilitation. *Social Science and Medicine, 2,* 185–200.

Newacheck, P. W., & Halfon, N. (1986). The association between mother's and children's use of physician services. *Medical Care, 24,* 30–38.

Newacheck, P. W., Halfon, N., & Budetti, P. P. (1986). Prevalence of activity limiting chronic conditions among children based on household interviews. *Journal of Chronic Diseases, 39,* 63–71.

Newbrough, J. R., Simpkins, C. C., & Maurer, H. (1985). A family development approach to studying factors in the management and control of childhood diabetes. *Diabetes Care, 8,* 83–92.

Nichols-Casebolt, A. M. (1988). Black families headed by single mothers: Growing numbers and increasing poverty. *Social Work, 33,* 306–313.

Nicholson, B. L., & Matross, G. N. (1989). Facing reduced decision-making capacity in health care: Methods for maintaining client self-determination. *Social Work, 34,* 234–238.

Nishiura, E., Whitten, C. F., & Jenkins, D. (1980). Screening for psychological problems in health settings. *Health and Social Work, 5,* 22–28.

Noble, D. N., & Hamilton, A. K. (1981). Families under stress: Perinatal social work. *Health and Social Work, 6,* 28–35.

Norbeck, J. S., & Tilden, V. P. (1983). Life stress, social supports, and emotional disequilibrium in complications of pregnancy: A prospective, multivariate study. *Journal of Health and Social Behavior, 24,* 30–46.

Northen, H. (1969). *Social work with groups.* New York: Columbia University Press.

Northen, H. (1982). *Clinical social work.* New York: Columbia University Press.

Northen, H. (1983). Social work in health settings: Promises and problems. In G. Rosenberg & H. Rehr (Eds.), *Advancing social work practice in the health care field.* New York: Haworth Press.

Northen, H. (1987). Assessment in direct practice. *Encyclopedia of Social Work, 18th ed.* (pp. 171–183). Washington D.C.: National Association of Social Workers.

Northen, H, (1988). *Social work with groups, 2d ed.* New York: Columbia University Press.

Northen, H. (in press). Social work practice with groups in health care. *Social Work with Groups, 12.*

Northen, H., & Roberts, R. W. (1976). The status of theory. In R. W. Roberts & H. Northen (Eds.). *Theories of social work with groups.* New York: Columbia University Press.

Northouse, L. (1985). The impact of cancer on the family: An overview. *International Journal of Psychiatry in Medicine, 14,* 215–242.

Northouse, L. (1988). Social support in patients' and husbands' adjustment to breast cancer. *Nursing Research, 37,* 91–95.

Northouse, L., & Swain, M. A. (1987). Adjustment of patients and husbands to the initial impact of breast cancer. *Nursing Research, 36,* 221–225.

Northouse, P. G., & Northouse, L. L. (1988). Communication and cancer: Issues confronting patients, health professionals, and family members. *Journal of Psychosocial Oncology, 5,* 17–46.

Nuckolls, C. H., Cassel, J., & Kaplan, B. H. (1972). Psychosocial assets, life crisis, and the prognosis of pregnancy. *American Journal of Epidemiology, 95,* 431–441.

Nuehring, E. M., & Barr, W. E. (1980). Mastectomy: Impact on patients and families. *Health and Social Work, 5,* 51–57.

Oakly, G., & Patterson, R. (1971). The psychological management of leukemic children and their families. In R. L. Noland (Ed.). *Counseling parents of the ill and handicapped.* Springfield, IL: Charles C. Thomas.

Oberst, M., & James, R. H. (1985). Going home: Patient and spouse adjustment following cancer surgery. *Topics in Clinical Nursing, 7,* 46–57.

Olds, D. L., Henderson, C. R., Tatelbaum, R., & Chamberlin, R. (1988). Improving the life-course development of socially disadvantaged mothers: A randomized trial of nurse home visitation. *American Journal of Public Health, 78,* 1436–1445.

Oliveri, M. E., & Reiss, D. (1981). A theory-based empirical classification of family problem-solving behavior. *Family Process, 20,* 409–418.

Oliveri, M., & Reiss, D. (1984). Family concepts and their measurement: Things are seldom what they seem. *Family Process, 23,* 33–48.

Olson, D. H. (1985). Commentary: Struggling with congruence across theoretical models and methods. *Family Process, 24,* 203–207.

Olson, D. H. (1986). Circumplex model VII: Validation studies and FACES III. *Family Process, 25,* 337–351.

Olson, D. H. (1988). Family assessment and intervention: The circumplex model of family systems. *Child and Youth Services, 11,* 9–48.

Olson, D. H., & Killorin, E. (1985). *Clinical rating scale for circumplex model* (revised version) St. Paul, MN: Family Science University of Minnesota.

Olson, D. H., & McCubbin, H. I. (1982). Circumplex model of marital and family systems V: Application to family stress and crisis intervention. In H. I. McCubbin, A. E. Cauble & J. M. Patterson (Eds.), *Family Stress, Coping, and Social Support* (pp. 48–68). Springfield, IL.: Charles C. Thomas.

Olson, D. H., Sprenkle, D. H., & Russell, C. S. (1979). Circumplex model of marital and family systems: I. Cohesion and adaptability dimensions, family types and clinical applications. *Family Process, 18,* 3–28.

Oppenheimer, J. R., & Rucker, R. W. (1980). The effect of parental relationships on the management of cystic fibrosis and guidelines for social work intervention. *Social Work in Health Care, 5,* 409–419.

Orcutt, B. A. (1977). Stress in family interactions when a member is dying: A special case for family interviews. In E. R. Prichard et al. (Eds.), *Social work with the dying patient and the family.* New York: Columbia University Press.

O'Reilly, P. (1986). Social support networks and maintenance of improved cardiovascular risk status. *Circulation, 74,* (Supp. II). 320.

O'Reilly, P. (1988). Methodological issues in social support and social network research. *Social Science Medicine, 26,* 863–873.

Orr, S. T., & James, S. (1984). Maternal depression in an urban pediatric practice:

Implications for health care delivery. *American Journal of Public Health, 24,* 363–365.

Orth-Gomer, K., & Johnson, J. V. (1987). Social network interaction and mortality. *Journal of Chronic Diseases, 40,* 949–957.

Osterweis, M., Bush, P. J., & Zuckerman, E. (1979). Family content as a predictor of individual medicine use. *Social Science and Medicine, 23A,* 287–291.

Osterweis, M. Solomon, F. & Green, M. (Eds.). (1984). *Bereavement: Reactions, consequences, and care.* Washington, D.C.: National Academy Press.

Page, W. F., & Kuntz, A. J. (1980). Racial and socioeconomic factors in cancer survival: A comparison of veteran's administration results with selected studies. *Cancer, 45,* 1029–1040.

Palinkas, L. A. (1985). Techniques of psychosocial epidemiology. In P. Karoly (Ed.), *Measurement strategies in health psychology* (pp. 49–114). New York: John Wiley and Sons.

Palley, H. A., Feldman, G., Gallner, I., & Tysor, M. (1985). Legislating health care coverage for the unemployed. *Health and Social Work, 10,* 174–182.

Papadopoulos, C., Larrimore, P., Cardin, S., & Shelley, S. I. (1980). Sexual concerns and needs of the postcoronary patient's wife. *Archives of Internal Medicine, 140,* 38–41.

Parad, H. (1963). Brief ego-oriented casework with families in crisis. In H. Parad & R. Miller (Eds.), *Ego-oriented casework,* (pp. 145–164). New York: Family Service Association of America.

Parad, H. & Caplan, G. (1968). A framework for studying families in crisis. In H. Parad (Ed.), *Crisis intervention: Selected readings* (pp. 53–74). New York: Family Service Association of America.

Parad, H. J., Selby, L., & Quinlan, J. (1976). Crisis intervention in families and groups. In R. W. Roberts & H. Northen (Eds.), *Theories of social work with groups.* New York: Columbia University Press.

Parsonet, L., & Weinstein, L. (1987). A volunteer program for helping families in a critical care unit. *Health and Social Work, 12,* 21–28.

Parsons, R. J. & Cox, E. O. (1989). Family mediation in elder caregiving decisions: An empowerment intervention. *Social Work, 34,* 122–126.

Pascoe, J. M., Chessare, J., & Baugh, E. (1985). Which elements of prenatal social support improve neonatal morbidity? *Pediatrics Research, 19,* 206A.

Pasley, K. & Ihinger-Tallman, M. (1988). Remarriage and stepfamilies. In C. S. Chilman, F. M. Cox & E. W. Nunnally (Eds.), *Variant family forms: Families in trouble series, Vol. 5* (pp. 204–221). Newbury Park, CA.: Sage.

Patterson, J. M. (1985). Critical factors affecting family compliance with home treatment for children with cystic fibrosis. *Family Relations, 34,* 79–89.

Patterson, J. M. (1988a). Chronic illness in children and the impact on families. In C. S. Chilman, E. W., Nunnally & F. M. Cox (Eds.). *Chronic illness and disability: Families in trouble series,* Volume 2. Newbury Park: Sage Publications.

Patterson, J. M. (1988b). Families experiencing stress I. The family adjustment and adaptation response model II. Applying the FAAR model to health-related issues for intervention and research. *Family Systems Medicine, 6,* 202–237.

Patterson, J. M., & McCubbin, H. I. (1983). The impact of family life events and changes on the health of a chronically ill child. *Family Relations, 32,* 255–264.

Patti, R. J., & Ezell, M. (1988). Performance priorities and administrative practice in hospital social work departments. *Social Work in Health Care, 13,* 73–90.

Payne, J. S., Goff, J. R., & Paulson, M. A. (1980). Psychosocial adjustment of families following the death of a child. In Schulman, J. L. & Kupst, M. J., *The child with cancer,* (pp. 183–192). Springfield, IL: Charles C. Thomas.

Payne, R. L., & Jones, J. G. (1987). Measurement and methodological issues in social support. In S. V. Kasl & C. L. Cooper (Eds.), *Stress and health: Issues in research methodology* (pp. 167–205). New York: John Wiley & Sons Ltd.

Pearlin, L. D., Lieberman, M. A., Meneghan, E. G., & Mullan, J. T. (1981). The stress process. *Journal of Health and Social Behavior, 22,* 337–356.

Pearlin, L. I., & Turner, H. A. (1987). The family as a context of the stress process. In S. V. Kasl & C. L. Cooper (Eds.), *Stress and health: Issues in research methodology* (pp. 143–165). New York: John Wiley & Sons Ltd.

Pederson, D. R., Bento, S., Chance, G. W., Evans, B., & Fox, A. M. (1987). Maternal emotional responses to preterm birth. *American Journal of Orthopsychiatry, 57,* 15–21.

Pelletier, K. R. (1984). Healthy people in healthy places: Health promotion programs in the workplace. In C. Van Dyke, L. Temoshok & L. S. Legans. (Eds.), *Emotions in health and illness: Applications to clinical practice*. New York: Grune and Stratton.

Peniston, R. L., Miles, N., Lowery, R. C., Kirkland, L., Landes, F., Warner, O. G., Simmons, R. L., Janani, J., Fletcher, J. W., Curry, C. L., Diggs, J. A., Lewis, J. F., & Randall, O. S. (1987). Coronary artery bypass grafting in a predominately Black group of patients. *Journal of the National Medical Association, 79,* 393–599.

Penn, P. (1983). Coalitions and binding interactions in families with chronic illness. *Family Systems Medicine, 1,* 16–25.

Peplau, L. A. & Gordon, S. L. (1985). Women and men in love: Gender differences in close heterosexual relationships. In V. E. O'Leary, R. K. Unger & B. S. Wallston (Eds.). *Women, gender and social psychology*. Hillsdale, NJ: Erlbaum.

Perlman, D., & Rook, K. S. (1987). Social support, social deficits, and the family: Toward the enhancement of well-being. In S. Oskamp (Ed.), *Family processes and problems: Social Psychological Aspects*. Newbury Park: Sage Publications.

Perlman, H. (1961). Family diagnosis in cases of illness and disability. *Family-centered social work in illness and disability: A preventive approach*. New York: National Association of Social Workers.

Perlman, H. (1970). Social casework: A problem-solving process. In R. W. Roberts & R. H. Nee (Eds.), *Theories of social casework* (pp. 129–180). Chicago: University of Chicago Press.

Perlman, H. (1979). *Relationship. The heart of helping people*. Chicago: University of Chicago Press.

Perlman, R., & Giele, J. Z. (1983). In R. Perlman (Eds.), *Family Home Care: Critical Issues for Services and Policies*. New York: The Haworth Press.

Perrault, C., Coates, A. L., Collinge, J., Pless, I. B., & Outerbridge, E. W. (1986). Family support system in newborn medicine: Does it work? Follow-up study of infants at risk. *The Journal of Pediatrics, 108,* 1025–1030.

Perrin, J. M. (1985). Special problems of chronic childhood illness in rural areas. In N. Hobbs & J. M. Perrin (Eds.). *Issue in the care of children with chronic illness* (pp. 402–415). San Francisco: Jossey-Bass.

Perry, C. L., Luepker, R. V., Murray, D. M., Kurth, C., Mullis, R., Crockett, S., & Jacobs, D. R. (1988). Parent involvement with children's health promotion: The Minnesota home team. *American Journal of Public Health, 78,* 1156–1160.

Petchers, M. K., & Milligan, S. E. (1988). Access to health care in a Black urban elderly population. *The Gerontologist, 28,* 213–217.

Peters, L. C., & Esses, L. M. (1985). Family environment as perceived by children with a chronically ill parent. *Journal of Chronic Disease, 38,* 301–308.

Peters, M. F., & Massey, G. (1983). Mundane extreme environmental stress in family stress theories: The case of Black families in White America. In H. I. McCubbin, M. B. Sussman & J. M. Patterson (Eds.), *Social stress and the family: Advances and developments in family stress theory and research.* New York: The Haworth Press.

Peters-Golden, H. (1982). Breast cancer: Varied perceptions of social support in the illness experience. *Social Science and Medicine, 16,* 483–491.

Peterson, K. J. (1985). Psychosocial adjustment of the family caregiver: Home hemodialysis as an example. *Social Work in Health Care, 10,* 15–32.

Peterson, K. J. (1987). Changing needs of patients and families in the acute care hospital: Implications for social work practice. *Social Work in Health Care, 19,* 1–14.

Peterson, P. (1984). Effects of moderator variables in reducing stress outcome in matters of children with handicaps. *Journal of Psychosomatic Research, 28,* 337–344.

Petitte, K. & Anderson, H. J. (1986). Major systems will be shaped by payers in the next decade. *Modern Healthcare, 16,* 53–57.

Peyrot, M., McMurry, J. F. Jr., & Hedges, R. (1988). Marital adjustment to adult diabetes: Interpersonal congruence and spouse satisfaction. *Journal of Marriage and the Family, 50,* 363–376.

Philipp, C. (1984). The relationship between social support and parental adjustment to low-birthweight infants. *Social Work, 29,* 547–550.

Phillips, H. U. (1957). *Essentials of social group work skill.* New York: Association Press.

Phillips, N. K., Gorman, K. H., & Bedenheimer, M. (1981). High risk infants and mothers in groups. *Social Work, 26,* 157–161.

Piening, S. (1984). Family stress in diabetic renal failure. *Health and Social Work, 9,* 134–141.

Piersma, H. L. (1985). The family with a chronically ill child. In J. C. Hansen (Ed.). *Health promotion in family therapy.* Rockville, MD: Aspen.

Pilisuk, M., Boylan, R., & Acredolo, C. (1987). Social support, life stress, and subsequent medical care utilization. *Health Psychology, 6,* 273–288.

Pilisuk, M., & Parks, S. H. (1983). Social support and family stress. In H. I. McCubbin, M. B. Sussman & J. M. Patterson (Eds.), *Social stress and the family: Advances and developments in family stress theory and research* (pp. 137–156). New York: The Haworth Press.

Pilisuk, M., & Parks, S. H. (1988). Caregiving: Where families need help. *Social Work, 33,* 436–440.

Pincus, H. A. (1980). Linking general health and medical health systems of care: Conceptual models of implementation. *American Journal of Psychiatry, 137,* 315–320.

Pincus, H. A. (1986). Linking general health and medical health systems of care: Conceptual models of implementation. *American Journal of Psychiatry, 137,* 315–320.

Pinkston, E. M., & Linsk, N. L. (1984). Behavioral family intervention with the impaired elderly. *The Gerontologist, 24,* 576–583.

Pizzo, P. (1987). Parent-to-parent support groups: Advocates for social change. In S. L. Kagan (Ed.), *America's family support programs: Perspectives and propects* (pp. 228–242). New Haven, CN: Yale University Press.

Pless, B. I., & Haggerty, R. J. (1985). Child health: research in action. In R. N. Rapoport (Ed.), *Children, youth, and families* (pp. 206–235). New York: Cambridge University Press.

Pless, I. B., Roghmann, K., & Haggerty, R. J. (1972). Chronic illness, family functioning, and psychological adjustment: A model for the allocation of preventive mental health services. *International Journal of Epidemiology, 1,* 271–277.

Pless, I. B., & Satterwhite, B. (1973). A measure of family functioning and its application. *Social Science and Medicine, 7,* 613–621.

Plumb, M. M., & Holland, J. (1977). Comparative studies of psychological function in patients with advanced Cancer - 1. Self-Reported Depressive Symptoms. *Psychosomatic Medicine, 39,* 264–276.

Pollin, I. S., & Cashion, M. M. (1984). Community-based social work with the chronically ill. In R. J. Estes (Ed.), *Health care and the social services: Social work practice in health care* (pp. 261–298). St. Louis, Missouri: Warren H. Green, Inc.

Poole, D. (1987). Social policy and chronic illness. *Health and Social Work, 12,* 246–249.

Poole, D. L., & Carlton, T. O. (1986). A model for analyzing utilization of maternal and child health services. *Health and Social Work, 11,* 209–222.

Porritt, D. (1979). Social support in crisis: Quantity or quality? *Social Science & Medicine, 13,* 715–721.

Poulshock, S. W., & Demling, G. T. (1984). Families caring for elders in residence: Issues in the measurement of burden. *Journal of Gerontology, 39,* 230–239.

Poverny, L. M. & Finch, W. A. (1988). Gay and lesbian domestic partnerships: Expanding the definition of family. *Social Casework, 69,* 116–121.

Powazek, M., Payne, J. S., & Goff, J. (1980). Psychological ramifications of childhood leukemia: One year past diagnosis. In J. Schulman & M. J. Kupst (Eds.), *The Child with Cancer.* Springfield, IL.: Charles C. Thomas.

Power, P. W. (1977). The adolescent's reaction to chronic illness of a parent: Some implications for family counseling. *International Journal of Family Counseling, 5,* 70–78.

Power, P. W. (1985). Family coping behaviors in chronic illness: A rehabilitation perspective. *Special Article, 46,* 78–83.

Power, P. W., & Dell Orto, A. E. (Eds.). (1980). *Role of the family in the rehabilitation of the physically disabled.* Baltimore: University Park Press.

Pratt, L. (1976). *Family structure and effective health behavior: The energized family.* Boston: Houghton-Mifflin.

Pratt, L. (1982). Family structure and health work: Coping in the context of social change. In H. I. McCubbin, A. E. Cauble & J. M. Patterson (Eds.), *Family stress, coping, and social support.* Springfield, IL: Charles C. Thomas.

Price, K. (1989). Quality of life for terminally ill children. *Social Work, 34,* 53–60.

Pueschel, S., & Yeatman, S. (1977). An educational and counseling program for phenylketonuric adolescent girls and their parents. *Social Work in Health Care, 3,* 29–36.

Quadagno, J., Sims, C., Squier, D. A., & Walker, G. (1987). Longterm care community services and family caregiving. In T. H. Brubaker (Ed.), *Aging, health, and family: Long-term care.* Newbury Park: Sage Publications.

Quinn, M. E., Fontana, A. F., & Reznikoff, M. (1986). Psychological distress in reaction to lung cancer as a function of spousal support and coping strategy. *Journal of Psychological Oncology, 4,* 79–90.

Quinn, W. H., & Herndon, A. (1986). The family ecology of cancer. *Journal of Psychosocial Oncology, 4,* 45–59.

Rabkin, J. G. (1986). Mental health needs assessment. *Medical Care, 24,* 1093–1109.

Radley, A., & Green, R. (1986). Bearing illness: Study of couples where the husband awaits coronary graft surgery. *Social Science and Medicine, 23,* 577–585.

Rando, T. (1985). Bereaved parents: Particular difficulties, unique factors, and treatment issues. *Social Work, 30,* 19–24.

Ransom, D. C. (1986). Research on the family in health, illness and care—state of the art. *Family Systems Medicine, 4,* 329–336.

Rapoport, L. (1962). The state of crisis: Some theoretical considerations. *Social Service Review, 36,* 22–31.

Rapoport, L. (1966). Working with families in crisis: An exploration in preventive intervention. In H. J. Parad (Ed.), *Crisis intervention: Selected readings* (pp. 129–139). New York: Family Service Association of America.

Rapoport, L. (1970). Crisis intervention as a mode of brief treatment. In R. W. Roberts & R. Nee (Eds.), *Theories of social casework* (pp. 265–312). Chicago: University of Chicago Press.

Raveis, V. H., Siegel, K., & Sudit, M. (1988–1989). Psychological impact of caregiving on the careprovider: A critical review of extant research. *The Journal of Applied Social Sciences, 13,* 40–79.

Ramsey, C. N. Jr. (Ed.). (1989). *Family Systems in Medicine.* NY: The Guilford Press.

Ray, F. (1961). The family as a group. *Family centered social work in illness and disability: A preventive approach.* New York: National Association of Social Workers.

Reddish, P. & Blumenfield, M. (1984). Psychological reactions in wives of patients with severe burns. *Journal of Burn Care and Rehabilitation, 5,* 388–390.

Reddish, P. & Blumenfield, M. (1986). A typology of spousal response to the crisis of severe burn. *Journal of Burn Care and Rehabilitation, 7,* 328–330.

Redl, F. (1953). The art of group composition. In Schulze, S. (Ed.), *Creative group living in a children's institution.* New York: Association Press.

Reece, D., Walz, T., & Hageboeck, H. (1983). Intergenerational care providers of non-institutionalized frail elderly: Characteristics and consequences. *Journal of Gerontological Social Work, 5,* 21–34.

Rehr, H. (1986). Discharge planning: An ongoing function of quality care. *Quality Review Bulletin, 12,* 47–50.

Rehr, W., Berkman, B., & Rosenberg, G. (1980). Screening for high social risk: Principles and problems. *Social Work, 25,* 403–406.

Reichert, K. (1982). Human services and the market system. *Health and Social Work, 7,* 173–182.

Reichert, K. (1983). Mixed economy of welfare. *Social Work, 28,* 412–416.

Reid, W. J. (1981). Family treatment within a task-centered framework. In E. R. Tolson & W. J. Reid (Eds.). *Models of family treatment* (pp. 306–331). New York: Columbia University Press.

Reid, W. J. (1985). *Family problem solving.* New York: Columbia University Press.

Reis, E., Linhart, R., & Lazerson, J. (1982). Using a standard form to collect psychosocial data about hemophilia patients. *Health and Social Work, 7,* 206–214.

Reiss, D. (1981). *The family's construction of reality.* Cambridge MA: Harvard University Press.

Reiss, D. (1982). The working family: A researcher's view of health in the household. *American Journal of Psychiatry, 139,* 1412–1420.

Reiss, D., Gonzalez, S. & Kramer, N. (1986). Family process, chronic illness, and death. *Family Process, 43,* 795–804.

Reiss, D. & Oliveri, M. E. (1983). Family stress as community frame. In H. I. McCubbin, M. B. Sussman & J. M. Patterson (Eds.), *Social stress and the family* (pp. 61–83). New York: The Haworth Press.

Reiss, I. L., & Lee, G. M. (1988). *Family systems in America* (4th ed.). New York: Holt, Rinehart & Winston.

Relman, A. S. (1980). The new medical-industrial complex. *The New England Journal of Medicine, 303,* 963–970.

Rene, A. (1987). Racial differences in mortality: Blacks and Whites. In W. Jones, & M. F. Rice (Eds.), *Health care issues in Black America: Policies, problems, and prospects.* Westport, CT: Greenwood Press.

Retsinas, J., & Garrity, P. (1985). Nursing home friendships. *The Gerontologist, 25,* 376–381.

Revenson, T. A., Wollman, C. A., & Felton, B. J. (1983). Social supports as stress buffers for adult cancer patients. *Psychosomatic Medicine, 45,* 321–331.

Rice, S. & Kelly, J. (1988). Choosing a gay/lesbian lifestyle: Related issues of treatment services. In C. S. Chilman, F. M. Cox & E. M. Nunnally (Eds.). *Variant family forms: Families in trouble series, Vol. 5* (pp. 114–132). Newbury Park, CA.: Sage Publications.

Richmond, M. E. (1917). *Social diagnosis.* New York: Russell Sage Foundation.

Richmond, M. E. (1922). *What is social casework.* New York: Russell Sage Foundation.

Rinaldi, R. C. (1985). Positive effects of psychosocial interventions on total health care: A review of the literature. *Family Systems Medicine, 3,* 417–426.

Rissman, R. & Rissman, B. Z. (1987). Compliance: I Non compliance: A review, II Facilitating compliance. *Family Systems Medicine, 5,* 446–467.

Rix, S. E. (1987). *The American woman 1987–88: A report in depth*. New York: W. W. Norton and Company.

Roback, H. B. (1984). Conclusion: Critical issues in group approaches to disease management. In H. B. Roback (Ed.), *Helping patients and their families cope with medical problems* (pp. 527–543). San Francisco: Jossey-Bass.

Roberts, C. S., & Strange, M. K. (1986). Defining the family in family medicine: Implications for social workers. *Social Work in Health Care, 12,* 51–60.

Robinson, B. C. (1983). Validation of a caregiver strain index. *Journal of Gerontology, 38,* 344–348.

Robinson, D., & Pinch, S. (1987). A geographical analysis of the relationship between early childhood death and socioeconomic environment in an English city. *Social Science and Medicine, 25,* 9–18.

Rogers, C. R. (1975). Empathic: An unappreciated way of being. *Counseling Psychologist, 5,* 2–10.

Rohrbaugh, M., & Bartels, B. D. (1975). Participants' perceptions of curative factors in therapy and growth groups. *Small Group Behavior, 6,* 430–456.

Rolland, J. S. (1987a). Chronic illness and the life cycle: A conceptual framework. *Family Process, 26,* 203–221.

Rolland, J. S. (1987b). Family illness paradigms: Evolution and significance. *Family Systems Medicine, 5,* 482–503.

Rolland, J. S. (1988a). A conceptual model of chronic and life-threatening illness and it's impact on families. In C. S. Chilman, E. W. Nunnally & F. M. Cox (Eds.), *Chronic illness and disability: Families in trouble series, volume 2* (pp. 17–68). Newbury Park: Sage Publications.

Rolland, J. (1988b). Chronic illness and the family life cycle. In B. Carter & M. McGoldrick (Eds.), *The changing family life cycle: A framework for family therapy*. New York: Gardner Press.

Romano, M. D. (1975). Outcome of marriage existing at the time of a male's spinal cord injury. *Journal of Chronic Diseases, 28,* 383–388.

Romano, M. D. (1974). Family response to traumatic head injury. *Scandinavian Journal of Rehabilitation Medicine, 6,* 1–4.

Romig, C. A., & Thompson, J. G. (1988). Teenage pregnancy: A family systems approach. *The American Journal of Family Therapy, 16,* 133–143.

Rosengarten, L. (1986). Creating a health-promoting group for elderly couples on a home health care program. *Social Work in Health Care, 11,* 83–93.

Rosin, A. J. (1977). Reactions of families of brain-injured patients who remain in a vegetative state. *Scandinavian Journal of Rehabilitative Medicine 9,* 1–5.

Rosman, B. L., & Baker, L. (1988). The "Psychosomatic Family" reconsidered: Diabetes in context: A reply. *Journal of Marital and Family Therapy, 14,* 125–132.

Ross, J. L., Phipps, E. J., & Milligan, W. L. (1985). Irritable bowel syndrome in an adolescent adjusting to divorce: A case report. *Family Systems Medicine, 3,* 334–339.

Ross, J. W. (1979). Coping with childhood cancer: Group intervention as an aid to parents in crisis. *Social Work in Health Care, 4,* 381–391.

Ross, J. W. (1982). Ethical conflicts in medical social work: Pediatric cancer care as a prototype. *Health and Social Work, 7,* 95–102.

Rounds, K. A., & Israel, B. A. (1985). Social networks and social support: Living with chronic renal disease. *Patient Education and Counseling, 7,* 227–247.

Roy, C. A., Flynn, E., & Atcherson, E. (1982). Group sessions for home hemodialysis assistants. *Health and Social Work, 7,* 65–71.

Roy, R. (1985). The interactional perspective of pain behavior in marriage. *International Journal of Family Therapy, 7,* 271–283.

Ruberman, W., Weinblatt, E., Goldberg, J. D., & Chaudhary, B. S. (1984). Psychosocial influences on mortality after myocardial infraction. *The New England Journal of Medicine, 311,* 552–559.

Rubin, L. (1985). *Just friends: The role of friendship in our lives.* New York: Harper & Row.

Rudolph, C., Andrews, V., Ratcliff, K. S., & Downes, D. A. (1985). Training social workers to aid chronically ill children and their families. In N. Hobbes & J. M. Perrin (Eds.), *Issues in the care of children with chronic illness.* San Francisco: Jossey-Bass.

Runyan, C. W. (1985). Health assessment and public policy within a public health framework. In P. Karoly (Ed.), *Measurement strategies in health psychology* (pp. 601–628). New York: John Wiley & Sons.

Sabbeth, B. R., & Leventhal, J. M. (1984). Marital adjustment to chronic childhood illness: A critique of the literature. *Pediatrics, 73,* 762–768.

Safer, M. A., Tharps, Q. J., Jackson, D. R. & Leventhal, H. (1979). Determinants of three stages of delay in seeking care at a medical clinic. *Medical Care, 17,* 11–29.

Salkever, D. S. (1985). Parental opportunity costs and other economic costs of childrens' disabling conditions. In N. Hobbs & J. M. Perrins (Eds.), *Issues in the care of children with chronic illness* (pp. 864–879). San Francisco: Jossey-Bass.

Sallis, J. F., & Nader, P. R. (1988). Family determinants of health behaviors. In D. S. Gochman (Ed.), *Health behavior: Emerging research perspectives.* New York: Plenum Press.

Saltzberg, M., & Bryant, D. (1988). Family systems theory and practice at the workplace. *Social Work Papers, 21,* 16–27.

Sampson, R. J. (1987). Urban Black violence: The effect of male joblessness and family disruption. *American Journal of Sociology, 93,* 348–382.

Sandefur, G. D., & Tienda, M. (1988). *Divided opportunities: Minorities, poverty, and social policy.* New York: Plenum Press.

Sanders, C. M. (1978). A comparison of adult bereavement in the death of a spouse, child, and parent. *Omega, 10,* 303–323.

Sandler, I. N. (1980). Social support resources, stress, and maladjustment of poor children. *American Journal of Community Psychology, 8,* 41–52.

Sarason, B. R., Shearin, E. N., Pierce, G. R., & Sarason, I. G. (1987). Interrelations of social support measures: Theoretical and practical implications. *Journal of Personality and Social Psychology, 52,* 813–832.

Sardell, A. (1988). The U.S. experiment in social medicine: The Community Health Center Program, 1965–1986. Pittsburgh, PA: The University of Pittsburgh Press.

Sargent, J. (1985). Physician-family therapist collaboration: Children with medical problems. *Family Systems Medicine, 3,* 454–465.

Satariano, W. A., Belle, S. H., & Swanson, G. M. (1986). The severity of breast cancer at diagnosis: A comparison of age and extent of disease in Black and White women. *American Journal of Public Health, 76,* 779–782.

Satariano, W. A., Minkler, M. A., Langhauser, C. (1984). The significance of an ill spouse for assessing health differences in an elderly population. *Journal of the American Geriatrics Society, 32,* 187–190.

Satir, V. M. (1964). *Conjoint family therapy: A guide to theory and techniques.* Palo Alto, CA: Science and Behavior Books.

Satir, V. M., Stachowiak, J., & Taschman, H. A. (1975). *Helping families to change.* New York: Jason Aronson.

Satterwhite, B. B. (1978). Impact of chronic illness on child and family: An overview based on five surveys with implications for management. *International Journal of Rehabilitation Research, 1,* 7–17.

Schaefer, D. S. (1983). Issues related to psychosocial intervention with Hispanic families in a pediatric cancer setting. *Journal of Psychosocial Oncology, 14,* 39–48.

Schaffer, J. B. (1983). Teaching about families in family practice: A call for a debate. *Family Medicine, 15,* 173–176.

Scharlach, A. E. & Boyd, S. L. (1989). Caregiving and employment: Results of an employee survey. *The Gerontologist, 29,* 382–387.

Schein, E. H. (1985). *Organizational culture and leadership.* San Francisco: Jossey-Bass.

Scherz, F. (1970). Theory and practice of family therapy. In R. Roberts & R. Nee (Eds.), *Theories of social casework* (pp. 219–264). Chicago: University of Chicago Press.

Schilling, R. F., Gilchrist, L. D., & Schinke, S. P. (1984). Coping and social support in families of developmentally disabled children. *Family Relations, 33,* 47–54.

Schilling, R. F., Schinke, S. P., & Kirkham, M. A. (1985). Coping with a handicapped child: Differences between mothers and fathers. *Social Science and Medicine, 21,* 857–863.

Schipper, H., Clinch, J., McMurray, A., & Levitt, M. (1984). Measuring the quality of life of cancer patients: The functional living index-cancer: Development and validation. *Journal of Clinical Oncology, 2,* 472–483.

Schipper, H., & Levitt, M. (1985). Measuring quality of life: Risks and benefits. *Cancer Treatment Reports, 69,* 1115–1123.

Schmid, W. W. (1982). Teen mother-well baby clinic: Maternal and child health. In T. S. Kerson (Ed.), *Social Work in Health Settings.* New York: Longman.

Schmidl, F. (1950). A study of techiques used in supportive treatment. *Social Casework, 32,* 413–419.

Schmidt, D. D. (1978). The family as the unit of medical care. *Journal of Family Practice, 7,* 303–313.

Schmidt, D. D. (1983). When is it helpful to convene the family? *Journal of Family Practice, 16,* 967–973.

Schmidt, G. L., & Keyes, B. (1985). Group psychotherapy with family caregivers of demented patients. *The Gerontologist, 25,* 347–350.

Schoeneman, S. Z., & Reznikoff, M. (1983). Personality variables in coping with the stress of a spouse's chronic illness. *Journal of Clinical Psychology, 39,* 430–435.

Schoenfeld, M., Berkman, B., Meyers, R. H., & Clark, E. (1984). Attitudes toward marriage and childbearing of individuals at risk for Huntington's disease. *Social Work in Health Care, 9,* 73–81.

Schopler, J. H., & Galinsky, M. J. (1985). The open-ended group. In M. Sundel, P. Glasser, R. Saari, & R. Vinter (Eds.), *Individual change through small groups, 2nd ed.* New York: Free Press.

Schorr, A. L. (1972). Family values and public policy: A venture in prediction and prescription. *Journal of Social Policy, 1,* 33–43.

Schuts, A. A, & David J. R. (1981). Combating the scapegoat in family therapy: Selected strategies. *Social Thought, 7,* 14–34.

Schultz, S. K. (1980). Compliance with therapeutic regimes in pediatrics: A review of implications for social work practice. *Social Work in Health Care, 5,* 267–278.

Schwartz, G. E. (1982). Testing the biopsychosocial model: The ultimate challenge facing behavioral medicine? *Journal of Consulting and Clinical Psychology, 50,* 1040–1053.

Schwartz, P., & Ogilvy, J. (1979). The emergent paradigm: Changing patterns of thought and belief. (Analytic Report 7, Values and Lifestyle Program) Menlo Park, CA: SRI International.

Schwartzman, J. (1985). Health, illness, and the family: An evolutionary perspective. *Family Systems Medicine, 3,* 447–452.

Scott, J. P., Roberts, K. A., & Hutton, J. T. (1986). Families of Alzheimer's victims. Family support to the caregivers. *Journal of American Geriatrics Society, 34,* 348–354.

Seabury, B. A. (1971). Arrangement of physical space in social work settings. *Social Work, 16,* 43–49.

Seabury, B. A. (1980). Communication problems in social work practice. *Social Work, 25,* 40–44.

Sealing, P. A. (1989). *Profile of child health in the United States.* Alexandria, VA: NACHRI.

Seattle Times (1988, December 4). p. 32.

Sebring, D. L., & Moglia, P. (1987). Amyotrophic lateral sclerosis: Psychosocial interventions for patients and their families. *Health and Social Work, 12,* 113–120.

Selan, B. H., & Schuenke, S. (1982). The late life care program: Helping families cope. *Health and Social Work, 7,* 192–197.

Selby, L. G. (1956). Supportive treatment: The development of a concept and a helping method. *Social Service Review, 30,* 400–414.

Selby, L. (1979). Support revisited. *Social Service Review, 53,* 573–585.

Selby, P. J., Chapman, J. A. W., Etazadi-Arnoli, J., Dalley, D., & Boyd, N. F. (1984). The development of a method for assessing the quality of life of cancer patients. *British Journal of Cancer, 50,* 13–22.

Seltzer, M. M., Ivry, J., & Litchfield, L. C. (1987). Family members as case managers: Partnership between the formal and informal support networks. *The Gerontologist, 27,* 722–728.

Selye, H. (1956). *The stress of life.* New York: McGraw-Hill.

Sempos, C., Cooper, R., Kovar, N. C., & McMillen, N. (1988). Divergence of the recent trends in coronary mortality for the four major race-sex groups in the United States. *American Journal of Public Health, 78,* 1422–1427.

Shanas, E. (1979). The family as a social support system in old age. *The Gerontologist, 19,* 169–174.

Shanfield, S. B., Benjamin, A. H., & Swain, B. J. (1984). Parent's reactions to the death of an adult child from cancer. *American Journal of Psychiatry, 141,* 1092–1094.

Shapiro, C. H. (1980). Termination: A neglected concept in social work curriculum. *Journal of Education for Social Work, 16,* 13–19.

Shapiro, J. (1983). Family reactions and coping strategies in response to the physically ill or handicapped child: A review. *Social Science and Medicine, 17,* 913–931.

Shapiro, J. & Shumaker, S. (1987). Differences in emotional well-being and communication styles between mothers and fathers of pediatric cancer patients. *Journal of Psychosocial Oncology, 5,* 121–131.

Shaw, M. E. (1981). *Group dynamics: The psychology of small group behavior, 3rd ed.* New York: McGraw.

Sheahen, M. C. (1984). Review of a support group for patients with aids. *Topics in Clinical Nursing, 6,* 38–44.

Sheehan, N. W. & Nuttal, P. (1988). Conflict, emotion and personal strain among family caregivers. *Family Relations, 37,* 92–98.

Sheinberg, M. (1983). The family and chronic illness: The treatment diary. *Family Systems Medicine, 1,* 26–36.

Sheldon, A., Chir, B., Ryser, C. P., & Krant, M. J. (1970). An integrated family oriented cancer care program: The report of a pilot project in the socio-emotional management of chronic disease. *Journal of Chronic Diseases, 22,* 743–755.

Shellhase, L. J., & Shellhase, F. E. (1972). Role of the family in rehabilitation. *Social Casework, 53,* 544–550.

Shenkel, R., Rogers, R., Perfetto, G., & Levin, R. A. (1985–86). Importance of "Significant Others" in predicting cooperation with diabetic regime. *International Journal of Psychiatry in Medicine, 15,* 149–155.

Sheridan, M. S. (1985). Things that go beep in the night: Home monitoring for apnea. *Health and Social Work, 10,* 63–70.

Sherman, S. N. (1965). Practice implications of psychodynamic and group theory in family interviewing. *The family is the patient: The group approach to treatment of family health problems.* New York: National Association of Social Workers.

Sherman, S. N. (1981). A social work frame for family therapy. In E. R. Tolson & W. J. Reid (Eds.), *Models of family treatment* (pp. 7–72). New York: Columbia University Press.

Sherwood, R. J. (1983). Compliance behavior of hemodialysis patients and the role of the family. *Family Systems Medicine, 1,* 61–72.

Shulman, L. (1979). *The skills of helping: Individuals and groups*. Itaska, IL.: F. E. Peacock.
Shulman, L., & Tuzman, L. (1980). Discharge planning—a social work position. *Quality Review Bulletin, 6,* 3–8.
Shumaker, S. A. &, Brownell, A. (1984). Toward a theory of social support: Closing conceptual gaps. *Journal of Social Issues, 40,* 11–36.
Siefert, K., Thompson, T., Bensel, R. W., & Hunt, C. (1983). Perinatal stress: A study of factors linked to the risk of parenting problems. *Health and Social Work, 8,* 107–121.
Siegal, R. (1982). A family centered program of neonatal intensive care. *Health and Social Work, 7,* 50–58.
Siegal, B. R., Calsyn, R. J., & Cuddihee, R. M. (1987). The relationship of social support to psychological adjustment in end-stage renal disease patients. *Journal of Chronic Diseases, 40,* 337–344.
Sigafoos, A., & Reiss, D. (1985). Rejoiner: Counterperspectives on family measurements: The pragmatic interpretation of research methods. *Family Process, 24,* 207–211.
Sikes, W. W., & Rodenhauser, P. (1987). Rehabilitation programs for myocardial infarction patients: A national survey. *General Hospital Psychiatry, 9,* 182–186.
Silliman, R. A., Earp, J. L., & Wagner, E. H. (1988). Stroke: The perspective of family caregivers. *The Journal of Applied Gerontology, 6,* 363–371.
Simmons, K. H., Ivry, J., & Selzter, M. M. (1985). Agency-family collaboration. *The Gerontologist, 25,* 343–346.
Simmons, J. W. (1986). Planning for discharge with the elderly. *Quality Review Bulletin, 12,* 68–71.
Simmons, J. W. (1987). A philosophical perspective on social work administration. Unpublished paper.
Simon, R. (1983). Issues in the referral for family therapy. *Family Systems Medicine, 1,* 56–61.
Simonds, J. (1977). Psychiatric status of diabetic youth matched with a control group. *Journal of the American Diabetes Association, 26,* 921–925.
Simos, B. (1977). Grief therapy to facilitate healthy restitution. *Social Casework, 58,* 337–42.
Singer, B. A. (1983). Psychosocial trauma, defense strategies and treatment considerations in cancer patients and their families. *The American Journal of Family Therapy, 11,* 15–21.
Siporin, M. (1975). *Introduction to social work practice*. New York: MacMillan.
Siporin, M. (1980). Ecological systems theory in social work. *Journal of Sociology and Social Welfare, 7,* 507–532.
Sivarajan, E. S., Newton, K. M., Almes, M. J., Kempf, T. M. Mansfield, L. W., & Bruce, R. A. (1983). Limited effects of outpatient teaching and counseling after myocardial infarction: A controlled study. *Heart & Lung, 12,* 65–73.
Slaby, A. E., & Glicksman, A. S. (1985). *Adapting to life-threatening illness*. New York: Praeger.
Slaughter, D. T., & Dilworth-Anderson, P. (1988). Care of Black children with sickle

cell disease: Fathers, maternal support, and esteem. *Family Relations, 37,* 281–287.

Sluki, C. E. (1985). Family consultation in family medicine: A case example. *Family Systems Medicine, 3,* 160–170.

Smilkstein, G. (1975). The family in trouble—How to tell. *Journal of Family Practice, 2,* 19–24.

Smilkstein, G. (1978). The family APGAR: A proposal for a family function test and its use by physicians. *Journal of Family Practice, 6,* 1231–1239.

Smilkstein, G. (1979) The family APGAR index: A study of construct validity. *Journal of Family Practice, 8,* 577–582.

Smilkstein, G., Helsper-Lucas, A., Ashworth, C., Montani, D., & Pagel, M. (1984). Prediction of pregnancy complications: An application of the biopsychosocial model. *Social Science and Medicine, 18,* 315–321.

Smith, E. M., Redmond, R., Burns, T. L., & Sagert, K. M. (1985). Perceptions of social support among patients with recently diagnosed breast, endometrial and ovarian cancer: An explanatory study. *Journal of Psychosocial Oncology, 3,* 65–81.

Smith, J. C., Mercy, J. A., & Conn, J. M. (1988). Marital status and the risk of suicide. *American Journal of Public Health, 78,* 78–80.

Smith, L. L. (1978). A review of crisis intervention theory. *Social Casework, 59,* 396–405.

Snyder, B., & Keefe, K. (1985). The unmet needs of family caregivers for frail and disabled adults. *Social Work in Health Care, 10,* 1–14.

Solomon, B. B. (1976). *Black empowerment: Social work in oppressed communities.* New York: Columbia University Press.

Somers, A. R. (1987). Insurance for long-term care. *New England Journal of Medicine, 317,* 23–29.

Somers, M. L. (1965). Group processes within the family unit. *The family is the patient: The group approach to treatment of family health problems* (Monograph VII). New York: National Association of Social Workers.

Somers, M. L. (1976). Problem-solving in small groups. In R. W. Roberts & H. Northen (Eds.). *Theories of social work with groups* (pp. 331–367). New York: Columbia University Press.

Sommers, T., & Shields, L. (1987). *Women take care: The consequences of caregiving in today's society.* Gainsville, FL: Triad Communications.

Soricelli, B. A., & Utech, C. L. (1985). Mourning the death of a child: The family and group process. *Social Work, 30,* 429–434.

Sourkes, B. M. (1980). Siblings of the pediatric cancer patient. In J. Kellerman (Ed.), *Aspects of Childhood Cancer.* (pp. 47–69). Springfield, IL: Charles C. Thomas.

Speedling, E. (1982). Heart attack. The family response at home and in the hospital. N.Y.: Tavistock.

Spiegel, D., Bloom, J. R., & Gotthiel, E. (1983). Family environment as a predictor of adjustment to metastatic breast carcinoma. *Journal of Psychosocial Oncology, 1,* 33–44.

Spiegal, J. P. (1981). An ecological model with an emphasis on ethnic families. In E. R. Tolson & W. J. Reid (Eds.), *Models of family treatment* (pp. 121–158). New York: Columbia University Press.

Spinetta, J. J., & Maloney, L. J. (1978). The child with cancer: Patterns of communication and denial. *Journal of Consulting and Clinical Psychology, 46,* 1540–1541.

Spinetta, J. J., Swarner, J. A., & Sheposh, J. P. (1981). Effective parental coping following the death of a child from cancer. *Journal of Pediatric Psychology, 6,* 251–263.

Springer, J. R. (1983). The family with a chronically ill adult. In J. C. Hansen (Ed.). *Health Promotion in Family Therapy* (pp. 83–91). Rockville, Maryland: Aspen.

Spink, D. (1976). Crisis intervention for parents of the deaf child. *Health and Social Work, 1,* 140–161.

Sourkes, B. M. (1980). Siblings of the pediatric cancer patient. In J. Kellerman (Ed.). *Aspects of Childhood Cancer* (pp. 47–69). Springfield: Charles C. Thomas.

Stamm, I. (1972). Family Therapy. In F. Hollis *Casework: A psychosocial therapy* (pp. 203–227). New York: Random House.

Staples, R., & Mirande, A. (1980). Racial and cultural variations among American families: A decennial review of the literature on minority families. *Journal of Marriage and the Family, 42,* 157–173.

Starr, P. (1982). *The Social Transformation of American Medicine.* New York: Basic Books.

Starr, P. (1986). Health care for the poor: The past twenty years. In S. H. Danziger & D. H. Weinberg (Eds.), *Fighting Poverty: What works and what doesn't* (pp. 106–159). Cambridge, MA: Harvard University Press.

Stavraky, K. M., Kincade, J. E., Stewart, M. A., & Donner, A. P. (1987). The effect of socioeconomic factors on the early prognosis of cancer. *Journal of Chronic Diseases, 40,* 237–244.

Steidl, J. H., Finkelstein, F. O., Wexler, J. P., Feigenbaum, H., Kitsen, J., Kliger, A. S., & Quinlan, D. M. (1980). Medical condition, adherence to treatment regimens, and family functioning. *Archives of General Psychiatry, 37,* 1025–1027.

Stein, H., & Pontious, J. M. (1985). Family and beyond: The larger context of noncompliance. *Family Systems Medicine, 3,* 179–189.

Stein, M., & Schieifer, S. J. (1985). Frontiers of stress research: Stress and immunity. In M. Zales (Ed.), *Stress in health and disease* (pp. 97–114). New York: Brunner/Mazel.

Stein, R. E. K., & Jessop, D. J. (1984). Does pediatric home care make a difference for children with chronic illness? Findings from the pediatric ambulatory care treatment study. *Pediatrics, 73,* 845–853.

Stein, R. E. K., & Jessop, D. J. (1985). Delivery of care to inner-city children with chronic conditions. In N. Hobbs & J. M. Perrins (Eds.), *Issues in the care of children with chronic illness* (pp. 382–401). San Francisco: Jossey-Bass.

Stein, R. E. K. & Riessman, C. K. (1980). The development of an impact-on-the-family scale: Preliminary findings. *Medical Care, XVIII,* 465–472.

Steinglass, P., Gonzalez, S., Dosovitz, L., & Reiss, D. (1982). Discussion groups for chronic hemodialysis patients and their families. *General Hospital Psychiatry, 4,* 140–161.

Stephens, M. A. P., Kinney, J. M., Norris, V. K., & Ritchie, S. W. (1987). Social networks as assets and liabilities in recovery from stroke by geriatric patients. *Psychology and Aging, 2,* 125–129.

Stern, M. J., & Pascale, L. (1979). Psychosocial adaptation post-myocardial infarction: The spouses's dilemma. *Journal of Psychosomatic Research, 23,* 83–87.

Stockwell, E., Swanson, D., & Wicks, J. (1988). Economic status differences in infant mortality by cause of death. *Public Health Reports, 103,* 135–142.

Stoesz, D. (1986). Corporate health care and social welfare. *Health and Social Work, 11,* 165–172.

Stoesz, D. (1987a). Policy gambit: Conservative think tanks on the welfare state. *Journal of Sociology and Social Welfare, 14,* (4): 3–20.

Stoesz, D. (1987b). Privatization: Reforming the welfare state. *Journal of Sociology and Social Welfare, 14,* (3): 3–19.

Stolar, E. (1982). Coping with mastectomy: Issues for social work. *Health and Social Work, 7,* 26–34.

Stone, R., Cafferta, G. L. & Sangl, J. (1987). Caregivers of the frail elderly: A national profile. *The Gerontologist, 27,* 616–626.

Strain, J. J., & Beallor, G. (1978). *Psychological intervention in medical practice.* New York: Appleton-Century-Crofts.

Strober, M., & Humphrey, L. L. (1987). Familial contributions to the etiology and course of anorexia nervosa and bulimia. *Journal of Consulting and Clinical Psychology, 55,* 654–659.

Stuifbergen, A. K. (1987). The impact of chronic illness on families. *Family and Community Health, 9,* 43–51.

Stull, D. E., & Borgatta, E. F. (1987). Family structure and proximity of family members: Implications for long-term care of the elderly. In T. H. Brubaker (Ed.), *Aging, Health, and Family: Long-Term Care* (pp. 247–261). Newbury Park: Sage Publications.

Subramanian, K. & Ell, K. (in press). Developing a group treatment model for low-income Anglo, Black and Hispanic patients coping with a first heart attack. *Social Work with Groups.*

Sulway, M., Tupling, H., Webb, K., & Harris, G. (1980). New techniques for changing commpliance in diabetes. *Diabetes Care, 3,* 108–111.

Susman, E., Hersch, S., Nannis, E., Strope, B., Woodruff, P., Pizzo, P., & Levine, A. (1982). Conceptions of cancer: Perspectives of child and adolescent patients and their families. *Journal of Pediatric Psychology, 7,* 253–261.

Susser, M. (1981). Widowhood: A situational life stress or a stressful life event. *American Journal of Public Health, 71,* 793–795.

Syme, S. L. (1984). Sociocultural factors and disease etiology. In W. D. Gentry (Ed.), *Handbook of Behavioral Medicine* pp. 13–37). New York: The Guilford Press.

Taksa, J. L (1982). Open communication: Families of children with leukemia. In T. S. Kerson (Ed.), *Social work in health settings* (pp. 112–125). New York: Longman.

Tamlyn, D., & Arklie, M. M. (1986). A theoretical framework for standard care plans: A nursing approach for working with chronically ill children and their families. *Issues in Comprehensive Pediatric Nursing, 9,* 39–45.

Tangerose, S., & James, S. (1984). Maternal depression in a pediatric practice: Implications for health care delivery. *American Journal of Public Health, 74,* 363–365.

Tarran, E. C. (1981). Parents' views of medical and social-work services for families with young cerebral-palsied children. *Development of Medical Children Neurology, 23,* 173–182.

Task Force on Long-Term Health Care Policies (1988). *Report to Congress and the Secretary by the Task Force on technology dependent children* (DHHS Publication No. HCFA 88-02171). Washington, DC: Government Printing Office.

Tavormina, J. B., Boll, T. T., Dunn, N. J., Luscomb, R. L., & Taylor, J. R. (1981). Psychosocial effects on parents of raising a physically handicapped child. *Journal of Abnormal Child Psychology, 9,* 121–131.

Taylor, S. E. (1983). Adjustment to threatening events: A theory of cognitive adaptation. *American Psychologist, 28,* 1161–1173.

Taylor, S. E., & Dakof, G. (1988). Social support and the cancer patient. In S. Spacapan & S. Oskamp (Eds.), *The social psychology of health* (pp. 95–116). Beverly Hills, CA: Sage Publications.

Taylor, S. E., Falke, R. L., Shoptaw, S. J., & Lichtman, R. R. (1986). Social support, support groups, and the cancer patient. *Journal of Consulting and Clinical Psychology, 54,* 608–615.

Taylor, S. E., Folks, R. L., Mazel, R. M., & Hilsberg, B. L. (1988). Sources of satisfaction and dissatisfaction among members of cancer support groups. In B. Gottlieb (Ed.), *Creating support groups: Formats, processes, and effects* (pp. 187–208). Beverly Hills, CA: Sage Publications.

Tebbi, C. K., Stern, M., Boyle, M., Mettlin, C. J., & Mindell, E. R. (1985). The role of social support systems in adolescent cancer amputees. *Cancer, 56,* 965–971.

Tew, B., & Laurence, K. M. (1973). Mothers, brothers, and sisters of patients with spina bifida. *Developmental Medicine and Child Neurology, 15,* 69–76.

The Children's Roundtable of Los Angeles (1989). *Services for children with disabilities in Los Angeles County.* Los Angeles, CA: University of Southern California School of Social Work.

Thockloth, R. Mc., Ho, S. C., Wright, H., & Seldon, W. A. (1973). Is cardiac rehabilitation really necessary?. *The Medical Journal of Australia, 2,* 669–674.

Thomas, L. (1977). On the science and technology of medicine. *Daedalus, 106,* 35–46.

Thomas, P. D., Goodwin, J. M., & Goodwin, J. S. (1985). Effect of social support on stress-related changes in cholesterol level, uric acid level, and immune function in an elderly sample. *American Journal of Psychiatry, 142,* 735–737.

Thomas, R. B. (1987). Methodological issues and problems in family health care research. *Journal of Marriage and the Family, 49,* 65–70.

Thrower, S. M., Bruce, W. E., & Walton, R. F. (1982). The family circle method for integrating family systems concepts in family medicine. *Journal of Family Practice, 15,* 451–457.

Toffler, Alvin. (1980). *The Third Wave.* New York: Bantum Books.

Tolson, E. R. (1981). Conclusion: Toward a metamodel for eclectic family therapy, In E. R. Tolson & W. J. Reid (Eds.), *Models of family treatment* (pp. 332–354). New York: Columbia University Press.

Tolson, E. R. & Reid, W. J. (Eds.). (1981). *Models of family treatment.* New York: Columbia University Press.

Tomlinson, P. S. (1986). Applying family stress theory to nursing practice. *Theoretical/Research Record, 11,* 81.

Tompkins, C. A., Schulz, R., & Rau, M. T. (1988). Post-stroke depression in primary support persons: Predicting those at risk. *Journal of Consulting and Clinical Psychology, 4,* 502–508.

Townsend, A. (1986). *Family caregivers' perspectives on institutionalization decisions.* Memphis: The University of Tennessee, Center fro Health Services and Department of Medicine.

Tritt, S. G., & Esses, L. M. (1988). Psychosocial adaptation of siblings of children with chronic medical illnesses. *American Journal of Orthopsychiatry, 58,* 211–220.

Truax, D. B., & Carkhuff, R. R. (1967). *Toward effective counseling and psychotherapy: Training and practice.* Chicago: Aldine Atherton.

Truax, D. B., & Mitchell, K. H. (1971). Research on certain therapist interpersonal skills in relation to process and outcome. In A. E. Bergin & S. L. Garfield (Eds.), *Handbook of psychotherapy and behavior change: An empirical analysis* (pp. 299–344). New York: John Wiley.

Trute, B., & Hauch, C. (1988). Building on family strength: A study of families with positive adjustment to the birth of a developmentally disabled child. *Journal of Marital and Family Therapy, 14,* 185–194.

Tsaltas, M. O. (1976). Children of home dialysis patients. *Journal of American Medical Association, 236,* 2764–2766.

Turk, D. C. & Kerns, R. D. (1985). *Health, illness and families.* New York: John Wiley and Sons.

Turner, F. J. (1974). *Psychosocial therapy: A social work perspective.* New York: Free Press.

Turner, R. J., & Avison, W. R. (1985). Assessing risk factors for problem parenting: The significance of social support. *Journal of Marriage and the Family, 47,* 881–892.

Tylke, L. (1980). Family therapy with pediatric cancer patients: A social work perspective. In J. L. Shulman & M. J. Kupst (Eds.). *The child with cancer* (pp. 16–25). Springfield, IL: Charles C. Thomas.

Umberson, D. (1987). Family status and health behaviors: Social control as a dimension of social integration. *Journal of Health and Social Behavior, 28,* 306–319.

Unger, D., & Powell, D. (1980). Supporting families under stress: The role of social networks. *Family Relations, 29,* 566–574.

U.S. Department of Health and Human Services, Health Care Financing Administration. (1981). Long-term care: Background and future directions. Washington D.C.

Urwin, C. (1988) AIDS in Children: A family concern . *Family Relations, 37,* 154–159.

Vachon, M. L. S., Lyall, W. A. L., Rogers, J., Freedman-Letofsky, K., & Freeman, S. J. J. (1980). A controlled study of self-help intervention for widows'. *American Journal of Psychiatry, 137,* 1380–1384.

Valancy, B. B. (1981). A staff-directed group for parents of neurologically impaired children. In P. Azarnoff & C. Hardgrove (Eds.), *The family in child health care* (pp. 189–198). New York: John Wiley.

Vance, J. C., Fazan, L. E., Satterwhite, B., & Pless, I. B. (1980). Effects of nephrotic syndrome on the family: A controlled study. *Pediatrics, 65,* 948–955.

Vandik, I. H., & Storhaug, K. (1985). Family-focused services for children with rare disorders, exemplified by bladder exstrophy. *Clinical Pediatrics, 24,* 94–100.

Vaux, A. (1985). Variations in social supports associated with gender, ethnicity and age. *Journal of Social Issues, 41,* 89–110.

Vega, W. A., Patterson, T., Sallis, J., Nader, P., Atkins, C., & Abramson, I. (1986). Cohesion and adaptability in Mexican-American and Anglo families. *Journal of Marriage and the Family, 48,* 857–867.

Velasco de Parra, M. L., Cortazar, S. D. de, & Covarrubias-Espinoza, G. (1983). The adaptive pattern of families with a leukemic child. *Family Systems Medicine, 1,* 30–35.

Venters, M. (1981). Familial coping with chronic and severe childhood illness: The case of cystic fibrosis. *Social Science and Medicine, 15A,* 289–297.

Venters, M. H. (1986). Family life and cardiovascular risk: Implications for the prevention of chronic disease. *Social Science and Medicine, 32,* 1067–1074.

Verbrugge, L. M. (1977). Marital status and health. *Journal of Marriage and the Family, 7,* 267–285.

Vess, J. D., Moreland, J. R., & Schwebel, A. I., (1985a). A follow-up study of role functioning and the psychological environment of families of cancer patients. *Journal of Psychosocial Oncology, 3,* 1–13.

Vess, J. D., Moreland, J. R., & Schwebel, A. I., (1985b). An empirical assessment of the effects of cancer on family role functioning. *Journal of Psychosocial Oncology, 3,* 1–14.

Videka-Sherman, L. (1982). Effects of participation in a self-help group for bereaved parents: Compassionate friends. *Prevention in Human Services, 1,* 69–77.

Videka-Sherman, L. (1987). Research on the effect of parental bereavement: Implications for social work intervention. *Social Service Review, 61,* 103–116.

Videka-Sherman, L., & Lieberman, M. (1985). The effects of self-help and psychotherapy intervention on child loss: The limits of recovery. *American Journal of Orthopsychiatry, 55,* 70–82.

Vigilante, F. W., & Mailick, M. D. (1988). Needs-resources evaluation in the assessment process. *Social Work, 33,* 101–104.

Viney, L. L., Clarke, A. M., & Benjamin, Y. N. (1986). A general systems approach to the patient, hospital staff, family, and community: Implications for health care services. *Behavioral Science, 31,* 239–253.

Vingerhoets, A. J. J. M., & Marcelissen, F. H. G. (1988). Stress research: Its present status and issues for future developments. *Social Science and Medicine, 26,* 279–291.

Violon, A. (1985). Family etiology of chronic pain. *International Journal of Family Therapy, 7,* 235–244.

Wagner, R. M. (1988a). Changes in extended family relationships for Mexican American and Anglo single mothers. *Journal of Divorce, II,* 69–87.

Wagner, R. M. (1988b). Changes in the friend network during the first year of single parenthood for Mexican American and Anglo women. *Journal of Divorce, II,* 89–109.

Waldo, D. R., & Lazenby, H. C. (1984). Demographic characteristics and health care and expenditures by the aged in the United States: 1977–1984. *Health Care, 6,* 1–29.

Walker, G. (1983). The pact: The caretaker-parent/ill-child: Coalition in families with chronic illness. *Family Systems Medicine, 1,* 6–29.

Walker, L. S., McLaughlin, F. J., & Greene, J. W. (1988). Functional illness and family functioning: A comparison of healthy and somaticizing adolescents. *Family Process, 27,* 317–324

Walkover, M. (1988). Social policies: Understanding their impact on families with impaired members. In C. S. Chilman, E. W. Nunnally, F. M. Cox (Eds.), *Chronic illness and disability: Families in trouble* (pp. 220–247). Series 2, Vol. 2. Newbury Park: Sage Publications.

Wallston, B. S., Alagna, S. W., DeVellis, B. M., & DeVellis, R. R. (1983). Social support and physical health. *Health Psychology, 2,* 367–391.

Waltz, M. (1986a). Marital context and post-infarction quality of life: Is it social support or something more? *Social Science and Medicine, 22,* 791–805.

Waltz, M. (1986b). Type A, social context, and adaptation to serious illness: A longitudinal investigation of the role of the family in recovery from myocardial infarction. In T. H. Schmudt, T. M. Dembroski, & G. Bluumchen. (Eds.), *Biological and Psychological Factors in Cardiovascular Disease, II* (pp. 594–613). New York: Springer-Verlag.

Waltz, M., Bandura, B., Pfaff, H., & Schott, T. (1988). Marriage and the psychological consequences of a heart attack: A longitudinal study of adaptation to chronic illness after 3 years. *Social Science & Medicine, 22,* 149–158.

Walwork, E. (1984). Coping with the death of a newborn. In H. B. Roback (Ed.). *Helping parents and their families cope with medical problems*. San Francisco: Jossey-Bass.

Wandersman, L. P. (1982). An analysis of the effectiveness of parent-infant support groups. *Journal of Primary Prevention, 3,* 99–115.

Ware, J., Johnson, S., Davies-Avery, A., & Brook, R. (1979). *Conceptualization and measurements of health for adults in the Health Insurance Study, III,* Mental Health, Santa Monica, CA: The Rand Corporation, R-1987/3-HEW.

Warren, D. I. (1981). *Helping networks: How people cope with problems in the urban community*. Notre Dame: University of Notre Dame Press.

Wasilewski, Y., Clark, N., Evans, D., Feldman, C. H., Kapkin, D., Rips, J., & Mellins, R. B. (1988). The effect of paternal social support on maternal disruption caused by childhood asthma. *Journal of Community Health, 13,* 33–42.

Wasserman, H. & Danforth, H. E. (1988). *The human bond: Support groups and mutual aid.* New York: Springer.

Watkins, S. C., Menken, J. A., & Bongaarts, J. (1987). Demographic foundations of family change. *American Sociological Review, 52,* 346–358.

Weatherly, R. A., Perlman, S. B., Levine, M., & Klerman, L. V. (1985). *Patchwork programs: Comprehensive services for pregnant and parenting adolescents* (Monograph No. 4). Seattle: School of Social Work, University of Washington, Center of Social Welfare Research.

Weeks, K. H. (1985). Private health insurance and chronically ill children. In N.

Hobbs & J. M. Perrins (Eds.), *Issues in the care of children with chronic illness* (pp. 880–991). San Francisco: Jossey-Bass.

Wegam, M. E. (1985). Contributor's section: Annual summary of vital statistics-1984. *Pediatrics, 76,* 861–871.

Weinberger, M., Hiner, S. L., & Tierney, W. M. (1985). In support of hassles as a measure of stress in predicting health outcomes. *Journal of Behavioral Medicine, 10,* 19–29.

Weissbourd, B. (1985). Family support programs: Partners to pediatricians. In M. Green (Ed.), *The psychosocial aspects of the family* (pp. 79–88). Lexington, MA: Lexington Books.

Weissbourd, B. (1987). Design, staffing, and funding of family support programs. In S. L. Kagan (Ed.), *America's family support programs: Perspectives and prospects* (pp. 245–281). New Haven, CN: Yale University Press.

Weissman, M. M., Sholomskas, D., & John, K. (1981). The assessment of social adjustment. *Archives of General Psychiatry, 38,* 1250–1258.

Welch, D. (1981). Planning nursing intervention for family members of adult cancer patients. *Cancer Nursing, 4,* 365–369.

Weller, D. J., & Miller, P. M. (1977). Emotional reactions of patient, family, and staff in acute-care period of spinal cord injury. *Social Work in Health Care, 3,* 7–17.

Wellisch, D. K. (1979). Adolescent acting out when a parent has cancer. *International Journal of Family Therapy, 1,* 238–241.

Wellisch, D. K. (1981). On stabilizing families with an unstable illness: Helping disturbed families cope with cancer. In M. R. Lansky (Ed.), *Family therapy and major psychopathology* (pp. 281–300). New York: Grune & Stratton.

Wellisch, D. K., Jamison, K. R., & Pasnau, R. O. (1978). Psychosocial aspects of mastectomy: II. The man's perspective. *American Journal of Psychiatry, 135,* 543–546.

Wellisch, D. K., Mosher, M. B., & Van Scoy, C. (1978). Management of family emotional stress: Family group therapy in a private oncology practice. *International Journal of Group Psychotherapy, 28,* 225–232.

Weissman, M. M., Sholomskas, D. & John, K. (1981). The assessment of social adjustment. *Archives of General Psychiatry, 38,* 1250–1258.

Westin, M. T., & Reiss, D. (1979). The family role in rehabilitation. *Journal of Rehabilitation, 11,* 25–29.

Wethington, E., & Kessler, R. C. (1986). Perceived social support, received support, and adjustment to stressful life events. *Journal of Health and Social Behavior, 27,* 78–89.

Whitehead, B. A., Fusillo, A. E., & Kaplan, S. (1988). The design of physical environments and health behavior. In D. S. Gochman (Ed), *Health Behavior: Emerging Research Perspectives* (pp. 231–242). New York: Plenum Press.

Whittaker, J. K., Garbarino, J., & Associates (1983). *Social support networks, informal helping in the human services.* New York: Aldine de Gruyter Publishers.

Whittaker, J. K., Schinke, S. P., & Gilchirst, L. D. (1986). The ecological paradigm in child, youth, and family services: Implications for policy and practice. *Social Service Review, 60,* 483–503.

Wiegerink, R., & Comfort, M. (1987). Parent involvement: support for families of children with special needs. In S. L. Kagan (Ed.), *America's family support programs: Perspectives and prospects* (pp. 182–206). New Haven, CT: Yale University Press.

Wikler, L. M. (1986). Family stress theory and research on families of children with mental retardation. In J. L. Gallagher & P. M. Vietze (Eds.), *Families of handicapped persons* (pp. 167–197). Baltimore: Paul H. Brookes Publishing Co.

Wikler, L., Wasow, M., & Hatfield, E. (1981). Chronic sorrow revisited: Parent vs. professional depiction of the adjustment of parents of mentally retarded children. *American Journal of Orthopsychiatry, 51*, 63–70.

Wilensky, G. R., & Berk, M. L. (1982). Health care, the poor, and the role of medicaid. *Health Affairs, 1*, 93–100.

Wilensky, H. L., & Lebeaux, C. N. (1965). *Industrial society and social welfare.* New York: Free Press.

Willems, E. P., & Halstead, L. S. (1978). An eco-behavioral approach to health status and health care. In R. G. Barker and Associates (Eds.), *Habitats, environments, and human behavior* (pp. 169–189). San Francisco: Jossey-Bass Publishers.

Williams, R. B. (1985). Neuroendocrine response patterns and stress: Biobehavioral mechanisms of disease. *Perspectives on Behavioral Medicine, 2*, 72–101.

Williams, R. R., Hunt, S. L., Barlow, G. K., Chamberlain, R. M., Weinberg, A. D., Cooper, H. P., Carbonari, J. P., & Gotto, A. M. (1988). Health family trees: A tool for funding and helping young family members of coronary and cancer prone pedigrees in Texas and Utah. *American Journal of Public Health, 78*, 1283–1286.

Williams, S., & Torrens, P. (Eds.). (1984). *Introduction to Health Services* (2nd ed.). New York: John Wiley and Sons.

Wilson, G., & Ryland, G. (1964). The family as a unit of service. *Social Work Practice*. National Conference on Social Welfare. New York: Columbia University Press.

Wilson, W. J., & Neckerman, K. M. (1986). Poverty and family structures: The widening gap between evidence and public policy issues. In S. H. Danziger & D. H. Weinberg (Eds.), *Fighting poverty: What works and what doesn't* (pp. 232–259). Cambridge, MA: Harvard University Press.

Winett, R. A. (1985). Ecobehavioral assessment in health lifestyles: Concepts and methods. In P. Karoly (Ed), *Measurement Strategies in Health Psychology* (pp. 147–182). New York: John Wiley and Sons.

Wing, S., Casper, M., Riggan, W., Hayes, C., & Tyroler, H. A. (1988). Socio-environmental characteristics associated with the onset of decline of ischemic heart disease mortality of the United States. *American Journal of Public Health, 78*, 923–926.

Winogrond, I. R., Fisk, A. A., Kirsling, R. A., & Keyes, B. (1987). The relationships of caregiver burden and morale to Alzheimer's disease patient function in a therapeutic setting. *The Gerontologist, 27*, 336–339.

Wise, P. H., Kotelchuck, M., Wilson, M., & Mills, M. (1985). Racial and socioeconomic disparities in childhood mortality in Boston. *New England Journal of Medicine, 313,* 360–366.

Wissow, L. S., Gittelsohn, A. M., Szklo, M., Starfield, B., & Mussman, M. (1988). Poverty, race, and hospitalization for childhood asthma. *American Journal of Public Health, 78,* 777–781.

Woehrer, C. E. (1978). Cultural pluralism in American families: The influence of ethnicity on social aspects of aging. *The Family Coordinator, 27,* 329–339.

Wohl, S. (1984). *The Medical Industrial Complex.* New York: Harmony Books.

Wolinsky, F. D. (1982). Racial differences in illness behavior. *Journal of Community Health, 8,* 87–101.

Wolock, I., & Schlesinger, E. (1986). Social work screenings in New Jersey hospitals: Progress, problems, and implications. *Health and Social Work, 2,* 15–24.

Wood, J. B., & Estes, C. L. (1988). "Medicalization" of community services for the elderly. *Health and Social Work, 13,* 35–42.

Woodward, C. A., Santa-Barbara, J., Levin, S., & Epstein, N. B. (1978). The role of goal attainment scaling in evaluating family therapy outcome. *American Journal of Orthopsychiatry, 48,* 464–476.

Worby, C. M., & Babineau, R. (1974). The family interview: Helping patient and family cope with metastatic disease. *Geriatrics, 29,* 83–94.

Wright, K., & Dyck, S. (1984). Expressed concerns of adult cancer patients' family members. *Cancer Nursing, 7,* 371–374.

Yalom, I. (1970). *The theory and practice of group psychotherapy.* New York: Basic Books.

Yalom, I. (1980). *Existential psychotherapy.* New York: Basic Books.

Yalom, I. D. (1983). *Inpatient group psychotherapy.* New York: Basic Books.

Yalom, I. D. (1985). *The theory and practice of group psychotherapy, 3rd. ed.* New York: Basic Books.

York, J., & Casyln, P. (1977). Family involvement in nursing homes. *The Gerontologist, 17,* 500–503.

Zales, M. (1985). *Stress in health and disease.* New York: Brunner/Mazel.

Zarit, S. H., Reeves, K. E., & Bach-Peterson, J. (1980). Relatives of the impaired elderly: Correlates of feelings of burden. *The Gerontologist, 20,* 649–654.

Zarit, S. H., Todd, P. A., & Zarit, J. M. (1986). Subjective burden of husbands and wives as caregivers: A longitudinal study. *The Gerontologist, 26,* 206–266.

Zelinka, J. D. (1982). Discharge planning: Acute medical service. In T. S. Kerson (Ed.), *Social work in health settings* (pp. 161–179). New York: Longman.

Zigler, E., & Weiss, H. (1985). Family support system: An ecological approach to child development. In R. N. Rapoport (Ed.), *Children, youth, and families* (pp. 166–205). New York: Cambridge University Press.

Zimmer, J. G., Groth-Juncker, A. & McCusker, J. (1985). A randomized controlled study of a home health care team. *American Journal of Public Health, 75,* 134–141.

Zimmerman, S. L. (1976). The family and its relevance for social policy. *Social Casework, 59,* 547–554.

Zimmerman, S. L. (1978). Reassessing the effect of public policy on family functioning. *Social Casework, 59, 451–457.*

Zimmerman, S. L. (1980). The family: Building block or anachronism. Social Casework, 61, 195–204.

Zimmerman, S. L. (1988). State level public policy choices as predictors of state teen birthrates. *Family Relations, 37*, 315–320.

Index